Australian Sign Language (Auslan)

This is first comprehensive introduction to the linguistics of Auslan, the sign language of Australia. Assuming no prior background in language study, it explores each key aspect of the structure of Auslan, providing an accessible overview of its grammar (how sentences are structured), phonology (the building blocks of signs), morphology (the structure of signs), lexicon (vocabulary), semantics (how meaning is created), and discourse (how Auslan is used in context). The authors also discuss a range of myths and misunderstandings about sign languages, provide an insight into the history and development of Auslan, and show how Auslan is related to other sign languages, such as those used in Britain, the USA and New Zealand. Complete with clear illustrations of the signs in use and useful further reading lists, this is an ideal resource for anyone interested in Auslan, as well as those seeking a clear, general introduction to sign language linguistics.

TREVOR JOHNSTON is Associate Professor in the Department of Linguistics, Macquarie University. A sign linguist with an international reputation, he was author of the first dictionary of Auslan, and has published a number of papers describing the Auslan grammar.

ADAM SCHEMBRI is Postdoctoral Research Fellow in the Department of Linguistics, Macquarie University. Highly acclaimed for his work on Auslan, he has presented papers on the topic at a number of conferences, and has ten years' teaching experience in linguistics.

Australian Sign Language (Auslan)

An Introduction to Sign Language Linguistics

Trevor Johnston and Adam Schembri

CAMBRIDGE
UNIVERSITY PRESS

CAMBRIDGE UNIVERSITY PRESS
Cambridge, New York, Melbourne, Madrid, Cape Town, Singapore, São Paulo, Delhi

Cambridge University Press
The Edinburgh Building, Cambridge CB2 8RU, UK

Published in the United States of America by Cambridge University Press, New York

www.cambridge.org
Information on this title: www.cambridge.org/9780521832977

First published 2007
Third printing 2009

Printed in the United Kingdom at the University Press, Cambridge

A catalogue record for this publication is available from the British Library

Library of Congress Cataloguing in publication data

ISBN 978-0-521-83297-7 hardback
ISBN 978-0-521-54056-8 paperback

To our parents: Patricia and Eric Johnston &
Marie and Charles Schembri

Contents

Acknowledgements

We would both like to acknowledge the debt we owe to all our deaf friends and colleagues (and for Trevor, this also includes many relatives) who have put up with our separate obsessions with Auslan and other signed languages over the years. Of course, more generally, the cooperation of scores and ultimately literally hundreds of people from the deaf community throughout Australia has been crucial. You have all informed the writing of this book by answering questions and by being involved in various ways in research projects. Without you it would not have been possible. Thank you.

We would like to thank our reviewer, Terry Janzen, for constructive criticism that helped improve this book. We are also indebted to Louise de Beuzeville for very useful feedback on an earlier draft of the entire book; Della Goswell and Donovan Cresdee for comments and sharing their native signer intuitions with us; Breda Carty for some of the ideas in Chapter 3 and Jemina Napier for thoughts on Chapter 9. We are also grateful to the following individuals and organisations for their assistance and support: Alistair McEwin, Julia Allen and the New South Wales Association of the Deaf; Robert Adam, Ann Darwin, Karen Lloyd and the Australian Association of the Deaf; Mandy Dolejsi, Della Goswell (again!) and the Australian Sign Language Interpreters Association; Ian Rogers and the Auslan Educators Network; Rebecca Ladd and the Deaf Society of New South Wales; Darlene Thornton, Patti Levitzke-Gray, Kevin Cresdee, Stephanie Linder and Kim Pickering.

We are especially grateful to the Australian Communication Exchange. A grant under their 'Friends of ACE Support' scheme made it possible for Adam to take leave from other projects and to spend three months in early 2005 concentrating on the writing of the book. We would also like to gratefully acknowledge the following organizations for financial support for research that informed this work: the Australian Research Council (ARC grants A59131903 and LP346973), the Royal Institute for Deaf and Blind Children (Sydney) and the Hans Rausing Endangered Languages Documentation Project (London) (grant MDP0088).

Some parts of this book draw on material that first appeared in the following publications (although most of the material has been considerably reworked): Chapter 2 and the appendix to *Signs of Australia* (Johnston, 1998) published by North Rocks Press; Chapters 4, 5 and 6 and *The Structure and Formation of Signs in Australian Sign Language (Auslan)* (Schembri, 1996) also published by North Rocks Press; Chapter 3 and *BSL, Auslan and NZSL: Three languages or one?* (Johnston, 2003a) published by Signum Press; Chapter 10 and *Sign Language: Morphology* (Johnston, 2006) in K. Brown (ed.), 2006, *Encyclopedia of Language and Linguistics 2nd Edition,* (p. 324) published by Elsevier.

Original drawings by Shaun Fahey first appeared in *The Survival Guide to Auslan* (Johnston & Schembri, 2003) published by North Rocks Press. Additional images not found in *The Survival Guide to Auslan* are derived from the original drawings by Shaun Fahey (see above) or from those by Peter Wilkin in the *Auslan Dictionary* (Johnston, 1989). They were created through the magic of digital manipulation by Trevor. Handshape drawings used in Figures 4.8 and 4.14 are reprinted with permission from Prillwitz *et al.* (1989) published by Signum Press. The Taiwan Sign Language handshape illustration in Figure 4.14 is reproduced with permission from Baker & Cokely (1980) published by Gallaudet University Press. Finally, the Warlpiri Sign Language handshapes in Figure 4.14 (Kendon, 1988) and the illustrations in Figures 8.10 and 8.11 (Taub, 2001) have been reproduced with permission from the cited publications by Cambridge University Press.

Last but not least, Adam would like to thank Joe Sabolcec for all the love and support during the long days and weekends spent writing this book (and at other times too).

Conventions for sign notation

General example	Specific instances	Explanation and example
SIGN	CAR	The English gloss of a sign is written in small capitals. It is the most commonly associated and/or nearest translation of the sign. Video clips of all Auslan signs cited in this book can be viewed by visiting the on-line Auslan dictionary at www.auslan.org.au.
SIGN-SIGN	LOOK-BACK	A sign glossed with more than one word. The words are separated by hyphens.
PRO-	PRO-1 I, me PRO-2 you PRO-3 he/him, she/her, it	A personal pronoun.
POSS-	POSS-1 my, mine POSS-2 your, yours POSS-3 his, her, hers, its	A possessive pronoun.
PT+	+f forward/front +c centre/self +lf left +rt right +dn down	A pointing sign. The gloss is followed by specification, after a plus symbol, of the location it points to.
SIGN+lf lf+SIGN+rt SIGN+gen	+f forward/front +c centre/self +lf left +rt right +dn down +rept repeated +exh exhaustive ('all') +mult multiple ('each') +fast +slow +hold +gen genitive (possessive)	A manual modification made to a sign is described by letters after a plus symbol, as listed here. The modification may involve a location, a direction, a manner of movement, or the addition of an affix (+gen). For example: ASK+lf = 'the sign ASK directed towards the left of the signing space ("ask him/her")'. lf+ASK+rt = 'the sign ask moves from the left of the signing space to right side ("he/she asked him/her")'. MOTHER+gen = 'the sign mother with the possessive affix ("mother's")'.
A-B-C-D.....	T-O-Y-O-T-A	A fingerspelled sign is represented by letters in small capitals separated by hyphens.
SIGN^SIGN	MOTHER^FATHER	The two elements of a compound are separated by a caret symbol (^). For example, MOTHER^FATHER = PARENTS.

General example	Specific instances		Explanation and example
<u>expression</u> SIGN SIGN SIGN	br bf hs hn hb ht htf htb fl rl ll mm oo th gr cs ! rs:	brow raise furrowed brow head shake head nod head back head tilted head tilted forward head tilted back forward lean right lean left lean pursed lips rounded lips protruding tongue grimace cheek to shoulder with stress role shift (specified after colon)	A bar above a sign or series of signs is used to show the scope of a facial expression or non-manual behaviour. Letters at the right hand end of the bar are used as labels, with meanings as listed. For example, <u> br </u> PRO-2 DEAF *Are you deaf?* = the signer raises the eyebrows while the signs PRO-2 and DEAF are produced. An English translation (*in italics*) may be added underneath, as shown.
CL:G-PERSON-PASS-BY			A depicting sign is represented by CL (for 'classifier') followed a colon and a label representing the handshape. It is followed by a description of what is depicted.
CA:WINK			Constructed action is represented by CA (for 'constructed action') followed a colon and a description of the action.
sh SIGN2 2h SIGN1 dh SIGN3	sh = subordinate hand 2h = two hands dh = dominant hand		The notation of subordinate (usually left) and dominant (usually right) hands is placed on separate tiers to show simultaneous articulation of two signs, one on each hand. For example, sh CL:B-flat 2h BALL dh PT+dn = 'after the two-handed sign BALL is produced the dominant hand points under subordinate flat hand'.
B, 1, 5, Bent 5, A, H, X, 7, O, gO, O>, C, V, F, I, W, Y, ILY, 3.			Letter, names or numbers are used to refer to handshapes in the text. A complete list of handshapes used in Auslan can be found in Table 4.9

1   Signed languages and linguistics

In this chapter, we discuss the discovery of signed languages as real languages and describe their place within modern linguistics. We begin by defining language and linguistics. First, we explore some of the properties language shares with other systems of communications, as well as features that may make language unique. Second, we introduce the field of linguistics—the scientific study of language—and its major areas of investigation. We then discuss signed language linguistics and its history, examine common myths and misconceptions about signed languages, and describe the relationship between signed languages and other forms of gestural communication.

1.1   What is language?

One of the aims of the field of linguistics is to understand exactly what language is, so providing a definition is difficult because the study of language is very much work in progress. In addition, many contemporary textbooks in linguistics discuss definitions of language that were proposed before signed languages were recognised as real languages. Thus, in order to provide a working definition of language, we will draw on a useful summary first provided by the researchers Charlotte Baker and Dennis Cokely (1980): a language is a complex system of communication with a vocabulary of conventional symbols and grammatical rules that are shared by members of a community and passed from one generation to the next, that changes across time, and that is used to exchange an open-ended range of ideas, emotions and intentions.

This working definition draws on a number of key features that were proposed by Charles Hockett (1960) to be central aspects of language structure and function: the use of arbitrary symbols, grammaticality, discreteness, duality of patterning, cultural transmission, inter-changeability, reflexiveness, displacement and creativity. Some of these features are shared by language and other communication systems, while others may be unique to human language. We describe each of these characteristics in the following sections.

1.1.1   Arbitrary symbols

All communication systems (including, for example, traffic lights, monkey calls, the dance of honey bees and human language) rely on the use of symbols to produce meaning. In traffic lights, for example, we have a set of three coloured lights—green, amber and red. Each of these coloured lights has a relation to a specific meaning: green, for example, means 'go' while red means 'stop'. Among vervet monkeys, there are three different calls that mean 'snake', 'leopard' and 'eagle' respectively (Seyfarth, Cheney & Marler, 1980). In response to the 'snake' call, other members of a vervet monkey troupe will stand up and scan the ground, while the 'leopard' call will see them run into the trees. The tail-wagging dance of bees is used to communicate information about sources of nectar (Frisch, 1967). The direction of the dance indicates the direction of the flight path to the food, the speed of the dance signals how rich the source of nectar is, and the tempo of the movement provides information about the distance. In each communication system, we see that the symbols involve a relationship between some form (e.g., a coloured light, a specific call or a movement) and a meaning.

The words and signs used in languages such as English and Auslan may also be considered examples of symbols. This link between form and meaning in signed and spoken language may be *arbitrary*. Arbitrary words or signs show no link between their form and meaning. The sound of the word *cat*, for example, does not resemble any sound made by a cat. It only means 'cat' by a completely conventional association of this sequence of sounds with this meaning. There is nothing natural about this link between form and meaning—it results entirely from the long-established use of this word in English-speaking communities. Other language communities have similar meanings associated with different sequences of sounds, so that 'cat' is *neko* in Japanese and *paka* in Swahili.

Similarly, the sign SISTER in Auslan is produced by tapping the X handshape twice on the nose. Neither the shape of the hand used in this sign nor its location or movement have any physical resemblance to the concept of 'sister'. The association between this sign and its meaning is nothing more than customary usage in the Auslan signing community. In fact, this sign also has this meaning in British Sign Language (BSL) and New Zealand Sign Language (NZSL), because these three languages are historically related. In other signed languages, such as American Sign Language (ASL) and Taiwan Sign Language (TSL), the sign is quite different. In fact, in TSL, there are two signs—ELDER-SISTER and YOUNGER-SISTER.

| SISTER (Auslan) | SISTER (ASL) | ELDER-SISTER (TSL) | YOUNGER-SISTER(TSL) |

Figure 1.1: *Signs for 'sister' in three signed languages.*

The Swiss linguist Ferdinand de Saussure claimed that arbitrariness was in fact a defining feature of language, differentiating it from other communication systems (Saussure, 1983 [1915]). As we see from the discussion above, however, arbitrary symbols are not unique to human language. There is no apparent link between the colours of traffic lights and their meanings, nor between the particular sound used in the 'leopard call' of vervet monkeys and any sound produced by a leopard. Furthermore, many symbols in human language are not arbitrary at all. Language also includes *iconic* symbols in which some aspect of symbol's form resembles some aspect of its meaning. The word for 'cat' in Thai, for example, is *meo*. Clearly, there is a link between the sound of this word and the sound made by a cat. English includes some words that use *onomatopoeia* (a term used to refer to sound-based iconicity), such as *chiffchaff* (the name of a particular songbird whose song alternates from a higher to a lower note), *cuckoo, tap, crash, click, slurp* and *bang*. English also uses links between form and meaning in other ways as well. In a phenomenon known as *sound symbolism*, related sounds tend to occur in words that are similar in meaning, such as the *gl-* sequence in *glisten, glow, glitter* and *gleam*. Moreover, the order of sentences in a story usually follows the sequence of events as they actually occurred (Haiman, 1985). Thus, there is more iconicity in spoken languages than previously believed.

Many symbols in signed languages are iconic, such as the signs CAT in Auslan and Japanese Sign Language (Nihon Shuwa or NS). The first appears to suggest an action typically associated with a cat (i.e., stroking its fur), while the second seems to represent the typical actions involved in a cat washing itself.

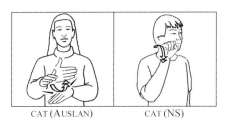

CAT (AUSLAN)   CAT (NS)

Figure 1.2: *Signs for 'cat' in Auslan and NS.*

Although some signs in Auslan are arbitrary, signs that are in some way iconic are more common. In spoken languages, however, the reverse is true—the link between form and meaning in most words is arbitrary. This greater degree of iconicity in visual-gestural languages is not particularly surprising because objects and actions in the external world tend to have more visual than auditory associations. Many objects (such as a table or cup) make no distinctive sounds at all, but have characteristic shapes, or are associated with typical human actions that can be used as the basis of signs. Thus, one form of the Auslan sign TABLE traces the shape of a tabletop and legs, and one variant of CUP represents holding a cup and bringing it to one's lips.

Despite these differences, what arbitrary and iconic words and signs have in common is that their association with particular meanings is based on customary usage within a particular community and thus must be learned by children, as we will see in §1.1.4. Thus, what is important about the use of symbols in language is their conventionalisation—the fact that members of a community share an understanding that particular meanings are conveyed by particular forms (Deuchar, 1984). Because most symbols in spoken languages are both arbitrary and conventionalised, it seems some linguists mistakenly assumed that a defining feature of language was arbitrariness. In fact, it is conventionalisation that is the key to understanding the relationship between a symbol's form and its meaning.

1.1.2 Grammaticality

Human languages have *grammaticality*. No human language consists of a vocabulary of conventional symbols alone—they also have rules for the appropriate combination of these symbols. This means they have grammars—rules for the correct grammatical structure of words and sentences. Other communication systems also have rules of combination. In the case of traffic lights, for example, the green light can follow a red light, but an amber light always precedes a red light. The term *grammar*, however, is usually reserved for the rules that exist in human languages.

An example of a grammatical rule in English would be the word order in the phrase *the woman has seen the man*. Here the subject noun phrase *the woman* comes before the verb phrase *has seen*, and the object noun phrase *the man* comes last (the terms *noun phrase* and *verb phrase* are explained in Chapter 7; *subject* and *object* are discussed in both Chapters 7 and 10). This is a grammatically correct sequence of words in English, but it may not be grammatical in other languages. In German, for example, a different order would be used for this example: *Die Frau hat den Mann gesehen*. Literally, this translates as 'The woman has the man seen'. Here we can see that part of the verb phrase (i.e., *gesehen* 'seen') comes at the end of the sentence, and the word for 'the' has two forms (i.e., *die* and *den*). In Auslan, the equivalent may be signed in the following way: PT+lf WOMAN FINISH SEE PT+rt MAN (see *Conventions* in the introductory pages to this volume for an explanation of these and other Auslan examples). Note that the Auslan sentence does not include a sign meaning 'has', unlike both English and German. Instead, a completed action is signalled in Auslan by the use of the sign FINISH. Also note that in this example, pointing signs work in the same way as the words *the* in English, or *die* or *den* in German, but they also may include information about the relative locations of the two individuals being discussed. This potential for spatial information is not present in the spoken language examples. Despite these differences between the three languages, it is clear that they each share the property of grammaticality.

1.1.3 Discreteness and duality of patterning

Language structure has discreteness: its symbols are made up of a limited set of smaller, separate units. The words of spoken languages are made from a limited set of sounds (e.g., Australian English uses just 44 distinctive sounds), and the signs of Auslan appear to be made of a limited number of handshapes (i.e., approximately 35 handshapes are important in the core vocabulary of the language, as we will see in Chapter 4). Discrete units have clear, definable boundaries, and do not show gradience. In English, for example, the sounds /s/ and /z/ are perceived as distinct—speakers appear to disregard intermediate sounds between the two. Similarly, the handshapes 4 and 5 in Auslan are distinct. Although the position of the thumb may vary in FOUR, once it is fully extended and visible, the sign becomes FIVE. Even though spoken and signed languages are both produced as a continuous stream of sounds and gestures, users are able to segment this connected speech and signing into a finite number of separate (i.e., discrete) units.

Moreover, language appears to have *duality of patterning*—it has two distinct levels of organisation. All languages are able to build meaningful units (e.g., words or signs) out of smaller units that have no meaning in themselves. Thus, words in English enter into two patterns of contrast at once. The word *man* differs from other words in meaning, contrasting with *woman, boy, girl,* etc. The word also differs from other words formationally, contrasting with *can, ban, mat,* etc. The sounds in the word *man* (i.e., the sounds represented by the letters /m/, /a/, and /n/) have no meaning of their own. Only a combination of these sounds in the correct order produces a word with meaning in English—*man*.

Signed languages also exhibit duality of patterning. For example, the sign SISTER contrasts in meaning with other signs such as BROTHER, MOTHER, FATHER, etc. We can see that the sign has a handshape, movement and location that do not in themselves have any meaning, and that changes in one of these features of the sign create a different sign. Changing the location to the cheek produces the sign STRANGE, for example, while moving it to the chin makes a sign meaning WHO in New South Wales and Queensland. In each case, the handshape, movement and location do not have meaning of their own—it is only when the parts are combined into the correct combination that we produce meaningful signs.

Duality of patterning may be a unique feature of language, although it is present to a limited extent in some forms of animal communication (e.g., bird song has individual notes that are combined into particular calls with specific meanings, see Tchernichovski *et al.*, 2001). Duality is most well developed in human language, however—it is this feature that makes it possible for the thousands of words in English and signs in Auslan to be built up from a much smaller set of units.

Nonetheless, just as words and signs are not all arbitrary, so not *all* words or signs in a language need to display discreteness and duality of patterning—the minimal units of some words or signs may have their own meanings, and some aspects of language may be gradient. As we shall see in Chapters 4, 5 and 10, many signs are composed of minimal units which may indeed carry their own meaning or that may be modified to show gradient meanings.

1.1.4   Cultural transmission

Spoken and signed languages differ from one part of the world to the next, as we shall see in §1.3.1. Children born into each different language community have to learn the vocabulary and grammar of the language (or languages) used by adult members of that community. This learning is referred to as *cultural transmission*. In this regard, language differs from many communication systems used by animals, such as the calls of the vervet monkey or tail-wagging dance of the bee. Although some aspects of their appropriate use may be learned in some animals, many of these non-human communication systems appear to be entirely innate. Zebra finches that are deafened during development or reared in isolation will develop the typical song of their species, although it may not completely match those used by hearing finches raised with other birds (Lombardino & Nottebohm, 2000). Some aspects of human behaviour also appear to develop without learning, such as how to swallow liquids or how to recognise our parent's voices, but understanding and producing the specific vocabulary and grammar of one's first language is not one of these innate abilities. If language were entirely innate, then languages would be the same across the globe and children would not need to learn them. Although children are undoubtedly born with an innate capacity to make language learning very rapid and effortless in the first few years of life (and some linguists believe that some general aspects of language structure may be innate, as we shall see in Chapter 10), it is clear that the vocabulary and grammar of specific languages are transmitted from one generation to the next by learning and are not genetically pre-programmed in the brain.

1.1.5   Inter-changeability and reflexiveness

All users of human language may send information to and receive it from other users. This is known as *inter-changeability*. This makes language different from some other communication systems. Although drivers can understand the message sent to them by traffic lights, it is not possible to communicate with traffic lights by attempting to send information back to them. Similarly, only worker bees perform the tail-wagging dance (i.e., other types of bee, such as the queen bee, cannot communicate in this way), and only male zebra finches can produce their distinctive song. Because speakers and signers can both send and receive information, this makes it possible for humans to monitor their own use of language based on the feedback they receive from their own language production (e.g., users of spoken language can hear their own talk, while signers can see and feel their own signing). The ability to monitor one's own use of language also directly leads to another possibly unique feature of human language—the ability to use language to talk about language itself, just as we are doing now. This characteristic is known as the *reflexiveness*.

1.1.6 Displacement

Displacement refers to the unique ability of language users to refer to objects and actions that are removed from the immediate time and place in which the language is being used. Thus, speakers and signers can talk about events in the past or in the future, or at distant locations. Systems of communication used by animals are generally limited to conveying information about objects or events in present and immediate situations. Thus, a vervet monkey cannot discuss a leopard it saw last week, for example. It can only refer to leopards that are present at the time the call is used. Furthermore, the property of displacement allows language users to talk about people and places that exist only in the imagination.

1.1.7 Creativity

Creativity, like displacement, appears to be another feature that is unique to human language. All natural languages are able to expand their vocabulary to express new meanings. For example, signs have developed since the 1990s for new technology, such as INTERNET (Figure 1.3), EMAIL, MOBILE-PHONE and DVD. New signs are also appearing in Auslan because of increasing contact with deaf people from other countries. Many Auslan signs for countries are now being replaced by signs used by the deaf community in that country. For example, there are new and old signs for AMERICA, ITALY (Figure 1.3) and CHINA. This property of language means that languages change across time, as new words and signs are created, and older ones abandoned.

INTERNET	ITALY	ITALY
(new concept, new sign)	(old concept, old sign)	(old concept, new sign)

Figure 1.3 *Old and new signs in Auslan.*

Creativity does not appear to be found in other communication systems. Despite changes to their environment, vervet monkeys have not created any new calls, and honeybees have not modified their tail-wagging dance to differentiate between different sources of nectar.

1.2   What is linguistics?

Having proposed a definition of language and discussed some of its key characteristics, we will now turn our attention to the study of language known as *linguistics*. More precisely, linguistics may be described as *the scientific study of language*. We refer to linguistics as *scientific* because linguists approach the study of language in a scientific manner. As Geoffrey Finch (2000) explained, this means that (1) linguists adopt an objective view of language and (2) they use scientific methods in their study of language (i.e., they use observation, description and explanation).

What does it mean to say that linguists adopt an 'objective' view of language? Linguists are mostly interested in how people actually use language, and less in how people think they should use language. The approach taken by linguists is thus a *descriptive* approach. Linguists aim to give a complete and accurate account of how a language is used at a particular point in time. Linguists collect and study facts about language through interviews, experiments and tests. They also gather information from written sources such as books and newspapers, and by tape-recording or video-recording people as they use language in real life situations. These observations are the basis for a description of the language, which attempts to explain the objective reasons for the ways language is structured, used and acquired by a community. In our case, our aim in this book is to provide an unbiased and objective introduction to some aspects of the history, structure and use of Auslan. We wish to provide information about the structure of language, for example, that is based on a description of how native signers in the community actually use the language (*native signers* are deaf or hearing people that grew up with the language from birth).

This is in sharp contrast to the *prescriptive* approach. Prescriptivists set out rules for what is believed to be correct ways to use language. Often, they use beliefs about language purity, logic and tradition to create rules of 'correct' language use (Crystal, 1997). One well-known example is the Académie Française, which was established in France in 1635 (Eastman, 1983). It is a group of 40 individuals that acts as an official authority on the French language. They publish a dictionary of the language, and make rulings about norms of French grammar and vocabulary. In particular, they publish lists of French words that are recommended as replacements for words that are 'borrowed' from other languages, particularly English. For example, the Académie has ruled that the English words *Walkman* and *browser* that are commonly used in France ought to be replaced by the French equivalents *baladeur* and *logiciel de navigation*. These recommendations are made because the Académie believes it must try and protect the 'purity' of the French language which they see as threatened by the growing influence of

English. These rulings have no legal power, however, and are often ignored by the French government, media and education system who continue to use words borrowed from English (McCrum, Cran & MacNeil, 1986). Recently, the British Deaf Association has established a 'British Sign Language Academy' to protect, promote and preserve BSL. It will be interesting to see whether this organisation will experience the same fate as its French cousin.

The English language lacks an organisation like the Académie Française, but English does have a strong tradition of prescriptivism. Beginning in the eighteenth century, prescriptive books about the structure and use of the English language began to be published, many of which became very influential in education (Leith, 1997). Many of these grammar books did not aim to record actual usage in the community, but instead proposed rules of English grammar based on the structure of Latin or on the laws of logic. At the time, Latin was a language still held in high esteem in Europe. For a thousand years prior, it had been the language used for international communication in scientific and political affairs, and its grammar was considered an example of great logic and clarity (although, in fact, it is no more so than any other human language). Thus, these books suggested that certain common usages in English should be abandoned because they did not follow the same grammatical rules found in Latin. A few well-known examples of 'correct' usage proposed by prescriptivists are listed in Table 1.1.

Table 1.1: *Examples of English prescriptive rules (adapted from Crystal, 1997).*

Common usage	'Correct' usage
It is me.	It is I.
Who are to you speaking to?	To whom are you speaking?
I want to quickly walk home.	I want to walk home quickly.
I haven't done nothing wrong.	I haven't done anything wrong.

Some of these usages (such as the use of double negatives like *I haven't done nothing wrong*) were supposedly 'incorrect' because they were considered illogical. Double negatives, however, have existed in English for several centuries as an emphatic way of expressing negation, and double negatives are the norm in other languages, such as French. It must be pointed out that all these so-called 'incorrect' ways of speaking and writing reflect extremely common usage across the entire English-speaking world, and that it is not clear why Latin grammar or logic should form the basis for determining standard forms of English.

Prescriptivism also exists in the Auslan signing community. Many Auslan teachers reject the use of particular signs even though they are used in the deaf community. This is especially true of those signs that have come into the language recently from Australasian Signed English (we discuss Australasian Signed English in Chapter 2) or from foreign signed languages, particularly

ASL. Many signers also reject signs that were originally only used in specific regions of Australia, or that have been created by hearing people, such as sign language interpreters. Some Auslan teachers instead advocate the preservation and teaching of older and traditional vocabulary, even when many younger deaf people do not use or are even unaware of such signs.

In contrast to the prescriptive approach, linguists do not attempt to evaluate variation in language, or to halt language change, but simply to record the facts. David Crystal (1997:2) pointed out, however, that it is not easy for any of us to study language objectively. Good language skills are important and highly valued, and people make judgements about a person's family background, education, intelligence and even attractiveness based on how they speak or sign. As a result, most readers will come to a book on linguistics like this one with strong views about what English and Auslan are, and how these two languages should be used. As Crystal explained, 'language belongs to everyone; so most people feel they have a right to hold an opinion about it. And when opinions differ, emotions can run high.'

1.2.1 Areas of linguistics

The field of linguistics is divided into a number of major areas.

First, some linguists may work in areas that focus on the structure of languages. The study of the nature of speech sounds and how they are produced and perceived is known as *phonetics*. This contrasts with *phonology*, which is the study of how sounds are organised into the words and phrases of different languages. Although phonetics and phonology both originally referred to the study of sounds in spoken language, they are also used by sign language researchers to refer to the physical properties of signs (signed language phonetics) and how signs are created from smaller formational units (signed language phonology). We explore some aspects of the phonetics and phonology of Auslan in Chapter 4.

The study of grammar is divided into two areas: *morphology* (the study of the grammatical structure of words) and *syntax* (the study of the grammatical structure of word sequences, such as phrases and sentences). *Lexicology* is the term used to refer to the study of the vocabulary (or the *lexicon*) of a language. *Discourse analysis* is the study of how sequences of sentences are organised into larger structures, such as conversations or stories. The study of the grammatical structure of Auslan signs and sentences is explored in Chapters 5 and 7, while a description of the Auslan lexicon is provided in Chapter 6. We describe some aspects of Auslan discourse in Chapter 9.

Second, linguists also work in areas that focus on how language is used. *Semantics* is the study of how language structures are used to make meaning, while *pragmatics* is the relationship between language structure, meaning and context. These aspects of Auslan are covered in Chapters 8 and 9. The study of the relationship between language and society, including variation in language structure and how it relates to social factors (such as gender, age or region), is known as *sociolinguistics* (this is discussed briefly in Chapter 2).

A particularly important area of sociolinguistics is the study of bilingualism (i.e., knowing two or more languages) and language contact (how languages influence each other as a result of contact between different linguistics communities). The study of how language changes over time is known as *historical linguistics* (we look at the history of Auslan in Chapter 3).

Third, linguists are also interested in how languages are learned and processed by the mind and brain. The study of how children learn language is called *first language acquisition. Psycholinguistics* is the study of how the mind produces and processes language, and is a subfield of both linguistics and psychology. *Neurolinguistics* is specifically concerned with the biological aspects of language and the brain (which parts of the brain are involved in producing and processing language and how they work), and thus overlaps with other fields such as medicine and psychiatry.

Last, the field of *applied linguistics* refers to the application of knowledge about the structure and use of language to other areas, particularly to language teaching (known as *second language acquisition*), translation and interpreting, and dictionary making (or *lexicography*).

Despite these well-established divisions and specialisations within the field of linguistics, it would be a mistake to see these areas as strictly separate and to believe that each could be pursued without reference to the others. Many linguists stress the essential interconnectedness of all the different levels of language structure and use. They emphasise that grammar cannot be properly described or studied without reference to semantics. Such linguists see the lexicon, morphology and syntax as forming a continuum of language structures that are not separated by clear and unambiguous boundaries in the way our brief introduction may suggest. We will return to the issue of the nature of language and linguistic theory in Chapter 10.

1.3   Signed languages: Myths and misconceptions

Signed languages (also known as *sign languages*) are the natural languages of deaf communities. In this book, we used the terms *signed language linguistics* or *sign linguistics* to refer to the scientific study of visual-gestural languages of deaf communities rather than the auditory-oral languages of hearing people.

It is very common for books on signed languages to begin with a discussion of myths and misconceptions. Although Auslan was first formally recognised as a community language by the Australian government in 1984 (Lo Bianco, 1987), a number of dictionaries have been available since 1989, and the language has been taught in schools, colleges and universities across the country, many misunderstandings about the language persist, even within the signing community itself. As a result, we outline some of the most common misconceptions in the following sections. Note, however, that we attempt to point out the reasons that these misunderstandings have emerged, and indicate that in some cases, there is a grain of truth in each of them.

1.3.1   Sign language is not universal

As we will see in §1.4 below on the history of signed language research, it was sometimes assumed in late eighteenth-century Europe that signed languages used by deaf people were a form of universal language. The Abbé de l'Epée, for example, who established one of the first public schools for deaf children in the world in 1760, believed that the signed communication used in his school in Paris could serve as the basis of universal language (Kendon, 2004). This belief has continued to this day, with many people outside the signing community surprised to learn that Auslan is a signed language variety only used in Australia (Auslan is, however, closely related to BSL and NZSL).

Signed language is not, however, a universal language. There are many different signed languages around the world, and many of these have developed independently of each other. Even a brief comparison of any of the documented signed languages used in various parts of the world today will show that signed languages are not identical in their vocabulary or grammatical structure. If we compare the sign SISTER in Auslan, ASL and TSL (Figure 1.1) we see that very different signs exist for this concept in these different signed languages. Signed languages also do not all use the same building blocks to create signs. We will see in Chapter 4 that the set of handshapes used in Auslan is not the same as those in other signed languages (e.g., Auslan does not use a handshape that has only the ring finger extended, but this handshape is used in the sign SISTER in TSL). The basic sentence structure of different signed languages also may not be similar. We will show in Chapter 7 that, in some situations, Auslan appears to prefer a sign order in which the actor precedes the verb and the undergoer follows it (e.g., MAN KNOW WOMAN). It is claimed that, in the same context, NS and Argentinian Sign Language use an actor-undergoer-verb order (e.g., MAN WOMAN KNOW) (Nakanishi, 1994; Massone & Curiel, 2004). In Auslan, a headshake may be used to signal negation (e.g., a headshake produced while signing WOMAN CAN DRIVE will produce an utterance meaning 'the woman cannot drive'), but in Greek Sign Language, it appears that a backward head tilt may also be used for the same function (Antzakas & Woll, 2002).

Furthermore, not only do signed languages vary from one part of the world to the next, but (like spoken languages), variation can be found in the vocabulary and grammar within particular signed language communities. Thus, different signers of Auslan may use different signs for the same concept because of their regional origin, educational background and age (this point is explored in more detail in Chapter 2).

Despite these differences, however, studies appear to indicate that the vocabulary of unrelated signed languages often have a proportion of similar or identical signs (Kyle & Woll, 1985), and that the grammar of signed languages are also similar in many ways (Johnston, 1989a; Newport & Supalla, 2000). We explore this point in more detail in Chapter 3. Thus, although signed language is not universal and instead varies from one part of the world to the next, it appears that different signed languages may be more similar to each other than the spoken languages of the world.

1.3.2 Signed languages are not based on spoken languages

As we will see in Chapter 2, signed languages of deaf communities are not based on spoken languages. Many people assume that Auslan is simply English in signed form. This, however, is not the case. Many aspects of the vocabulary and grammar of Auslan are quite unrelated to English. For example, the English word *light* has several meanings. English speakers describe an object as *light* if it does not weigh very much; they would say something is a *light* colour if it is very pale; or they would say 'turn on the *light*' when referring to an electric light in a house or other building. All three of these meanings would be translated into Auslan by different signs (as shown in Figure 1.4), despite the fact that the same form is used in English. We explore more examples of the vocabulary of Auslan in Chapter 6.

'not heavy'　　　　　　'not dark'　　　　　　'electric light'

Figure 1.4: *Three Auslan signs for the separate senses of the English word 'light'.*

In terms of grammar, Auslan uses rules that differ from those found in English. One of the grammatical features of English is the marking of plurality (i.e., the concept of more than one) by the use of the ending *–s* on nouns. English also marks past tense (i.e., that some action occurred in the past) by the use of the ending *–ed* on verbs or by a system of modified verb forms (e.g., *run* versus *ran*). It also includes strict rules about the ordering of words in sentences (e.g., *the woman asked the boy* means something quite different from *the boy asked the woman*). For each of these grammatical phenomena, Auslan and English differ. Auslan does not use an ending on nouns to show plurality, but, as we shall see in Chapter 5, this does not mean that Auslan cannot signal information about number. Auslan does not mark past tense by an ending on verb signs, but the language can indicate important time-related information in other ways (see Chapters 6 and 7). The order of signs is more flexible in Auslan than English, and thus strategies other than word order (as used in the English example above) might be employed to show who does what to whom (see the discussion on the use of space and indicating verbs in Chapter 7 for details).

Despite these differences, Auslan is the language of a minority surrounded by a much larger English-speaking majority. As is also typical of many minority languages in the same social situation, contact between the two languages has resulted in Auslan drawing on English in many areas of its vocabulary and grammar. Many signs are based on fingerspelling the first letter of the corresponding English words (e.g., D-D for DAUGHTER, B-B for BRISBANE) or are fingerspelled abbreviations (e.g., J-A-N for JANUARY and S-Y for SYDNEY). Other words are regularly fingerspelled in full (e.g., S-O-N, J-U-L-Y). The influence of English on Auslan is explored in more detail in Chapters 2 and 6 (the two-handed fingerspelling system used in Australia is illustrated in Figure 2.2).

Thus, signed languages of deaf communities are not based on spoken languages, but they may in fact be significantly affected by the language of the surrounding community.

1.3.3 Signed languages are not simply pantomime and gesture

Sometimes it is mistakenly believed that signed languages are nothing more than forms of pantomime and gesture. By this, it is often meant that signs, and rules for their combination, are made up on the spot. Communication between signers, it is sometimes believed, is achieved by simply pointing at objects, drawing pictures in the air or by acting out descriptions of events. People often use the term 'sign language' to refer to this kind of improvised visual-gestural communication that occurs when two people who do not speak each other's language meet (e.g., 'The man in the market place in Bali did not speak English, so we had to use sign language to communicate'). Research in linguistics, as explained above, has demonstrated that the natural signed languages are in fact real human languages, and not simply pantomime and gesture in this sense.

It is true, however, that the visual-gestural languages of deaf communities share some properties with the gestural communication used by non-signers (Kendon, 2004). The extent of these similarities is currently a matter of controversy among sign language researchers. We explore this point in more detail in §1.5 below, and the debate in signed language linguistics about the relationship between signed language and gesture is taken up in Chapter 10.

1.3.4 Signed languages are not always iconic

Related to the misconception about the relationship between signed languages and gesture is the widespread belief that the meaning of all signs comes from their being 'pictures' of what they represent. We discussed the notion of iconicity in language in §1.1.1 above, and we pointed out that iconicity is more common in signed languages than in spoken languages. A range of different kinds of evidence can be presented to demonstrate that the presence of iconicity in signed languages should not, however, be overemphasised (Woll, 1990). First, like words in all languages, signs also may be arbitrary. Some signs in Auslan have no apparent iconic relationship to their meanings (e.g., PRETEND, MELBOURNE, YOUNG and BEACH (Figure

1.5)). This lack of a clear form-meaning relationship is also found in other signed languages. In addition, the formation of signs in visual-gestural languages is never determined solely by their resemblance to an object or action. As we will see in Chapter 4 on the formational structure of signs, the structure of signs is also influenced by the complex interactions of visual perception and manual production as well as language-specific formational patterns (e.g., the handshape in the TSL signs ELDER-SISTER and YOUNGER-SISTER is not found in any Auslan sign). Furthermore, processes of historical change in signs result in some iconic signs developing into arbitrary symbols over time (Frishberg, 1975; Kyle & Woll, 1985). For example, one sign for LIBRARY (Figure 1.5) in Auslan originally meant 'hairclip' and was the name sign of the librarian at the Victorian school for deaf children. For many signers today who are unaware of the sign's history, the sign is an arbitrary one with no clear connection to its meaning. Together these facts mean that the sign vocabularies of unrelated signed languages, such as NS and Auslan, often develop many different signs.

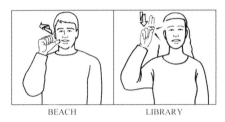

BEACH   LIBRARY

Figure 1.5: *Two signs that lack a form-meaning relationship.*

Second, even when signs are iconic in origin, the particular relationship represented can be specific to that language, as we saw with the different forms of the sign CAT in Auslan and NS above. Similarly, the most common Auslan sign for WOMAN (Figure 1.6) is signed with a B hand moving down the cheek, perhaps indicating the smooth cheeks of a woman's face (in contrast to the Auslan sign MAN which suggests a man's beard). In Israeli Sign Language, the index and thumb pinch the earlobe, while in Danish Sign Language (DSL), the sign indicates the shape of the breasts (Woll, 1990).

Auslan   Israeli Sign Language   DSL

Figure 1.6: *Signs for 'woman' in three unrelated signed languages.*

Third, there is also no evidence that children from signing families learn signed languages quicker than hearing children learn spoken ones, despite the greater degree of iconicity in sign vocabulary and grammar. In a summary of many years of research comparing the acquisition of spoken and signed languages, Laura Petitto (2000:452) presented the following conclusions:

> Deaf children who are exposed to sign languages from birth acquire these languages on an identical maturational times course as hearing children acquire spoken languages. Deaf children acquiring sign languages from birth do so without any modification, loss, or delay to the timing, content, and maturational course associated with reaching all the linguistic milestones observed in spoken language. Beginning at birth, and continuing through age 3 and beyond, speaking and signing children exhibit identical stages of language acquisition.

Finally, interesting evidence comes from experimental studies of short-term memory and language production errors ('slips of the hand') that suggests that signers use the structural components of handshape, orientation, location and movement (see Chapter 4) when remembering and producing signs rather than their iconic properties alone (Emmorey, 2002). As we shall see in §1.3.6 below, there is much evidence that visual-spatial information, such as photographs and maps, and linguistic information, such as spoken and written words, are processed in different areas of the brain. For sign language researchers, the question naturally arose: are signs processed more like pictures or more like words? Researchers wondered if highly iconic signs (e.g., DRINK, TABLE, CUP) might be easier to recall for signers than less iconic ones, perhaps because of strong connections with visual memories or representations. Klima and Bellugi (1979) reported, however, that experimental studies comparing signers' ability to remember lists of signs low in iconicity with lists of highly iconic signs showed no difference in recall. This does not mean that the iconicity does not have other effects on the processing of signed languages by the brain—for example, iconic signs may be easier for adult learners to remember (see Lieberth & Gamble, 1991)—but only that iconic and non-iconic signs both share similar structural properties.

Unfortunately, however, this evidence has been interpreted by some linguists to mean that iconicity plays no significant role at all in signed languages (see, for example, Pinker, 1994). This is not the case: most signs in Auslan do in fact have some link between their form and meaning, and iconicity plays an important role in the grammar (see Chapters 5, 6, 7 and 8).

1.3.5 Signed languages have the same expressive capacity as spoken languages

Contrary to what is sometimes believed, signed languages have the same potential for expressing subtle, technical and complex meanings as spoken languages. Although signed languages share some properties with gesture and include many iconic signs, this does not mean that they are limited in their expressive capacity. There are well-established Auslan signs for a range of complex concepts, such as CULTURE, DISCRIMINATION, PHILOSOPHY and LINGUISTICS. Moreover, any word that exists in English (or any language with a Roman script) can be introduced into Auslan by means of fingerspelling.

Nevertheless, the sign vocabulary of Auslan is smaller that the vocabulary of English (Johnston & Schembri, 1999). This, however, does not indicate that the expressive capacity of Auslan is limited, only that the language has not been used in as wide a range of situations as English. This is true of all languages—the vocabulary of the language reflects the way it has been used. Auslan has only recently begun to be employed again as a language of instruction in schools for deaf children. It is only over the last two decades that it has started to be used by deaf students at universities and college, and by deaf employees in a wide-range of professional and technical jobs. As a result, the sign vocabulary of Auslan is undergoing a period of rapid development and expansion.

1.3.6 Signed and spoken languages are processed by the brain in similar ways

Signed languages are produced by the hands, face and body, and perceived through vision. This makes them very different from spoken languages that are produced by the speech organs and perceived by hearing. Research has shown, however, that this does not make as great a difference to how signed and spoken languages are processed by the brain as might be expected.

The human brain is divided into two halves (known as *hemispheres*). In most human beings, the left hemisphere controls many language functions, while the right hemisphere controls many visual-spatial skills (as was mentioned in §1.3.4 above). After a stroke, particular parts of the brain may be damaged which can result in the loss of specific skills. Patients with damage to parts of the right hemisphere, for example, may lose their ability to draw. Others with left hemisphere damage may suffer from language problems (known as *aphasia*), such as the inability to produce grammatically correct sentences. This does not mean that the right hemisphere does not have a role in language processing (it is important for the production of intonation and for making sense of stretches of spoken discourse, for example), only that parts of the left hemisphere play a particularly important role for spoken language grammar.

Because many people are aware of the different roles played by the two sides of the brain, some assume that signed languages must be entirely processed by the right hemisphere because, unlike spoken languages, they are visual languages that make use of space. Research into the signed communication and visual-spatial skills of deaf people with brain damage in the 1980s has, however, suggested that this is not the case (Poizner, Klima & Bellugi, 1987). Deaf signers with damage to certain areas of the left hemisphere (such as Broca's area or Wernicke's area of the brain) showed very similar types of aphasia to hearing people who use spoken languages. Signers with left hemisphere damage had difficulties with signed language grammatical skills, and yet retained the ability to draw. Moreover, some signers with right hemisphere damage exhibited a breakdown of visual-spatial skills, and yet were still able to use some key aspects of signed language grammar.

Recent research using new technologies, such as functional magnetic resonance imaging (or fMRI) or positron emission tomography (or PET), has enabled researchers to see which areas of the brain are active in normal healthy individuals during language production. Although recent work has shown that the right hemisphere does indeed have a role in certain aspects of signed language processing (such as in the use of space and facial expression during signing), it has confirmed the initial findings based on the study of people with aphasia. For many key aspects of the production and comprehension of signed languages, the left hemisphere is dominant, just as it is with spoken languages (Emmorey, 2002), though it is becoming increasingly clear that language, especially face-to-face communication that is signed or spoken, also uses the right hemisphere.

1.3.7 Children learn spoken and signed languages in similar ways

There have been no longitudinal studies of children learning Auslan (i.e., no studies that have investigated how children develop Auslan from birth to early adulthood). Research on children learning other signed languages (such as ASL and BSL), however, suggests that signed languages are acquired by children in the same way as spoken languages (Emmorey, 2002). For deaf children with signing parents, signed language acquisition begins at birth and continues through childhood. These children appear to reach all the same developmental milestones at the same age as hearing children learning spoken language (Petitto, 2000). From the age of approximately six months, these deaf children begin to 'babble' on their hands, producing sign-like actions in imitation of the signed language they see around them. They produce their first sign at around their first birthday. Although some researchers claimed that deaf children's first signs are acquired earlier than hearing children's first words, more recent research suggest that this finding was incorrect, and that there is no significant difference in the timing of the first sign versus the first word.

The one-sign stage (like the one-word stage in speaking children) continues for some time, as the children add more and more new signs to their vocabulary. Signing children produce signs like FATHER, MOTHER, DOG, BATH, HOT, EAT and GOODBYE, as is also typical of young children learning spoken languages. They also make the same kinds of errors in production, producing signs with incorrect handshapes or movements in the same way speaking children are unable initially to pronounce all the sounds used in English words. Just before they are two years of age, children begin to combine their signs in two-sign combinations, such as WANT MILK or FIND

BALL. By two and a half, vocabulary begins to grow more rapidly, and sentences become much longer as children begin to acquire complex grammatical rules. They learn how to negate sentences with headshakes and using signs like NOT and NOTHING, and begin to form questions, and make use of space in their signing. By age five, most of the basic grammar of the signed language is learned, although it takes a few more years before all aspects of the language are mastered completely.

Hearing children from deaf families who learn both signed and spoken languages (for example, in cases where one parent signs and another speaks) move through the same stages, and show no preference for spoken language in their early years, even though they can hear (Petitto, 2000). This shows that, for young children, language is language, regardless of whether it is spoken or signed.

1.3.8 Signed languages were not invented by hearing people

There is no evidence that any single individual, hearing or deaf, invented natural signed languages such as Auslan, BSL, ASL and French Sign Language (Langue des signes française or LSF). Signed languages appear to have been in use among deaf people in Australia, Britain, the United States and France (and elsewhere in the world) before schools for deaf children were established in the eighteenth and nineteenth centuries (we discuss the history of Auslan in Chapter 3). In fact, there are references to the use of signed language by deaf people in the writings of Plato (Rée, 1999). The work of the eighteenth-century deaf writer, Pierre Desloges, describes an active signing community in Paris at the time, most of whom had no formal education. In fact, the Abbé de l'Epée is known to have first learned LSF from deaf people, and later used a variety of this signed communication as the medium of instruction in the first public school for deaf children in Paris (Lane, 1984). This very approach was recommended by John Wallis in England in the late seventeenth century, who suggested that educators must learn deaf people's signed language in order to teach them English (Rée, 1999).

Thus, it can be assumed that signed languages developed naturally when deaf people first came together to form deaf communities. We can see that same process at work today in countries such as Nicaragua where a new signed language has developed only relatively recently. In 1979, a socialist government came to power after a revolution in Nicaragua. The new government created the first school for the deaf, and deaf children were brought together for the first time. Although the language of instruction in the school was Spanish, the deaf children began to create a signed language in the classroom and in the playground to communicate with each other. At first, they used *home signs*—a limited vocabulary of signs that they had individually created to communicate with their hearing family members. Over time, more and more of these signs began to be shared among the deaf students, and rules for the combination of these signs into sentences began to develop naturally. A new language—Nicaraguan Sign Language—was born (Kegl, 1994; Kegl, Senghas & Coppola, 1999).

The misconception that signed languages were invented by hearing people probably comes about for two main reasons. First, some artificial sign systems have been created (at least in part) by hearing individuals, and there is little doubt that such systems have in fact influenced natural signed languages. This includes the Australasian Signed English system that was developed by a committee (which included both hearing and deaf people) between 1974 and 1982. The purpose of this system for representing English in signed form was to teach English to deaf children. We discuss artificial sign systems in Chapter 2.

Second, it seems that fingerspelling systems that are used by deaf signers were first used by hearing people. For example, the two-handed manual alphabet used in Auslan today appears to have its origins in fingerspelling systems used by hearing people as secret codes (Sutton-Spence & Woll, 1999). Later, this alphabet began to be used by some deaf people and was adopted as a tool for teaching literacy to deaf children. The one-handed alphabet used in many other signed languages, such as ASL and LSF, appears to have been introduced in the early seventeenth century by Juan Pablo Bonet as a method of teaching reading and writing to deaf individuals (Padden & Gunsauls, 2003). It may have its origins in a manual alphabet used by monks during periods of ritual silence.

1.3.9 Signed languages can be written down

Members of the Australian deaf community do not have any everyday written form of the language, and English is used as the written language by all literate signers. Some people mistakenly believe that signed languages cannot be 'real' languages because they lack a written form. This misunderstanding reflects the fact that writing is such a large part of our culture, and as a result, some of us find it difficult to imagine using a language that has no written form. There are, however, many spoken languages around the world today that have no writing system and no written literature, and few would question whether these are real languages. Thus, the issue of a writing system is irrelevant to the question of whether or not signed languages are real languages.

Sometimes, however, the point about Auslan lacking a written form is misinterpreted as a claim that signed languages, by their very nature, cannot be written down (Bernal & Wilson, 2004). People sometimes point out that Auslan make use of the space around the signer, as well as a range of facial expressions, and this poses a challenge for the design of a writing system for the language. There is, however, much in the spoken message that is routinely omitted from the written form (such as accent, intonation etc). In fact, a number of writing systems for signed languages have been proposed. Some have become widely used by sign language researchers for specific purposes, and others have even begun to be used in schools for deaf children in some countries as an educational tool.

Signed language writing systems come in two forms: *glossing* and *notation*. Glossing refers to the practice of using spoken language translations of signs, together with special symbols to represent the use of space and facial expression. This is the type of writing system used in this book to represent Auslan (see *Conventions*). Notation, in contrast, involves the use of special symbols to represent the physical features of signed language itself. The most well-known examples would be Stokoe Notation, first created by William Stokoe, and HamNoSys or the Hamburg Notation System from the Institute for German Sign Language in Hamburg, Germany. None of these systems, however, are intended as practical ways of communicating in a written form of a signed language: they are intended to represent signs and signed utterances for linguistic analysis (an example of two Auslan signs written in HamNoSys can be found in Chapter 4).

One signed languages notation system that does aspire to be a practical way of communicating in the written form is Sutton Sign Writing. This uses simplified illustrations of handshapes, facial expressions and the body together with movement symbols to represent signs. It is used by researchers, teachers and some members of the deaf community in the USA and some other countries (e.g., Belgium, Colombia, Denmark, Japan, Nicaragua, Peru, South Africa and Spain).

1.4   A brief history of the study of signed languages

As mentioned above, recognition of signed languages may be traced back to the work of Plato in Ancient Greece. In his philosophical work *Cratylus* (written in 360 BC), Plato wrote that if we had no voice or tongue, 'should we not, like the deaf and dumb, make signs with the hand and head and the rest of the body?'. In the eighteenth century, the French philosopher René Descartes suggested that the signed languages of deaf people represented examples of true human languages (Rée, 1999). Similar beliefs were shared by nineteenth-century scholars such as Edward Tylor in Britain, Wilhelm Wundt in Germany and Garrick Mallery in the United States of America (Kendon, 2004). The educator Roch-Ambroise Bébian even attempted to develop a writing system for signed languages based on his discovery that signs can be analysed into smaller components (Fischer, 1995). For a number of reasons, however, signed language research went into decline during the early twentieth century, and many of these earlier insights were forgotten.

Modern signed language linguistics is often considered to have begun with the publication in 1960 of *Sign Language Structure* by William Stokoe, a hearing lecturer at Gallaudet College in Washington DC. This was the first analysis of ASL structure using linguistic methodology, and Stokoe presented persuasive evidence that ASL was indeed a language with a grammar and vocabulary independent of English. This was followed five years later by the *Dictionary of American Sign Language on Linguistic Principles* (Stokoe, Casterline & Croneberg, 1965). Stokoe's publications were, however, preceded by work published in Dutch by Bernard Tervoort. He described the signed communication used by deaf children in the residential school at St Michielsgestel in The Netherlands. Tervoort recognised this signing as a language, but his study was less influential than the later work by Stokoe.

Despite these beginnings, however, the signed language research being carried out by Stokoe and his colleagues at Gallaudet in the 1960s aroused little interest elsewhere, and some hostility from other members of the college academic and administrative staff who believed that signed languages were not 'real' languages and questioned the value of this research (Maher, 1996). By the early 1970s, however, interest in ASL was growing, led by the researchers Klima and Bellugi at the Salk Institute for Biological Studies. Klima and Bellugi recognised that the study of human language would be incomplete without research into the visual-gesture communication of deaf communities, and they trained a whole generation of deaf and hearing sign language researchers in their sign language laboratory in San Diego (Emmorey & Lane, 2000). News of the groundbreaking work on ASL began to spread out across the world in the 1970s. Signed language research started in the United Kingdom and Europe in the mid 1970s, and began in Australia in the 1980s with the work of Trevor Johnston. He wrote the first published descriptions of Auslan including a sketch grammar and a dictionary (1987a, 1987b) as well as a curriculum guide for the teaching of Auslan as a second language (1987c). This was followed by the first doctoral dissertation on Auslan (1989a) and a comprehensive illustrated dictionary of the language (1989b).

Since the 1980s, signed language research has begun to become a truly international field of research, with research papers published on signed languages from South and Southeast Asia, the Middle East, Africa and South America. In 2004 at the Eighth International Conference on Theoretical Issues in Sign Language Research in Barcelona (Spain) papers on over 25 signed languages from all parts of the world were presented.

1.5   Signed languages and gesture

In §1.3.3 above, we showed that signed languages are not identical to gesture and mime. Nevertheless, *gesture* is a very broad term, and one whose use is easily misunderstood. Adam Kendon (2004), for example, suggests that gestures are visible actions of the hands, face and body that are intentionally used to communicate. When human beings interact face to face, a range of different bodily actions conveys information about their intentions, feelings and ideas. For example, a speaker's posture and gaze direction can make their addressee aware of the focus and nature of their attention, even though this information may not be under conscious control. Kendon suggests, however, that this body language should not be considered an example of gesture, as gestures are deliberately communicative actions.

Gesture is often contrasted with signed languages, but we can see that Kendon's (2004) definition would certainly encompass the visual languages of deaf communities. How then are gesture and signed languages to be distinguished? Is such a distinction possible or useful?

In earlier work, Kendon suggested there were a number of main kinds of gestural communication: (1) gesticulation, (2) mime, (3) pointing, (4) emblems and (5) signed languages. The psychologist David McNeill (1992) placed these gesture types on a continuum that he termed 'Kendon's continuum', reflecting their relationship to language. A version of this continuum is shown in Figure 1.7. For our purposes, we will compare each type of gesture to signed language so that differences and similarities can be highlighted.

From least linguistic   *to most linguistic*

Gesticulation → Mime → Pointing → Emblems → Signed languages

Figure 1.7: *Kendon's continuum*

Gesticulation refers to the type of spontaneous gesturing that occurs as people speak. McNeill (1992:9) illustrated this nicely with an example from his own research. In these studies, a speaker watched a film or animated cartoon, and then later recounted the story to a second person. The example in Figure 1.8 is a gesture produced by a participant while explaining how one character in the cartoon pursued another and attempted to hit the unfortunate individual with an umbrella. The speaker produces this gesture while saying '...and she chased him out again'. This example illustrates how the iconic gesture can complement the spoken utterance, conveying information that the speech leaves out, since the informant did not refer to the use of the umbrella by the cartoon character in spoken words, only in the gesture.

Figure 1.8: '*...and she chased him out again'.*

Although such use of gesture may convey specific meanings in particular contexts, this does not necessarily mean that such gestures could be considered equivalent to words in a spoken language, nor to signs in a signed language. Gesticulation lacks most of the main properties of language. There is no fixed vocabulary of such gestures, for example, and the use of gesticulation varies from one person to the next. These gestures tend to occur on their own, rarely joining together into sentence-like patterns. Instead, these gestures appear to be closely synchronised with the rhythm of speech, and to serve to supplement spoken language in particular ways. However, like signed languages, gesticulation makes meaningful use of handshapes, locations and movements: the gesture in Figure 1.8 resembles a sign in Auslan for HIT, for example.

Mime involves imitating real-life activities without the object and people normally involved being physically present. A mime artist 'may act out the process of riding a bike, going to bed or driving a bus without any props other than her or his own gestures and body movement' (Brennan, 1992:12). It differs from the use of gesticulation shown in Figure 1.8 in two ways. First of all, mime may rely less on accompanying speech to convey its meaning, and it involves more than the use of the hands. If the umbrella-waving gesture discussed above were combined with movement of the head and body, then it would be properly considered an example of mime. Like gesticulation, however, there is no vocabulary of mime standardised across a community of users. As a result, the mimed communication of the types seen in television game shows or in the theatre may sometimes require too much time and space to work as an effective communication system (Brennan, 1992:13). The mime artist must tell a story by acting it out in real time, as if it were happening in the present, and must walk around the stage in order to suggest the location and spatial arrangement of the objects and people being described. As Mary Brennan explained:

> If the artist wishes to convey the meaning expressed by the sentence 'I over-indulged last night by eating an enormous meal' an elaborate replay of the activity involved would be required. In contrast, sign languages can exploit the potential of space and gesture while honing the medium into a fast and efficient linguistic tool.

The existence of a standardised vocabulary of signs means that users of signed languages can refer freely to events in the past, present or future, and do not require such elaborate acting out of activities to communicate basic information. The grammatical organisation of signed languages also allows signers to quickly and efficiently communicate who did what to whom. Thus, signers may remain in one place, using only the space around them as a 'stage' in which to represent people, objects and actions. Despite this, many aspects of signed language have a basis in mime. As we shall see in Chapters 8 and 9, both individual signs such as SWIM and RUN as well as the use of role shift during stretches of signed discourse resemble mimed representations of actions.

Unlike other forms of gesture, emblems usually involve the use of very specific handshapes, locations and movements that are linked to specific meanings. In Britain and Australia, for example, Churchill's palm-forward 'V for victory' gesture differs only slightly from the palm-backwards 'up-yours' insult. Emblems also have a different relationship to speech, often replacing it completely. These gestures have particular functions, being used mainly as forms of greeting, command, request, insult, or threat. Examples of emblematic gestures include hand waving for 'hello' or 'goodbye', the 'okay' sign, and the 'thumbs-up' gesture.

The precise meaning of particular emblematic gestures is often only known to a particular cultural group. Thus, like the words of spoken languages, emblems vary from one part of the world to the next. McNeill (1992) explained that the 'hand purse' gesture (made by placing the fingers and thumb together, pointing upwards) is used to signal a 'question' or 'query' in Italy, 'good' in Greece, and to express fear in France, Belgium and Portugal. Similarly, the 'okay' sign, so widely known throughout Europe, is considered a threatening gesture in North Africa.

Emblematic gestures may thus be comparable to the signs in signed languages. Unlike signs, however, such gestures tend to be restricted in number and function. Non-signers tend to use very few emblems and there do not appear to be rules for producing new emblematic gestures. Emblematic gestures are rarely systematically combined into phrases and sentences. Despite this, however, emblems are incorporated into signing and form the basis of many Auslan signs. Examples would include GOOD and CONGRATULATE (from the 'thumbs up' gesture), and PERFECT (from the 'okay' gesture) (Figure 1.9).

CONGRATULATE   PERFECT

Figure 1.9: *Auslan signs derived from emblematic gestures.*

Pointing falls on the continuum between gesticulation and mime at one end and emblems at the other. This is because pointing has forms that are conventionalised within a particular culture (McNeill, 2000). In English-speaking cultures, the usual form for pointing involves the use of an index finger extended from a fist, but in some Aboriginal cultures, this form exists alongside other types of pointing using different handshapes (Wilkins, 2003). However, within Western culture, two fingers or a full flat hand would still be understood as pointing, showing that this convention is not as standardised in our culture as the use of some emblems (e.g., the 'thumbs up' sign). Pointing is also midway along Kendon's continuum because in some contexts (e.g., pointing while saying 'no, I want this book, not that one'), the use of pointing with spoken language may appear obligatory, but pointing is also fully comprehensible without speech. In fact, the use of pointing by non-signers shares many characteristics with pointing in Auslan, and is the source of the pointing signs that act as pronouns and determiners in the language (see Chapters 6 and 7).

1.6   Summary

As all of the points above have demonstrated, research in linguistics over the last four decades has shown that signed languages are 'real' languages, having many of the same characteristics as spoken languages. Like spoken languages, signed languages fulfil all the criteria in the definition of *language* provided in the definition in §1.2 above. They are natural languages that were not invented by any single individual. They are shared by the members of a community and passed down from one generation of users to the next. Signed languages do not form a universal language used by deaf people all over the world, nor are they identical to the types of gesture and mime used by hearing people. They have a similar expressive capacity as spoken languages and are organised around similar grammatical rules. Signed languages have rules for creating new vocabulary and may change across time, and they are learned by children and appear to be processed by the brain in similar ways to spoken languages.

1.7   Further reading

This chapter is best read in conjunction with other opening sections of introductory textbooks on linguistics. Finch (2000), Hudson (2000), Trask (1999) and Yule (1996) provide good basic overviews. Crystal (1997) is a useful compendium of interesting facts about language. For an Australian perspective, see Finegan *et al.* (1997) and Fromkin *et al.* (2005). The latter book includes a little information on Auslan.

For introductions to the linguistics of signed languages, see Valli, Lucas & Mulrooney (2005) for ASL, and Sutton-Spence & Woll (1999) for BSL. Baker & Cokely (1980) on ASL is useful, although intended for sign language teachers. Brennan (1992) is an excellent and accessible overview of the vocabulary and some aspects of the grammar of BSL. Klima & Bellugi (1979) and Kyle & Woll (1985) are classic introductions to signed language research, although much important work has happened since they were published.

For an overview on the study of signed language and the brain, see Emmorey (2002). This book also includes a useful summary of findings in the field of signed language acquisition. The research on Nicaraguan Sign Language is summarised in Kegl (1994). For an introduction to gesture studies, see Kendon (2004). This book, together with Kyle & Woll (1985) and Rée (1999), provide overviews of the history of signed language research. Maher (1996) is an interesting biography of William Stokoe.

2   Auslan in social context

In the previous chapter, we saw that signed languages are now recognised as real languages. In this chapter, we place signed languages in their social context and describe how language use in signing communities differs from that found in spoken language communities. For example, we explain how signed languages are often only found as primary languages in deaf communities which are small linguistic minorities embedded within much larger communities using spoken languages. These spoken languages, in turn, often have written forms, which are used by literate signers. The types of signed communication that evolve in deaf communities given this relationship between signed and spoken (written) languages—such as natural signed languages, artificial sign systems and natural sign systems (Fischer, 1998)—is explained in this chapter. Importantly, the question of variation in signed language is also examined.

2.1   The deaf population, the deaf community and the Auslan-using population

Only a very small percentage of the Australian population is severely or profoundly deaf. The prevalence of deafness in developed societies has long been estimated to be about 0.1 per cent of the population (i.e., one in one thousand people) (Schein, 1968; Schein & Delk, 1974). If this were the case, there would be approximately 20,000 deaf Auslan users out of a population of approximately 20 million in 2005. The precise number of signing deaf people in Australia is, however, unknown. Published estimates have ranged from as low as 7,000 (Power, 1987) to as high as 30,000 (Deaf Society of NSW, 1989). For the past decade, research by Merv Hyde and Des Power (1991), which suggested a figure of approximately 15,000 signing deaf people, has been considered the most reliable (Ozolins & Bridge, 1999).

In the two most recent Australian Census of Population and Housing, however, only some 4,425 individuals in 1996 and 5,305 individuals in 2001 claim to use a signed language in the home (Johnston, 2004). Furthermore, in a study comparing the demographics of deafness in twenty countries around the world, the American researcher Jerome Schein (1987) noted that the Australian figure is 35.1 per 100,000 of population, which he reported as the lowest of all 20 countries he surveyed. This would suggest a current figure of approximately 6,700 signing deaf people in Australia (based on a total population of 20 million), again much lower than suggested by Hyde and Power (1991). Uldis Ozolins and Marianne Bridge (1999) pointed out, however, that Schein (1987) based his figures on data from the 1933 census, the last time statistics on disability were included in a national survey.

Recent research indicates that there may be fewer people with severe and profound deafness than has previously been assumed (Johnston, 2004). This suggests that the figures from Schein (1987) may in fact still be accurate. The research looked at evidence from the number of children enrolled in each of Australia's major residential schools for deaf children up to 1954 (when mainstreaming was introduced). This was combined with data on the prevalence of deafness from National Acoustic Laboratories (NAL) surveys of children under the age of eighteen years who were tested for hearing loss between 1949 and 1980. These were compared with results from neo-natal hearing screening programmes in Australia, the United Kingdom and the United States of America. Together the evidence suggests that the number of severely and profoundly deaf Auslan users may be approximately 6,500. Enrolment and NAL data also provide evidence of a marked increase in incidence rates during two rubella epidemics. The data suggest there will be a decline in numbers over the next twenty to twenty-five years.

Of course, a much larger proportion of the population has various types and degrees of hearing impairment. For example, according to a survey by the Australian Bureau of Statistics in 1993, almost one million people (or approximately 5 per cent of the population) had some hearing loss. However, most of this hearing impairment was mild or moderate and acquired in adulthood (Wilson *et al.*, 1998). Often it was due to disease, regular exposure to loud noise or the result of the ageing process. In terms of the size and make up of the deaf community, one should therefore not confuse such individuals (variously known as 'hard of hearing', 'hearing impaired', or 'deafened' people) with signing deaf people. Very few deafened individuals, for example, know (or perceive the need to know) any signed language because prior familiarity with spoken English greatly improves their ability to lip read, and they can often maintain their ability to speak intelligibly.

In contrast, the use of a signed language is one of the defining characteristics of a deaf community. People who have been deaf from early childhood form the core of the signing deaf community. Members of the deaf community spend a large part of their leisure and social life with other deaf people. Most, however, are employed in the wider (hearing) community, and may have many hearing family members. The signing deaf community is thus similar to the various minority ethnic communities in an immigrant country like Australia (e.g., the Greek or Vietnamese communities) in terms of where and when the language of the community is used. Signed language is used in the home, at social events, at the various deaf clubs, deaf associations and organisations, and in some schools. Interactions with the wider community are either conducted in some form of written (or sometimes spoken) English or in signed language with the aid of interpreters.

The deaf community also resembles other minority communities in that it forms a distinct subculture within the Australian community. Deaf people share many experiences, values and traditions. Aspects of the Australian deaf subculture include regular gatherings at the Australian deaf games and national conferences, as well as state-based regular deaf festivals. Traditionally, smaller-scale gatherings took place in deaf clubs, although increasingly such clubs are closing and deaf people are meeting in other venues. Deaf people value membership in the signing community, and participation in its organisational networks. This is reflected in a strong pattern of endogamous marriage—80-90 per cent of deaf people who get married marry other deaf people (Schein & Delk, 1974; Kyle & Woll, 1985).

The vast majority of deaf adults' children are hearing and many of them use some form of signed language in order to communicate with their parents. Some of these hearing children of deaf parents (often called 'children of deaf adults' or 'CODAs') are involved in the social life and welfare of the deaf community and thus use signed language outside the family. The signing population therefore includes some CODAs as well as hearing individuals who have learned signed language through classes, socialise with deaf people or work in deaf community organisations.

The signing population, the signing deaf community and the deaf and hearing-impaired population are thus not identical. They do not map simply and neatly onto one another because not all deaf people use a signed language, not all users of a signed language are deaf, and not all signers participate in or identify with the deaf community.

2.2 Auslan and the deaf community

In Australia, Auslan is the primary or preferred language of the majority of deaf people who have been severely or profoundly deaf since early childhood. It is the native language (i.e., the language acquired from birth) of only a minority of deaf signers, which has been traditionally estimated at between 5-10 per cent of the deaf community (Schein & Delk, 1974, although see Mitchell & Karchmer, 2004).

Recent Australian research does indeed show that only a small fraction of signers are raised in households with at least one parent or sibling who uses a signed language. For example, a survey of the deaf community in New South Wales found that only 32 of all the 706 deaf adults who responded to the survey questions (equal to 4.7 per cent of the total) came from families where Auslan was used in the home (Deaf Society of NSW, 1998). Indeed, a study by Johnston (2004) noted that between 1871 and 1954, fewer than 3 per cent of children enrolling in the Royal Institute for Deaf and Blind Children in Sydney were identified as having a deaf parent, uncle or aunt, or grand-parent (though up to 10 per cent had a deaf sibling). Given that most of these deaf parents would themselves not be native signers, this suggests very few signing deaf children have significant exposure to native signers as adult language models.

Regardless of whether the parents are themselves native signers, those deaf children who are born to signing deaf parents appear to acquire signed languages in the same way as hearing children acquire spoken language from their parents and other family members, as we saw in Chapter 1. For most adults in the deaf community, however, Auslan is acquired either as a (possibly delayed) first language at some time during their school years, or as a second language in later life. In a small number of cases, deaf people learn Auslan as a late-acquired first language in early adulthood, after partial or unsuccessful exposure to English.

Thus an important difference between deaf communities and other linguistic minorities is that, in most cases, the language is not passed on from parent to child, but often from child to child, or is learned by children from adults outside the family. In the past, near-native and non-native signers have usually acquired the language in centralised schools for the deaf or in specialised units attached to a regular school, often learning it from other deaf children who have deaf parents, older deaf children, or deaf ancillary staff (Johnston, 1989a). Increasingly, however, the effect of educational policies of mainstreaming children with special needs has been that many other deaf adults have learnt the language through social exposure to signing deaf people only after school.

As Auslan has only recently become the language of instruction in some schools for deaf children, those deaf adults who learnt the language at school probably have overwhelmingly acquired it in residential school dormitories, or in the playground, rather than through formal instruction. Indeed, prior to the establishment of sign bilingual programmes for deaf children in Australia (where Auslan and English are both used in the classroom), the use of Auslan was almost entirely confined to deaf people's homes, social events, and deaf clubs. Since its recognition by the Australian government in the 1980s, however, the language has begun to be used in a wider range of social, educational and employment situations (Lo Bianco, 1987; Branson & Miller, 1991).

2.3   The language of the deaf community

Auslan exists in a complex linguistic environment and, as with all languages, there are different forms of signing which are appropriate to different social situations. However, it is important to realise that not all the signing behaviour that one may observe individuals engaging in is properly characterised as 'Auslan'. Rather, several distinct varieties of signed language exist within the community. Even if delineating clear boundaries between the varieties of signed language used in the Australian deaf community is problematic, we will attempt to describe this complex sociolinguistic situation here because this is essential for understanding the type of language data upon which our description of Auslan is based.

In this section, the relationship between Auslan (or most deaf community signed languages) and English (or many hearing community spoken languages) is described. Though the nature and extent of the relationship between signed and spoken languages remains difficult to characterise (Johnston, 1991a; Lucas & Valli, 1992; Sutton-Spence, 1995), it is clear that there are many similarities, as well as differences, with other situations of contact between language communities. Importantly, although Auslan is not English in signed form, it must be recognised that signed communication can be used to represent the spoken language of the surrounding community (this type of language-mixing may in fact be unique to deaf communities). However, the ability of signed communication to represent spoken languages does not undermine the essential autonomy and uniqueness of natural signed languages (Johnston, 1991a).

2.3.1　Natural sign languages

As we saw in Chapter 1, deaf people in deaf communities use signed languages which (a) are not identical to the majority spoken language of the majority hearing community, and (b) are not identical to the signed languages of other deaf communities. *Auslan* is the name given to the *natural sign language* (also known as a *native sign language* or NSL) of the Australian deaf community. Many signed languages are identified and named in a similar way to the majority spoken language of the speech community in which they are found (e.g., LSF, NS, Swedish Sign Language, Italian Sign Language and so on). It would be a mistake, however, to believe that each of these signed languages is a mirror of the spoken language of it majority linguistic community, as we pointed out in Chapter 1. After all, ASL and BSL are quite different and mutually unintelligible (i.e., signers from each community would have difficulty understanding each other if they simply used their own signed language), yet both deaf communities are in countries that have English as their majority spoken language. We have seen in the previous chapter that signed languages fulfil all the criteria of a natural language.

This rest of this book is dedicated to describing Auslan, the natural signed language used in Australia. However, like other minority languages in the Australian community, it is impossible for users of Auslan to avoid contact with English, the majority language of the country. Consequently, as explained above, there are several distinct types of English-influenced signing behaviour. These will be identified and described in the following sections.

2.3.2   Artificial sign systems

An *artificial sign system* is developed with the specific purpose in mind of representing the vocabulary and grammar of spoken languages using manual signs (Fischer, 1998). Both in Australia and elsewhere in the English-speaking world, this type of 'engineered' signing is also sometimes called *manually coded English* (or MCE). Artificial sign systems have generally been created by educators in order to increase deaf children's exposure to spoken language by making it visible. When using an artificial sign system, one makes a manual sign (or uses fingerspelling) for each word and word ending of the spoken language, almost as if signing were a type of writing. In most cases, this signing is presented simultaneously with the spoken message. An example is presented in Figure 2.1.

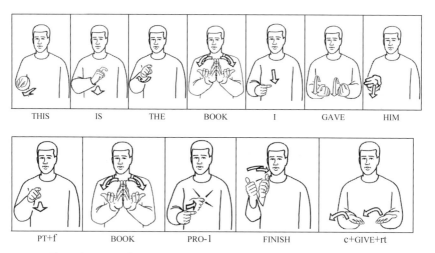

Figure 2.1: *Example in Australasian Signed English (top) and Auslan (bottom).*

The manual representation of spoken language for use in the education of deaf children has a long history. In eighteenth-century France, the Abbé de l'Epée created a system of what he called 'methodical' signs (Lane, 1984). He took vocabulary items from LSF, combined them with signs he created for French grammatical markers, and produced a system to represent spoken French in signed form. Recent varieties of artificial sign systems used in North America include: Seeing Essential English (SEE I), Signing Exact English (SEE II), Linguistics of Visual English (LOVE) and Signed English (SE) (Bornstein, 1990; Supalla & McKee, 2002). In the United Kingdom, the two main systems used are British Signed English (BSE), and the Paget-Gorman Sign System (PGSS) (Kyle & Woll, 1985). The sign system which educators have introduced in Australia and New Zealand is a single, standardised system called Australasian Signed English (ASE), often referred to simply as 'Signed English' (Jeanes & Reynolds, 1982). It has also been adopted in some other parts of the Pacific, such as in Papua New Guinea and Fiji.

During the last three decades of the twentieth century, ASE was the most widely used medium of instruction in programmes for signing deaf children (Leigh, 1995). Unlike a natural language, however, ASE is a system devised by a committee in the 1970s as an exact representation of English in signed form (MacDougall, 1988). Although its lexicon draws heavily on signs from Auslan, the vocabulary items in ASE are standardised for specific English meanings. In some cases, this usage did not always reflect the sign's original meaning in Auslan. For example, a sign meaning originally something like 'checked-pattern' was made the sign for the English word *check* in all its senses, and a modified form of the sign meaning 'light colour' was used for all senses of the word *light* (see Chapter 1). These standardised signs were combined with invented signs (such as the signs THE and HIM in Figure 2.1) that represent English determiners, pronouns, prepositions and other function words necessary to represent English grammar (these grammatical terms are defined in Chapter 7). A set of signs to represent the irregular past tense forms of English verbs was also created (in most cases, original Auslan verbs were modified in some way, as we see in the example of GAVE in Figure 2.1).

Despite its widespread use in deaf education, several studies overseas have raised questions about the capacity of teachers to use artificial sign systems for manually encoding English (Supalla 1991; Drasgow & Paul, 1995). Perhaps the most serious problem for these systems was demonstrated in a classic experiment by Ursula Bellugi and Susan Fischer (1972). This study showed that signs on average take twice as long to articulate as words, due partly to the relatively larger size of the articulators involved in the production of signs (i.e., the hands and arms versus the speech tract). In order to represent English in signed form, the rate of articulation must thus decrease to an unnaturally slow pace, or many of the signs must be dropped.

The implications of this finding for artificial sign systems have been confirmed by research in Australia. The work of Greg Leigh (1995) has shown that while some pre-school teachers seem able to represent English accurately using ASE in interactions with very young children, the greater linguistic demands of upper primary and secondary school education lead to much lower levels of accuracy in the simultaneous use of signed and spoken English. Leigh's (1995) study demonstrated that less than 30 per cent of all utterances signed by secondary school teachers using ASE were considered to be grammatically acceptable representations of English in signed form by independent raters, compared to 53 per cent and 78 per cent for primary and pre-school situations respectively.

The impact of such inconsistent linguistic role models on the language development of deaf children from hearing families is not well understood. ASE is not widely used in the Australian deaf community (Deaf Society of NSW, 1998), and research overseas has reported that deaf children in schools using an artificial sign system may not always use it to communicate with each other (Supalla, 1991). The effect of two decades of instruction in ASE on the signed language used by younger members of the deaf community has not yet been the subject of any research, but there is some evidence that it has had a significant impact on the Auslan lexicon (Johnston, Adam & Schembri, 1997). This is especially true for younger deaf signers, particularly those who live in the smaller communities outside the larger urban centres.

2.3.3 Fingerspelling

Fingerspelling refers to the use of hand configurations to represent the letters of a writing system, with different systems used in different parts of the world (Carmel, 1982). While fingerspelling is an essential part of Auslan and some other signed languages, it should not be confused with signed language as such. When one fingerspells fully, one more or less 'writes in the air', spelling words out manually, letter by letter. Fingerspelling may thus be regarded as an artificial sign system. However, it is regularly used as part of a natural system (see §2.3.4) and, in the case of Auslan, even as part of the native sign language (see Chapter 6).

The fingerspelling system used in Australia is the two-handed alphabet that has its origins in Britain (Figure 2.2). There is also a one-handed alphabet in Australia, but its use is restricted. This one-handed manual alphabet had its immediate origins in Ireland and—together with Irish Sign Language (ISL)—was used in Australian Catholic schools for the deaf from 1875 until the 1950s (see Chapter 3). The use of this one-handed alphabet has long been discontinued in Catholic deaf education and its regular use in the deaf community is confined to an older generation of signers. However, the American one-handed alphabet (the one used by deaf signers of ASL) is increasingly commonly known by deaf Australians, especially younger people or those who travel overseas frequently, because of the prestige of ASL and the use of similar alphabets in a number of deaf communities around the world (Figure 2.3). The ASL manual alphabet was also used in the Perth school for deaf children from its foundation in 1896 until 1927, and is thus familiar to older members of the Western Australian deaf community (Blackmore, 1996). There are a number of differences between the ISL and the ASL one-handed alphabets. For example, the handshapes for the letters *f, g, h, k, l, p, q, t* and one variant of *s* are different in the ASL and ISL alphabets (Figure 2.4). These differences surface in some of the initialised signs in Auslan that have their origins in the Catholic deaf community (see Chapters 5 and 6).

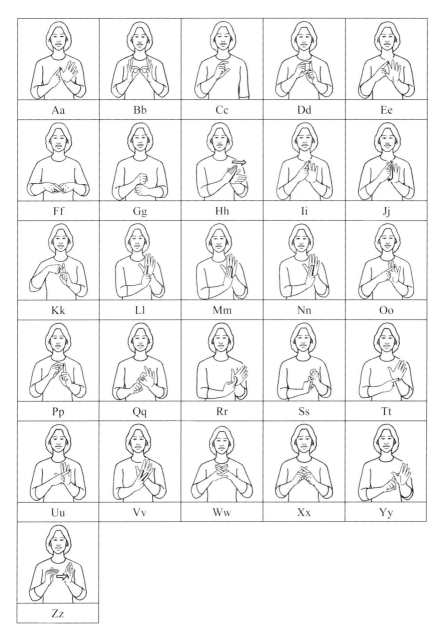

Figure 2.2: *The two-handed alphabet.*

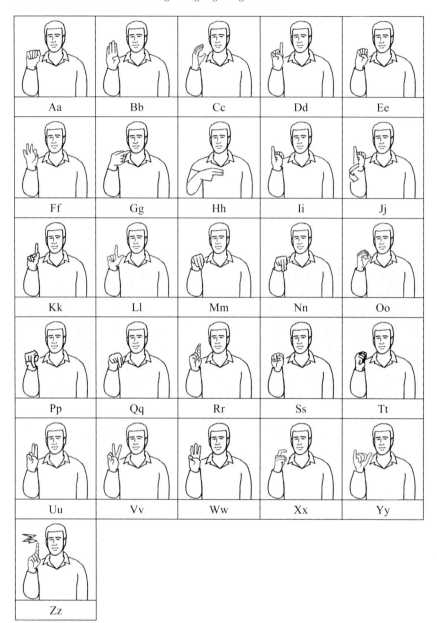

Figure 2.3: *The ASL one-handed alphabet.*

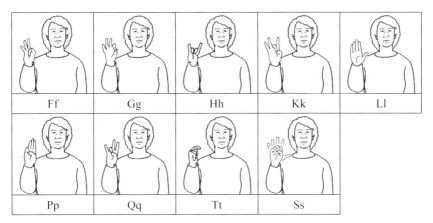

Figure 2.4: *Letters in the ISL one-handed alphabet which are different from ASL letters.*

Though fingerspelling is an important part of a signing deaf person's manual communication skills, virtually no signer uses fingerspelling exclusively to communicate, except perhaps in situations when communicating with some individuals who are deaf-blind (in which case, one fingerspells onto the hand of the other person, using a modified version of the standard two-handed manual alphabet). Alone, fingerspelling is a manual code for representing the letters of the English alphabet and is thus not a signed language in and of itself. Fingerspelling is generally mixed in with signing and is especially used for spelling nouns (place names, people's names, names of everyday objects, etc.), or for spelling English words that have no direct signed equivalent (Johnston, 1989a). However, research shows that fingerspelling of English lexical items often occurs even when there is also a perfectly adequate signed equivalent (Schembri & Johnston, in press). This may be in order to achieve some communicative effect (e.g., to emphasise some point, impress one's addressee, or to hide your meaning from an onlooking child, etc.).

The use of the body and the hands to represents letters of the alphabet has a long history and references to the practice have been found in ancient Greek and Roman writings (Padden & Clark Gunsauls, 2003). It is possible to trace the origins of the one-handed alphabet to at least the sixteenth century when it was used as a system of communication by monks during periods of ritual silence and prayer (as noted in Chapter 1). The earliest form of the modern two-handed alphabet appears in a British pamphlet 'Digita Lingua' published anonymously in 1698 and may have first developed as a code created for secret communication by spies (Sutton-Spence & Woll, 1993).

Thus fingerspelling appears to be an invented system for the representation of the written form of spoken languages used by hearing people long before it was introduced to deaf people (Sutton-Spence, 1995; although for an alternative view, see Branson, Toms, Bernal & Miller, 1995). However, both the one-handed and the two-handed alphabets are of long standing within many deaf communities and are so integrated into natural signing that they may also be regarded as part of an entirely natural sign system for the representation of written languages within these communities. Moreover, they are also the source of many partially and fully lexicalised signs within various native signed languages (see Chapter 6).

2.3.4   Natural sign systems

Not only is it possible to represent spoken or written words letter by letter using fingerspelling, it is also possible to represent the words of a spoken language using a combination of fingerspelling, signs and mouthing (i.e., the silent articulation of spoken words). When one's signing is little more than the representation of speech or writing, one cannot properly say that one is using a natural sign language, rather one is using a form of a *natural sign system* (or NSS) (Fischer, 1998). In Australia, when using a natural sign system, one is either 'signing in English' (intentionally fully representing each English word) or using a type of contact signing (representing a mixture of features of Auslan and English in various proportions).

2.3.4.1 Signing in English

Within the signing community, the desire or need to represent English exactly in signs often stems from that the fact that the language of writing for Auslan users is English, and there is often a need to represent writing. For example, one may wish to read out a document, such as correspondence received by the secretary of an organisation, to a group of people or to see, in manual form, what someone (e.g. a lawyer in a court of law) is saying word for word in English. In such situations, there is little doubt that the signers are actually thinking in English and that the addressee is actually 'reading' English in signed form. In signed language interpreting, the use of this form of signing is sometimes known as *transliteration* because it is not unlike the representation of the written form of one spoken language using the script of another language. It is also sometimes known as Conceptually Accurate Signed English in the USA (Humphrey & Alcorn, 1996), and as Sign Supported English in the UK (Sutton-Spence & Woll, 1999).

   Signing in English is a natural and spontaneous development within the signing community, and in this respect differs from contrived artificial sign systems such as ASE. It is also differs from ASE in that content words of English are represented by Auslan signs that are equivalent in meaning (e.g., SHOP, REMEMBER, YELLOW, QUICK) and grammatical items are fingerspelled (e.g., I-S, T-H-E, A-N) rather than represented by contrived signs. Some signers may opt to fingerspell prefixes (e.g., D-I-S- or U-N-) and suffixes (e.g.,

-I-N-G, -E-D), and combine them with signs (e.g., U-N-HAPPY, BUY-I-N-G), whereas other signers may prefer to fully fingerspell these grammatically modified lexical items (Bernal & Wilson, 2004). The Auslan signs and the fingerspelling are often accompanied by appropriate mouthing (or even vocalisation) of the intended English words.

Even though someone signing in English only has to replace a vocal (or graphic) representation with a manual one, this is no simple matter. There is a very high level of skill in being able to sign in English proficiently, and it can be difficult to do effectively. In particular, one needs excellent productive and receptive fingerspelling skills, clear and rapid signing ability, and a good English vocabulary together with a solid knowledge of the Auslan lexicon in order to know which signs are best suited to represent particular English words in a given context.

Auslan signers are immersed in a sea of English speakers and environmental text in English is everywhere, so it is not surprising that this kind of English-based signing occurs (see Chapter 7). Although an English text signed using Auslan signs is not a text in Auslan, it is still language, just as much as written English is a language and (like written English compared to spoken English) it has functions and roles specific to its modality. Our understanding of a signing community cannot ignore the fact that signing in English occurs, but the linguistic description of a natural signed language as a language in its own right must be properly distinguished from a natural sign system.

The use of English-based signing will only succeed if one's deaf interlocutor has lip-reading skills, a good knowledge of English syntax and a wide English vocabulary. One should not expect to be understood by a deaf person with an inadequate knowledge of English simply because one is signing in English. Something which is not understood by a deaf adult when written in English is only marginally more likely to be understood when signed in English.

2.3.4.2 Contact signing

Signing deaf communities are excellent examples of communities which are characterised by language contact because, as noted above, deaf people always represent small minorities which are embedded within larger speaking and hearing communities. Whenever two or more speech communities come into contact (as geographical neighbours or by the introduction of a language from one speech community into sectors of another speech community through the dynamics of conquest, colonisation, trade or cultural prestige), there will inevitably be linguistic consequences. One of the outcomes of this language contact is *lexical borrowing* (we explore borrowing in Chapter 6). Language contact can also lead to the development of new varieties of language which may be ad hoc and temporary (often producing a language variety called a *pidgin*, defined below) or which may grow and develop into a new and essentially independent natural language that is learnt by children from their parents (often called a *creole*).

In addition to the natural sign system described above which is consciously used as a means of representing English, there are other forms of signing which are clearly heavily influenced by contact and mixing between the wider community's spoken and written language and the deaf community's signed language. This mixed form of signed communication is known as *contact signing* (Lucas & Valli, 1992).

In Australia, deaf people are constantly exposed to English, albeit imperfectly. As children, most deaf people grow up with parents and teachers who are hearing and who do not use Auslan but instead use some form of English-based sign system, if they use signs at all. As adults, most deaf people work and conduct their daily business with hearing people who similarly do not know any signed language. Parents, teachers, friends and fellow workers regularly mouth or speak when they use signs. All writing and reading is done in English, as Auslan has no written form for everyday use. Deaf children and adults, signing or not, cannot fail to be influenced by the language and attitudes of the people around them. Consequently, though Auslan and English are far from identical, the former is very much influenced by the latter. It should come as no surprise therefore that many signers conceive of the meaning of many individual signs as anchored to the meanings of related English words. Many of their signed utterances are essentially utterances in English (or attempts at utterances in English), especially when they are trying to communicate with someone who is hearing and has little familiarity with Auslan (although signing in English is often also used between deaf people themselves, see Lucas & Valli, 1992).

Because of this linguistic environment, there also exists a form of signing that 'combines' aspects of both Auslan and English. A significant amount of signing behaviour among deaf people themselves and with hearing people is not actually conducted in Auslan or English but, rather, in a language system that results from a mixture of features of both languages. This variety of signing was previously called *pidgin sign English* (or PSE) by most signed language linguists (Reilly & McIntire, 1980; Woodward & Markowicz, 1980), but is now commonly referred to as *contact signing*.

Strictly speaking, a pidgin is usually the result of language contact between adult users of mutually unintelligible languages which occurs for very specific purposes, such as trade. The vocabulary may come from either of the languages used by these adults, or predominantly from one of the languages, especially if the speakers of that language represent a dominant group in some way (Arends, Muysken & Smith, 1995). In some cases, the lexical items may come from a third language that neither group speaks fluently (Mühlhäusler, 1986). Contact signing was formerly called a pidgin by many signed language linguists because of the superficial similarity this mixed kind of signing has with spoken language pidgins. It is now realised that such a description is inaccurate because contact signing does not share all the characteristics of a pidgin. For example, although contact signing results from the mixing of two languages (e.g., Auslan and English), it may actually occur between fluent users of a signed language and be used in a range of situations. Thus, it has little in common with situations where speakers of different languages come together and try to use another language to communicate for trade purposes. It also has some unique features that distinguish it from spoken language pidgins, such as the use of fingerspelling and mouthing (Lucas & Valli, 1992).

Observation of contact signing in the Australian deaf community suggests that it involves a mixture of Auslan and English vocabulary and grammar, as well as some idiosyncratic uses of both languages depending on the signer's degree of bilingualism. Signers may use Auslan signs and fingerspelled items combined with mouthing, and with a mix of Auslan and English meanings. They may use some of the spatial and non-manual features found in Auslan, as well as English word order patterns. Thus, contact signing is more variable than the full representation of English using either a natural or artificial system. Importantly, contact signing is what hearing people are often exposed to when communicating with deaf people. However, research suggests that it would be incorrect to assume that deaf people only use a natural sign language with each other, and contact signing with hearing people. Work in the American deaf community has demonstrated that some deaf signers use ASL with both deaf and hearing conversational partners, and contact signing with each other (Lucas & Valli, 1992). It is even possible that the majority of deaf signers are most comfortable with, and most familiar, with a mixed signing system like this rather than a 'pure' form of a natural sign language (cf. Corker, 1997; Turner, 1999).

The form and meaning of lexical items used in each variety of signed communication, together with their characteristic morphological and syntactic patterns, are presented in Table 2.1.

2.4   Bilingualism and diglossia

Thus, Auslan exists in a complex linguistic environment and, as with all languages, there are different forms of signing which are appropriate to different social situations (see Chapter 9). However, as we have shown, two of these forms of signing represent not only two quite different languages (Auslan at one extreme and English at the other) but each has its own quite distinct modality—visual-gestural versus auditory-oral. Thus deaf communities are unique types of bilingual communities.

Table 2.1: *Features of the different signed varieties used in the Australian deaf community (adapted from Lucas & Valli, 1992).*

Features	Auslan	Contact signing	Signing in English	Australasian Signed English
Lexical form	Auslan and fingerspelling, with or without English mouthing	Auslan signs and fingerspelling, English mouthing	Auslan signs and fingerspelling, English mouthing	Some Auslan signs and some contrived signs, spoken English
Lexical meaning	Auslan	Auslan, English, idiosyncratic	English, but with Auslan influences	English, sometimes in conflict with Auslan meanings
Morphology	Auslan sign modifications and non-manual features	Reduced Auslan modifications and English endings, fewer non-manual features	Fingerspelling for English bound morphemes and grammatical items	Fingerspelling for English bound morphemes, and contrived signs for grammatical items
Syntax	Auslan word order, use of space and non-manual features	Simplified English word order, reduced use of space and non-manual features, and some idiosyncratic patterns	English	English

Bilingualism is a characteristic that the deaf community shares with many other societies around the world—in fact, it is possible that a majority of the world's population is bilingual (Grosjean, 1982). The two languages are, however, quite unequal in status with English indisputably the dominant and highly valued language in the wider community. Auslan is an unwritten language used most often face to face and in restricted domains such as within the family, with school peers and as part of social events in the deaf community. It has only recently been formally taught and become the object of scholarly study, and only in the last two to three decades has it begun to be used in a wider variety of settings, such as in court, medical or university situations. English, on the other hand, is a written language used in a whole range of domains ranging from family to international scientific discourse: it has been studied over a long period of time and has a commonly accepted standard form which is formally taught and is itself the language of instruction across the curriculum. Until recently, Auslan has been associated only with informal situations and events within the deaf community such as playing sport and socialising, while English has been associated with more formal situations and events such as religious ceremonies, sports management and meetings of community organisations.

The different status of native sign languages and spoken/written languages in deaf communities has been compared to diglossic situations in spoken language communities (Stokoe, 1969; Deuchar, 1978). *Diglossia* is a term used to refer to communities that use two distinct forms of the same language, with each language being assigned a distinct role in the community (Romaine, 1995). For example, in German-speaking Switzerland, standard German is used as the language of instruction in schools and in writing, but Swiss German is the language spoken at home. Bilingual diglossic communities also exist, in which two different languages are in a similar relationship. In Paraguay, Spanish is the language used in government and education, and the indigenous language Guarani is used in less formal contexts.

However, there are some problems with this comparison of deaf communities and spoken language diglossic situations (Lee, 1982). The relationship between Auslan and English is complicated by the existence of sign systems and contact signing which mixes features of both. Furthermore, the use of English-based signing may vary according to one's conversational partner, the topic, situation and desire to express identification with the deaf community (Lucas & Valli, 1992). English is no longer tied exclusively to some particular situations—Auslan is now the language of instruction in some schools for deaf children, for example. Nonetheless, English remains the only written language. Despite attitudinal change since the 1980s that have begun to value Auslan more highly, English remains the language with the higher social status.

2.5   Sociolinguistic variation in the deaf community

The historical, social, and linguistic context of the signing deaf community in Australia, in particular the relationship between Auslan and English, results in considerable variation in the use of all forms of signed language discussed above. Although it has developed a core lexicon of signs and aspects of its grammatical organisation that are independent of English, there are nonetheless influences from this spoken and written language on both the vocabulary and grammar of Auslan.

However, the language of the majority hearing community is not the sole driving factor in variation. Other language internal and language external factors play a role separately and in complex interrelation. Language external social factors include age, gender, education, social networks, religious affiliation and socio-economic status. Language internal linguistic factors include phonological processes (e.g., influences from the preceding or following signs in a sentence) and register. Language internal factors will be discussed at each relevant section in the discussion of the structure of Auslan in Part II of this book (e.g., Chapter 4 discusses phonological processes, and Chapter 9 looks at register). In this section, we will look at some aspects of variation that reflect external social factors.

2.5.1   Variation in grammar

We have already discussed one major type of grammatical variation in signed communication—the influence of English. Clearly, language mixing means that in some contexts, signers will use aspects of English rather than Auslan grammar. There is a second kind of variation in Auslan grammar, however, which remains not very well understood. In some contexts, for example, signers will vary in their choice and combination of the morphological, syntactic and discourse structures that are described in Chapters 5, 6, 7 and 9. In Chapter 6, for example, we discuss the use of classifier signs, such as those used to describe the motion of humans and vehicles. We will see how the upturned 2 handshape and the upright 1 may be used to represent a person moving, and a B handshape with the palm oriented sideways or downwards may represent vehicles. We also look at noun-verb pairs, in which subtle differences in movement and other features may be used to distinguish signs referring to objects from those used to indicate actions. Not all signers use classifier signs or noun-verb pairs (or other aspects of sign formation and modification) in this way on all occasions, however (Schembri *et al.*, 2002). Similarly, in Chapters 7 and 9, we outline some of the different possibilities for combinations of signs in sentences. We will see that Auslan signers have at least two strategies available to them when producing sentences. First, they may use the order of signs to tell us clearly who is the person doing the action and who is affected by it (e.g., MOTHER ASK FATHER to mean 'mother asks father'). Second, they may convey this information by spatial modifications to the signs (e.g., MOTHER+lf FATHER+rt lf+ASK+rt 'mother asks father) (Johnston *et al.*, in press). The factors that influence these types of choices have not yet been the focus of any research.

It should be remembered that there is a range of acceptable grammatical patterns that users of a language have available to express various meanings. These are not examples of variation in the sense we have just been discussing. They represent systematic alternatives that the grammar of the language uses to explicitly encode different meanings or shades of meaning. The nature of some of these alternative structures, and their meanings, are discussed in Chapters 7 and 9.

2.5.2 Variation in vocabulary

In addition to variation in grammar, different users of Auslan may use different individual signs to express the same concept for reasons relating to their own background, or that of their addressee. These factors may be separately identifiable, but are all interrelated. For example, an individual's regional origin, school, age and religion influence their sign vocabulary (Johnston, 1989a). These factors all interact because, in the past, most deaf people in a particular state attended a large central residential school for the deaf that was found in each state capital. Those who did not, a small minority, tended to be Catholic children who attended separate schools (there were two Catholic schools for deaf children in New South Wales, and one in Victoria).

Before we discuss this variation in vocabulary, we will define two key terms often used in relation to describe sociolinguistic variation: *accent* and *dialect*. Accent refers to variation in spoken language due to differences in pronunciation. For example, some speakers of Australian English (especially those with a 'broad' rather than a 'cultivated' Australian accent) would systematically pronounce the /ai/ sound in words like *buy* and *sign* closer to the /oy/ in *boy* and *soy* (Horvath, 1985). There is not yet any evidence that different subgroups of Auslan signers consistently differ in accent (i.e., in the way they produce specific handshapes, locations or movements in a range of signs), although some recent research suggests that some differences may be emerging (see below).

On the other hand, a dialect is a distinct variety of a language that differs from other varieties in pronunciation, vocabulary and grammar. Therefore, in the Scottish dialect of English, someone may say *I didnae send the bairn out to do the messages*, meaning *I didn't send the child out to run errands*. Not only would this first example be typically pronounced with a Scottish accent, but we can also see that there are differences between the two utterances in vocabulary (e.g., *bairn* versus *child*). Like English, Auslan has differences in vocabulary that are due to dialect.

2.5.2.1 Region

There are two main regional varieties of Auslan—a northern dialect (in New South Wales and Queensland) and a southern dialect (all the other states). Most noticeably, these two dialects differ on the basis of signs for numbers, colours and certain other concepts, such as temporal information (e.g., YESTERDAY, LAST-WEEK) and question signs (e.g., WHO). Indeed, there are important core sets of vocabulary in certain semantic areas (e.g., colour signs) in which every basic term is different in the northern and southern dialects (Figure 2.5).

| RED | BLUE | GREEN | YELLOW | BLACK |

Figure 2.5: *Colour signs in the northern (top) and southern (bottom) dialects of Auslan.*

There are also a number of state-based lexical differences that cut across this major dialect division, such as AFTERNOON (Figure 2.6). Relatively few concepts, however, have more than four distinct state-based sign variants.

| Queensland | New South Wales | Victoria | South Australia and Western Australia | Tasmania |

Figure 2.6: *The sign AFTERNOON in various states.*

Within the deaf community, signers are usually familiar with most of the common signs from other states because the dialect variation does not account for a very large percentage of the vocabulary of Auslan as a whole. Regional lexical variation rarely leads to confusion or misunderstanding among native signers (cf. Woodward, Erting & Oliver, 1976).

Some regional variants may be the result of natural formational changes being taken further in one region than in another (cf. Woodward, 1973). For example, data on sociolinguistic variation in Auslan (Schembri, Johnston & Goswell, in press) suggests that signers in Perth, Brisbane and Adelaide are less likely to lower signs such as THINK, NAME and CLEVER than signers in Sydney and Melbourne. As is explained in Chapter 4, when these signs are produced in isolation, they are usually located in the forehead region. In connected signing, however, a sign like NAME is often produced at lower locations, such as near the cheek, jaw or in the space in front of the signer's body. However, this lowering of signs occurs more often in the varieties of Auslan used by signers from the larger state capitals. If this pattern developed further, this could lead to regional differences in signs, with Sydney signers producing NAME at the jaw, for example, while Perth signers produce it at the forehead.

Overall, some of the regional differences discussed above remain strongest in older age groups. There appears to be a lessening of the differences in some areas of the lexicon (particularly in number signs, for example) in younger signers, particularly those who have been exposed to a more standardised use of ASE-based signing in school (many of the signs used in ASE were based on signs used in the southern dialect of Auslan).

2.5.2.2 School

Each state (but not the Australian Capital Territory or the Northern Territory) had, until the 1970s, one large public residential school for the deaf. The signs used by the children of the largest school in a city were naturally also the signs of the deaf community both by force of numbers and through peer transmission. In New South Wales and Victoria, alternative schools existed in order to provide a Catholic education. Thus, the variety of Auslan used by many signers is a function of both the school they attended and their religious denomination (e.g., Catholic and Protestant signers traditionally used distinctive signs for AUNT, as shown in Figure 2.7).

Figure 2.7: *The sign AUNT used by elderly Catholic (left) and Protestant signers (right).*

Signers at the smaller schools for the deaf usually also knew the signs of the dominant group, and as adults almost all signers adopted the majority community signs though they never completely abandoned their school signs, especially when talking with their school and age peers.

The large central residential schools for the deaf began to lose their important role in the education of deaf children from the 1970s onwards. Within a decade, all but limited residential facilities were shut down and the schools themselves greatly reduced in size. Some of the schools themselves were closed. This followed a long period in which spoken English was the exclusive means of instruction in some schools, and deaf children were expected to learn to speak, lip-read and rely on their residual hearing with the use of hearing-aids (this approach is known as *oralism*). During this time, the use of signed communication was forbidden. Importantly, between the 1970s and the late 1980s, sign-based school programmes were reintroduced, but ASE was used, rather than Auslan. From the late 1980s, however, a number of rather small sign bilingual programmes were established in which Auslan was used as one of the languages of instruction. Because of these developments, the school a young deaf person attended, and thus the variety of signed language they use or are familiar with, is now more a function of their age than religion. Indeed, following the phasing out of ISL as the medium of instruction in Catholic schools in the 1950s, religion has ceased to be a significant factor in deaf education or in Auslan use among younger signers.

2.5.2.3 Age

Signers from a similar age group or generation tend to share the same kind of signs, especially if they went to school together. Technological changes may also mean that one generation's sign for something is quite different from the next generation's sign. For example, TELEPHONE has three forms which reflect the changes from the now obsolete two-piece receiver and mouthpiece with a hand crank to the combined receiver and mouthpiece (Figure 2.8). Most recently, of course, a number of signs for MOBILE-PHONE have emerged.

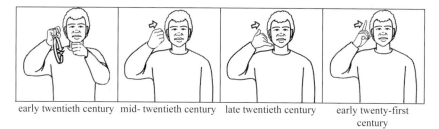

early twentieth century   mid- twentieth century   late twentieth century   early twenty-first century

Figure 2.8: *Signs meaning 'telephone' during the past century.*

Age is also closely related to fingerspelling (Schembri & Johnston, in press). In Australia, fingerspelling is used more extensively by older members of the deaf community (particularly those over seventy years of age), and older signers also tend to fingerspell more English functors than younger signers. This reflects the educational method, called the Rochester Method (Padden & Gunsauls, 2003), used in the 1930s and earlier, both in Australia and elsewhere. Essentially the Rochester Method involved the exclusive use of fingerspelling as a means of instruction. Observations suggests that older deaf people are also inclined to use a great deal of fingerspelling in formal situations or when communicating to a hearing person in order to display their knowledge of English spelling, vocabulary and grammar.

A larger percentage of so-called 'new signs' are likely to be used by many younger members of the deaf community than older members (Schembri &

Johnston, in press). Some of these signs are based on the ASE vocabulary that has been in widespread educational use for over three decades, but they also reflect influences on Auslan from ASL and other signed languages, and other factors related to external influences on language change.

2.5.2.4 Religion

Apart from the most striking difference due to schooling (the use of the ISL one-handed alphabet and a large number of initialised signs from ISL), religion is also manifested in the different signs that religious groups have for various religious concepts (e.g. BAPTISM, CATHOLIC, PROTESTANT, etc.). Frequently religious signing is heavily influenced by individual religious leaders and there appears to be little uniformity in sign use between different congregations (Knights & Knights, 1989). Religious groups with strong North American connections (Jehovah's Witnesses and some fundamentalist groups, such as the Deaf Christian Fellowship) have also introduced significant numbers of borrowings from ASL.

2.5.2.5 Gender

In terms of vocabulary, there are only a small number of signs that are considered more typical of or appropriate for men or women. The sign DOFF (from doffing a hat) was once used as a greeting exclusively by men. Today, the sign HI, which is based on a salute, is perhaps more typical of men or youths than women, who might prefer HELLO.

| DOFF | HI | HELLO |

Figure 2.9: *Various greeting signs.*

In elderly groups, it has been suggested that men may use more fingerspelling than women (Johnston, 1989a). This may reflect a period of time in which males had greater educational opportunities and work experiences than women. Until the 1970s, more effort was made to teach boys English and/or a trade than women in order to prepare them for the workforce. Subsequent experience in the workforce and exposure to English often meant that males had greater use for and knowledge of English than their female contemporaries.

2.5.2.6 Signed language exposure

Signers who have acquired Auslan as a first language from deaf parents tend to use a grammatically richer type of signed language and have a much wider sign vocabulary than signers who learned it at school or even later. Although this has not been the focus of specific research in Australia, this impression is supported by a number of studies that have shown significant differences in the comprehension and production of aspects of ASL grammar between native signers and early and later learners of signed language (Newport, 1990; Mayberry & Eichen, 1991; Morford & Mayberry, 2000). Native signers also appear to make more frequent use of lowered variants of signs made in the forehead region (Schembri *et al.*, in press), perhaps as a result of greater fluency.

2.5.2.7 Contact with other signed languages

Deaf people who have travelled to the United States or studied at Gallaudet University are likely to be familiar with, if not fluent in, ASL. Consciously or unconsciously, they are likely to use a number of ASL signs. Given the relatively powerful influence of ASL in Australia and internationally, there is relatively little resistance to borrowings from ASL when they do not replace existing signs. There is some rejection of ASL signs (especially initialised signs) among some members of the community, however, such as Auslan teachers (e.g., some signers may consciously choose to use the fingerspelled form D-I-C or the BSL sign LINGUISTICS instead of the initialised ASL borrowings DICTIONARY and LINGUISTICS). Influences from International Sign have also become more evident following the World Congress of the World Federation of the Deaf held in Brisbane in 1999, and the Deaflympics in Melbourne in 2005 (International Sign is discussed in Chapter 3).

2.6 Summary

In this chapter, we have examined the size and nature of the signing deaf community. We distinguished between the different varieties of signed communication used in the deaf community (such as natural sign languages, natural sign systems and artificial sign systems), described the relationship between Auslan and English, and provided some examples of variation in the grammar and vocabulary of the language. In the next chapter, we will look at the history of Auslan and its relationship to other signed languages used around the world.

2.7 Further Reading

Like this chapter, Sutton-Spence & Woll (1999) provides a useful summary of the social context of signed languages. For accounts of the deaf community that focus on the social and cultural aspects of deafness, see Padden & Humphries (1988, 2005), McKee (2000) and Ladd (2003). For information about the numbers of signing deaf people in Australia, see

Johnston (2004) and Hyde & Power (1991). Lucas and Valli (1992) provide detailed description of language contact in the American deaf community, while Ann (2001) covers the same issue from a cross-linguistic perspective. Johnston (2002) discusses 'signing in English'. Emmorey (2002) provides an overview of the research on the late acquisition of signed languages. See Schembri *et al.* (in press) for a description of the first large-scale study of sociolinguistic variation in Auslan.

3   Auslan and other signed languages

In this chapter, we look at the relationship between Auslan and other signed languages. First, we examine the traditional use of signed languages in Aboriginal Australia, before moving on to discuss the links between Auslan and other signed languages from the BSL family, including BSL itself and NZSL. We briefly describe the influence of ISL on Auslan, and the relationship between ASL and other signed languages in the BSL family. We close with a discussion of International Sign, and emerging signed languages in the developing world.

3.1   Signed languages of Aboriginal Australia

Signed languages were used by Aboriginal Australians prior to the British occupation and settlement of the continent in 1788. Indeed, some indigenous signed languages, such as Warlpiri Sign Language, have survived to the present day (Kendon, 1988). Unlike the signed languages of deaf communities however, all available evidence suggests that Aboriginal signed languages have always been alternate signed languages used instead of or together with speech for a range of purposes, such as to ensure silence while stalking prey during hunting (Sebeok, 1978) or while observing periods of speech taboo when in mourning (Kendon, 1988). Among the Warlpiri and Warumungu people, these natural sign systems (which Kendon referred to as *alternate sign languages*) are quite rich, allowing communication about any topic in daily life. For the most part, each Aboriginal signed language represents the spoken language(s) of a particular tribe rather than being a natural (or *primary*) signed language. It is doubtful that there would have been the concentration of deaf individuals in the traditional small-scale societies of Aboriginal Australia to support the development of the type of deaf signed languages that were discovered by linguists in the twentieth century.

There is not yet any evidence to suggest that any existing or extinct Aboriginal signed languages were adopted or adapted by deaf communities in Australia. It has been reported, however, that the signed communication of some deaf indigenous individuals from regional areas (such as far north Queensland) includes signs that differ from Auslan signs (Karin Fayd'herbe, personal communication, 2005). This lexical variation remains to be properly documented, however, and there are certainly no widely used Auslan signs that are commonly attributed to any pre-existing Aboriginal sign.

3.2   The origins of Auslan

Although Auslan might be considered a comparatively young language (the deaf community in Australia being less than 200 years old at the beginning of the twenty-first century), it is related to varieties of signed language that may have been used in Britain for several centuries. Historical records clearly indicate that Auslan developed from the varieties of BSL that were introduced into Australia by deaf immigrants, teachers of the deaf (both deaf and hearing) and others concerned with the welfare of deaf people from the early nineteenth century (Johnston, 1989a). *Auslan* is thus only a new name given to a language that is not itself new. Rather, Auslan—with its British origins—appears to be a relatively 'old' signed language when compared to many of the signed languages that have been recently identified in other parts of the world. For example, Taiwan Sign Language (TSL) dates only from the late nineteenth century (Smith, 1989), and Israeli Sign Language from the early twentieth century (Aronoff, Meir, Padden & Sander, 2003).

Prior to the establishment of the first schools for the deaf, a number of signing deaf people from Great Britain had immigrated to Australia. The earliest known non-Aboriginal deaf person was Elizabeth Steel who arrived in Sydney in 1790 as a convict aboard the *Lady Juliana* (Branson & Miller, 1995). There is no direct evidence, however, that she used any signed language. The earliest known signing deaf person was the Sydney engraver John Carmichael who arrived in 1825 on the *Triton* (Carty, 2000). Unlike what is known about Steel, there is a great deal of evidence that Carmichael used BSL and was indeed a talented storyteller in signed language. He was educated at the Edinburgh Deaf and Dumb Institution with Thomas Pattison, who later founded the first school for the deaf in Australia. There are no records to indicate whether Carmichael was alone or formed part of a community of deaf people in Sydney at the time, but it seems unlikely that he would have remained in Sydney without the company of fellow signed language users until his death in 1857 (Pattison did not arrive in Sydney until 1858).

It is not known if there were any Australian-born deaf people among the non-Aboriginal population in Australia before the arrival of John Carmichael. There may have been small numbers of deaf children and adults before this time, but no written records of deaf Europeans in Australia other than Steel and Carmichael have been found. It seems probable that the small number of deaf individuals who immigrated to Australia and lived in the larger settlements at the time may have formed very small deaf communities, but that deaf people outside the largest urban centres may have never encountered another deaf person. Thus, apart from some basic home signs that may have developed for limited communication with their immediate family and friends, it is unlikely that most deaf people would have known a signed language. This is still the case for many deaf people today who grow up isolated in poor rural areas of countries of the developing world (Kuschel, 1973; Kendon, 1980).

The recorded history of the distinct Australian variety of BSL is closely bound up with the education of deaf children and the establishment of schools for the deaf which did not occur before 1860. Nevertheless, as part of the same family of signed languages as BSL, the earliest history of Auslan extends back into the history of signed language use in Great Britain.

3.3 British Sign Language (BSL)

The origins of BSL itself are unknown. The earliest historical records discovered to date show that some form of signed language was used by deaf people in Britain by at least the sixteenth century, although the relationship between modern BSL and these early forms of signed communication is not well understood. Despite this, the British deaf historian Peter Jackson (1990:3) claimed 'BSL was in common usage among deaf people, and some hearing people, by the early 1630s, and had probably been in existence for centuries before that as well.' There is, however, insufficient historical evidence for this, as descriptions of signed language use in centuries past are sketchy at best (Rée, 1999).

The parish register of St. Martin's in Leicester, for example, mentions that in February 1575, a deaf man by the name of Thomas Tillsye was married to a woman named Ursula Russel, and that Thomas made his wedding vows in sign (Sutton-Spence & Woll, 1999), but provides very little detail of the signs he actually used. It is therefore impossible to know whether Tillsye used a home sign system, or an older variety of signing related to modern BSL.

Amongst the earliest records which describe the signed language(s) in use in seventeenth-century Britain are two books by John Bulwer, *Chirologia* and *Philocophus*, published in 1644 and 1648 respectively. The latter book was dedicated to a baronet and his brother, both of whom were deaf. The following passage from the dedication shows that Bulwer (1648) recognised the signed language used by the two brothers was the equal of spoken languages in expressive power:

> You already can expresse yourselves so truly by signes, from a habit you have gotten by always using signes, as we do speech: Nature also recompensing your want of speeche, in the invention of signes to expresse your conceptions.

Bulwer (1648) provided mostly written descriptions of the signs used by the deaf brothers, but it appears that some of these descriptions closely resemble signs with a related form and meaning used in BSL, Auslan and NZSL today, such as GOOD, BAD, WONDERFUL, SHAME, CONGRATULATE and JEALOUS.

A number of other written sources make it clear that some deaf people were using forms of signed language before the first schools and institutions for the deaf opened in Britain. The famous diarist, Samuel Pepys, described an encounter with a deaf servant who signed to his master, George Downing, to tell him of the Great Fire of London in 1666 (Sutton-Spence & Woll, 1999). In the novel *The Life and Adventures of Mr. Duncan Campbell, Deaf Mute* published in 1732, Daniel Defoe described signs and fingerspelling as being widely used by deaf people (Woll, 1987). Although the majority of deaf people in rural communities were isolated from each other at this time, Rachel Sutton-Spence and Bencie Woll (1999) claim that these sources suggest that small signing deaf communities existed in the larger towns and cities in Britain in the seventeenth and eighteenth centuries, and may have done so for many years prior to these written accounts.

The more widespread use of signed communication among British deaf people, however, most certainly began with the advent of the industrial revolution from the 1750s and its accompanying social and economic changes. The resulting population explosion and the mass migration to cities led to a significant increase in the number of deaf children in urban centres, and this seems to have played a significant role in the introduction of public education for deaf children (Johnston, 1989a). The first British school for deaf children (and perhaps the first school of its kind the world) was opened in 1760 by Thomas Braidwood in Edinburgh, a few months before de l'Epée's institution (Jackson, 2001). From work published in the early nineteenth century by his grandson (Watson, 1809), Braidwood's teaching methods apparently involved some combination of signed communication, reading, writing and spoken English. Based on the important role played by schools for deaf children in the emergence of signed languages—a recent well-documented case is that of Nicaraguan Sign Language (Kegl, 1994)—it is likely that the signed language used in the Braidwood school has a direct historical relationship with modern BSL and Auslan.

By 1870, some 22 schools for the deaf had been established in the UK (Kyle & Woll, 1985). In the early years of deaf education, the most common method of instruction was the 'combined method' (i.e., the use of signs and speech) reportedly used by Braidwood. According to Jim Kyle and Bencie Woll (1985) records suggest that that all instruction was in sign (probably some form of BSL or of a BSL-based natural sign system) by the middle of the nineteenth century, with literacy in English (rather than speech) the main educational goal. Most schools were residential and many of the staff were themselves deaf. These schools allowed for the creation and consolidation of the British deaf community and of modern BSL. It was in the schools for the deaf that the home signs of pupils, the natural signed language(s) of the urban deaf communities, and artificial signs created by educators would have mixed together. A similar mixing process appears to have occurred in North

America. French signs were introduced by educators of deaf children (Lane, 1984), but these appear to have mixed with an existing signed language to create modern ASL. Many of the students who attended the first school for deaf children in Hartford, Connecticut, came from the island of Martha's Vineyard where a signed language had developed naturally due to a disproportionately high percentage of hereditary deafness in that community (Groce, 1985).

The existence of central schools for the deaf thus helped to stabilise and standardise the many varieties of signed language in use throughout the UK (although considerable social and regional variation continues to this day). Many of these newer schools were set up by former students and ex-teachers of the older established schools (Kyle & Woll, 1985), and this probably helped to further standardise signed language use. This pattern was repeated in Australia where the first two schools in Sydney and Melbourne were opened by former pupils of the schools for the deaf in Edinburgh and London respectively.

3.4   From BSL to Auslan

The first two schools for the deaf were opened within a few weeks of each other in 1860, first in Sydney and then in Melbourne. As mentioned above, Pattison founded the Sydney school, while another deaf man, Frederick J. Rose (a former pupil of the Old Kent Road School for the Deaf and Dumb in London), opened the Melbourne school (Flynn, 1984). Rose had arrived on the Victorian goldfields in 1852 and had travelled back and forth between England and Australia several times before establishing the school. The method of instruction in both schools seems to have involved some use of fingerspelling and signed language, although whether this was an older variety of BSL, some form of a natural sign system, or a combination of the two is not known.

Connections with BSL throughout the nineteenth and early twentieth centuries were reinforced and maintained by the immigration of deaf individuals and teachers of the deaf to Australia, or by deaf children being sent to Britain for their education (Carty, 2004). For example, two twin deaf brothers, Adam and William Muir, travelled from Melbourne to the Institution for the Deaf in Glasgow (Scotland) to be educated. After their return in 1878, Adam Muir began to conduct Sunday morning services for the deaf community. Similarly, an early teacher of the deaf at the Victorian Deaf and Dumb Institution in Melbourne was Samuel Johnson (1882-1885). He immigrated to Victoria in 1882 from Dublin, Ireland, where he had taught at the Claremont Deaf and Dumb Institution. Apparently British-based signed language and fingerspelling were used at this school for Protestant children (see §3.6 below for further details). He too conducted services for the deaf community. Importantly, the first full-time missioner to the deaf community was Ernest Abraham who arrived in Australia in 1901 at the age of 34. Though hearing himself, he was a fluent signer, having been adopted by the deaf minister of the South London Gospel Mission at the age of 14. He worked in deaf education and community welfare in London and Manchester until his emigration to Australia. Moreover, until the late 1960s, it was quite common for Australian teachers of the deaf to receive supplementary training in the United Kingdom or for British teachers of the deaf to migrate to or have periods of employment in Australia. Large-scale immigration from Britain in the post-war period also included small numbers of British deaf people (mostly children). Thus the connection of Auslan with BSL through education and immigration was never totally broken.

As already mentioned, modern BSL exhibits a significant amount of regional lexical variation (Brien, 1992), and it seems probable that lexical differences existed in the signed language used in the Edinburgh and London schools for the deaf where Pattison and Rose were educated. On the basis of this, it appears that well-established lexical differences which characterise the signing used in the northern and southern dialects of Auslan stem from differences in the varieties of BSL used in each of the original schools for the deaf (Johnston, 1989a), although direct historical evidence for this is lacking. Certainly, an initial study has suggested that the traditional lexicon of signs used in Melbourne continues to closely resemble those used in the London variety of BSL (Day & Elton, 1999) and this is supported by anecdotal evidence (Robert Adam, personal communication, 2004). The number systems and colour vocabulary traditionally used in both of these cities is almost identical, for example, but a greater understanding of the degree of lexical similarity awaits further research.

The history of Auslan is thus a relatively smooth transition from BSL, with an uninterrupted pattern of transmission of signed language from Melbourne and Sydney to schools for the deaf in Adelaide (1874), Brisbane (1893), Perth (1896) and Hobart (1904). It appears that deaf children from Queensland were sent to the Sydney school until the opening of the Brisbane institution, and that children from elsewhere in the country were initially sent to the Melbourne school. This pattern appears to have formed the basis for the northern and southern dialects mentioned in Chapter 2.

Historical records suggest that signed languages may have been in use amongst deaf people in these cities prior to the establishment of schools for the deaf. A deaf boy named Henry Hallett, for example, is known to have arrived in Adelaide on the *Africaine* in 1836 (Carty, 2004). He was just a small child when he arrived with his family (none of whom were deaf), but he later married a deaf woman, Martha Pike, who had been born in South Australia, and they were the forerunners of several generations of deaf Halletts. Although there is no direct evidence, it seems likely that Hallett and

Pike (and perhaps other deaf South Australians) may have used some kind of signed language.

In 1875, a deaf nun, Sister Mary Gabrielle Hogan, came from Ireland to open the Rosary Convent school for Catholic deaf children in Waratah (now a suburb of Newcastle), New South Wales (Fitzgerald, 1999). In the classroom, Hogan used signs adapted from ISL and the one-handed manual alphabet used in Ireland. In the later half of the nineteenth century and early twentieth century, additional Catholic schools for the deaf were opened in other parts of Australia (St Gabriel's school in Castle Hill, New South Wales, and the St Mary's Delgany school in Portsea, Victoria).

The use of signs and fingerspelling continued for some students in Australian schools for the deaf through the late nineteenth century and into the early twentieth century, but many other students were also taught to speak and lip-read (Carty, 2004). This was increasingly true after the Congress of Milan in 1880 where the majority of educators called for a ban on the use of signed communication in the classroom and demanded purely oral methods of instruction. School records from this period in Great Britain show falling numbers of deaf teachers of the deaf, and a decreasing reliance on signs in teaching (Brennan, 1992). Though oral methods or the exclusive use of fingerspelling combined with speech became widespread in Australia in the early decades of the last century, signed language was never completely abandoned in many of the large central residential schools, and certainly continued to be used in dormitories and playgrounds (Johnston, 1989a).

From the 1950s onwards, educational methodologies became increasingly focused on the sole use of spoken English as a medium of instruction. This was made possible by technological advances in hearing aids and other assistive devices (Carty, 2004). Following changes in educational philosophies in the 1960s, the emphasis shifted to 'normalising' the education of deaf children as much as possible, and residential schools began to close down. By the 1980s, deaf children were increasingly integrated into classes with hearing children or attended classes in small units attached to regular schools. The use of signed language came to be seen only as a last resort for those who failed to acquire spoken English. The closure of centralised, residential schools for deaf children meant that many deaf children did not have children from deaf families or deaf ancillary staff as linguistic role models (Johnston, 1989a). This has made the transmission of Auslan from one generation of deaf people to the next more disrupted than before, as we outlined in Chapter 2.

Despite the many changes in approaches to the education of deaf children in the last 145 years, it seems that varieties of Auslan have remained the primary or preferred language of the deaf community throughout much of that time. There can be little doubt, however, that the various educational philosophies which dominated deaf education over the last century—all of which have variously emphasised skills in signed, spoken, fingerspelled, and/or written English (with different degrees of success) rather than the use of Auslan—have had considerable impact on the signed language of the deaf community.

3.5   BSL and Auslan compared

Even after having been used for almost two centuries in Australia, Auslan was universally recognised as closely related to BSL, if not still regarded by many people in the Australian deaf community as 'essentially the same language' as BSL. Signers of Auslan and BSL report only some lexical differences between the two languages, not grammatical ones. Indeed, it is part of the folk linguistics of these communities, and perhaps justifiably so, that there are no major grammatical differences between the signed language used in Britain and Australia. This issue has, however, not yet been the focus of any empirical research, so there may be subtle differences in the grammars of the two varieties that have thus far escaped attention (e.g., differences in the variants of FINISH used to mark perfective aspect). As a result, we will focus here on comparative studies of the lexicons of BSL and Auslan. This research shows clearly that these two varieties have developed many distinctive signs of their own.

In a recent paper, Woll, Sutton-Spence and Elton (2001) suggested that Auslan retains a significant number of older BSL signs that are no longer in use in the British deaf community. While this claim may be partly accurate, the reverse appears also to be true. Signers of all ages in the British deaf community, for example, continue to use signs for the numbers six (using the I handshape), seven (the Old 7 handshape), and eight (the pinky, ring and middle fingers extended from the first) that are only used by older signers in the northern dialect of Auslan. The processes of language change in both BSL and Auslan appear to have resulted in some older signs disappearing in one community, while being retained in the other.

There have not yet been any empirical studies of the degree of mutual intelligibility between Auslan and BSL. However, generations of immigrants to Australia, reports from deaf families with members in both countries and travellers, tourists and teachers throughout the twentieth century leave little doubt that these signed languages are closely related. It would be wrong to dismiss such intuitions as 'merely anecdotal'.

Thus both languages appear, for the most part, to be mutually intelligible even if they had, and continue to have, quite distinctive regional variation in non-core and even core areas of the lexicon (e.g., colour terms). As mentioned above, it is on this level—the lexical—that some comparative research has been done. Conclusions about the degree of lexical similarity between the languages have varied depending on a number of factors. Studies have used word lists or samples of different size and composition and involved different numbers of native signers in the research. The type of criteria applied to categorise signs as identical, similar or different has differed from one investigation to the next. The quality of the lexicographical work that produced the dictionaries consulted by the researchers, especially in regard to the recording of regional variants, has also varied between studies. Furthermore, because of iconicity, identical or similar signs may or may not be cognates (*cognates* are words from different languages that derive from a word in a common ancestor language). Similar signs may have developed completely independently in different signed languages. All of these issues explain why the various studies discussed below report different figures for the percentage of similar lexical items in BSL and Auslan.

Bencie Woll (1987), for example, reported a similarity score of 90 per cent for the 257 'core' lexical items in her study comparing Auslan and BSL. In comparative research of this kind (known as *lexicostatistics*), it has traditionally been accepted that a result of 36 per cent to 81 per cent identical or related lexical items indicates that two languages belong to the same family, while languages with above 81 per cent shared vocabulary are considered dialects of the same language (Crowley, 1992). Figures such as those reported by Woll would thus tend to suggest that Auslan and BSL are most appropriately considered dialects of the same signed language. However, there are methodological problems with this approach. For example, 'core' signs (such as those for family relationships, common actions, basic descriptions of size and shape, etc.) are likely to have a high degree of stability over time due to their high frequency of use and thus may not represent the overall lexicons of the languages well. In order to study a more representative sample of lexical items, the comparison of randomly selected signs from published dictionaries, rather than just the comparison of the signs for a limited set of core vocabulary, is required. However, prior to the publication in the 1980s and 1990s of the first linguistically informed and comprehensive dictionaries of Australian and British signed languages it was difficult to make even lexical comparisons between the two languages with a degree of confidence. The first Auslan dictionary was completed in 1989 (Johnston, 1989b) and the first BSL dictionary appeared in 1992 (Brien, 1992).

Studies by David McKee and Graeme Kennedy (2000) and Johnston (2003a) used both a list of basic vocabulary items prepared by James Woodward (this list was originally designed by the American linguist Morris Swadesh but was later modified by Woodward for use with signed languages), and a second, random method of comparison. The studies showed a lexical overlap of 87 per cent and 98 per cent respectively (using basic concepts as the basis of comparison), and 93 per cent and 82 per cent respectively (using randomly selected signs from the two above-mentioned published dictionaries). There can be little doubt from these findings that the intuitions of native signers do in fact have a basis in reality.

It is important not to misinterpret these results, however. The signed languages of Britain and Australia both display a high degree of internal variation in vocabulary (and grammar, if we include contact signing in our description of these languages). A large part of the lexicon of these two 'languages' may be shared, but each of the communities is not homogeneous. As we saw in the previous chapter, region, age, religion and educational background are responsible for significant variation. A high degree of overlap in the entries in comprehensive dictionaries of these languages need not prevent certain groups or regions in a community using BSL or Auslan from having a very distinctive core vocabulary that could lead to frequent initial misunderstandings with signers from the other country (even within the same country). Signers could, however, easily adjust their vocabulary for this by selecting signs that they understand and know to be less regionally restricted. The less sophisticated, non-native signer from a small or isolated community in either of these countries is likely to find another variety or dialect used by a deaf person from the other country a little difficult to follow, especially if they too are from a small or remote region.

3.5.1   Auslan, BSL and New Zealand Sign Language (NZSL)

No other signed language appears as closely related to Auslan, and hence BSL, as NZSL for the very simple reason that New Zealand has a very similar history to Australia in terms of colonisation by the British. There are also important parallels, and differences, in the history of their deaf communities with respect to the use of BSL. Indeed, some deaf children from New Zealand travelled to Australia or Britain to attend deaf schools in these countries before, and even after, the establishment of the first school for the deaf in Christchurch in 1880 (Collins-Ahlgren, 1989).

Some indication of the degree of overlap between all three signed languages was made possible with the publication of *A Dictionary of New Zealand Sign Language* (Kennedy *et al.*, 1997). With data from that dictionary now available it was possible for McKee & Kennedy (2000) and Johnston (2003a) to compare the languages based on both a Swadesh list (Figure 3.1) and randomly selected signs from dictionaries of each language (Figure 3.2).

The comparisons between each set of signed languages indicated that the percentage of identical and similar or related signs in each pairing was consistently high. For NZSL and Auslan, this ranged from 87 per cent to 96 per cent and for NZSL and BSL from 79 per cent to 96 per cent depending upon how criteria were applied and consideration given to regional and phonological variants in each language.

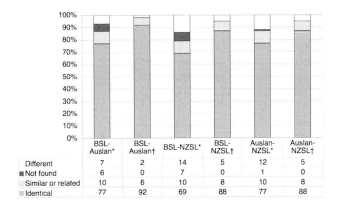

	BSL- Auslan*	BSL- Auslan†	BSL-NZSL*	BSL- NZSL†	Auslan- NZSL*	Auslan- NZSL†
Different	7	2	14	5	12	5
■ Not found	6	0	7	0	1	0
Similar or related	10	6	10	8	10	8
▦ Identical	77	92	69	88	77	88

Figure 3.1: *The similarity of signs in a Swadesh list in three pairs of signed languages*
(*McKee & Kennedy, 2000; †Johnston, 2003a).

For random based comparisons of the lexicons the degree of similarity is, not surprisingly, lower. Nonetheless it is only as low as 59 per cent between BSL and NZSL, and as high as 82 per cent between Auslan and the two other signed languages (Figure 3.2).

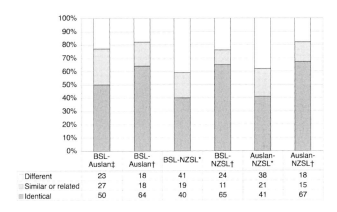

	BSL- Auslan‡	BSL- Auslan†	BSL-NZSL*	BSL- NZSL†	Auslan- NZSL*	Auslan- NZSL†
Different	23	18	41	24	38	18
Similar or related	27	18	19	11	21	15
▦ Identical	50	64	40	65	41	67

Figure 3.2: *The similarity of randomly selected signs in Auslan, BSL and NZSL*
(*McKee & Kennedy, 2000; †Johnston, 2003a).

Despite the high percentages of similarity in core vocabulary described above, they are not identical. Indeed, small as the divergence in the core vocabulary of the three languages may be, it might still be considered higher than one would expect for three dialects of the same language having only recently diverged from a common parent language. For example, a comparative study of thirteen spoken languages with a long tradition of written records showed an average vocabulary retention of 80.5 per cent for every thousand years (Crowley, 1992). In the case of identical signs between NZSL and BSL (Figure 3.1), to retain 'only' 69 per cent of core vocabulary in common (the lowest score by the McKee & Kennedy study) after less than 200 years of separation may, therefore, imply a relative rapid divergence. It certainly appears to have created greater differences in core vocabulary than one might find between the varieties of English spoken in each country (Crystal, 1995).

The exclusive use of spoken English in deaf education between 1880 and 1979 (when ASE was introduced into New Zealand schools) may have resulted in a comparatively more disrupted transmission of signed language in New Zealand from one generation of deaf children to the next. This may have been compounded by the relatively small size of the deaf community in New Zealand, and the smaller resulting number of deaf families. The use and knowledge of fingerspelling in New Zealand may reflect this history: research suggests that NZSL signers make significantly less use of fingerspelling than appears to be true of signers from the Australian and British deaf communities (Schembri & Johnston, in press). Anecdotally, many NZSL signers appear to be less fluent with the manual alphabet and to report difficulties in comprehending fingerspelling. Indeed, some NZSL signers, now elderly, only use 'aerial spelling' (i.e., spelling out words by tracing out their shapes with an index finger in the air) (Forman, 2003).

Gerrit Van Asch, the founder of the first school for deaf children in New Zealand, is known to have been an ardent oralist and is said to have refused admission to signing children (i.e., those with deaf parents or those who had received part of their education by means of the 'manual' method in Australia or Britain). This policy appears to have continued for several decades after the school was first opened (Collins-Ahlgren, 1989), and differs markedly from the experiences in Australia where some use of signed communication was retained in several schools for deaf children for most of the last 140 years. Signed communication did, however, develop naturally amongst the school children in New Zealand and was used in the school dormitories, but it is difficult to know how much this school-based signing was influenced by BSL. Certainly, a number of signs developed in NZSL that do not appear related to anything documented in BSL (e.g., variants of MOTHER, FATHER, NINE, ELEVEN and TWELVE).

The continued use of these novel school-based signs may partially explain the figures that suggest that NZSL shares fewer lexical items with both Auslan and BSL than these two languages do with each other. Nonetheless, it is clear that NZSL is part of the same signed language family as BSL and Auslan. Indeed, it has been suggested that all three signed languages are really dialects of a single signed language (British-Australian-New-Zealand Sign Language or BANZSL) that has evolved from a signed language that emerged in Britain during the early nineteenth century (Johnston, 2003a).

Recent suggestions that NZSL is entirely an indigenous creole language that developed from the spontaneous school-based signing without significant influence from either Auslan or BSL appear implausible in the light of the reported lexical comparisons (Forman, 2003).

3.6   Auslan and Irish Sign Language (ISL)

As has already been mentioned, Auslan was also influenced, but to a much lesser extent, by another signed language—ISL.

Many of the signs and the manual alphabet used in Ireland appear to have been borrowed or adapted from LSF and perhaps even ASL, but there has also been contact with BSL (Matthews, 1996). The first Irish school for deaf children was opened at the Smithfield Penitentiar, Dublin, in 1816, and the first headmaster was trained in Edinburgh at the Braidwood school. It thus seems likely that some form of signing and fingerspelling may have been used at the Smithfield school, perhaps influenced by BSL. This school later became the Claremont National Institution for Education of the Deaf and Dumb, which taught many Protestant deaf children for most of the nineteenth and twentieth centuries until its closure in 1971. Some elderly Irish deaf people who attended this school still use the British two-handed manual alphabet (Matthews, 1996).

LSF and a system of signed French were the languages used at the Le Bon Sauveur school for the deaf in Caen, France, and it was to this school that two Dominican sisters, a priest and two deaf girls were sent from Ireland in 1846 (Burns, 1998). The nuns and girls returned later that year to establish a Catholic school for deaf girls in Cabra (Dublin) that used signed language (LeMaster & Foran, 1987). The girls' school (St Mary's School) was followed in 1849 by a boys' school (St Joseph's School). The signing system at St Mary's school was an adapted form of the French system, modified to reflect English grammar by Father John Burke, the school's chaplain (Matthews, 1996). It has been reported that the Christian Brothers, who took over the administration and teaching of the boys' school in Cabra, used in their school some ASL signs that they had learnt from an American publication (*Course of Instruction* published by the New York Institution in the United States) (Crean, 1997). Furthermore, Catholic children who were transferred to these schools from the Smithfield school probably brought with them some British signs and the one-handed manual alphabet. The signs used by Sister Hogan, the founder of the Waratah school for deaf children in Australia, may have thus been a mixture of indigenous Irish signs, BSL and LSF signs, with perhaps some ASL signs.

From the earliest days of signed language use in Australia, there were thus two signing traditions—a minority Catholic ISL-based system and a majority Protestant BSL-based system—though by the latter half of the twentieth century the ISL-based variety was no longer being passed down to the younger generation (Johnston 1989a). The BSL-based signing tradition has always formed the bedrock of the signed language of the Australian deaf community, however, even though there has been some mixing with and borrowing from ISL. Users of the ISL one-handed alphabet invariably also knew the two-handed alphabet which they used, together with the BSL-based signs, when mixing in the wider deaf community. Most users of the two-handed alphabet did not, however, appear to have learned the use of the one-handed alphabet.

Evidence of contact with ISL is manifested in the existence of a number of Auslan signs such as HOME, COUSIN, UNCLE, GARDEN, YESTERDAY and MORNING which are identical to signs still used in ISL (Foran, 1996) (see Figure 3.3). Interestingly some of these signs are also used in regional varieties of BSL and appear to have come into that language also through independent borrowing from ISL (Brennan, 1992; Sutton-Spence & Woll, 1999).

It should be noted that in previous work by Stokoe (1974), Auslan is shown as a direct descendant of ISL. The historical evidence does not support this conclusion. The direct line of descent is indisputably from BSL with, however, some influence from ISL.

HOME   COUSIN   MORNING

Figure 3.3: *Auslan signs which are identical to ISL signs.*

3.7   Auslan and other signed languages with some BSL contact

Auslan is not the only signed language that can trace its origins to Britain. There are a number of deaf communities around the world that, like the ones in Australia, are found in cities, countries or cultures that have had historical connections with Britain. They were once part of the British colonial empire that reached the peak of its power and influence during the late nineteenth and early twentieth centuries.

One might expect that just as the spoken and written language of Britain (i.e., English) was spread around the world, its signed language—BSL, or at least, the varieties of British-based signing used at the time—may likewise have spread. As we have seen, in Australia, and to a lesser extent New Zealand, this certainly seems to have been the case. However, apart from

South Africa and Ireland, one can only find the remnants of a possible influence from BSL in some isolated lexical signs and a residual knowledge of the two-handed manual alphabet in some countries of the former colonial empire such as India and Pakistan (Woll *et al.*, 2001). For example, in a dictionary of the Bangalore variety of Indo-Pakistani Sign Language (Vashista *et al.*, 1985), there are a few signs that are identical in form and meaning to Auslan and BSL signs (e.g., SAVE, SCHOOL, SEE, SWEAR and TOMORROW). Of these signs, a small set clearly derives from the British two-handed manual alphabet (e.g., YEAR, IF, MONDAY and QUESTION) (Figure 3.4).

Maltese Sign Language (Lingwa tas-Sinjali Maltija) also shows evidence of contact with BSL (the Mediterranean island of Malta was once a British colony). Signs such as SISTER, BROTHER, WOMAN, GOOD, BAD and the numbers ONE to NINE are the same as BSL signs (Bezzina, n.d.)

SCHOOL YEAR MONDAY

Figure 3.4: *Some Indo-Pakistani Sign Language signs that derive from BSL and are still used in BSL and Auslan.*

Overall, however, the long-term impact of some of the schools for the deaf established in the days of the British Empire was minimal because the overwhelming majority of deaf children of school age in countries like India did not in fact receive an education. The numbers of deaf children who did attend the special schools of the time were insufficient to have a lasting impact on the signed language of emerging deaf communities, even if some of those schools employed British teachers, or teachers trained in Britain, who may have been familiar with BSL-related signed language.

In South Africa, it appears that the influences were many and varied (Herbst, 1987). Like Australia, schools were established by the Catholic church (e.g., Grimley Dominican School for the Deaf was established in Cape Town in 1874 by Irish Dominicans who used ISL-based signing). Other schools reportedly used BSL-based signing. A school for children from Afrikaans-speaking homes was established in 1881. However, South Africa has long been extremely culturally and racially diverse. Not only do there appear to be many varieties of signed language in South Africa which are quite unlike or unrelated to Auslan (through BSL and ISL), but those varieties in white English-speaking areas that have had contact with both

BSL and ISL appear to share much lower levels of vocabulary with BSL (Woll, 1987), and hence Auslan, than NZSL.

3.7.1 Signed language in the United States and Canada

ASL is used in the United States and parts of Canada. Like most signed languages, the beginnings of ASL are closely related to the establishment of formal education for deaf children. The language developed from a variety of LSF brought to America by Thomas Gallaudet and Laurent Clerc when they established the first school for the deaf in the United States in Hartford, Connecticut, in 1816. Bender (1970), Woodward (1980) and Lane (1984) are among the many that have documented the well-known relationship of LSF to ASL.

Like Australia, it appears that none of the signs used by the indigenous peoples were introduced into the early communities of European colonists. Rather, aside from the spontaneous development of signs within families and communities with a high proportion of deafness, it seems that early forms of signing in North America were probably influenced by older forms of BSL. ASL may be distantly related to the BSL signed language family through Martha's Vineyard Sign Language, but this remains speculation based on known historical links with Great Britain and some shared lexical items (see Groce, 1985; Woll, 1987). Lexical similarities remain in only a few regional varieties of ASL, especially that used in the Atlantic, or maritime, provinces of Canada. Recorded in *The Canadian Dictionary of ASL* (Bailey & Dolby, 2002) are a number of signs of Maritime Sign Language (as this dialect used in the provinces of Nova Scotia, New Brunswick and Newfoundland is sometimes called) such as ALIVE, ANNUAL, ASK, BAD, BEFORE, BOY, BREAD, BROTHER, BROWN, EASY, FATHER, GOOD, MOTHER, SLEEP and TRAIN. These are identical in form and meaning to existing signs in Auslan or BSL. Others, such as AGE, APPLE, MORE, SISTER, SURE and NOT-YET, closely resemble variants of signs found in Auslan or BSL. Interestingly, because only the one-handed manual alphabet is used in North America, a few of these BSL relics actually derive from lexicalised two-handed fingerspelling (e.g., FATHER and MOTHER) (see Chapter 6 for a discussion of lexicalised fingerspelling).

These historical relics notwithstanding, Auslan and BSL are not mutually intelligible with ASL (see Bellugi & Klima, 1975; Stokoe *et al.*, 1976; Battison & Jordan, 1976, regarding BSL and ASL). Granted, there are similarities in the types of English language contact phenomena manifested in each signed language community (such as fingerspelling, mouthing, word order preferences and so on) but these phenomena may not consistently assist mutual comprehension. For these reasons, signed language users from different English speaking communities with different signed languages would only experience each others' signed languages as slightly less impenetrable than other unrelated signed languages. However, the impact of these contact phenomena has not been the focus of any published research. The fact remains that most varieties of ASL and BSL/Auslan appear to be mutually unintelligible.

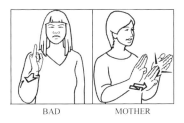 

Figure 3.5: *Maritime Sign Language signs that appear to derive from BSL and are identical to signs still used in BSL and Auslan (on left) or closely resemble BSL and Auslan signs (on right).*

There has been some published research on lexical similarities between ASL and signed languages in Britain, Australia and New Zealand (McKee & Kennedy, 2000; Johnston, 2003a). In particular a comparison of Auslan signs and ASL signs based on the modified Swadesh list, on the one hand, and a comparison of signs in three published ASL dictionaries (O'Rourke, 1978; Lane, 1993; Tennant, 1998) on the other, showed a fairly high percentage of identical or similar signs, ranging from 38 per cent to 44 per cent (Figure 3.6).

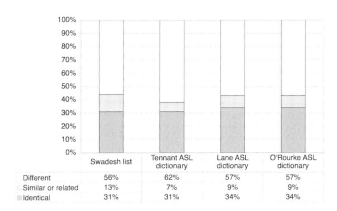

Figure 3.6: *The similarity of signs in Auslan and ASL.*

The degree of overlap of ASL with Auslan in both the Swadesh list and randomly selected sets of signs is quite high given that we are dealing with two pairs of essentially unrelated signed languages. By the criteria of lexicostatistics, these figures would suggest that ASL and Auslan could be considered varieties from the same language family. Historically, it would appear that such a conclusion is not justified even though Auslan has had some historical contact with ASL, however slight, through the proxy of ISL and its relationship with both ASL to LSF discussed above, and through the contact of early and regional varieties of ASL with BSL.

Clearly, the degree of overlap in the lexicons suggests a closer underlying similarity in the meaning of signs cross-linguistically that cannot be explained by historical relationships alone (i.e., they may not actually be cognate), in contrast to the interpretation of similar degrees of lexical overlap in spoken languages (Woll, 1983). Other factors may help explain the high proportion of apparently cognate signs.

First, the iconicity of many signs found in signed languages will naturally contribute to higher percentages of identical or similar signs between any two signed languages, related or not. For example, there is no known historical relationship between TSL and Auslan, and yet each of these languages has a small number of apparently identical signs, such as DUCK, FORGET, HEAVY, ICE-CREAM, JUMP and MOON (Smith, 1979). A study of two unrelated signed languages – Mexican Sign Language and NS – found that 23 per cent of a sample of 166 signs were similar (Guerra Currie, Meier & Walters, 2002). An older and larger study reported in Kyle and Woll (1985) compared 257 lexical items in 15 signed languages and found that an average of 35-40 per cent of these signs were similar. Indeed, a study by Parkhurst and Parkhurst (2003) which compared four unrelated signed languages concluded that the effects of iconicity were so great that the percentages of lexical overlap between any two signed languages need to be considerably increased (to >81 per cent) for there to be evidence that they are essentially one language.

| FORGET | HEAVY | ICE-CREAM |

Figure 3.7: *Three signs that are identical in Auslan and TSL.*

Second, the existence of words for various concepts in majority spoken languages appears likely to encourage very similar distinctions being made in community signed languages. This is exemplified by the changes in the sign COUSIN in ASL (now neutral for gender) from LSF MALE-COUSIN and FEMALE-COUSIN (Stokoe *et al.*, 1976:125), or in the existence of signs found for older/younger sibling found in East Asian signed languages (see Chapter 1), but not in European signed languages. The similarity of the signs between two essentially unrelated signed languages might thus be further amplified through contact with majority languages. In other words, the saturation of the culture with English-based meanings and concepts in the United States and Australia (and Britain and New Zealand) may encourage the 'alignment' of signed and spoken vocabularies and amplify the effects of iconicity.

Another explanation of the overlap is the growing impact, and relative importance, of ASL internationally. Signs from ASL have been borrowed by Auslan signers for many years, and particularly over the last two decades. Some of this borrowing has been unconscious with many deaf community members, especially younger signers, being unaware that some signs they use on a daily basis are recent ASL-isms. Consequently, many of these borrowed signs are identical in Auslan and ASL. When lexicostatistical comparisons are made, a percentage of the overlap can therefore be attributed to relatively recent lexical borrowing. McKee & Kennedy (2000) made a similar observation but only with regards to the lexical overlap between NZSL, Auslan and BSL. They suggested that recent lexical borrowing from ASL, in each of these languages and in similar semantic domains, could have contributed to the high degree of lexical overlap that was observed.

The many lexical items that appear to have been borrowed in contemporary Auslan from ASL are discussed in Chapter 6. Although influences from ASL are also evident in BSL (Brien, 1992; Sutton-Spence & Woll, 1999), native signers from Britain, New Zealand and Australia anecdotally report that the number of ASL loan signs in the non-core lexicon of Auslan appears to be greater. The degree of influence on the Auslan lexicon from signed languages such as ISL and ASL, along with a greater understanding of the relationship between Auslan, BSL and NZSL, awaits further investigation.

3.8   Auslan and other unrelated signed languages of the world

As explained in Chapter 1, signed language is not universal and an Auslan signer cannot simply step into a foreign deaf community and converse freely with other deaf people on any topic. However, it has often been observed that two deaf people who do not know each other's signed language will do better at communicating with each other than most hearing people meeting a foreigner who speaks another language (Battison & Jordan, 1976). However, the reasons for this ability do not support the common and false notion that signed language is a single international language (but see §3.8.1 below).

First, deaf people have a lifetime's experience at making themselves understood by hearing people through mime and gesture and they are adept at quickly developing a 'compromise sign system' (Deuchar, 1984) or 'interlanguage' (Kyle & Woll, 1985) with a stranger. If this stranger is also deaf then the speed with which a basic sign vocabulary can be negotiated can astound non-signers and mislead them into believing in a universal signed language. The highly predictable exchanges typical of such encounters ('What is your name?', 'Where do you live?', 'What's your job?', 'What country are you from?', 'What city do you live in?', 'Are you married?' and so on) also greatly facilitates this process.

Second, a shared culture enables deaf signers of different signed languages to draw on the stock of signs and gestures common in the surrounding hearing community to communicate with each other. Major world cultural groupings (e.g., European, Middle Eastern, South Asian, East Asian) have a wide repertoire of signs and gestures that are understood and used across large regions (Critchley, 1939; Brun, 1969). Moreover, the high iconicity of many signs in signed languages means that the meaning of some signs of a foreign signed language may be transparent in context, so are at least able to be guessed at. Of course, the iconic motivation of a sign is almost totally lost if it relates to some aspect of culture or technology that is not shared by the interlocutors.

Third, it appears that many of the grammatical features of Auslan we will discuss in Chapters 5, 6, and 7 are shared with most signed languages studied to date (Newport & Supalla, 2000; Meier, 2002a). Many signed languages' grammars make similar use of locations and orientations in space, the direction, quality and speed of movements, facial expressions and sign orders. The largest differences between signed languages appear to be lexical in nature. As Kyle and Woll (1985:168) observed:

> Sometimes it is claimed by deaf people themselves that they are simply using mime, but since hearing people do not follow this sign 'interlanguage' very well (as they would if it were simply mime) it is more likely that at least some grammatical processes used in the visual medium are shared across cultures despite differences in vocabulary. Once basic vocabulary items are negotiated, conversation can flow since people use similar means of putting signs together.

Some of these shared grammatical features of signed languages are, however, also features commonly found in pidgin and creole languages (Fischer, 1978; Deuchar, 1984). For example, creoles often have no equivalent to the verb *to be* in English, use words meaning 'finish' to signal that something has happened before the time of speaking, and rely on features such as intonation (or its equivalent in signed language—facial expression) for distinguishing statements and questions. Though the significance of this similarity with pidgins and creoles will be looked at in detail in Chapter 10, for now let us note that it lies at the root of the fourth factor that contributes to a degree of commonality between unrelated signed languages and, hence, deaf people's skill in cross-linguistic communication. Namely, signed languages are young languages both in the history of the deaf communities, and individually in the lifetimes of deaf people. This is to say, natural signed languages have emerged, for the most part, with the establishment of institutionalised education for the deaf children over the past 200 years, and individually, most deaf people have acquired these languages in a situation in which care-givers and educators have been non-native users of the language themselves. Thus, signed languages are young languages, and also ones that are only rarely passed on from one generation of native users to the next.

Of course, there are signed languages which are related and similar to each other in the same way that spoken languages form families (Woll *et al.*, 2001). As we have seen, there exists the BSL family of signed languages. It would appear that a number of European signed languages are also related: for example, LSF appears to be related to signed languages used in Ireland, Belgium, Canada, the USA, Mexico and Brazil. This reflects the history of signed languages in Europe which began with the establishment of schools for the deaf founded by teachers trained at or at least familiar with the signs and the methods used at de l'Epée's institute for the deaf in Paris (Lane, 1984).

Apart from the above-mentioned possibility of a number of shared features, the vocabulary of Auslan is, for the most part, quite unlike that found in other, unrelated signed languages in non-English speaking countries. In most situations, these signed languages appear to be unintelligible to an Auslan observer just as Auslan seems to be unintelligible to these foreign signers.

3.8.1 International Sign Language

The term *International Sign Language* (or *Gestuno*) was used by the World Federation of the Deaf in a 1975 publication to describe a form of signed language using a special lexicon devised to assist communication between deaf people who had no language in common (either signed or written). However, the publication simply represented an attempt to encourage the use of a standard lexicon at international meetings of deaf people, whether political, sporting or cultural. It does not mean that an agreed upon and codified international signed language exists or that messages of equal complexity to those conveyed in natural sign languages can easily be communicated using International Sign (or IS), as it is now referred to (Rosenstock, 2004). More importantly, neither does it mean that when IS is provided as a language of interpretation at international conferences, workshops and meetings, one can assume that as much information is being conveyed or understood as would be in a source language (signed or spoken). In most cases, a much simpler message is being conveyed.

By using a basic standardised vocabulary (much of which appears to be drawn from a mix of ASL and various European signed languages), IS attempts to make maximum use of common grammatical features found in signed languages (see above), especially those relating to the use of space, to convey messages in the most visual way possible (Supalla & Webb, 1995; McKee & Napier, 2002). In the three decades since 1975, the international deaf community and signed language interpreters who work at international events have gained increasing experience with IS and exposure to each other's signed languages, especially ASL. It would now seem the basic vocabulary is not as accessible to as many deaf people in as many regions as might once have been imagined. Deaf people from Africa and parts of Asia do not find some of the signs as obvious or suggestive as North American and European signers do (Rosenstock, 2004). Indeed, because ASL is the most commonly and widely seen and used signed language, there has been a tendency for ASL vocabulary items to become 'internationalised'. They tend to occur not only in the spontaneous international contact pidgin used between deaf people, but also in the more formal attempts to provide interpretation in IS.

3.9 Emerging signed languages of the developing world

In many of the world's poorer, developing countries, patterns of urbanisation and economic constraints have meant that deaf people have usually been isolated from each other and lacked educational opportunities. They remained within their family or village and it was rare if they even knew other deaf people, let alone had regular interactions with them. In these cases, home sign systems develop. These idiosyncratic home sign systems used in the homes or villages of individual deaf people may develop a relative degree of sophistication (Goldin-Meadow, 2003; Singleton & Newport, 2004). However, it is doubtful whether bona fide signed languages can be said to exist at all in these circumstances (cf. Washabaugh, 1986).

One should not assume, therefore, that relatively high levels of hearing impairment or deafness in parts of the developing world have automatically meant that there are deaf communities and signed languages to be found everywhere. Some threshold or 'critical mass', similar to what seems to have occurred in Nicaragua, appears necessary for this development to take its natural course (Kegl, 1994).

Nonetheless, there have been a few recorded instances where signed languages have emerged in a non-urban setting without institutionalised education. Martha's Vineyard is one example we have already come across (see above). Another, contemporary, example is the village of Kata Kolok on the island of Bali, in Indonesia where endemic hereditary deafness over many generations has led to the existence of a well-established community signed language (Branson *et al.*, 1996). Other examples include a Mayan village in the Yucatan (Johnson, 1991), a community in the Enga province of Papua New Guinea (Kendon, 1980), the villages of Ban Khor in Thailand (Woodward, 2000) and Adamorobe in Ghana (Frishberg, 1986), and the signed language found in groups of Bedouin of the Negev desert in Israel (Sandler, Meir, Padden & Aronoff, 2005). Recently, another such signed language has been found in the village of Kosindo in Surinam (van den Bogaerde, 2005), and undoubtedly others have yet to be identified.

However, the global situation is rapidly changing. The early twenty-first century is unfolding as the greatest period of mass migration from countryside to cities in human history. The extent and speed of urbanisation in East Asia, for example, far outpaces that of Europe in the nineteenth century. Either through the concentration of numbers of deaf people in cities and the subsequent growth of social networks, or through the establishment of schools for the deaf in developing countries, we can expect this process to result in the emergence of new deaf communities and new signed languages, just as has already been documented in Nicaragua (Kegl, Senghas, & Coppola, 1999). Indeed, this currently appears to be happening in Cambodia.

3.10 Summary

In this chapter, we have reviewed the history and origin of Auslan, and showed that it appears to have no known relationship with Australian Aboriginal signed languages. We d escribed the development of Auslan from BSL, and presented the evidence for the claim that BSL, Auslan and NZSL might all be considered dialects of the one signed language. We examined the links between Auslan and two other signed languages—ISL and ASL—and discussed the emergence of IS and new signed languages in other parts of the world. In the following chapter, we begin an examination of the structure of Auslan with a focus on the formational characteristics of signs.

3.11 Further Reading

For a detailed account of Australian Aboriginal signed languages, see Kendon (1988). For a history of signed language use and the deaf community in the United Kingdom, see Kyle & Woll (1985), Jackson (1990) or Rée (1999). Groce (1985) is a fascinating study of Martha's Vineyard Sign Language, and Lane (1984) traces the beginnings of ASL and deaf education in North America. Although focused on the early twentieth century, Carty (2004) is the most significant work to date on Australian deaf history. See also Carty (2000) for the story of John Carmichael. Johnston (2003a) and McKee & Kennedy (2000) are the key lexicostatistical works on the relationship between Auslan and other signed languages in the BANZSL family.

4   Phonetics and phonology: the building blocks of signs

One of the defining features of language is that the symbols that are used in language can be broken down into smaller discrete parts or *segments* (Hockett, 1960). In this chapter, we explore in detail how segmentation applies to the signs used in a signed language. As linguistics has traditionally focused on the study of speech, many of the key concepts and much of the terminology used in the study of signed languages have been adapted from the description of spoken languages. We thus begin with a brief outline of the internal structure of words in spoken languages. We then move on to discuss the internal structure of signs, how they may be classified into different types based on their formational characteristics, and how their structure is influenced by a number of constraints.

4.1   The internal structure of words

The words in a spoken language like English are not produced simply as a random combination of sounds, but are made from a limited set of sounds. Sounds from this limited set are used to build all the hundreds of thousands of words in the English language. In traditional models of spoken language phonology, these sounds act as the smallest contrastive units of the language, because a change in even one of these sounds can change the meaning of the word, as in the contrast between the words *pet* versus *bet.* Following Bloomfield (1933), the smallest segments of sounds that are used to distinguish two words have come to be known as *phonemes*. The number of phonemes varies from language to language, although most languages appear to have between 20 and 40 (Crystal, 1997). The variety of English spoken in Australia, for example, has 44 phonemes.

4.1.1   Minimal pairs

How do linguists know which sounds act as phonemes, the smallest formational units in a language? One method traditionally employed to determine whether two sounds are phonemic is to identify *minimal pairs.* A minimal pair is a pair of words that differ only by a single sound where this sound is in the same position in both words. As mentioned above, the words *pet* and *bet* have different meanings, yet they differ in only one sound: *pet* begins with a /p/ and *bet* begins with /b/. This is the smallest amount by which the two words could differ. Any smaller difference would be impossible in English, because English speakers are not usually aware of any way to divide /p/ and /b/ into smaller parts (Aitchison, 1992). These two sounds are two of the 44 phonemes in Australian English (see Fromkin *et al.*, 2005, for more information about English phonemes).

It is often difficult to see how the basic contrastive sounds or phonemes work in such minimal pairs, because the English spelling system does not always accurately reflect the number and type of sounds in a particular word. Although the pronunciation of English has changed over the last few centuries, much of the writing system has not. English has also borrowed many words from languages with different writing systems. Linguists and lexicographers have attempted to overcome this problem by using a phonemic transcription system that directly represents the sounds themselves. The minimal pairs in Table 4.1 are presented both using English spelling and the symbols of the International Phonetic Alphabet (IPA).

Table 4.1 *Examples of minimal pairs in English.*

English			IPA		
pit	:	fit	pɪt	:	fɪt
fit	:	fought	fɪt	:	fɔt
fought	:	fawn	fɔt	:	fɔn
fawn	:	born	fɔn	:	bɔn
born	:	barn	bɔn	:	ban
barn	:	bath	ban	:	baθ

If we look just at the sounds of these words represented in the 'IPA' column in Table 4.1, we see that each pair contrasts in only a single sound. This set of minimal pairs illustrates some of the basic distinctive formational units (i.e., phonemes) of English, and how these smallest units are used to build words. Often there may be slight differences in the sound of the phoneme itself, depending on its position in the word. English speakers will notice that the /k/ sound at the beginning of *cat* is slightly different from the /k/ sound at the end of *beak*. When it is at the beginning of a word, as in *cat,* the /k/ sound is pronounced with aspiration (i.e., a puff of breath). At the ends of words, such as *beak,* this puff of breath does not occur. This is also true of the sounds /t/ and /p/. These slight differences in the pronunciation of /t/, /p/ and /k/ may be important in other languages (such as Thai), but they are not contrastive in English (Ladefoged, 1982). Non-contrastive variants of phonemes are known as *allophones.* There are many other examples of allophones in English. The human speech organs are thus capable of producing an enormous number of different speech sounds. Every spoken language, however, uses only a limited set of sound contrasts as its most basic building blocks.

4.2   The internal structure of signs

It was not until comparatively recently that the similarities between the linguistic uses of sounds in languages and of gestural elements in signed languages were recognised. With the publication of *Sign Language Structure* in 1960, Stokoe was the first researcher to demonstrate that the signs used by deaf people actually had internal structure in the same way as spoken words. Before Stokoe, signs had been generally regarded as simple, unanalysable gestures with no internal organisation, rather like those used in gesticulation (Bloomfield, 1933). This meant that signs were thought to be unlike words because they could not be broken down into smaller, recurring segments. Stokoe (1960) showed, however, that just as hundreds of thousands of English words are produced using a very small number of different sounds, the signs of ASL were produced using a limited number of gestural features. Stokoe found that the action of a sign had three main parts or *aspects*: a *handshape* oriented in a specific way, at a specific *location* and with a specific type of *movement*. He proposed that these aspects be known as *cheremes*, analogous to the phonemes of spoken languages. This term, however, never gained widespread acceptance.

4.2.1   Handshape, location and movement

Handshape, as the name suggests, refers to the shape of the hand used in a sign. In the Auslan sign NOT-KNOW, for example, the fingers of the hand are held flat and close together. The human hand is, however, capable of assuming a vast array of other possible shapes. It may be closed into a fist, or the fingers may be spread out or held together. The hand may be bent at the wrist, or the fingers may be bent at the knuckles or joints. The thumb may be extended, held parallel to the fingers or held across the palm or closed fist. The index, middle, ring or little finger may be extended, bent, or in contact with each other. As we will see below, despite the great number of possible hand configurations that can be produced, each particular signed language tends to use only a limited number of handshapes to create signs in the core lexicon (see Chapter 6 for a discussion of the Auslan lexicon).

NOT-KNOW

Figure 4.1: *Handshape, location and movement in a simple sign.*

Location refers to the position of the hand on the body or in the space around the signer. In NOT-KNOW, the hand is held near the forehead. As with handshapes, there are a great number of different locations on the body and in space that may be used. Signs in the core lexicon, however, tend to use a relatively limited set.

Movement is perhaps the most complex of the three basic aspects. The movement in the sign NOT-KNOW is quite simple: the hand moves away from the signer. In other signs, the hand moves away from the body, towards it, upwards, downwards, to and fro, in an arc, a circle, or spiral. The handshape may change, or the direction of the palm and fingers may be altered. Many signs use simple movements, while others may be realised as complex combinations of different types of movement. As with handshape and location, the core signs of a signed language appear to use only a subset of all those movements of the fingers, hands and arms that are physically possible.

4.2.2   Other aspects of sign structure

Since Stokoe's original work, further research has shown that other features of sign structure need to be taken into account. The Canadian researcher Robbin Battison (1978) suggested that *orientation,* which refers to the direction of the palm and fingers, is also an important component of sign phonology. A particular handshape can be oriented in a number of different ways in relation to the signer's body. The palms and fingers may be oriented left, right, up, down, towards or away from the signer. In the sign MOTHER, for example, the palm of the dominant hand faces down or away from the signer. If the sign were produced with the palm of the dominant hand oriented towards the signer (so that the back of the dominant hand made contact with the palm of the subordinate hand), it would not be well formed (Figure 4.2).

MOTHER   WORK

Figure 4.2: *Correct forms of MOTHER and WORK.*

Some signs also make contrastive use of *hand arrangement* and *point of contact* (Klima & Bellugi, 1979). In signs that involve two hands, such as the sign WORK, hand arrangement refers to the placement of the hands in space with respect to each other. Note that in this sign, the hands cross each other near the wrist. In a two-handed sign like WORK, only one hand (i.e., the dominant hand) repeatedly contacts the other hand (i.e., the subordinate hand). The point of contact describes the part of the dominant hand that may be used to contact the subordinate hand. In this sign, it is the little finger side of the dominant hand which makes contact (Figure 4.2).

Other features, such as the *stress* and *duration* of sign production, and the *rate of repetition* of movement are also employed in the formation of signs in Auslan (Johnston, 1989a). Many linguists also suggest that *non-manual features* (such as facial expression, eye gaze, mouth gestures, mouthing of spoken language lexical items, and movements of the head and body) play an important role in the internal structure of signs (e.g., Sutton-Spence & Woll, 1999; Valli *et al.*, 2005).

Of these additional features, signed language linguists now generally include orientation in their descriptions of signs and many appear to agree that it counts as one of the four most basic building blocks in sign structure (Woll, 1990). The other features listed above, however, do not appear essential to describe every sign in Auslan and other signed languages. In this account, we will not discuss in detail hand arrangement, point of contact, stress, duration and rate of repetition unless these appear to be necessary to describe a particular sign. Non-manual features will be discussed separately since they can appear with or without manual signs, and because they appear to play a variety of different roles in signed languages.

4.2.2.1 The signing space
Users of signed languages tend to use only those parts of the body and locations in space which fall into what linguists call the *signing space.* The signing space refers to an area which 'extends from approximately just above the head to the waist, and in width from elbow to elbow when the arms are held loosely bent' (Brennan, 1992:22). It is in this area that the hands and arms can move and make contact with the body and each other easily and naturally.

4.3   Sign parameters and notation systems

Thus far, we have seen that we can analyse signs as being articulated using one or more handshapes oriented in a specific direction and performing one or more distinct movements at a location or locations in the signing space or on the signer's body. Some signs may also be accompanied by a particular non-manual feature. These five gestural features are known as the *parameters* of sign production. Just as in spoken languages, notation systems have been developing using symbols for each of the contrastive units involved in sign production (as we saw in Chapter 1). These systems have enabled researchers to describe the production of signs in written form. In general, we shall refer to signs in this book by means of glossing and illustrations only. We could, however, represent signs using a phonemic notation system, as in the following examples, using HamNoSys: SISTER [∂↖0⅄⊥⅄⁺] and THANK-YOU [◯ᵣo∪⊥]. HamNoSys has been used by some linguists in Australia and New Zealand as a way of recording signs in written form (Johnston, 1991b; Kennedy *et al.*, 1997). Each symbol is explained in Table 4.2.

Table 4.2 SISTER *and* THANK-YOU *in the Hamburg Notation System (HamNoSys).*

		SISTER		THANK-YOU
Handshape	∂	hook	◯	flat
Orientation	↖	hand up, palm left	ᵣ	hand diagonally up, palm towards the singer
	0		o	
Location	⅄	nose	∪	chin
Movement	⊥	towards	⊥	move away from signer
	⅄	contact		
	+	twice		
Non-manual features		n/a		n/a

4.4   Minimal pairs in Auslan

How have linguists determined which formational units are of importance in a signed language like Auslan? As in the study of spoken languages, linguists have isolated the basic parts of signs through the study of minimal pairs found in pairs or sets of signs, especially *citation forms*. The citation form of a sign refers to the form of a sign used in isolation, for the purposes of discussion or analysis (e.g., in response to a question like 'What is the sign for mother?'), rather than in a stretch of connected signing. Many citation forms of signs in Auslan differ in only one parameter, and these can be compared.

For example, the signs WORK and TALK are the same in orientation, location and movement. The signs differ in meaning, yet the only difference occurs in the handshape used in each sign. Thus, we can see that handshape is an important part of signs, and that it is used to distinguish signs from each other. Other signs, such as ON and TRUE, differ only in orientation. Here the handshape is the same, and only the orientation of the palm distinguishes the two signs. Similarly, BEAUTIFUL and WELL differ only in location, and BROTHER and PAPER differ only in movement. Additional examples of sign minimal pairs are included in Figure 4.3 but for a more extensive discussion, see Johnston (1989a).

Figure 4.3: *Examples of minimal pairs in Auslan citation forms.*

4.5   Sign types

Brennan (1992) grouped BSL signs into three main formational types: *manual* signs, *non-manual* signs and *multi-channel* signs. Table 4.3 provides examples of each type from Auslan.

Not surprisingly, manual signs are by far the most frequent type in Auslan, followed by multi-channel signs (Johnston, 1989a). The use of non-manual features without a manual sign can occur, though it is relatively rare. When this occurs, as in the example of the headshake meaning 'no', this use of non-manual features may be considered an example of a non-manual sign. Non-manual features tend to co-occur with manual signs, either as part of an individual multi-channel sign, or in combination with a whole string of signs. When combined with individual signs, non-manual features may modify the meaning of the sign in some way, perhaps intensifying or adding other nuances to its meaning (this is explained in Chapter 5). This is true of the example RECENT+cs ('just recently') where the non-manual feature 'cs' ('cheek to shoulder' movement) intensifies the meaning of the sign RECENT. If they are used with an entire signed phrase, non-manuals usually fulfil a grammatical function, being used to distinguish questions from statements, for example, or to mark the topic of a sentence, as explained in Chapter 7.

Note that for Brennan (1992), multi-channel signs are those that obligatorily co-occur with a specific set of non-manual features. We do not make this claim here, although we recognise that some particular facial expressions, eye gaze, mouth gestures, mouthings and movements of the head and body tend to be associated with specific signs.

Table 4.3 *Sign types.*

Sign type	Explanation	Example
Manual	Signs which can be made with only the hands. These signs are formed from the four basic components: handshape, orientation, location and movement.	 SIGN
Non-manual	Signs which are made with parts of the body other than the hands. The signs may involve facial expressions, mouth gestures, mouthing, changes in gaze, or movements of the head or body, or a combination of these features.	 NO
Multi-channel	Signs which are made with the hands together with other parts of the body. They thus have five component parts: handshape, orientation, location, movement and non-manual features.	 RECENT+cs

4.6   Manual signs

Manual signs can also be divided into three broad classes, based upon the involvement of one or both hands (Battison, 1978). Before we describe these classes, however, it is important to note that handedness is not contrastive in Auslan (or other documented signed languages, see Emmorey, 2002). There are no signs that are specified as always produced on the right or left hand for all signers. As we will see, some signs are produced with only one hand, and others are produced with one hand acting on the other. In both cases, signers use their dominant hand as the main articulator, depending on whether a signer is right-handed or left-handed.

As shown in Figure 4.4 and Figure 4.5, signs in Class A are one-handed, those in Class B are two-handed and those in Class C are combinations of one-handed and two-handed elements. Signs within these classes may be further categorised into subclasses based on how they reflect particular patterns of combination.

Class A may be subdivided into Type 1 and Type 2. Type 1 signs are one-handed signs that are produced in the signing space, and do not involve contact on the body, such as HAVE and NOW. Type 2 signs are one-handed signs that make contact with the body, such as WHY and KNOW.

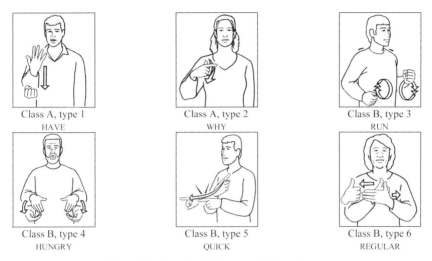

Figure 4.4: *Class A and B signs and their sub-types.*

Class B signs may be subdivided into four types. Type 3 signs are two-handed signs which both have the same handshape and in which both hands move in the signing space without making contact with the body, such as RUN and PLAN. Type 4 signs have the same handshape on both hands, but make contact with the body, such as HUNGRY and PRACTISE. Type 5 signs have the same handshape on both hands, but one hand acts on the other, such as TRUE or QUICK. Type 3, 4, and 5 signs are also known as *double-handed signs* in work on Auslan (Johnston, 1989a; Schembri, 1996). Type 6 signs are two-handed signs in which one hand acts on the other, but unlike Type 5, the two hands have different handshapes, as in REGULAR and CENTRE (these are also referred to as *two-handed signs*).

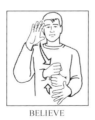

BELIEVE

Figure 4.5: *An example of a Class C sign.*

Class C signs also refer to signs that involve some combination of the above types, as in the signs BELIEVE (which appears originally to have been a combination of a Type 2 sign THINK and a Type 5 sign HOLD).

In later sections, we shall see how particular constraints in signed languages appear to operate differently on these subclasses of signs. Despite these differences, signs in all classes each consist of the hand or hands assuming a particular handshape, orientation, location and movement. In the sections below, we will examine the use of each these formational features in Auslan.

4.6.1 Handshape in Auslan

Before we begin our discussion of handshape, it is appropriate to note that the articulator in Auslan may involve more than simply the handshape. For example, non-manual signs may involve parts of the body other than the hand acting as the articulator of a sign, and a small number of manual and multi-channel signs involve the arm as well as the hand (e.g., the arm moves from the shoulder joint, not the elbow, in the sign SCOTLAND). We will, however, focus on handshape here.

SCOTLAND

Figure 4.6: *A sign involving the whole arm, not just the hands.*

There are sixty-two handshapes listed in the *Signs of Australia* dictionary of Auslan (Johnston, 1998). Johnston found it necessary to specify these sixty-two different handshapes in order to adequately describe the range of hand configurations used in the manual and multi-channel signs of Auslan. Of these handshapes, approximately thirty-seven appeared to act as distinctive hand configurations in signs from the core lexicon. Thus, twenty-five were classified as regular variants of these thirty-seven handshapes.

Variant handshapes are hand configurations which differ non-contrastively from each other, and which signers of a particular signed language may treat as equivalent despite small differences in production. This non-distinctive variation is similar to the slight differences in pronunciation of /k/ that were mentioned earlier and which are not contrastive in English. The S handshape (see Figure 4.8) is usually made in the sign MAKE with the thumb bent over the fingers, but can also be made with the thumb held near the index finger, as in the sign WASH (Figure 4.7).

MAKE   WASH

Figure 4.7: *Two non-contrastive forms of the S handshape.*

The positioning of the thumb in these handshapes is not significant in Auslan, as shown by variants of the sign POSS-2 'yours' which may use either form. These two handshapes may thus be considered phonological variants (or allophones) of the one handshape. There are many other examples of handshape allophones in Auslan signs and fingerspelling (e.g., the manual letter -B- has a number of allophones, as mentioned in Chapter 6).

The identification of distinctive handshapes was the result of a detailed study of signs in the database which produced the dictionary of Auslan. We focused on handshapes that appeared to work contrastively in signs from the core lexicon, adopting an analysis similar to earlier work on BSL (Brennan, Colville & Lawson, 1984). This list of basic handshapes does not include all those hand configurations which work contrastively in depicting (or 'classifier') signs, such as those which represent the size and shape of objects (depicting signs are discussed in Chapter 6). Research has suggested that handshapes in depicting signs tend to work differently from signs in the core lexicon. In the hand configurations used in some depicting signs, the number of fingers, their distance from each other and their degree of bending may be used to signal differences in meaning (Corina, 1990). In core signs, however, such differences may simply result in variant forms of the same handshape, as explained above.

4.6.1.1 Distribution of handshapes

The distribution of the major handshapes in the core lexicon of Auslan varies considerably (Johnston, 1989a). Just four of the total number of distinctive handshapes (i.e., 1, B, 5 and S) are used in over 50 per cent of all the signs in the 1998 edition of the Auslan dictionary (Johnston, 1998). One of these handshapes, the B hand, occurs in over 25 per cent of all signs. The fifteen most frequent handshapes account for 80 per cent, while the next twenty-two handshapes account for the remaining 20 per cent.

Some of these handshapes are very rare and may be considered to be of limited importance in the phonological structure of Auslan. Six of these handshapes (the Irish H, ILY, Old 7, M, ! and 9 handshapes) occur in only 1 per cent of all the Auslan signs in the Auslan dictionary (Johnston, 1998). This tiny percentage partly reflects the fact that these handshapes occur in a small number of *initialised signs* or in number signs. An initialised sign is one in which the handshape used in the sign represents the first letter of a common gloss of that sign (e.g., PROGRAM uses a -P- handshape). It may be unrelated to any other sign in the language in this way or, more commonly, it may represent the replacement of an original handshape of another sign by one that represents an initial letter of a gloss of that sign or a gloss of the new 'initialised' sign that it now creates. Many of the handshapes that occur in initialised signs are not native to Auslan and reflect direct borrowing from ASL, ISL and IS, or an indirect influence from one-handed American or Irish manual alphabets. Some have been adopted from artificial sign systems, such as ASE (Jeanes & Reynolds, 1982).

Consequently, signers tend to modify some of these less frequent handshapes so that they more closely resemble common handshapes in the language. Some Auslan signers do not distinguish between the 2 and P handshapes, so that the ASL loan signs PROGRAM and PHILOSOPHY are often signed with a variant of the 2, rather than the P, handshape. Similarly, signers often produce EUROPE with a variant of the O handshape rather than the E from the one-handed manual alphabet. It is also rare for these hand configurations, unlike the more basic handshapes, to appear in signs where one handshape changes to another. Thus, many handshapes found in initialised signs do appear to have a rather uncertain status in Auslan, and appear to be less relevant to the phonological system of the language. It is not clear, however, that they can be considered marginal, as ASL and IS continue to be an important source of borrowed signs for Australian signers.

Less common number-related handshapes include the handshape in NINE, or the configuration used in the old northern sign SEVEN. These use a particular combination of fingers that occurs only in number signs, perhaps to enable all the numbers from one to ten to be articulated coherently on one hand. This aspect of the handshape does not mean, however, that it is not used in everyday signed interactions. The 9 handshape does, for example, occur in a range of signs which incorporate numerical information, such as NINE-YEARS-AGO, NINETEEN-YEARS-OLD and so on.

Thus, particular handshapes may only occur in number signs or signs derived from one-handed fingerspelling. They are examples of what are called *marked* handshapes (discussed in more detail in §4.8.3 below).

4.6.1.2 Handshape minimal pairs
Figure 4.8 reproduces thirty-five of the major distinctive handshapes listed in the *Signs of Australia* dictionary (Johnston, 1998).[1] Examples of minimal

---

[1] We have excluded from Figure 4.8 two marginal handshapes (the handshapes for the one-handed letters N and M) because they do not seem to appear in any native lexical Auslan signs.

pairs for each of the handshapes have been included to illustrate their contrastive role in the language.

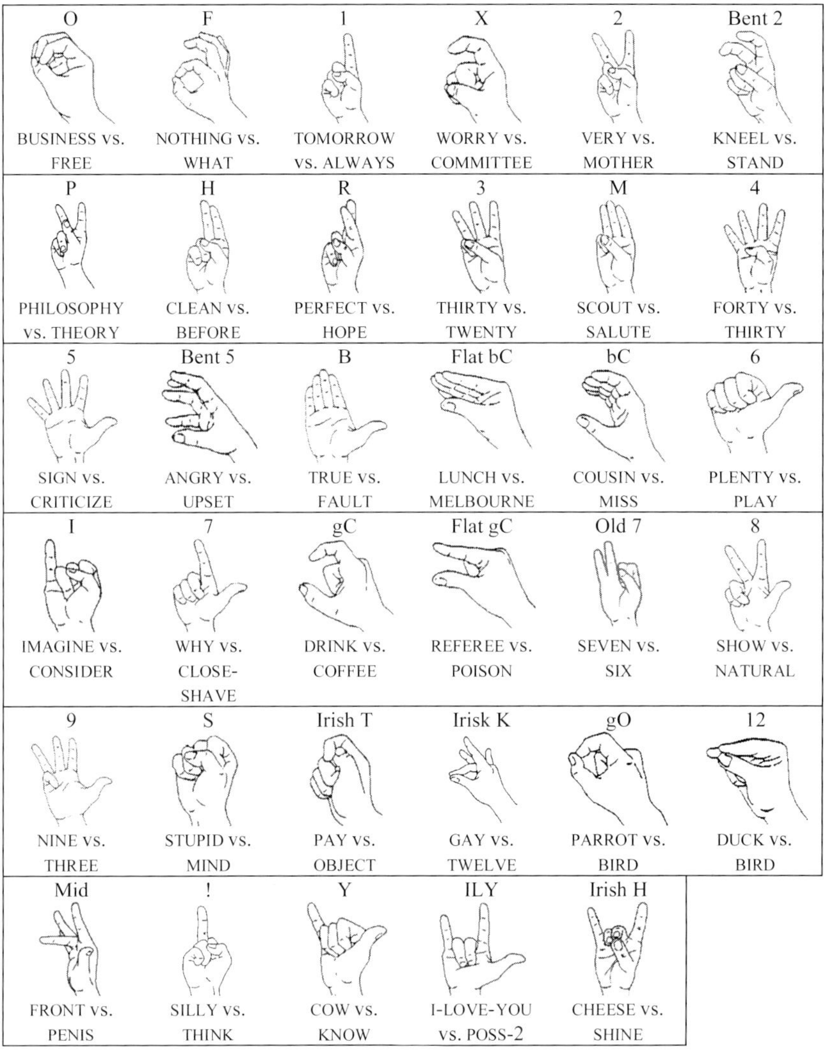

O	F	1	X	2	Bent 2
BUSINESS vs. FREE	NOTHING vs. WHAT	TOMORROW vs. ALWAYS	WORRY vs. COMMITTEE	VERY vs. MOTHER	KNEEL vs. STAND
P	H	R	3	M	4
PHILOSOPHY vs. THEORY	CLEAN vs. BEFORE	PERFECT vs. HOPE	THIRTY vs. TWENTY	SCOUT vs. SALUTE	FORTY vs. THIRTY
5	Bent 5	B	Flat bC	bC	6
SIGN vs. CRITICIZE	ANGRY vs. UPSET	TRUE vs. FAULT	LUNCH vs. MELBOURNE	COUSIN vs. MISS	PLENTY vs. PLAY
I	7	gC	Flat gC	Old 7	8
IMAGINE vs. CONSIDER	WHY vs. CLOSE-SHAVE	DRINK vs. COFFEE	REFEREE vs. POISON	SEVEN vs. SIX	SHOW vs. NATURAL
9	S	Irish T	Irisk K	gO	12
NINE vs. THREE	STUPID vs. MIND	PAY vs. OBJECT	GAY vs. TWELVE	PARROT vs. BIRD	DUCK vs. BIRD
Mid	!	Y	ILY	Irish H	
FRONT vs. PENIS	SILLY vs. THINK	COW vs. KNOW	I-LOVE-YOU vs. POSS-2	CHEESE vs. SHINE	

Figure 4.8: *The major handshapes in Auslan with glosses of minimal pairs.*

It is important to recognise that our understanding of the formational processes of signed languages is just beginning. As more data becomes available, descriptions such as those found here will naturally be subject to revision. Indeed, more systematic research is required before the exact number of handshapes needed to describe the signs of the Auslan lexicon can be specified. For instance, the complexity of depicting signs and the influence of other signed languages on Auslan make identifying a finite set of distinctive handshapes used in all types of signing, and not just in signs in the core lexicon (see Chapter 6), a difficult task.

4.6.2   Location in Auslan

The location of the sign may refer to the hand's actual point of contact on the body, or to the hand simply being significantly near some location on the body. When the sign has no contact with the body, or when it is not located near some part of the body, it is described as being articulated in *neutral space.* Most citation forms of signs with no body contact are made in the centre of neutral space, such as SIGN and CLASS, although others are specified for relatively higher (e.g., HEAVEN) or lower (e.g., FLOOR) locations.

As we have seen, signs involving contact or proximity to the body fall into two categories: those on the body itself (signs of Types 2 and 4), and those on the hands (signs of Types 5 and 6). Locations on the body are known as *primary* locations, those on the hand as *secondary* locations (Johnston, 1989a).

4.6.2.1 Primary locations
There are a large number of distinct locations on or near the body needed to describe signs in Auslan. Sets of minimally distinct signs illustrate the importance of this parameter, and how apparently subtle differences in location work to distinguish signs with different meanings.

HOW-OLD   HOW-MUCH   HOW-MANY

Figure 4.9: *Three signs in which location is the minimal distinction.*

Table 4.4 presents the thirty-nine primary locations in Auslan with an example of a sign from the core lexicon that is produced at each location. It should be noted that the location features in signs from the core lexicon can, for the most part, be specified and listed as shown in Table 4.4. Other uses of space in Auslan, however, do not lend themselves very well to such traditional structural analyses. The meaningful use of space in signed languages will be discussed in Chapters 5 and 6.

Table 4.4 *The major primary locations in Auslan with examples.*

Location	EXAMPLE	Location	EXAMPLE
Head		**Chin**	FRUIT
Above head	SHOWER	Under chin	NOT-CARE
Top of head	BALD	**Neck**	
Whole of face	EMBARRASS	Ipsilateral	MEAT
Side of head	NOISE	Central	VOICE
Forehead		**Shoulders**	
Ipsilateral	THINK	Above	BURDEN
Central	INDIA	Below	RESPONSIBLE
Eye		**Chest**	
Side of eye	LOOK	Ipsilateral	LIVE
Under eye	CRY	Central	PRO-1
Nose		Contralateral	HEART
Bridge of nose	SISTER	**Arm pit**	HUSBAND
Tip of nose	AGE	**Stomach**	HUNGRY
Under nose	SNOB	**Waist**	INCOME
Ear		**Back**	BACK
Whole ear	LISTEN	**Thigh**	DOG
Earlobe	EAR-RING	**Arm**	
Behind ear	COCHLEAR-IMPLANT	Upper arm	VIRGIN
Over ear	CHERRY	Elbow	BISCUIT
Cheek	STRANGE	Lower arm	POOR
Mouth		**Wrist**	TIME
Mouth	ORAL	**Hand**	
Teeth	METAL	Back of hand	THEATRE
Side of mouth	JEALOUS	Palm	CENTRE

4.6.2.2 Secondary locations

Although particular locations on the hand and fingers are important for a number of signs, it is difficult to produce a definitive account of the contrastive status of the various locations on the hand. One reason for the lack of clear minimal pairs involving secondary locations is that a change in the point of contact on the hands almost invariably requires a change in orientation and direction of movement of the hand or hands. This factor makes it difficult to collect and compare minimal pairs that contrast only in secondary location. As a result, specification of secondary locations is important for the accurate description of signs, but they appear to be of lesser contrastive significance than primary locations.

Nevertheless, it is clear that a range of secondary locations is regularly used in Auslan. Signs make contact with the tip of the thumb (e.g., ALCOHOL) or the side of the thumb (e.g., INITIAL), the tip of the index finger (e.g., POINT), the side of the index finger (e.g., ENGLISH), the tip of the middle finger (e.g., COINCIDENCE), the ring finger (e.g., SPOUSE) and the little finger (e.g., MENSTRUATION).

Signs can also make contact with the thumb side of the hand (e.g., WORK), with the little finger side (e.g., SKILL) or with the ends of the fingers as a group (e.g., DOLLAR). Signs may also be located between the thumb and fingers (e.g., INVOLVE) or between the fingers (e.g., THROUGH). Note that signers appear to vary in their use of locations between the fingers. Signs like THROUGH (and others such as LETTER, BETWEEN, etc.) may, for some signers, make contact between the index and middle, middle and ring, or ring and little fingers without contrasting in meaning.

4.6.3   Movement in Auslan

Movement types in sign phonological structure have been classified into two major categories: *primary* and *secondary* movements (Johnston, 1989a). Primary movements are sub-classified into *path* movements (movement from one location to another) and *local* (or *internal*) movements (changes in handshape and orientation) (Liddell, 1990; van der Hulst, 1993). Secondary movements refer to rapidly repeated local movements which can be performed during a path movement or while the hand is stationary.

4.6.3.1 Primary movements
Brennan (1992) suggested that path movement can involve changes in location along one of three axes. First, vertical path movements involve the contrasts up, down and up and down. Second, path movements along the bilateral axis involve contrasts right, left and side to side. Third, path movements along the horizontal depth axis involve contrasts towards the signer, away from the signer and to and fro. Movement may also be circular or elliptical along any of these axes.

Johnston (1989a) pointed out that path movements are not limited to these axes and can also be expressed by combining these features (e.g., 'up left' for 'diagonally up and towards the left', as might be used in a form of the sign AEROPLANE-TAKE-OFF). Linguists also recognise that oscillating movements along these axes may be either unidirectional or bidirectional (i.e., they may be repeated single upwards movements, or they may be combinations of upwards and downwards movements, produced with more or less equal stress in both directions). Examples of 10 major types of path movement are shown in Table 4.5.

Table 4.5 *Examples of path movement in Auslan.*

Mayor types of path movement	Sign examples
Up	LIFT
Down	SIT
Up and down	DOUBT
Sideways	DAY
Side to side	SCHOOL
Away	FORWARD
Towards	BACKWARD
Back and forth	COMMUNICATE
Horizontal circular	SWIM
Vertical circular	PLAY

Local movements refer to changes in handshape and orientation. Handshape change generally involves changes in *aperture* (Wilbur, 1987). This means that handshapes will change from open or spread hand configurations to closed, bent, flattened or hooked handshapes (or vice versa). An example of a closing handshape occurs in the sign HAVE (Figure 4.4). The same hand configuration opens in the sign FORGET (Figure 3.7). In the sign UNDERSTAND, the index finger flicks open, while in IDEA, it bends into a hooked handshape.

The fingers and palm may be oriented up, down, left, right, towards the signer or away, and in any manner of directions that combines these features. Finger and palm orientation changes are generally achieved through movements of the wrist and/or arm. In the sign REBEL, for example, the palm moves from a position facing the signer to one that is directed away from the signer. In the sign CAN'T, the opposite sequence of orientation occurs.

REBEL

CAN'T

NONE-OF-ONE'S-
BUSINESS

Figure 4.10: *Signs illustrating different types of path movement.*

Changes in handshape and orientation may combine with path movements. The sign BELIEVE involves both a handshape change (from 5 to S) and a path movement (from a location at the forehead to one contacting the base hand in front of the signer's chest). A sign such as NONE-OF-ONE'S-BUSINESS usually combines a change in palm orientation (from towards the signer to away from the signer) with a path movement (from a location on the face to one in the direction of the addressee). Many signs in Auslan (and in ASL, see Liddell, 1993) which involve local movements can be produced either with or without path movements (e.g., DIE which may consist of either a simple orientation change or an orientation change plus downward movement). Harry van der Hulst (1993) made the point that such complex combinations typically involve the complete synchronisation of the two types of movement, so that it is atypical to produce an aperture change at the end of a path movement. Examples of exceptions to this tendency can be found in Auslan, such as the sign TICKET (where the handshape appears to close at the end of a short path movement), but it seems complete synchronisation is more typical in signs from the core lexicon.

4.6.3.2 Secondary movements
The analysis of secondary movements is a matter of debate amongst signed language linguists (van der Hulst, 1993), but they typically involve rapidly repeated changes in handshape or orientation. Examples of nine secondary movement types found in Auslan are listed in Table 4.6.

Table 4.6 *Examples of secondary movement in Auslan (adapted from Liddell, 1990).*

	Without path movement	**With path movement**
Bending	ONE-MORE	PRAWN
Flattening	WET	GOSSIP
Squeezing	ORANGE	CATCH-UP
Wiggling	WHEN	MANY
Rubbing	SALT	PIZZA
Twisting	MAYBE	CHECK
Nodding	YES	VARY
Pivoting	WHAT	LIGHTNING
Circling	COFFEE	ROLL

4.6.4 Minor parameters in Auslan

4.6.4.1 Orientation
Orientation refers to the direction in which the fingers and palm of the hand are pointing during the production of a sign. Johnston (1989a) used a system of cardinal directions to describe orientation. The fingers and palm may be

oriented upwards, downwards, right, left, towards or away from the signer's body. Diagonal orientations may involve a combination of these elements. Although widely discussed in the literature (Klima & Bellugi, 1979; Baker & Cokely, 1980; Wilbur, 1987; Valli *et al.*, 2005), some signed language linguists appear to believe orientation is a relatively redundant feature (e.g., Brentari, 1998). Often other formational elements of a sign, such as the location on the body or in space or the point of contact on the hand, will mean that a particular sign can only be comfortably produced with certain orientations. It would not, for example, be very comfortable for a right-handed signer to produce the sign SAY with the dominant hand oriented with its palm to the right.

The use of different orientations also appears to be more variable than other features of sign phonological structure. The citation form or signs such as SAY, SEE or THINK show some variation in orientation (Brennan, 1992). The palm may be oriented towards the signer, or towards the side, and the choice between the two appears to be more or less arbitrary. Similarly, in signs such as PROGRAM or COURSE, the subordinate hand may have its palm oriented upwards or away from the signer.

Despite these observations, there is little doubt that many signs can only be accurately described by including orientation information. This is particularly true of signs that do not make contact with the body or hands. Minimal pairs such as THING versus SAME differ only in palm orientation (the palm in the first sign in each case is oriented upwards, downwards in the second). Signs such as DRUG (knuckles contacting) and BASTARD (knuckles upwards) differ only in finger orientation. Other signs, such as WORK and WINDOW, or HOLIDAY, SWIM and PLAY contrast in both the direction of the palm and fingers.

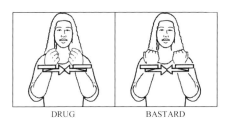

DRUG   BASTARD

Figure 4.11: *A minimal pair based on finger orientation.*

4.6.4.2 Hand arrangement
In signs involving two hands, the hands may be arranged in a variety of locations with respect to each other. The two hands may be held side by side as in GIVE, move together as in COMPARE, interlink as in JOIN, move apart as in DISCONNECT, or cross as in CONFLICT. The dominant hand may be held above the subordinate hand as in WIPE, below the subordinate hand as in

BAKE, behind it as in HIDE, in front of it as in ADVERTISE, or inside it as in DROWN.

Brennan (1992) showed that minimal pairs can be found in BSL that contrast only in hand arrangement. Similarly, in an Auslan sign like PARALLEL, the two 1 handshapes are held beside each other, whereas in FOLLOW, one is held behind the other with the index finger contacting the back of the hand. These signs are identical in all other respects. Such signs, however, could also be described adequately using a combination of other features, such as location and point of contact.

4.6.4.3 Point of contact

For those signs that make contact with the body or hand, the point of contact sometimes needs to be specified. This is because different parts of the hands may be involved in contacting the location. If we take signs that involve the 6 handshape, for example, we can see that different parts of the thumb and fist may act as the point of contact. In the signs KNOW and MONEY, it is the tip of the thumb which contacts the location on the body or passive hand. In BEST and BETTER, it is the side of the thumb that makes contact. In RIGHT, it is the palm side of the hand, in the sign NUMBER it is the little finger side, and in REGULAR, the back of the hand is the point of contact. There is a similar range of options for other handshapes. Although it is sometimes predictable from the combination of other parameter choices (given the handshape, orientation and location of the dominant hand in the sign MONEY, for example, the contacting surface of the hand is obvious), the point of contact appears nevertheless to be an important part of sign description.

4.7   Non-manual and multi-channel signs in Auslan

4.7.1   Non-manual signs

The term *non-manual* groups together a wide range of possible features. The non-manual means of articulation in signed languages include movements of the eyes, head and body, various kinds of facial expression, mouthing and mouth gestures. Mouthing based on spoken English words is discussed in Chapters 2 and 5, so we will focus here on the other non-manual features.

Table 4.7 provides an overview of the range of facial expression and mouth gesture types (as well as head and body movements) that are available to the Auslan signer, subdivided into movements and actions of the head, eyebrows, eyes, nose, mouth and cheeks.

Table 4.7 *Non-manual features.*

Body part	Action	Body part	Action
Head	Shaking	**Mouth (cont.)**	Poking out the tongue
	Nodding		Protruding the lips
	Turning to the left		Rounding the lips
	Turning to the right		Vibrating the lips
	Tilting to the left		Pressing the lips together
	Tilting to the right		Drawing the lips back
	Tilting backwards		Stretching the lips
	Tilting forwards		Turning up the corners of the mouth
	Moving backwards		Turning down the corners of the mouth
	Moving forwards		Pushing the tongue into the cheek
	Moving side to side		Pushing the tongue down below the lower lip
Eyebrows	Raising		Biting the lip
	Lowering		Sucking in air
Eyes	Closing		Blowing out air
	Opening	**Cheeks**	Puffing out
	Blinking		Sucking in
	Widening	**Shoulders**	Hunching
	Narrowing		Moving forwards
	Gazing forward and down		Moving backwards
	Gazing forward and upwards		Turning to the left
	Gazing to the left		Turning to the left
	Gazing to the right		Turning to the right
Nose	Wrinkling	**Body**	Leaning forwards
Mouth	Opening		Leaning backwards
	Closing		Leaning sideways

Despite this enormous potential for creating contrasts in meaning, however, it seems that signed languages rarely use non-manual features alone to form signs (Brennan, 1992). Non-manual signs may include the head movements meaning 'yes' and 'no', and the shoulder shrug for 'I don't know'. Some of these forms are identical to conventional gestures found in the non-signing community. Others appear to be unique to Auslan and other signed languages, such as the non-manual signs meaning 'menstrual period' (produced as a repeated movement of the tongue against the cheek) or 'have sex' (a repeated puffing of the cheeks) that are used by some signers. For the most part, however, non-manual signs are rare. In fact, non-manual features usually co-occur with manual signs, forming multi-channel signs.

4.7.2 Multi-channel signs

Multi-channel signs combine actions of the hands with those made by other parts of the body. For Brennan (1992), the distinguishing characteristic of multi-channel signs is that the manual and non-manual features form a single integrated sign, with both components being obligatory. Examples in Auslan seem to include signs that might be glossed as REALISE and AT-LAST (both produced with a mouth gesture that resembles a silent articulation of the syllable 'pah'), FORBID ('hup') and BIZARRE ('bah bah') which are regularly accompanied by particular mouth gestures. Signs such as IN-CASE and TYPICAL may be produced with puffed cheeks. The sign GULLIBLE is often produced with a forward tilt of the head.

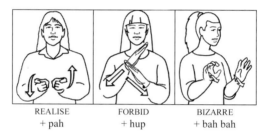

| REALISE | FORBID | BIZARRE |
| + pah | + hup | + bah bah |

Figure 4.12: *Examples of multi-channel signs.*

Brennan (1992) suggested that some lexical items in BSL may be distinguished from one another solely on the basis of non-manual features. Such minimal pairs do seem also to occur in Auslan. The signs PROPER and MAKE-DO, for example, appear to differ only in non-manual features (MAKE-DO is often produced with a protrusion of the tongue). For some signers, the sign MOUSE (neutral facial expression) forms a minimal pair with a sign that may be glossed as ORGASM (often produced with the lips rounded and cheeks sucked in).

However, it is not clear how many of these signs obligatorily take a non-manual component. Discussions with native signers thus far suggests that not all appear to agree on whether certain non-manual features are actually obligatory for particular multi-channel signs. Certainly, other researchers have similar difficulty in eliciting these judgements from signers. The Danish researcher Elisabeth Engberg-Pedersen (1993:23) found that DSL signers appear to be very aware of the role of non-manual features in the expression of emotion, but less aware of their many other roles in signed languages. In her own research on the function of facial expressions in DSL, she was told by her informants that 'if you use the sign HAPPY, you should look happy'. This did not appear to be completely true, however, since signers would use quite a different facial expression while uttering the sign equivalent of the question 'Are you not happy?' This may be due to the fact that many non-manual features co-occur with individual manual signs to signal grammatical functions such as negation, questions, affirmations and topicalisation (all of these are discussed in Chapter 7) and thus it can be difficult to identify exactly what the role of the specific non-manual features might be in any given context. In some cases, there is little difference between the non-manual features that may appear to be characteristic components of multi-channel signs (such as the tongue protrusion in MAKE-DO) and those which are optional means of modifying manual signs. The 'cs' facial expression that may accompany the sign RECENT, for example, is used with some signs (e.g., YESTERDAY, NOW) to indicate that something is extremely close in space or time. Detailed analysis of the many non-manual features available to the Auslan signer and their role in both the formation of individual signs and in the grammar needs to be carried out before we can have a clear understanding of the use of multi-channel signs in Auslan.

| PROPER | MAKE-DO | MOUSE | ORGASM |

Figure 4.13: *Examples of possible minimal pairs based on non-manual features.*

4.8   Constraints on word and sign structure

We have shown that Auslan signs, like the words of spoken languages, are made from smaller formational units. Another fundamental aspect of language, both spoken and signed, is that any particular language exploits only a selected subset of all possible formational components (Fromkin *et al.*, 2005). Furthermore, each language has a set of rules that determine which combinations of these units are allowed, and which combinations may be impossible. These language-specific constraints restrict the number and possible combinations of formational units that can occur in a language.

The first constraint is true of all spoken languages. Standard Australian English, as we have seen, draws on a limited set of 44 sounds. This set represents a small subset of all the sounds which are physically possible and which occur in the world's spoken languages. English, for example, does not use the nasal vowels of French, nor the click sounds that occur in African languages such as Zulu (Katamba, 1989). Even when the sounds of two languages appear to be similar, they may actually differ in phonetic detail. The English sounds /t/, /d/ and /n/, for example, are made with the tongue tip contacting the alveolar region of the mouth (the gum behind the teeth). In Italian and French, the same sounds are made with the tip of the tongue contacting the upper teeth (Ladefoged, 1982).

Under the second constraint, not all combinations of these language-particular sounds may occur. If users of English look at the following nonsense words, most will agree which combinations of English phonemes would make possible new words in the language, and which would not make possible new words: *klosp, trest, charp, fliss, psken, srbob, ptlit.* English speakers would tend to agree that the last three words in this list do not follow the usual patterns of word formation in the language because the English sound system generally does not have combinations of consonants like 'srb-' or 'ptl-'.

In English, a word which begins with three consonants uses a limited subset of phonemes and combines them in a particular sequence as follows: if the first phoneme is /s/, the second phoneme will be /p/ or /t/ or /k/, and the third phoneme will be /l/ or /r/ or /w/ or /j/. As a result, words such as *spring, string, squeal, splendid* and *stew* are found, whereas lexical items such as *thbneal, bdlack, sgtingl* and *wbtonk* are not attested in English (Aitchison, 1992). In Russian, on the other hand, initial clusters of three or even four consonants (such as /tkn-/ or /vzdr-/) are more frequent and less restricted (Ostapenko, 2005).

In signed languages, too, not all possible combinations of formational features occur. Instead, there are particular sets of phonological constraints that restrict combinations of handshape, location and movement. Many of these constraints seem to be common to many of the world's signed languages (Emmorey, 2002), while some others appear to differ from one signed language to another.

4.8.1 Linguistic constraints

Constraints on sign structure are realised in two ways in Auslan. First, Auslan signers do not appear to use all possible combinations of handshapes, locations and movements that can be produced by the body. For example, no Auslan signs use the hand configurations shown in Figure 4.14, just as English does not use all possible combinations of sounds. These handshapes are found in other signed languages, however, just as sound combinations not possible in English are found in other spoken languages.

Second, even when Auslan signers do use the same handshapes, locations and movement found in other signed languages, they may not always combine these formational units in the same way. Although detailed comparative work has not yet been carried out for Auslan, data collected in a study by Klima and Bellugi (1979), comparing ASL and Chinese Sign Language (CSL), appear to hold true for Auslan. For example, they found a range of formational differences, ranging from parameter combinations in CSL that seemed impossible or at least odd in ASL, to subtle differences in the production of similar hand configurations.

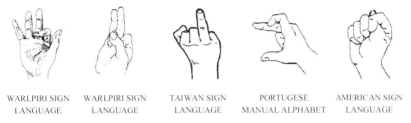

| WARLPIRI SIGN | WARLPIRI SIGN | TAIWAN SIGN | PORTUGESE | AMERICAN SIGN |
| LANGUAGE | LANGUAGE | LANGUAGE | MANUAL ALPHABET | LANGUAGE |

Figure 4.14: *Examples of handshapes not found in Auslan.*

The comparison of Auslan signs with signs from other signed languages suggests that Auslan, like English, has distinctive formational constraints. We can see that certain handshapes, locations and movements may occur in one signed language and not in another. Furthermore, two signed languages may use the same formational units, such as handshape, and yet have different restrictions on how these units can combine in the signs of the two languages (Klima & Bellugi, 1979).

Some of these differences seem quite arbitrary and unpredictable from language to language, and we will thus refer to them as *linguistic* constraints on sign structure. The differences between patterns of sign structure in CSL and Auslan cannot be explained by physical limitations on handshapes, locations and movements. Many of the patterns in sign formational structure in Auslan, however, do seem to reflect such physical limitations. The signs in signed language need to be clearly seen by other people and to be produced easily by the signer's body, allowing communication to occur quickly and efficiently (Baker & Cokely, 1980). The limits of the human visual system and the workings of the muscles of the arms, hands and fingers appear to have influenced the way that signs are produced in Auslan. These constraints (referred to as constraints on the *perception* and *production* of signs below) mean that some handshapes, locations and movements, and some combinations of these parameters, occur much more frequently in Auslan signs than others (as we have already seen previously), and that some parameter combinations may never occur.

4.8.2 Perceptual constraints

Signed languages differ from mime in a number of important ways, as the discussion in Chapter 1 showed. Signers use a much more limited space for signed communication, for example. Brennan (1992) pointed out that in order to mime tying a shoelace, one might bend down and simply enact the concept. In contrast, signs that are related semantically to parts of the body outside the signing space tend to occur within the signing space, such as STILETTOS, SOCK (Figure 4.15) and CONDOM. Some of these signs, such as CONDOM, can be made in a more explicit location, but despite the fact that sign position can be influenced by real world physical locations, there is a strong tendency towards locating all signs within a more restricted signing space.

Constraints of perception seem to be part of the explanation for this use of the signing space. North American researchers have suggested that peripheral vision appears to have a significant effect on the location of signs on the body (Siple, 1978; Battison, 1978). Our eyes tend to focus on objects that are in the centre of our field of vision. Humans do, however, perceive a great deal with their peripheral vision. Research in the 1970s by Patricia Siple (1978) showed that signers usually look at each other's faces when they sign, and not at the hands (except perhaps when fingerspelling an unfamiliar word). Thus, the face of the signer and the area around the face is most clearly seen during signing. This, together with the production constraints discussed below, may partly explain why signs tend to be restricted to locations within the signing space (as mentioned in §4.2.2.1). Signs in other areas would fall outside the normal field of vision.

SOCK

Figure 4.15: *A sign located in the signing space despite being iconically and semantically linked to a location (the feet) which is outside it.*

Inside the signing space, there appear to be further restrictions. It is clear from the discussion in §4.6.2 above that signers exploit a range of different locations on the body. It appears, however, that the various possible locations on the body are not used to the same degree, as is demonstrated by examining the distribution of signs in *Signs of Australia* (Johnston, 1998) that are specified for contact with the head or trunk regions (Table 4.8). The unequal distribution of sign location becomes immediately apparent when we examine the number of signs made in each these two general regions of the body (note that we have disregarded signs made in the space in front of the signer's body because their location specifications are less fixed).

Table 4.8 *Distribution of signs involving body contact according to location.*

Location	Number of signs (percentage of total)
Head, Face, Neck locations	76.8% (n = 497)
Trunk and Arm locations	23.2% (n = 150)
Total	100% (n = 647)

We can see from this table that those signs in Auslan which have locations on the body are more often made in the face, head and neck area than in the chest or upper arm area. Thus, more than 76 per cent of these signs are made in the area where signers' visual acuity is greatest. But is this entirely due to the effects of visual perception, as suggested by Siple (1978)? Battison (1978) pointed out that the neck, face and head region has the largest number of visually distinguishable body parts (e.g., the lips, chin, mouth, nose, jaw, temple, eye, etc.), while the trunk region has relatively fewer distinctive areas. This greater diversity of locations in the head region may lend itself to a greater number of distinctive locations available for sign formation and thus a larger number of signs.

Vision does appear to influence sign structure, however, when one examines the overall number of differences between one-handed and double-handed signs in the head and trunk regions of the body. If we analyse all those signs in this subset that are made on or near the head and trunk regions (i.e., not just those making contact with the body), we can see that signs made on the trunk tend to be double-handed (such as HUNGRY, ACCEPT, TIRED) (Table 4.9). In contrast, more of those that are usually only one-handed (such as WOMAN, THINK and WATER) are made on the head, face and neck (Figure 4.16).

Table 4.9 *Distribution of one- and double-handed signs according to location (two-handed signs not included).*

	One-handed	Double-handed
Signs in head, face and neck locations (n = 1124)	78% (n = 878)	22% (n = 264)
Signs in trunk and upper arm locations (n = 2064)	30.5% (n = 630)	69.5% (n = 1434)

Battison (1978) suggested that this may be partly due to the fact that if two hands are acting in an identical fashion, then the visual system has more information for identifying the sign. This extra information may be important in locations that are perceived through the peripheral vision, such as the chest and stomach, but less important in locations such as the face and neck where visual acuity is greatest.

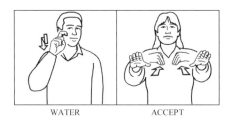

WATER   ACCEPT

Figure 4.16: *A one-handed sign on the face and a double-handed sign on the body.*

4.8.3   Production constraints

Not only perceptual constraints influence the form of signs. Auslan signs also appear to be shaped by the need to produce signs easily and with little effort. These constraints on production mean that only particular combinations of handshape, location and movement are possible in the language, and that some parameter combinations appear more frequently than others. We can especially see this in two rules, for forming signs that use two hands, known as the *symmetry condition* and the *dominance condition* respectively.

Battison (1978) was the first to observe that if the two hands in a sign move independently (as in the following Type 3 signs: PLAY, AUSLAN, TRAVEL, SIGN, PLAN and HOLIDAY), then they tend to have the same handshape, location and movement. If both hands moved around in different ways, this would naturally make the sign physically more difficult to produce. Although differences in handshape, location and movement may sometimes occur with depicting signs, it is typically not found in signs in the core lexicon (see Chapter 6 for a discussion of these different sign types). The symmetry condition was formulated by Battison (1978:33) as follows:

> (a) If both hands of a sign move independently during its articulation, then (b) both hands must be specified for the same location, the same handshape, the same movement (whether performed simultaneously or in alternation), and the specification for orientation must be either symmetrical or identical.

By 'same location', Battison meant that either (1) both hands would be in an identical location in the signing space (e.g., SIGN) or (2) both hands would be in mirror-image locations (e.g., PLAY). Similarly, 'symmetrical orientation' means that the fingers and the palms of the two hands must be arranged in mirror images of each other (e.g., in SIGN, one hand's palm points left while the other points right), or they must have 'identical orientation' (e.g., in PLAY where the fingers and palms of both hands point in the same direction). Thus, the symmetrical condition constraint on the production of core signs results in a large number of physically possible gestures in which two hands perform different movements being excluded from the core lexicon.

People are generally either right-handed or left-handed. A right-handed signer has a *dominant* right hand (this is also known as the *active* or *strong* hand in the literature) that is usually used in one-handed signs, and a *subordinate* left hand (or *passive, base* or *weak* hand). In Type 6 two-handed signs (those which have different handshapes on the dominant and subordinate hand) such as RIGHT, CENTRE, VIDEO, THEATRE, BUY, BLUE, only the dominant hand has independent movement. The subordinate hand usually will not move in an independent fashion. This constraint is referred to as the *dominance condition*. Thus, although having two different handshapes on each hand makes a sign more physically difficult to produce, this difficulty is reduced by allowing only one hand to move. It was formulated by Battison (1978:35) as follows:

> (a) If the hands of a two-handed sign do not share the same specification for handshapes (i.e., they are different), then (b) one hand must be passive while the active hand articulates the movement, and (c) the specification of the passive hand is restricted to be one of a small set.

Note that another important aspect of the dominance condition reduces the difficulty of Type 6 signs. The subordinate hand will usually only have one of seven handshapes: 6, S, B, 5, 1, bC or O. The reduction from some thirty-seven possible major handshapes to just seven configurations of the hand significantly reduces the complexity of this type of sign's production.

| PLAY (a) | RIGHT (b) | QUESTION (c) |

Figure 4.17: *Signs illustrating the symmetry condition (a), the dominance condition (b), and an example of an exception (c).*

An investigation of a sample of signs from the *Signs of Australia* dictionary showed that almost all Type 6 two-handed signs in Auslan use one of these handshapes on the subordinate hand, while a few two-handed signs use other handshapes. Signs such as COINCIDENCE, QUESTION, OTHER and LAST, for example, have the Mid, F, 2, and I handshapes on the subordinate hand. Thus the handshape restrictions in the dominance condition seem to have a small number of exceptions in Auslan, although the constraints on the movement of the subordinate hand appear to be the same. It is interesting to note that many of these exceptions to the dominance rule derive from fingerspelling or from the use of list buoys (see Chapter 6 for a discussion of how fingerspelled items differs from core Auslan signs, and Chapter 9 for a discussion of list buoys).

The seven hand configurations required by Battison's (1978) dominance condition are examples of what Baker and Cokely (1980:82) described as 'the most natural, basic and easy-to-make handshapes' in signed languages. These are known as *unmarked* handshapes in the linguistics literature (Battison, 1978). Brentari (1998) discussed a number of criteria for recognising unmarked handshapes. For example, they appear to be among the most frequent in signed languages. These seven handshapes (the 6, S, B, 5, 1, bC and O) occur in over 60 per cent of all the signs in the *Signs of Australia* Auslan dictionary (Johnston, 1998). They also occur in the greatest range of combinations with other elements of signs. Of a sample of signs from the Auslan dictionary produced with a local movement involving a change of handshape, over 80 per cent involve the use of at least one of these unmarked handshapes.

There seem to be two main reasons for this phenomenon. First, this small set of handshapes appears to be the most physically and perceptually distinct from each other. They form a set of basic visual-geometric shapes: the S is a maximally compact hand configuration; the B handshape is a simple flat surface; the 5 has the fingers spread and extended to the maximum extent; the 1 has a single finger projecting from a fist; the bC is an arc and the O handshape is a full circle (Brennan, 1992). They are the most basic possible handshapes (only the S and the 6 are minimally different from each other) and appear to be the easiest to produce and perceive (Lane, Boyes-Braem & Bellugi, 1976). They can be contrasted with the less frequently occurring handshapes, such as Old 7, 8, 9, Irish H, Irish K, ILY and Mid, which involve complex articulations, and are much less visually distinct from each other. This group of handshapes is known as *marked* handshapes (Battison, 1978).

Second, unmarked handshapes appear to be the first handshapes that signing children acquire (McIntire, 1977). Research shows that young children learning signed languages use the unmarked handshapes in place of the more marked configurations in the early stages of signed language acquisition (Marentette & Mayberry, 2000). It is common in children learning Auslan, for example, to replace the H handshapes in the sign FATHER with the less marked 1 hand configurations.

In comparison, marked hand configurations are used in far fewer signs in Auslan (the 30 more marked handshapes in Auslan account for less than 40 per cent of the signs in the Auslan dictionary). They also often interact with location, so that contrasts using the less perceptually distinct unmarked handshapes occur in locations further from the centre of the signing space, while contrasts using the less distinct marked handshapes tend to occur in the central parts of the signing space. If we draw on the signs from our Auslan sample again, we see that marked handshapes are thus more likely to occur in signs that are made around the face (see Table 4.10).

Table 4.10 *Distribution of marked handshapes according to location.*

	Head and Neck locations	**Trunk locations**
Unmarked handshapes	53%	65%
Marked handshapes	47%	35%

Handshape is not the only parameter that is influenced by physical constraints on sign structure. Signs that move from one location on the body to another, for example, tend to occur within the same major area of the body (Battison, 1978). Linguists have suggested that there appear to be four major body areas in which double-location signs tend to occur: the head, the trunk, the arm and the hand. Signs with two locations will generally fall within one of these major body areas. Examples of signs made in two separate locations include (a) on the head—FLOWER, DEAF, HEARING; (b) on the trunk—ARMY, MORNING, GOVERNMENT; (c) on the arm—PRIOR, MUSCLE; and (d) on the hand—SUBJECT, TOAST, LESSON. Signs that are exceptions, such as BELIEVE or BOYFRIEND, appear most often to be compounds or signs which are derived from compounds (see Chapter 5 for a discussion of compounds in Auslan).

| DEAF | GOVERNMENT | PRIOR | SUBJECT |

Figure 4.18: *Signs with two locations.*

Similarly, there also appear to be lateral restrictions on sign locations, with the greatest percentage of signs occurring centrally or ipsilaterally on the body (i.e., on the same side of the body as the dominant hand) rather than contralaterally (i.e., on the opposite side of the body to the dominant hand). Thus, for a right-handed signer, most signs that contact the body will be produced on the right side or in central locations on the body. Some contralateral signs (e.g., signs produced on locations on the left side of the body of a right-handed signer) do exist, such as ADMINISTRATION, RESPONSIBLE and PROFESSIONAL, but historically it appears that such signs tend to move into the centre of the trunk over time (Frishberg, 1975).

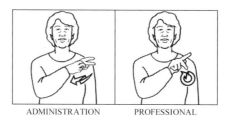

ADMINISTRATION   PROFESSIONAL

Figure 4.19: *Signs located contralaterally.*

Thus, like the words of spoken languages, signs in Auslan are made up of smaller formational units that appear to be constrained by phonological rules. Phonemes only occur in particular combinations in English: some combinations of sounds occur often, some less often, some never occur. Due to variation in language-specific rules (but also more importantly to numerous perceptual and production constraints on language in the visual-gestural modality), this may also be true of the combinations of handshape, orientation, location and movement parameters in Auslan signs.

4.9   Simultaneity and sequentiality in sign structure

In spoken languages, the basic formational units can be put together in a variety of ways into larger units that are known as *syllables*. In English, a syllable is usually a group of consonants clustered around a vowel sound. These units are organised in sequence, so a syllable may consist of an initial consonant or consonant cluster (known as an *onset*), then a vowel (or *nucleus*), and then one or more final consonants (forming a *coda*). The vowel and final consonant(s) together form, for obvious reasons, the *rhyme*.

A single word may consist of a number of syllables. The word 'computer', for example, is made up of three syllables: 'com', 'pu', 'ter' (or /kom/, /pju/, /tə/). The first syllable consists of a consonant-vowel-consonant (or CVC) combination forming an onset, nucleus and coda. The second is composed of two consonants followed by a vowel (CCV), and the third is made up of a consonant and a vowel (CV). These last two have only an onset followed by a nucleus. The CVC, CCV and CV combinations are typical of the possible syllable structures in English.

According to Stokoe's original description of sign structure in ASL, signs seemed to be organised differently. The three aspects of handshape, location and movement were thought to be produced simultaneously by the signer. For Stokoe (1960), it seemed clear that the nature of the formational units of a sign meant that simultaneous production was inevitable. It is, after all, physically impossible to produce a handshape that is not in some location on and near the body, and to produce some kind of movement that does not involve a change in location, handshape or orientation. Thus, there is always some degree of simultaneity in sign production.

This simultaneous characteristic of sign structure made signs initially appear quite different from the words of spoken language. As we have seen, spoken words, in contrast to Stokoe's simultaneous model of sign structure, result from the sequential combination of segments known as phonemes: there are few words in English that are made from a single phoneme. Syllables generally contain two or more phonemes strung together, and words may result from the combination of many such syllables. It is contrasts in such linear strings of phonemes that form the basis of the minimal pairs in English which we discussed in §4.1.1.

The contrast we find in many minimal pairs in Auslan, however, may be described as simultaneous contrast. Many signs consist of a single handshape, produced in a single location and combined with a single type of movement. These elements are produced simultaneously by the signer, and appear to lack any internal sequential organisation. A sign such as WHEN for example, is produced by placing the 5 hand on the cheek and wriggling the fingers. The sign HOW-MUCH differs only in location, as shown by Table 4.11 (for illustrations see Figure 4.9 above).

The internal structure of many signs in Auslan thus appears to differ fundamentally from the words of a spoken language, where the formational elements (consonants and vowels) are organised in a linear fashion.

Table 4.11 *Example of signs showing simultaneous contrast.*

	WHEN	HOW-MUCH
Handshape	5 handshape	5 handshape
Location	On the cheek	On the chin
Movement	Wriggling movement	Wriggling movement

Stokoe's analysis did recognise that there are examples of sequential contrast in ASL. He noted that the movement parameter often involved a sequence of movements from one handshape to another or from one location to another, and that many ASL signs were compound signs formed from the sequential combination of two individual signs. Work on ASL since the early 1980s, however, has made it clear that Stokoe's simultaneous model is not an adequate account of the phonological structure of the language (e.g., Liddell & Johnson, 1989; Sandler, 1989; Brentari, 1998), and this claim seems equally true for Auslan. Many signs in both ASL and Auslan show sequential patterning, and changes in sequence are used contrastively. In the Auslan sign HELP, for example, the contrast between the signs that mean 'I help you' and 'you help me' is a sequential contrast. To represent 'I help you', the sign begins at a location near the signer's body and ends at some location away from the signer. For 'you help me', the sequence of locations is reversed (see Figure 4.20).

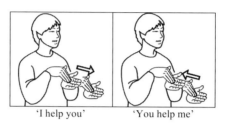

'I help you'   'You help me'

Figure 4.20: *Two signs in sequential contrast.*

There are many other examples where linear ordering of parameters is important in Auslan. One phonological variant of the sign HEARING, like the various forms of HELP, uses a sequence of locations. The handshape first contacts the ear and then moves to the chin where it may make a repeated contact. The ear location is not essential, however, so another common phonological variant of the sign consists of a repeated contact on the chin. Compound signs, on the other hand, consist of the sequential combination of individual signs. The sign PARENTS, for example, is derived from a combination of the signs MOTHER and FATHER. The correct ordering of these parts is required to produce both these signs. Reversing the sequence of either HEARING (i.e., moving the handshape from chin to ear) or PARENTS (i.e., combining the signs in reverse order as in FATHER^MOTHER) does not produce acceptable variants of these signs.

Thus, signed languages such as Auslan appear to employ both simultaneous and sequential patterns of organisation. The realisation that signed languages show sequential contrast has important ramifications for an understanding of sign formation processes, and has led many signed language linguists to suggest that the formational elements of signs, like the phonemes of spoken words, are organised into segments which are, in turn, organised into syllables (for an overview, see Sandler & Lillo-Martin, 2006). The notion of a sign syllable has proved important for understanding the constraints on location and handshape change in individual signs, as well as the processes at work in compounding and lexicalised fingerspelling discussed in Chapters 5 and 6.

4.10   Features, segments and syllables

Since the 1980s, several researchers have developed models to describe the sequential structure of signs. Perhaps the most influential account has been the movement-hold model developed by Scott Liddell and Robert Johnson (1989). The details of this approach are complex, and there is insufficient space to cover them all here. However, the basic claim about the structure of signs in the movement-hold model is that, just as spoken language syllables consist of various combinations of consonant and vowel segments, signs consist of sequences of *movement* and *hold* segments. In the same way that a consonant or vowel may be analysed as consisting of a bundle of articulatory features (e.g., a consonant is the result of a combination of specific features of voicing, manner and place of articulation, see Fromkin *et al.*, 2005), each sign segment is a combination of handshape, orientation, location and non-manual features. A *hold* segment is a period of time in which all aspects of the articulatory bundle do not change, and a *movement* segment are periods of time in which a handshape, orientation, location, or non-manual feature changes. More than one of these features may change at the same time. A sign may have only a change in handshape specifications, or in location, or it may have a change in both handshape and location. These changes occur as part of the movement segment.

The discussion in this chapter has thus far drawn on the parameter model proposed by Stokoe, treating the formational elements (such as handshape, location and movement) as analogous to the phonemes of a spoken language. Note that in the Liddell and Johnson model, it is the movements and holds specified for different combinations of handshape, orientation, location and non-manual features which are equivalent to the phoneme segments of spoken languages, not the features themselves.

One form of PLEASE would thus be described as beginning with a hold on the chin. The hand then moves down and ends with a second hold in the signing space below the chin. The sign begins with a B handshape and ends with a 6. In simplified movement-hold notation, it would be represented as in Table 4.12. Note that this sign would form a minimal pair with FRUIT in which the same handshape change occurs in the same sequence, but the hand remains in the chin location rather than moving downwards

This hold-movement-hold (HMH) structure is perhaps the most frequent type of sequential organisation in the language (e.g., MAN, FORGET, COPY). There appear to be at least five other structures in Auslan: M (e.g., WHO, SIGN, RUDE), H (e.g., HOW-MUCH, WHEN, ONE), MH (e.g., POSS-1, THINK, HOW), MHMH (e.g., CHILDREN, FLOWER), and MMMH (e.g., FATHER,

MOTHER, PAPER) as also reported in ASL (cf. Liddell & Johnson, 1989).[2] Some structures, such as HM or MMMMH, do not seem to be possible in either signed language. According to Liddell and Johnson (1989), this constraint is similar to the restrictions on phoneme combinations in the words of spoken languages, and some linguists have seen an analogy between the movements and holds of Liddell and Johnson's model and the consonants and vowels of spoken languages.

Table 4.12 *Movement-hold representation of* PLEASE *and* FRUIT.

	PLEASE			FRUIT		
	Segments					
Dominant hand	**H**	**M**	**H**	**H**	**M**	**H**
handshape	B		6	B		6
orientation	fingers up, palm towards		fingers up, palm towards	fingers up, palm towards		fingers up, palm towards
location	chin		in front of body	chin		chin
non-manual signal	-		-	-		-

Some of the claims made by this model have, however, been criticised by a number of linguists (Sandler, 1989; Wilbur, 1990, 1993; Perlmutter, 1993). Although there is no question that holds occur during the production of individual signs, and that they can be identified and measured, the majority of holds appear to be dropped in signed interaction (Wilbur, 1990). In conversation, signs are not produced with clear holds at the beginning or the end of signs. The signer instead produces signs in one continuous stream. Liddell and Johnson (1989) explained this as a result of a rule called *hold deletion*, which will be explained in §4.11 below.

---

[2] Note that signs in the MMMH category were originally analysed by Liddell and Johnson (1989) as MMH because the transitional movement between the two contacting movements was ignored.

Some researchers point out there appear to be few cases where signs are produced only as holds, despite the examples given above. Some researchers argue that signs appear not to be well formed unless they have some kind of movement, either movement from one location to another, a change from one handshape or orientation to another, or some other kind of movement (Brentari, 1998). Even those signs that appear to consist only of a hold, such as the signs HOW-MUCH or ONE, are often produced with either some secondary movement, or a transitional movement. Psycholinguistic studies of sign perception also suggest that movement is the most central formational category. Psychological studies of signers have shown that the perception of sign movement appears to be crucially different from that of the static parameters such as handshape and location (Poizner, Klima & Bellugi, 1987). Thus, movement appears to be central to sign production and perception, and to form the core of what has come to be known as the sign syllable.

A number of scholars argue that ASL signs are organised into syllables (e.g., Sandler & Lillo-Martin, 2006). Some claim that movement corresponds to the nucleus of the syllable, analogous to the vowels of spoken language syllables. Ronnie Wilbur (1993), for example, suggested that each of the following patterns of movement constitute a single syllable: (a) a single path movement (change of location, e.g., HELP); (b) a single local movement (change of handshape or orientation, e.g., HAVE, REBEL); or (c) combinations of path and local movement (change of location and handshape, e.g. BELIEVE, or location and orientation, e.g., NONE-OF-ONE'S-BUSINESS).

Elliptical movements constitute two syllables (as in WAIT+slow-rept), as do bi-directional (or back-and-forth) movements (e.g., BABY). A single circular movement is considered to be one syllable (e.g., PLATE), and the wiggling, fluttering and tremoring movements one finds in many signs (e.g., WHEN) are also counted as a single syllable. Some lexical items—in particular those derived from fingerspelled English words—involve a sequence of two or more handshape changes (e.g., S-O-N, C-L-U-B). These items would be considered multi-syllabic forms.

| WAIT+slow-rept | BABY | PLATE | WHEN | S-O-N |

Figure 4.21: *Movement and syllables.*

The concept of a sign syllable (although controversial amongst linguists) is significant because signed languages such as ASL and Auslan appear to favour signs that are monosyllabic (i.e., signs that have only one syllable) (Corina & Sandler, 1993). The vast majority of citation forms of Auslan signs appear to have only one change in handshape, orientation and location. This is part of the reason that the traditional view of sign structure (in which the simultaneous aspect of signs were emphasised) was useful for a long time. In fact, there appear to be no signs in the core lexicon that have a citation form that is longer than two syllables, and a number of processes appear to be at work in the language which reduce polysyllabic signs (i.e., signs with more than one change in location, handshape or orientation) into monosyllabic signs. As we will see in Chapter 5, this is true of compound signs that are derived from combinations of two individual signs (e.g., BELIEVE, BOYFRIEND). Although individual signs in a compound each form a separate syllable, the compounding process often produces a monosyllabic, rather than disyllabic, sign (compounding will be discussed more in Chapter 5).

4.11   Phonological processes

As we have mentioned earlier, segments in spoken and signed language interactions are not produced as single, isolated units, but in a continuous stream. When people use language to communicate, the forms of segments may be simplified in order to make communication more efficient. This may result in changes in how the formational units of the language are produced. For example, in casual conversation, a phrase such as *I don't know* is often produced as *I dunno*, where the final segment in *don't* has been deleted. Similarly, phrases such as *you have to go* may be realised as *you haf to go*. Here the final segment in the word *have* has lost its voicing (i.e., it has changed from the voiced sound /v/ to the voiceless /f/) because the first segment of the next word is also a voiceless sound (for discussions of these processes, see Fromkin *et al.*, 2005).

   These changes help make spoken language communication more efficient because the segments are fewer in number, or are made more similar to each other, and this means that less energy and time is required to produce them. The same kinds of processes can be found at work in rapid and casual signed interactions (Liddell & Johnson, 1989).

   One such phonological process is the deletion of some segment in a sign. *Hold deletion* is one of the most common processes of deletion. Signs that are usually produced with a hold as part of their citation form may be signed differently in connected signing. In the sign NOT-KNOW, for example, the sign is produced in citation form as HMH. In contrast, the same sign in a signed phrase, as in (4.1), may have no holds. The three signs PRO-1, NOT-KNOW and WHERE would be produced as a continuous stream of movement, with transitional movements added between the signs as part of a process known as *movement epenthesis*. This is represented in simplified movement-hold notation in Table 4.13.

(4.1)   _____br_____
      POSS-1 KEY PRO-1 NOT-KNOW WHERE
      I don't know where my keys are.

Table 4.13 *Movement-hold representation of hold deletion and movement epenthesis.*

Sign	PRO-1		NOT-KNOW		WHERE
Citation form	M H		H M H		M M M H
Movement epenthesis	M H	M	H M H	M	M M M H
Hold deletion	M	M	M	M	M M M H

Similarly, signs such as BOY or GIRL are usually produced with a repeated movement, but in a rapidly signed casual conversation, the second movement may be dropped. This *movement deletion* may happen to any sign with a repeated movement. Another common phonological process is *movement reduction*. This involves, for example, a sign being produced with a smaller movement than one might find in the citation form. In (4.2), the sign WHEN might be produced in rapid signing with only the slightest fluttering of the fingers.

(4.2)   br
      WHEN PRO-1 YOUNG BOY, RIDE-BICYCLE SCHOOL TO-AND-FRO
      When I was a young lad, I rode a bicycle back and forth to school.

Assimilation is another frequent phonological process. In *handshape assimilation*, the handshape of a sign becomes more similar to the handshape of the sign preceding or following it in a phrase. In a phrase like PRO-1 NOT-KNOW in (4.1), it would be extremely common for signers to use a B handshape for PRO-1 rather than a 1 handshape (this has been demonstrated for ASL in recent studies by Lucas *et al.*, 2001). Here the handshape of the sign PRO-1 becomes the same as the handshape in the following sign. *Location assimilation* is also common. In a signed phrase like PRO-1 NAME S-A-M, the sign NAME may be made relatively lower in the signing space (in front of the right side of the face, for example, rather than at the forehead) because the preceding sign is made in a lower location (Schembri *et al.*, in press) (see Figure 4.22).

Perseveration and *anticipation* may also occur. Typically, in a signed conversation, phrases will include both one-handed and two-handed signs. When a one-handed sign follows a two-handed sign, often the non-dominant hand will be held in place rather than return to a resting position. This is known as perseveration. Anticipation refers to the non-dominant hand moving into position while a one-handed sign is being produced in readiness for the two-handed sign that will follow.

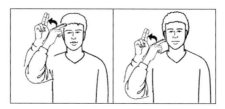

Figure 4.22: *The citation form of NAME (left) and a lowered form of the sign (right).*

Although we have provided specific examples here of deletion, reduction, assimilation, perseveration and anticipation, it is important to realise that these phonological processes apply to many (perhaps most) signs and fingerspelled items in casual, connected signing.

4.12   Summary

In this chapter, we have examined the building blocks of Auslan: handshape, orientation, location, movement and non-manual features. We have also examined how signs may be classified into different groups on the basis of shared formational characteristics, how their structure is influenced by linguistic, perceptual and production constraints, and how their form may vary as a result of a number of phonological processes. In the next chapter, we shall look at the relationship between the structure of signs and their meanings.

4.13   Further Reading

Fromkin *et al.* (2005) provides a useful introduction to the phonology of Australian English. See Valli *et al.* (2005) for an introduction to ASL phonology, and both Brennan (1992) and Sutton-Spence & Woll (1999) for BSL. For more advanced theoretical accounts of ASL, see Liddell & Johnson (1989) and Brentari (1998), and Sandler & Lillo-Martin (2006).

5 Morphology: sign formation and modification

The previous chapter showed that natural signed languages such as Auslan make use of individual meaningful gestures known as signs that have specific formational features. Signs can be broken down into five formational parameters: handshape, orientation, location, movement and non-manual features. It was shown that there are constraints on the combinations of parameters that a sign may have in Auslan, and that these parameters might also be analysed as being organised into formational units analogous to the segment and syllable.

In this chapter, we will introduce the notion of morpheme in Auslan by showing how the parameters of signed languages (which may act as meaningless formational units) described in the last chapter are used to create meaningful units, either alone or in combination. We also show how the use of morphemes in Auslan exists alongside other sources of meaning in the organisation of the language, and will introduce the main processes of sign formation (or derivation) and sign modification (or inflection).

5.1   The morpheme in signed and spoken language

In Chapter 4, we saw how the units of handshape, orientation, location, movement and non-manual features act as the smallest formational units of Auslan. The parameters in signs from the core lexicon such as PEOPLE, WORK or BLUE can be identified separately, but in this context they lack a separate meaning. In these signs, the features of handshape, orientation, location and movement combine to produce a unit with a single meaning.

The signs FOUR-YEARS-OLD and CL:1-PERSON-PASS-BY, however, differ from the signs PEOPLE, WORK and BLUE, because FOUR-YEARS-OLD and CL:1-PERSON-PASS-BY are more complex. In the case of FOUR-YEARS-OLD, at least two of the parameters have separate meanings of their own—the handshape signifies 'four', and the location on the nose signifies 'age in years'. If the 4 handshape in this sign is changed to a 3 handshape, this produces a sign meaning THREE-YEARS-OLD; and if the location is changed to the chin, this produces a sign meaning THREE-POUNDS. With the sign CL:1-PERSON-PASS-BY, the parameters of handshape, orientation, location or the movement may also be modified for different meanings. By changing the movement and orientation so that the palm faces the signer and the hand as a whole moves towards the body, for example, we could produce a sign meaning CL:1-PERSON-MOVE-TOWARDS. By changing the handshape and orientation from an upright 1 handshape to a B handshape with the palm held vertical, we have a sign meaning something like CL:B-VEHICLE-PASS-BY. (These handshapes are often referred to as 'classifier' handshapes, hence the abbreviation CL. For more discussion see Chapter 6.) Thus, although all signs can be analysed into separate formational parameters, in some signs these parameters combine to form a single meaning, while in other signs they can have a meaning of their own.

| FOUR-YEARS-OLD | THREE-YEARS-OLD | THREE-POUNDS | CL:1-PERSON-PASS-BY | CL:1-PERSON-MOVE-TOWARDS | CL:B-VEHICLE-PASS-BY |

Figure 5.1: *Signs in which one or more parameters are meaningful.*

The smallest meaningful units of a language are known as *morphemes* (Bloomfield, 1933). Morphemes are used in the language to create the larger units we call words and signs, as well as to modify existing words and signs. As we saw in signs like PEOPLE, a particular combination of parameters may form a single morpheme. This is similar to many words in English, such as *dog*, *walk* and *yellow*. These words are made from a combination of English phonemes, but the individual segments have no meaning of their own in the context of these words. They combine instead to form words that are single morphemes. Signs like PEOPLE, and words like *dog*, are thus referred to as *monomorphemic* lexical items.

In other cases, one or more of the parameters can act as separate morphemes, as in the sign FOUR-YEARS-OLD, a *bimorphemic* sign (i.e., a sign consisting of only two morphemes). Many linguists have suggested that CL:1-PERSON-PASS-BY is a *polymorphemic* sign (i.e., a sign consisting of at least two morphemes). Signs like these have been compared to words in English that result from a combination of two or more morphemes, such as polymorphemic lexical items like *un-believ-able*, *work-ing*, and *cat-s*.

An additional example from English may help further illustrate this difference between the formational units of words and signs and their morphological organisation. The English words *bun*, *sun* and *under*, for example, all contain the sequence of sounds /un/. The /un/ element does not, however, have a meaning of its own in these examples. It simply combines with the other sounds to create a single unit of meaning (i.e., the word *under* is a monomorphemic lexical item). On the other hand, in the word *unhappy*, the initial /un/ clearly has a meaning of its own, and in this case, the meaning is 'not'. The /un/ here is acting as a morpheme. The word *unhappy*, like the sign FOUR-YEARS-OLD, is thus composed of two morphemes.

5.1.1 Types of morpheme

Morphemes can be classified according to how they behave in a particular lexical item. Table 5.1 below presents the four main morpheme types found in spoken and signed languages.

Table 5.1 *Morpheme types.*

	Free	**Bound**
Root	Free root	Bound root
Non-root	Free non-root	Affix

The first major distinction between types of morphemes reflects whether they are *free* or *bound* (Bloomfield, 1933). Free morphemes in a language are those that can stand alone. They do not require additional morphemes, and can be produced as an independent lexical item. The English words *school* and *look,* and the Auslan signs THREE and HAVE, are examples of free morphemes. Bound morphemes, however, cannot stand alone as an independent word. They require the presence of some other morpheme. In English, the plural marker *-s* and the past tense marker *-ed* are bound morphemes. Neither of these is ever produced by users of English on its own. They always occur attached to other morphemes, as in *schools* and *looked*. An example of a meaningful unit that might be considered a bound morpheme in Auslan is the side-to-side movement in the sign THIRTEEN. This movement occurs in the signs ELEVEN through to NINETEEN (although different lexical variants of the sign ELEVEN and TWELVE also exist that do not use this movement).

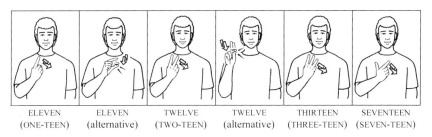

ELEVEN	ELEVEN	TWELVE	TWELVE	THIRTEEN	SEVENTEEN
(ONE-TEEN)	(alternative)	(TWO-TEEN)	(alternative)	(THREE-TEEN)	(SEVEN-TEEN)

Figure 5.2: *Numeral signs modified for –TEEN.*

We can see it adds the same meaning to all these signs, changing the numeral signs from ONE to NINE into ELEVEN to NINETEEN. Although we can compare this morpheme in Auslan to bound morphemes in English such as *-s* and *-ed*, this bound morpheme in Auslan is somewhat different. This is because the -TEEN morpheme in Auslan cannot be produced in isolation. It is physically impossible to produce a sign's movement without also simultaneously producing a particular handshape in a particular location. This is similar to tone morphemes in some spoken languages. In Chichewa (a language spoken in East Africa), verbs may signal changes in tense by changes in tone (Spencer, 1991). Clearly, changes in tone cannot be physically produced without accompanying other sounds.

The second major distinction is between *root* and *non-root* morphemes (Matthews, 1974). A root morpheme can potentially have other morphemes attached to it, whereas a non-root morpheme can never have any other morphemes attached. We can further classify both root and non-root morphemes as either free or bound.

A free root morpheme is a root which can stand alone, but which can also link up with other morphemes. The English words *school* and *look* are of this type. The Auslan sign ASK and AGREE may be considered free root morphemes. They can occur in their usual form, or they can be modified by combining with additional morphemes to produce changes in meaning. As we will see in §5.4.2.3, the movement in ASK may be modified so that the sign is produced with a final sweeping movement from one side of the signing space to the other. The resulting sign ASK+mult would mean 'ask all of you'. The same pattern of movement can be added to a range of other signs to produce a similar modification in meaning. Similarly, as we will see in §5.3.3, a separating movement and handshape change may be added to AGREE to produce the sign DISAGREE.

A bound root is a root which cannot occur as a free morpheme, but which clearly works as the semantic and structural core of the word in which it occurs. The English word *disgruntled* includes an example of a bound root. We clearly recognise that the bound morphemes *dis-* and *-ed* are attached to the root *-gruntle-*, but this root is not one that occurs on its own. In Auslan, we might argue that the handshape on the subordinate hand in the sign FOUR-O'CLOCK represents a root morpheme that cannot be produced on its own (see Figure 5.3). There is no free morpheme which means O'CLOCK. This handshape always combines with a numeral handshape in signs that represent hourly times on the clock. The -O'CLOCK sign here appears to be at the core of the meaning of this sign, since it is the only recurring element. It can combine with all of the number signs from ONE to TWELVE to produce different signs from ONE-O'CLOCK to TWELVE-O'CLOCK.

A free non-root is a morpheme that can stand by itself, but which cannot occur with another morpheme attached to it. Words in English which are free non-root morphemes include *at*, *from*, *and*, *whose* and *so*. Notice that other morphemes, such as *-ed* or *-ing*, cannot normally be attached to these words. In Auslan, signs with a similar grammatical role, such as BUT, FOR and WHO appear to fall into the free non-root category, as do many other types of signs, such as PEOPLE and NAME. It does not seem possible to attach other morphemes to these signs. Whereas free root morphemes in Auslan, such as ASK, may have an additional movement added to produce signs such as ASK+mult, invariant signs such as BUT and PEOPLE do not do this.

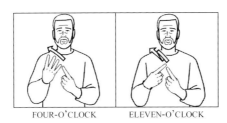

FOUR-O'CLOCK   ELEVEN-O'CLOCK

Figure 5.3: *Number signs combined with the -O'CLOCK root.*

Bound non-roots are also known as *affixes*. These are morphemes that cannot stand alone, but must always be attached to a root morpheme. Affixes differ from bound roots because they add to or modify the meaning of the root to which they are attached, but may not have any separate and clearly definable lexical meaning of their own. Examples of English affixes that we have already mentioned include *-ed* and *-ing*. Affixes fall into two categories: *prefixes* come before the root (such as *re-do, un-happy, dis-believe, non-smoking, pre-history, in-sincere*) and *suffixes* are added after a root (*school-s, teach-er, laugh-ed, gentle-ness, drink-ing, fair-ly*). An unambiguous example of an affix in Auslan is a nominal genitive ('possessive') suffix that can be used to signal possessive relationships between two nouns (this is explained in more detail in §5.3.3 below).

Finally, because there is a tendency towards monosyllabic signs in signed languages (see Chapter 4), many Auslan signs appear to result from the simultaneous rather than sequential combinations of meaningful units. Often, one or more of the parameters of a sign may be altered to signal different meanings, as we saw in the examples with FOUR-YEARS-OLD versus FIVE-YEARS-OLD where only the hand configuration was different. This often makes the analysis of complex signs into root and non-root morphemes a difficult task (something which researchers have also observed in other signed languages, such as Engberg-Pedersen, 1993).

5.1.2   Productivity in Auslan

One of the defining characteristics of human language is *creativity*. As we saw in Chapter 1, humans may use the grammatical resources of language systems to produce and understand an endless variety of meanings.

The concept of creativity is an important one in the study of the morphological structure of a language. In §5.1 above, the notion of the smallest meaningful unit or morpheme was introduced. In order for a particular item or feature to be clearly considered a morpheme, there needs to be some evidence of listability, separability and productivity (Bauer, 1988; Spencer, 1991; Okrent, 2002).

If we look at the English word *unfair*, for example, we can clearly distinguish two separate morphemes, *un-* and *fair*, and we can recombine these with other morphemes to produce different lexical items, such as *un-true* and *un-happy*, or *fair-ly* and *fair-ness*. Thus, this morpheme is productive because it can be used to produce new forms, and it has the same meaning in every word in which it is used. There are many separable and productive morphemes of this kind in English, but the list is not infinite. Lists of morphemes (such as *un-*) in English are given in dictionaries of the language, where information about their form and meaning is provided.

Many sign language researchers have suggested that the handshape in signs such as CL:1-PERSON-PASS-BY is a separable and productive morpheme (e.g., Supalla, 1982; Engberg-Pedersen, 1993; Schembri *et al.*, 2005) because it can be identified in this sign as a separate meaningful unit and it can combine with other meaningful units to create a range of possible forms: CL:1-PERSON-APPROACH, CL:1-PERSON-PASS-BY, CL:1-PERSON-MOVE-AWAY, CL:1-PERSON-WANDER-OFF, etc.

Separability and productivity, however, are not all-or-nothing notions. It is possible for morphemes to lose their separability and productivity over time, entering a linguistic 'twilight zone' where the meaning of the form no longer clearly adds to the meaning of the word. Many linguists see morphological productivity as existing on a cline, with morphemes in a language ranging from relatively unproductive to highly productive. Bauer (1988) provided examples from English of morphemes at opposite ends of this cline—the suffixes *–th* and *–able*.

If we look at words such as *truth, health, growth, depth, strength, warmth* and so on, we can see that we have a suffix *-th* which appears to create abstract nouns from verbs or adjectives (e.g., the adjective *true* + *-th* = *truth*, and the verb *grow* + *-th* = *growth*). It is possible to provide a complete list of all the lexical items of English that appear to contain this suffix. This is because the suffix is now unproductive. It cannot be added to other verbs or adjectives to produce new nouns—forms such as *blackth, coolth, walkth* are not possible, except perhaps as a joke.

Morphemes that appear to be at the unproductive end of the scale can also be found in Auslan. A small number of signs in Auslan, for example, are derived from the one-handed Irish manual alphabet, formerly used in Catholic schools for the deaf in Australia. Although the American one-handed alphabet has a considerable influence on the formation of signs in Auslan, this is less true of the one-handed Irish alphabet. Only a very small number of initialised signs based on Irish fingerspelling continue to be used.

The signs ST-GABRIEL'S-SCHOOL (a Catholic school for deaf boys in Sydney) and GARDEN appear to be derived from the Irish fingerspelled -G-, while the signs HOMOSEXUAL and HONEYMOON seem to be based on the Irish -H-. It is a simple task to list all those signs in the language that appear to use these two handshapes. This is because the system of initialisation using these Irish fingerspelling morphemes is not productive in Auslan (although it may remain so in ISL).

GARDEN HOMOSEXUAL

Figure 5.4: *Initialised signs based on Irish one-handed fingerspelling.*

At the other end of the scale, we can find many examples of highly productive morphemes in English. The suffix *-able* (or sometimes *-ible*) can be added to any transitive verb in the language (the notion of transitivity is discussed in Chapter 7). Unlike those words which end in *-th*, it would not be possible to make an exhaustive list of all those words that can take *-able*, because every time a new verb is coined, it is immediately possible to add this suffix to it. As Bauer explained (1988:60), 'you may not know what it means to *Koreanise* the US economy (because I have just this moment invented the word), but given that it exists, you know that it is possible to discuss the degree to which the US economy is *Koreanisable*'. Thus, we can see that *-able* is an extremely productive suffix.

Auslan, too, has a number of morphemes that are relatively more productive, such as the classifier handshape that occurs in CL:1-PERSON-PASS-BY (also mentioned above). The orientation, location and movement of this form may be modified in a great variety of ways to represent the motion, manner of motion, orientation and location of human beings and other upright vertical objects. These classifier morphemes are used for a wide range of possible verbs of motion and location (classifier handshapes are discussed in Chapter 6, and a discussion of debates about their status in signed language grammars can be found in Chapter 10).

5.2   Morphological processes: Derivation and inflection

We discussed earlier how morphemes are used both to create the units we call words and signs, and to modify existing lexical items. The process of creating words from morphemes is usually known as *derivation*, while the use of morphemes to modify words is referred to as *inflection* (e.g., Bauer, 1988; Spencer, 1991). This is a useful distinction, although it is important to recognise that the division between derivational and inflectional morphology is often not clear in many spoken and signed languages (see the discussions in Matthews, 1974, and Bauer, 1988, for example). Moreover, recently researchers have begun to re-examine the notion that signed language grammars include inflection at all (Liddell, 2003). As a result, we will refer to these processes as sign formation and sign modification respectively, but we will note which types of formational and modifying processes have been referred to as derivational and inflectional in published descriptions of signed languages.

An example of derivational morphology in English would be the suffix *-er*. This morpheme creates a word for referring to the person who is carrying out the action described by a verb. We can add this suffix to some verbs such as *teach*, *sell*, and *believe* to make the nouns *teacher*, *seller*, and *believer*. In contrast, inflectional morphology in English involves the use of morphemes that add grammatical information to words that already exist. It does not result in the creation of new words. An example would be the suffix *-ing*. We add this suffix to many verbs to show that the action continued for some length of time or is ongoing at the time of speaking, as in *teaching*, *selling* and so on. These words remain verbs with the same basic meaning, with the suffix adding grammatical information.

Because inflections add grammatical information, inflectional processes are usually obligatory in certain grammatical contexts in English and other spoken languages (e.g., Bybee, 1985). The choice between the use of different inflectional processes is determined by the grammar. This is not true of derivational processes that produce new words, each having their own grammatical properties.

5.3   Sign formation processes

The established lexicon of every language is constantly changing. Users of English need only look at the works of Shakespeare or Chaucer to see how much the vocabulary of the language has changed over the last few centuries (Aitchison, 1992). This is also true of the Auslan lexicon. New signs develop and are added to the established vocabulary, while existing signs change in meaning or fall out of usage. How does this change occur? The following sections provide a brief overview of the main processes of sign formation which occur in Auslan. The processes discussed below are *lexical extension*, *reduplication*, *affixation*, *compounding* and *numeral incorporation*.

5.3.1 Lexical extension

One important way a language may develop new words for new ideas is to simply 'extend' the meaning of an established word, creating a polysemous lexical item (see Chapter 9). If we look at examples of computer terminology in English, we see that many words for familiar objects like 'window', 'menu', and 'file', and for actions such as 'close', 'open', and 'save' are used in new ways. These terms have developed additional meanings within the specialised technical vocabulary of computer users, yet the words themselves remain the same. Similarly, Auslan signers may use the signs WINDOW, CLOSE, OPEN and SAVE to refer to the same computer-related concepts. This process is called an *extension of meaning* (or *lexical extension*) because the meaning of a word has simply been broadened or extended in new ways.

In Auslan and other signed languages, there appear to be different ways that lexical extension can work (Brennan, 1992). Sometimes the same sign will be used, as in WINDOW or SAVE, or sometimes a modified form of a sign might be used, as in INFORMATION which appears to be a lexicalised form of SAY+rept (for a discussion of lexicalisation, see Chapter 6). For some signers, PAY+rept (literally 'to pay regularly') is used as 'rent' or 'mortgage', and for others, EARN+rept ('to earn regularly') is lexicalised as 'income', 'wages', or 'pension'.

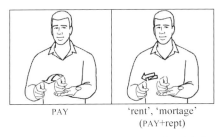

| PAY | 'rent', 'mortage' (PAY+rept) |

Figure 5.5: *The possible lexicalisation of modified signs.*

As we have already mentioned in §1.3.4, some signs in Auslan also began as name signs (i.e., signs used as names to refer to specific individuals, similar to nicknames in spoken language) that went on to gain wider meanings, such as LIBRARY (Figure 1.5). ADELAIDE is also believed to have started as the name sign for Samuel Johnson who was involved in establishing both the first school for deaf children and welfare services for deaf adults in that city. This has also apparently occurred with a brand name: the ASL sign originally used for 'Porta Printer' (an American brand of teletypewriter) has become the Auslan sign for TELETYPEWRITER (similar processes have occurred in English, as discussed in Fromkin *et al.*, 2005).

BRIDGE ⇒ SYDNEY   CHAT ⇒ AUSLAN

Figure 5.6: *Two examples of lexical extension.*

There are many other examples of lexical extension to be found in the established lexicon of the language. Indeed, the meaning of many signs has been 'extended' from a concrete image or action to something which is directly or indirectly associated with the underlying image (this is known as *metonymy*). AIRPORT has many variant forms, but one of these is based on a sign meaning literally 'aeroplane lands'. BOW-TIE can also be used to mean 'ball' or 'formal dance'. MASK is also used for 'thief', and BRIDGE has come to mean 'Sydney'. Other lexical extensions include the use of ONE-TO-ONE to mean 'tutorial' and CHAT (in signs) for 'Auslan'.

5.3.2 Reduplication (noun-verb pairs)

Many of the signs mentioned above are closely related semantically, but exploit differing patterns of movement to create variations in meaning. One of the most important of these modifications is *reduplication*. Reduplication is used here to refer to the repetition of the movement segment in a sign. This may be used to modify some aspect of the sign's meaning or to create a new lexical item.

Reduplication appears to play an important role in the distinction between some noun and verb signs in Auslan (for a discussion of nouns, verbs and other word classes, see Chapter 7). Ted Supalla and Elissa Newport (1978) were the first to observe that many related noun and verb signs in ASL have slightly different types of movement. They claimed that the ASL verb SIT has a single downward movement, while the related noun CHAIR has a repeated downward movement. The other parameters in these two signs (the handshape, orientation and location) are identical, but the movement appears to be reduplicated in CHAIR.

There is evidence that Auslan, like ASL, makes some use of reduplication to distinguish noun signs from related verb signs. The signs BUY and SELL usually have single movements, for example, while the signs for SHOPPING and SELLING may have reduplicated forms. The movement in noun signs that refers to concrete objects, such as those for KEY, DRAWER, BAG, BOOK and DOOR, is often reduplicated. Signs for the related actions, such as LOCK, OPEN-DRAWER, PICK-UP (bag), CLOSE-BOOK or OPEN-DOOR, involve a single twisting, closing, pulling or lifting movement.

OPEN-DOOR   DOOR

Figure 5.7: *An example of a noun-verb pair in Auslan.*

Although it is not difficult to find examples of this patterning in the language (see Schembri *et al.*, 2002), many native signers seem to feel that such differences in movement are not obligatory in all cases in Auslan (Johnston, 2001). In many cases, there may be no formational differences between noun and verb signs in the language (just as is true of lexical items in English, such as *file* or *cook*). This does not mean that Auslan signers do not clearly distinguish between nouns and verbs, but that the signers do not rely on a single grammatical feature, such as reduplication, to signal these differences. Other signs in the surrounding linguistic context can also provide information on a particular sign's grammatical class (see Chapter 7). For example, the sign WORK can mean 'job' in some contexts. This sign will be interpreted as a noun when it co-occurs with an adjective like NEW or a possessive sign like POSS-1 in phrases like NEW WORK 'new job' or POSS-1 WORK 'my job'. In other cases, the noun-verb distinction will only emerge when the sign has been modified (or inflected) in some way. The sign TELEPHONE may, for example, be used as a noun or a verb. As a verb, however, its movement is most often modified to signal 'I telephone you' (the sign moves from its location at the ear to a location near the addressee). Furthermore, the co-occurrence of non-manual adverbials (see §5.4.3) and role shift (see Chapter 9) with a sign also signal a verbal (or adjectival) interpretation of its meaning. Thus, nominal or verbal interpretations of many signs in Auslan (like *file* and *cook* in English) may depend on their use in context.

In some cases, nouns and verbs which are related in meaning may have quite distinct forms. The verb TEACH, for example, is morphologically unrelated to the noun TEACHER.

5.3.3 Affixation

Affixation is a process that forms new words by combining bound affixes and free morphemes. It appears to be relatively infrequent in the grammar of Auslan, as has also been reported for BSL (Brennan, 1990) and ASL (Liddell & Johnson, 1989) and many other signed languages (e.g., the discussion of Israeli Sign Language in Sandler & Lillo-Martin, 2006). Only a small number of affixes have been suggested for Auslan and the case for two of them being unambiguous examples of affixes is weak. They include a negative suffix, a reflexive suffix and a genitive suffix (and a possible prefix in age- and time-related signs in mentioned in §5.3.5 below). They are found with a limited set of signs, and do not appear involved in productive word formation processes.

Examples of pairs of signs in which a negative suffix may be present include: WILL and WON'T, WANT and NOT-WANT, TASTE and DISLIKE, BOTHER and CAN'T-BE-BOTHERED, WITH and WITHOUT. In each pair, the second sign ends in a B or 5 handshape twisted into a palm up position. This final element could be analysed as an affix (a similar form is found in Israeli Sign Language, see Aronoff *et al.*, 2004). Additional examples include the signs NOT-MINE, NEVER-AGAIN, NOT-ENOUGH, NOT-MIND, NOT-PLEASED, UNEMPLOYED, USELESS, DISBELIEVE and NOT-TRUE.

However, a sign exists which appears be the source of this 'negative suffix' in both BSL (Brennan, 1992) and Auslan (Johnston & Schembri, 1999). The negative sign means something like 'not have' in BSL, or 'not do' or 'not finish' in Auslan. The BSL sign appears, however, to be much more widely used than its Auslan equivalent. Indeed, Brennan (1990) referred to it as one of the most widely used markers of negation in BSL. Because this form can be used as an independent sign in both signed languages, this suggests that it should be considered a free morpheme rather than a bound morpheme. The status of this element as an affix in both Auslan and BSL is thus in doubt, and signs like DISAGREE might more appropriately be analysed as compounds (i.e., as AGREE^NOT-DO). The most appropriate analysis of these forms awaits further research.

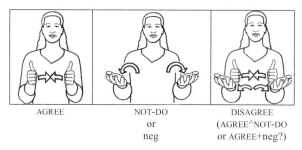

| AGREE | NOT-DO
or
neg | DISAGREE
(AGREE^NOT-DO
or AGREE+neg?) |

Figure 5.8: *Two alternative analyses of the sign DISAGREE.*

The reflexive affix is another case in point. It was suggested in Johnston (1989a) that the sign SELF could be analysed as a suffix in signs like PRO-1+SELF 'myself', PRO-2+SELF 'yourself' etc. However, since SELF also occurs as an independent sign (e.g., it can be directed towards the addressee to mean 'yourself'), its status as a suffix is doubtful.

As an interesting aside, older records of sign use in Australia (Jeanes *et al.*, 1972) suggest that the Auslan sign SELF (which does not occur in BSL) may have itself developed from a compound. This sign may have begun as a combination of a pointing pronominal followed by a possessive sign using a B handshape (e.g., PRO-2^POSS-2), or of another sign meaning INDIVIDUAL (which also may mean 'self' in Auslan, and is the only form used in BSL for this meaning) plus the B hand possessive sign (e.g., INDIVIDUAL^POSS-2).

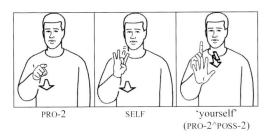

PRO-2	SELF	'yourself'
		(PRO-2^POSS-2)

Figure 5.9: *The signs PRO-2 and SELF are one possible explanation for the origin of SELF.*

One unambiguous example of an affix in Auslan is the genitive ('possessive') suffix. Although actually an example of sign modification (or inflection) rather than sign formation (or derivation), we will discuss this sign here. This morpheme can be used to signal possessive relationships between two nouns, as in MOTHER+gen SISTER+gen SPOUSE to mean 'mother's sister's husband'. This sign is not used as a free morpheme of any kind, but it appears to have been borrowed from English by means of fingerspelling (Branson *et al.*, 1995). It resembles fingerspelled -S-, although its upward movement is distinct from the downward contacting movement of the manual letter -S-. In older forms of fingerspelling (Jeanes *et al.*, 1972), this sign was used to represent the possessive -*s* suffix that follows nouns in English, as in the phrase *the woman's car*. As well as its traditional use in fingerspelling, it is also used to represent the possessive in Auslan by some signers, particularly when discussing family relationships. Thus, even this example of an unambiguous affix may be regarded as a borrowing from English and, therefore, perhaps only the result of language contact.

MOTHER'S (MOTHER+gen)

Figure 5.10: *The +gen affix.*

Finally, it is possible that some of the examples listed above do not actually represent potential affixation at all. It may be that NOT-WANT, for example, simply displays a reversal of the movement in WANT.

WANT   NOT-WANT

Figure 5.11: *Movement reversal vs. affixation.*

5.3.4 Compounding

Unlike affixation, compounding appears to be a relatively common way in which new signs develop (e.g., Klima & Bellugi, 1979 for ASL; Wallin, 1983, for Swedish Sign Language; Brennan, 1990 for BSL). Compounding, as already noted in Chapter 4, refers to the process of combining two or more free morphemes to form a new sign. Examples of compounds include signs such as PARENTS and DELICIOUS. The sign PARENTS is derived from a combination of the signs MOTHER^FATHER, while DELICIOUS appears to result from a compounding of TASTE^GOOD.

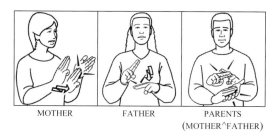

MOTHER   FATHER   PARENTS
                                (MOTHER^FATHER)

Figure 5.12: *An example of a compound in Auslan.*

Compounding is a process extensively used in spoken languages. In fact, according to Bauer (1988), there is no known language that does not have compounds. In many languages, such as Mandarin Chinese, compounding is the main way of producing new lexical items. Examples of English compounds include words such as *blackboard, bathroom, homework, strawberry, railway,* and *highway.*

When two or more separate words come together to form a compound in English, changes in the pronunciation and meaning of the words result (see, for example, Matthews, 1974). Although we can see how the word has been derived, we cannot predict the meaning of the word *greenhouse*, for example, from knowledge of the meaning of the words *green* and *house*. A greenhouse is not necessarily either green or a house. Instead, it is a structure, often made of glass, for the cultivation and protection of plants. In addition to the semantic change, there is also a change in the stress. Unlike the phrases *green house* and *black board*, the compounds *greenhouse* and *blackboard* are pronounced with the primary stress on the first element (i.e., **green**house, **black**board).

Thus, we can see that there are specific changes in the production and meaning of morphemes in English compounds which signal that we are dealing with a single word and not a phrase. In Auslan, as in other signed languages, evidence can be found of distinctive changes in the form and meaning of each compound as a result of the process of *lexicalisation* (lexicalisation is discussed in Chapter 6). The most detailed description of this compound lexicalisation process in a signed language comes from the work of Klima and Bellugi (1979), Liddell (1984), and Brennan (1990). It appears that these analyses of compounding in ASL and BSL provide an excellent framework for understanding compounds in Auslan.

Drawing on Klima and Bellugi's account (1979), Brennan (1990) lists five major types of formational changes in lexicalised compounds. First, there is a reduction or shortening of the movement in the first sign of a compound. Auslan examples include CHILD (LITTLE^SHORT), BOYFRIEND (BOY^FRIEND), CHECK (SEE^MAYBE), and FURIOUS (THINK^BAD). This change in movement is very clear in CHILD. When used as an individual lexical item, LITTLE is made with repeated or twisting contact. In the compound however, the first part of the sign is produced with a single contact. Similarly, in BOYFRIEND, the sideways brushing movement of BOY is dropped, and the hand moves straight off the chin to form the second part of the compound. In the compounds CHECK and FURIOUS, the formational characteristics of the first elements SEE and THINK are reduced, if not lost altogether. In CHECK, for example, the hand simply touches the face below the eye and moves down into neutral space as the handshape changes. The outward movement usually associated with SEE blends into the downward movement towards the location for MAYBE.

| SEE | MAYBE | CHECK (SEE^MAYBE) |

Figure 5.13: *An example of formational changes in the elements of a compound.*

Second, there is a loss of repetition of movement, if present, in the second sign. Auslan examples include PARENTS (MOTHER^FATHER) and TOMATO (RED^BALL). As can be seen from Figure 5.12, the double contact movement is lost in the second (and first) components of PARENTS—both MOTHER and FATHER are made with a single contact, rather than the usual repeated movement. TOMATO shows a similar pattern. In one variant, the twisting motion associated with BALL is lost completely. There appear to be exceptions to this rule, however, such as in EXPENSIVE (MONEY^SORE), where the second component may retain its repeated movement, and in CHECK (Figure 5.13) where the second sign sometimes maintains its twisting movement.

Third, if the second element of a compound is two-handed, the subordinate hand tends to take up its position at the start of the whole compound rather than simply at the start of the second element. Examples of this include BELIEVE (THINK^HOLD), MEMORIAL (MIND^STICK) and OBLIVIOUS (THINK^RUN-OUT). Generally, as Brennan (1990) explains, if the two signs that make up a compound like BELIEVE or MEMORIAL were produced as separate signs then the subordinate hand would not consistently assume its position before the start of the second sign. This may be less true in fluent, rapid signing in informal situations (as explained in Chapter 4). In citation forms of compounds like BELIEVE, however, the base hand will take up its position right from the beginning of the sign. This anticipation is typical of two-handed compounds, as is the anticipation and blending of the initial handshape of HOLD into that of THINK (Figure 5.14).

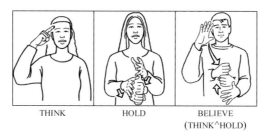

| THINK | HOLD | BELIEVE (THINK^HOLD) |

Figure 5.14: *The compound BELIEVE showing two types of anticipation and blending.*

Fourth, the compound is signed as a single unit with any transitional movements between the two elements being made more smoothly and fluidly. Many of the signs we have so far examined illustrate this principle. For example, Brennan (1990) showed how in CHECK (which has an identical form in Auslan and BSL: SEE^MAYBE), the sign undergoes assimilation of handshape. The citation form of the sign SEE uses a 1 handshape. The sign CHECK, however, usually begins with the ILY handshape placed beside the right eye rather than a simple 1 handshape as in the citation form of SEE.

Fifth, as a result of all or some of the above processes the overall duration of the compound sign tends to be similar to a simple sign, rather than two signs. PARENTS (MOTHER^FATHER) is a very clear example of this. In its citation form, MOTHER is usually produced with a repeated movement, as is FATHER. The compound PARENTS, however, is inevitably produced as one (or perhaps two) movements. Signs like MOTHER and FATHER could be analysed as consisting of two movements and ending with a hold, if we ignore the transitional movement between the two contacting movements (MMH). In PARENTS, although each sign is produced as a MMH alone, the resulting combination is not MMH^MMH, but simply MHMH or HMH. This process (and the other four changes in the production of compound signs listed above) reflects the general phonological constraints on monomorphemic forms mentioned in Chapter 6: no sign may have more than two changes in movement (not counting transitional movements), or two changes in handshape, orientation or location.

In addition to these formational changes, it may not be possible to predict the meaning of the compound simply by knowing the meaning of the two signs that form the compound (as in the English examples examined above). The sign LUCKY, for example, appears to be derived from a combination of the signs NOSE^GOOD. It is possible that this combination may have had a clearer link to its meaning at some earlier stage in the language's history, but the relationship between NOSE^GOOD and the meaning 'luck' or 'lucky' is now quite unpredictable (see Figure 5.15). This shift in meaning is typical of most compound signs in Auslan. Even though it is possible to see connections between the meanings of the component signs and the meaning of the compound as a whole in examples such as YOUR-RESPONSIBILITY (WORK^POSS-2) or WITNESS (SEE^FINISH), it seems clear that these signs have come to act as a single meaningful unit.

LUCKY
(NOSE^GOOD)

Figure 5.15: *The elements of a compound can combine to produce a sign with an unrelated or unexpected meaning.*

Table 5.2 shows examples of other possible compounds in Auslan. In many of these signs, the process of assimilation has resulted in forms of these signs that are perhaps more appropriately considered as *blends* (cf. Liddell, 1984). A blend (also known as a *portmanteau word*) is a new lexical item formed from a combination of other lexical items, but the original forms may be unrecognisable in the blend (Bauer, 1988). The sign EXPERIENCE, for example, appears to have developed from a compound, but it is not easy to say what the original signs in the compound were. The first part of EXPERIENCE may be related to the sign KNOW, but the second part of the sign is not recognisable as a free morpheme in Auslan.

Table 5.2 *Examples of lexicalised compound signs in Auslan.*

Elements of compound	Meaning of compound	Elements of compound	Meaning of compound
FACE^GOOD	HANDSOME	THINK^TRUE	BELIEVE
RED^FACE	EMBARRASSED	THINK^RIGHT	DECIDE
RED^FLOW	BLOOD	SAY^FORGIVE	APOLOGISE
LIKE^SELF	PLEASE-ONESELF	WHITE^FACE	PALE
THINK^STRONG	CONFIDENT	SAY^TRUE	PROMISE
THINK^AIM	INTEND	SAD^STRONG	GRIEF
KNOW^ALL	FAMOUS	BOOK^STAMP	PASSPORT
THINK^FINISH	RELIEF	WRONG^MIND	FEEL-BAD

Compounds are an important way in which Auslan continues to create new lexical items, particularly through the process known as loan translation (e.g., HOME^WORK for 'homework', see Chapter 6). As with all neologisms, however, only time will tell if recently coined compounds such as BOOK^LIST for 'bibliography' and EXPLAIN^DOCUMENT for 'define' will, in fact, become accepted lexical items in Auslan.

5.3.5 Numeral incorporation

A subset of time signs in Auslan, such as LAST-WEEK, NEXT-WEEK, LAST-YEAR, NEXT-YEAR, YESTERDAY and TOMORROW (Figure 5.16) can have their handshape modified by substituting its citation handshape for one of the integers from 2 to 9. This can be used to express the number of weeks, years, or days under discussion (note that in one variant of YESTERDAY, however, the signer extends additional fingers than are found in the citation form to signify each additional day).

In each of these signs, the location, orientation and movement remain the same when the numeral handshape is incorporated. It has thus been suggested that this combination may form a type of bound root morpheme, with the handshape a type of incorporated morpheme, producing a bimorphemic sign (Liddell, 1996). Other bound roots that combine with numerals in this way include the following: -DAY-OF-THE-MONTH (e.g., THIRD-OF-MONTH), -HUNDRED (e.g., THREE-HUNDRED), -MORE (e.g., THREE-MORE) as well as the various regional variants of the older signs -POUND (e.g., THREE-POUND) and -PENNY (e.g., FOUR-PENCE). Note that in Auslan, unlike ASL (Liddell, 1996), the most widely used signs WEEK and DAY are distinct from the signs discussed here and do not actually undergo numeral incorporation.

TOMORROW   TWO-DAYS-LATER/
                  DAY-AFTER-TOMORROW

Figure 5.16: *Numeral incorporation in a time sign.*

There are limits to the degree of numeral incorporation possible for specific signs. For example, though most signers readily accept the incorporation of the integers 2, 3 and 4 with the signs listed above, there is disagreement and variation in the acceptability and use of incorporated handshapes for 5 to 9.

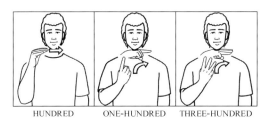

HUNDRED   ONE-HUNDRED   THREE-HUNDRED

Figure 5.17: *Numeral incorporation in a number sign.*

Two sets of signs that might be included as an example of numeral incorporation actually appear subtly different on closer inspection from the signs described above. We have already discussed the set of -O'CLOCK signs, in which numeral signs 1 to 12 move away from a subordinate 1 handshape. Similarly, in signs signifying a person's age, the number of years is made with reference to the tip of the nose (the location of the related signs AGE, OLD and YOUNG). The lexical number signs themselves are, however, made in neutral space. In signs like THREE-O'CLOCK or THREE-YEARS-OLD, for example, the signs begin with a hold, followed by a short movement away from the finger or nose, and a final hold. They thus both have a HMH structure. The sign THREE, however, may be produced as a MH or simply as a H. In both these signs, an initial segment appears to have been added to the sign. This is especially clear in the -O'CLOCK signs using ELEVEN and TWELVE, and age signs using ELEVEN to NINETEEN in which a movement away from the nose is produced prior to the side-to-side movement of the numeral sign. For this reason, Liddell (1996) has suggested that the additional segment ought to be analysed as a prefix, but it is not yet clear whether this is the most appropriate analysis for these Auslan examples.

5.4   Processes of sign modification

In this section, we examine common processes of sign modification associated with noun, adjective and verb signs in Auslan (word classes are discussed in Chapter 7). As the use of the space on and around the signer's body plays an important role in sign modification processes, we will begin with an overview of the role of space in signed language morphology.

As we saw in Chapters 1 and 4, locations on the body and in the space surrounding a signer can have a purely articulatory function. When used as part of the phonological structure of signs, locations in space may be used with no inherent meaning of their own (e.g., the location of the sign PEOPLE on the nose is a meaningless formational element in this sign).

Space can also be used in signed languages in ways in which location is not just purely articulatory, but has an inherent meaning. As we saw in Chapter 4, lexical units in signed languages are most often produced with the hands. Unlike the articulators in spoken language, it is physically possible to move the hands around in space as they produce some signed lexical items. Thus signs such as TABLE, HAVE and BLUE may have their location modified meaningfully (e.g., MAN PT+lf HAVE+lf TABLE+lf BLUE+lf 'The man on the left has a blue table'). This is not true of all signs, however. Many signs in citation form, such as WOMAN, WANT and RED, are produced in specific locations on the body, and may not be moved around the signing space. These are sometimes referred to as *body-anchored* signs (e.g., Baker & Cokely, 1980). With the exception of body-anchored signs, space can thus be used as a means of sign modification. In these cases, spatial modifications of signs may be used to refer specifically to spatial information, or to talk about other types of information (i.e., non-spatial information).

When space itself is used to talk about space, it may be used in two main ways (see Figure 6.6). First, utilising space in signed language grammar may involve the interaction with the physical space around the signer that the signer shares with his or her addressee (known as *real space* or as *shared space,* see Emmorey, 2002; Liddell, 2003). For example, signers may direct a pointing sign at an object that is between themselves and their addressee. In order to refer back to the same object, the addressee would point to the same location.

Alternatively, the use of space may involve the creation of a three-dimensional representation of the location and spatial arrangement of people and objects in the real world (which we will call *topographic space*). For example, when describing a scene in which a person on the right approaches another person on the left, signers would first place a 1 handshape person classifier handshape on the left side of the signing space. Then, the signer would move a sign such as CL:1-PERSON-MOVE from a location on the right to a location near the subordinate 1 handshape on the left. Uses of topographic space will be discussed in more detail in §5.4.1 below, and will be explored in Chapter 6.

Space can also be used to convey information that is essentially non-topographic (i.e., non-spatial). In this *abstract* use of space (also known as *token space*, see Liddell, 2003), locations may, for example, relate to the roles that the referents or participants are playing in the sentence and not necessarily to their positions in space. For example, a location on the left side of space can be associated with the referent of the sign TEACHER, and on the right with STUDENT. A signer may first produce these signs, and then point to the locations on the left and right. By pointing back to these locations, the signer may refer back to these referents, even though they are not at those locations in the real world. Abstract uses of space are discussed in more detail in §5.4.2.2 below.

Data from a growing number of signed languages has shown that all of them exploit modifications based on space and movement to convey information regularly encoded in the inflectional systems of many spoken languages (for an overview, see Newport & Supalla, 2000). These processes are involved in what have been described as nominal and verbal inflections in signed languages (e.g., Klima & Bellugi, 1979). The uses of real, topographic and abstract space will be exemplified and further explained in the following sections on noun and verb modification, as well as in Chapter 6. Note that space restrictions here do not allow us to discuss spatial modification of adjective, adverb and other classes of sign (see Liddell, 2003, for further discussion of these uses of space in ASL).

5.4.1 Noun modification

There are a limited number of modifications made to nouns in Auslan, some of which might be treated as examples of inflection (as are similar modifications in ASL and Italian Sign Language, see Wilbur, 1987; Pizzuto & Corazza, 1996). The first involves the placement of signs in locations in the signing space that are themselves spatially significant. The second involves reduplication in a subset of noun signs to represent plurality and spatial information. The third involves the modification of nouns to represent descriptive information. Finally, there are modifications of nouns that involve affixation (e.g., the use of a genitive suffix as discussed in §5.3.3 above).

In terms of modifications for spatial relationships and plurality, Auslan nouns can be divided into two major classes based on their formational features and the kinds of inflections that they usually take (cf. Pizzuto & Corazza, 1996). The first class includes noun signs articulated in citation form in a location in the signing space, such as HOUSE and CHILD, and the second one comprises nouns articulated with a fixed location on, or close to, the signer's body, such as WOMAN and APPLE (i.e., body-anchored signs). Some of the nouns in the first class may be modified in two ways: (1) for plurality (i.e., to indicate more than one) and (2) for location (in order to show grammatical relationships of the kind discussed above). This is also true, although to a lesser extent, for some nouns in the second class.

Signs that are not body-anchored, such as WINDOW or DOOR, are normally produced in the centre of the signing space in their citation form. Any other locations in which the nouns may be produced in the signing space, such as on the signer's right or left, for example, are potentially meaningful modifications of these signs. Thus, HOUSE signed at a particular location in the signing space (e.g., left or right, high or low) rather than at its normal default and neutral citation location can mean 'house at this location' (see Figure 5.18).

These modified places of articulation can be used to contrast or compare the locations of the referents in space. A signer may be describing the layout of a room, and may produce the sign WINDOW on the left side of the signing space and DOOR on the right side to represent the relative positions of the window and door from the signer's perspective. This is part of the topographic use of space described above. Once a location on the left is associated with WINDOW and one on the right with DOOR, as we have already seen, then a signer may point at these locations to refer back to the entities in question. The placement of a sign in a meaningful non-citation location is a type of modification used to signal locative information that may be unique to signed languages (although similar information is often conveyed by the use of co-speech gesture in English).

HOUSE HOUSE+lf

Figure 5.18: *The citation form and a located form of the noun HOUSE.*

The second type of modification involves repetition and location. In noun signs such as HOUSE and CHILD, the place of articulation of the sign, and the movement pattern, may also be modified to signal distinctions in the number of referents. A repeated displacement of the hands (often up to three points in the signing space) is used to signal that there is more than one referent. We can see that this is a type of reduplication of the sign, but in different locations. Reduplication to signal plurality is also found in some spoken languages (Bauer, 1988). In Indonesian, for example, *rumah* means 'house', and *rumahrumah* 'houses' (Crowely *et al.*, 1995). The movement in the sign CHILD may be reduplicated twice to specify two children, and it may also be reduplicated twice to mean three *or more* referents.

This reduplication for plural in Auslan appears to be optional in almost all cases. Signers will often produce the sign HOUSE without reduplication in phrases like THREE HOUSE 'three houses' or MANY HOUSE 'many houses', for example. Thus, the numeral and quantifier signs in these examples are sufficient to signal the notion of plurality. Not all signs in this class (i.e., those signs that are not body-anchored) can be reduplicated for plurality. Signs that are already specified for a repeated movement, such as CAR or KEY, tend not be reduplicated, for example. There are also other ways to signal plurality in Auslan, such as combining lexical signs with indicating verbs modified for number (see §5.4.2.3 below), with depicting verbs of location modified for distribution (see Chapter 6), or with pointing determiner signs that can indicate plurality (see Chapter 7).

Body-anchored signs, such as WOMAN and APPLE, may not be located and reduplicated in the same way because their places of articulation are fixed on the body. Some signers, however, accept a reduplicated form of these signs in which the body shifts or the face turns slightly from left to right. Thus, to signify 'two women', the first production of the sign WOMAN may occur with the signer's body or head leaning slightly to the left, followed by a second production with the body or head leaning slightly to the right. The sign can also be reduplicated up to three times in this way to signal three or more referents. It is not clear, however, that all signers consider this 'non-manual' reduplication acceptable in Auslan, and it is a clearly optional modification and seems rarer than the types of reduplication discussed above.

Shifting the body during the production of signs such as WOMAN and APPLE also allows the establishment of a location associated to the referent. This allows for the same grammatical use of space described above for the signs WINDOW or DOOR. Following a non-manually modified production of a body-anchored noun sign like WOMAN on the left, a signer may then refer back to the referent by pointing to the left side of the signing space.

A third type of modification involves information about size and shape of a referent included in the form of the noun sign itself (cf. Kyle & Woll, 1985). Although citation forms of signs such as TABLE, BOX, HOUSE, TENT and SINK tend to have a movement of a fixed size, this can be modified to show a relatively small or large table or box, for example. The hands simply extend or shorten the horizontal movement of TABLE, or delineate a smaller or larger area in BOX. Note that this appears to be possible only in those noun signs that are related to size and shape specifier (or SASS) constructions (these are discussed in Chapter 6).

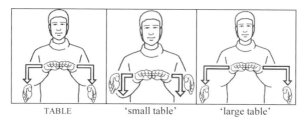

| TABLE | 'small table' | 'large table' |

Figure 5.19: *Modification based on size and shape.*

The fourth type of modification involves the addition of affixes, as in the example of the possible genitive affix in Auslan (discussed in §5.3.3 above). If accepted as an Auslan affix, +*gen* could be considered a *case* marker in Auslan, just as it is in English. Case refers to morphological markings on words that indicate their syntactic relationships with other words in the sentence. In Latin, for example, the form of the word for 'girl' (*puella*, *puellam*, *puellae,* etc.) differs according to the role of the noun in a sentence. Nominative case *puella* indicates that the noun is a subject; accusative case *puellam* indicates that the noun is the object (subject and object are discussed again in Chapters 7 and 10), and the genitive case *puellae* indicates ownership. Unlike Latin, English nouns are only inflected for genitive case, as in *the girl's ca*r. The noun MOTHER in the phrase MOTHER+*gen* SISTER is followed by the +*gen* suffix and thus could be said to be inflected for genitive case in the same way as the English example. Unlike the possessive suffix in English, however, the use of +*gen* is not obligatory. It is also highly variable. Many signers appear never to indicate possessive relationships in this way, preferring the use of a possessive sign (e.g., MOTHER POSS-3 SISTER, literally 'mother her sister' to mean 'mother's sister'). No explicit marking at all (e.g., MOTHER SISTER 'mother's sister') is also very common.

In summary, nouns may undergo a number of modifications which resemble inflections in spoken languages, such as +*gen* for genitive case and relocated reduplication for plurality, but they also exhibit a number of other modifications, such as changes to the place of articulation and movement of noun signs that have no clear parallel in spoken-language inflectional systems.

5.4.2 Verb modification

In this section we discuss in detail several types of verb modifications in Auslan that might be treated as examples of inflections (as they are, for example, in the work on ASL by Padden, 1988). These modifications are often analysed as carrying specific types of meaning relating to the traditional grammatical categories of person, number and aspect, as well as other features such as location, manner and intensification (e.g., Sutton-Spence & Woll, 1999: Sandler & Lillo-Martin, 2006). There are five major forms of verb modifications: (1) spatial and directional modifications to express who did what to whom (person), the location of the action or the participants involved (location) or both simultaneously (person and location); (2) modifications to express the number of referents or participants (number); (3) modifications of movement to express how the action referred to by the verb unfolds in time (aspect); (4) modifications to represent how an action happens (manner); and (5) modifications to express intensifications of meaning (intensification).

Before we describe in detail how verb signs may be modified to express meanings often encoded in the person and number systems in spoken languages, we actually need to look at how these systems work.

5.4.2.1 Person and number agreement in spoken languages

In examples from Spanish in Table 5.3, we can see that the verb *hablar* 'to speak' has various forms depending on who is speaking. Traditionally, the form *habl-* is analysed as a bound root with the endings *-o*, *-as*, *-a*, *-amos*, *-áis* and *-an* as suffixes, and these suffixes are said to mark agreement with person and number.

Table 5.3: *Person and number agreement in the Spanish verb 'hablar'.*

Singular		Plural	
Yo hablo	'I speak'	Nosotros hablamos	'we speak'
Tu hablas	'you speak'	Vosotros habláis	'you (plural) speak'
Él/ella habla	'he/she speaks'	Ellos/ellas hablan	'they speak'

The form of the verb *habla* is said to 'agree with' the pronoun *él* in a sentence such as *él habla inglés* 'he speaks English' because it is obligatory for the form of the verb to be *habla* in this context (i.e., other forms such as *hablas* or *hablamos* are ungrammatical with *él*). This agreement rule is based partially on the category of number because the pronoun in this case is singular. For plural *ellos* 'they', we can see that the form of the verb is not *habla* but *hablan*. This difference signals the change in the number of referents. The agreement in these Spanish verbs is also partly based on the category of person. Person refers to the distinction between first person (involving the speaker), second person (involving the person who is spoken to), and third person (involving any others). Thus, in *yo hablo inglés* 'I speak English' and *tu hablas inglés* 'you speak English', the forms of the verb are different because they reflect differences in person. Note that agreement here is with the subject of the verb.

In Spanish, all verbs take endings to indicate person and number agreement. In Auslan and other signed languages, only some verbs show person and number modifications (see below). Moreover, in Spanish, agreement marking is not optional. This appears to be one area of significant difference between the related systems of sign modification in many signed languages and inflectional systems in many spoken languages—in Auslan and other signed languages, modifying for person and number appears to be optional in some cases. For example, HAVE may change its location to reflect a location associated with its referent, as in P-A-T+lf HAVE+lf 'Pat has (something).' This modification, however, does not always occur.

As with nouns, not all verbs can be moved around in the signing space. Those that cannot be modified spatially to mark person, location, or number are *plain* verbs. Examples include LIKE, THINK and WANT. There is a strong tendency for this class of verbs to be body-anchored signs, but this is not always true (e.g., the plain verb RUN does not have a place of articulation on the body). Thus, the relative lack of spatial modification possible with these signs may partly reflect articulatory constraints.

The discussion of sign modifications for person, location and number does therefore not apply to plain verbs. Many plain verbs, however, can be modified for aspect, manner and intensification as explained in the remaining sections.

5.4.2.2 Person and location

Verb signs that are able to undergo modifications to express meanings associated with person and location inflection have been referred to as *directional* verbs (Fischer & Gough, 1978; Baker & Cokely, 1980) or *indicating* verbs (Liddell, 2003). This class of signs has also been further divided into the two sub-classes of *spatial* and *agreeing* verbs (Padden, 1988), but see Chapter 10 for a discussion of our reasons for not using this terminology.

Indicating verbs in Auslan include the signs GIVE, OBJECT and PAY. In their citation form, each of these three signs is produced with a movement away from the signer. This movement may be modified so that it is directed at physically present referents in real space. The dominant hand in the sign PAY, for example, can be moved from a location in front of the signer to the location of the addressee to mean 'I pay you.' To represent 'you pay me', the orientation of the hand and direction of its movement is reversed. All indicating verbs can be directed at present referents in this way.

If the signer wishes to talk about referents that are not physically present, it is still possible to use indicating verbs. As we have seen above, many signs may be associated with particular locations in the signing space. One could fingerspell K-I-M on the right, then P-A-T on the left to associate these referents with these locations. Then the indicating verb PAY might be moved from the right to the left to represent 'Kim pays Pat.' Whether or not Pat is (or has ever been) actually located anywhere on the signer's left may be irrelevant. In this example, the signer is using the spatial resources of the language primarily in order to distinguish between who is the *actor* (the referent who brings about or is directly involved in the action of the verb) and who is the *undergoer* (the referent which is in some way affected by the action).[3] As a result, we refer to this as an abstract use of space, as was previously mentioned.

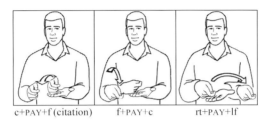

c+PAY+f (citation) f+PAY+c rt+PAY+lf

Figure 5.20: *The citation form and two spatially modified forms of PAY.*

The direction of the movement, and often the orientation of the hand(s), in these signs could be analysed as an inflection used to signal person agreement. In the case of the Auslan examples provided here, the initial position of the hands may be described as signalling the actor and the final position may express the undergoer of the verb. Indeed, these various locations in space have been analysed by Padden (1988) as affixes that attach to the root of the verb. First-person agreement affixes are locations near the signer's body (used to express the equivalent of English 'me', 'I', 'we' and 'us'), and second-person affixes are locations near or in the direction of the addressee (used to express the equivalent of English 'you'). If the referent is physically present, third-person agreement may be signalled by directing the sign towards the referent's real-world location (used to express the equivalent of English 'he', 'she', 'it', 'they' and 'them'). If it is absent, agreement for third person may use any other location away from both the signer and the addressee.

Thus, in (5.1), GIVE moves from the addressee in front of the signer to a location in the signing space on the right which corresponds to a third person. This involves modifications to the orientation, location, or both orientation and location of these signs. In some Auslan verbs, both orientation and location features are clearly modified to include information about the actor and undergoer of the verb. In order to sign the equivalent of 'you pay me', the dominant hand points towards the signer with the palm to the right (see f+PAY+c in Figure 5.20). The hand then moves towards the signer.

---

[3] The terms *actor* and *undergoer* are from Van Valin & LaPolla (1997).

(5.1)   <u>br</u>
        BOOK, FINISH f+GIVE+rt
        Have you given him (or her) the book?

In some indicating signs the orientation may not need to be modified at all, it is simply the direction of movement that is changed. For example, in the Auslan equivalent of 'I help her', HELP begins near the signer and moves towards some other person away from the addressee (e.g., c+HELP+lf). In the translation of 'she helps me', the sequence of locations would be reversed (e.g., lf+HELP+c) (cf. Figure 4.20). In yet others, there is little or no movement and the relative locations of actor and undergoer are indicated by orientation of the sign alone (e.g., LOOK). In this verb, the fingertips face the location of the undergoer, and the back of the hand signals the location of the actor. Thus a possible Auslan translation of the English sentence 'he stares at me' would be the sign LOOK held still and oriented with the fingertips pointing at the signer, and the back of the hand towards some another person away from the addressee (e.g., rt+LOOK+hold+c).

In other indicating verbs, no aspect of the sign's movement or orientation is modified meaningfully. Instead, the entire sign is displaced from its citation form location in front the signer's body to some other location. Examples of these locatable verb signs would include BUY, GROW and HAVE. Note that some researchers do not recognise the potential for many of these signs to be modified meaningfully and treat them instead as plain verbs (e.g., Padden, 1988; Sutton-Spence & Woll, 1999).

Verbs that can be spatially modified to indicate referents associated with both the actor and undergoer, such as LOOK, HELP and GIVE, are *double indicating verb* signs (referred to as *fully directional verbs* in previous descriptions of Auslan, see Johnston 1989a, 1989b). The beginning and end points are usually understood as representing the actor and undergoer respectively. This alignment of actor with the beginning point and undergoer with the end point, however, is not found with all indicating verbs. In some verbs, the spatial arrangement and movement from beginning to end can only be understood as moving from the undergoer to the actor. Padden (1988) called this small subset of indicating signs *backwards agreeing verbs*. This class includes INVITE, COPY, CHOOSE, BORROW and TAKE, because they begin at the location of the undergoer, and move towards the location of the actor (the non-backwards indicating verbs, such as PAY, are referred to by Padden as *regular agreeing verbs*). Thus, the Auslan equivalent of 'I invite you' begins near the location of the addressee and moves towards the signer (e.g., f+INVITE+c).

Second, some indicating verbs must begin or end their movement on the body and thus may only be modified spatially at one point. They are only able to indicate who or what corresponds to the undergoer of the verb. These are *single indicating verbs* (referred to as *end directional* and *beginning directional verbs* in previous descriptions of Auslan, see Johnston 1989a, 1989b). Verbs of this kind include SEE, THANK, TELL, REMIND, HAND-OVER-RESPONSIBILITY-TO and GIVE-BACK. The signs TELL, ASK and THANK begin near the mouth, SEE and VISIT near the eye, HAND-OVER-RESPONSIBILITY-TO from the shoulder and REMIND from the forehead. Locatable verbs such as HAVE would also fall into this class.

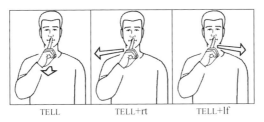

Figure 5.21: *An example of an end directional sign.*

In end directional signs, the initial location is fixed, but undergoer information is signalled by the final location of the sign. A separate sign is often required to represent information about the actor, as in (5.2).

(5.2) PRO-1 TELL+rt NOW
       I'll tell her now.

Many indicating verbs appear to use locations to signal information that is primarily or exclusively spatial. The modifications of the sign's location tell us where something is, or describe the path and trajectory of its motion through space rather than tell us who is doing what to whom.

Figure 5.22: *An example of an indicating verb primarily encoding spatial meanings.*

Thus, in the verbs MOVE and CARRY, the initial and final position of the hands express not the actor and undergoer, but the relationships between where something was located before and after it was moved or carried or driven, as the following examples show.

(5.3) _____ br
       CAN PRO-2 lf+CARRY+rt PLEASE
       Could you carry it (from there to there), please?

(5.4)   PRO-1 c+DRIVE-TO+lf ALONE
         I drove from Sydney to Melbourne alone.

In these examples, the movement from one side of the signing space to the other does not represent actor and undergoer, but the description of movement from one location to another (hence, these verbs are referred to as 'spatial verbs' by Padden, 1988).

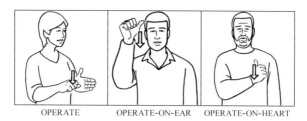

OPERATE   OPERATE-ON-EAR   OPERATE-ON-HEART

Figure 5.23: *A body locating sign.*

One subset of indicating verbs that are articulated on the body can change location if the meaning of the sign is connected to a body part. For example, the sign OPERATE can be moved on to the ear for 'operate on ear', to the chest for 'operate on the heart', and so on (see Figure 5.23). In this way signs like CUT, WASH and SHAVE can incorporate the location on the body where the action referred to by the verb was performed. With such signs there is usually a location specification found in the citation form, which is normally understood as neutral (e.g., OPERATE is produced in citation form on the palm). In previous descriptions of Auslan, such signs are labelled as *body locating signs* (Johnston, 1989a, 1989b).

Indicating verbs may also be modified to produce reciprocal forms. Verbs that may be produced with a single hand (e.g., LOOK, GIVE, INVITE) can be modified in such a way as to refer to two actors and undergoers simultaneously. For example, the dominant hand can sign LOOK and may be directed towards the subordinate hand while the subordinate hand is simultaneously producing the sign LOOK directed towards the dominant hand. This results in a form LOOK+recip meaning 'look at each other' (Figure 5.24).

LOOK+recip

Figure 5.24: *A reciprocal form of an indicating verb.*

Another class of verbs that exploits spatial modification are *classifier verbs* (which we refer to as *depicting verbs*). These are discussed in more detail in Chapter 6. For a summary of the different verb types in Auslan see Figure 5.25.

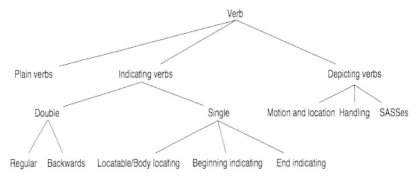

Figure 5.25: *Verb types in Auslan.*

5.4.2.3 Number

Indicating verbs can also be modified to express number. These verbs may be unmarked for number, as in (5.5).

(5.5)   br
        CLASS+lf TEACHER FINISH GIVE+lf BOOK
        The class was given the book by the teacher.

The sign GIVE can, however, be modified to indicate more than one referent. In fact, verbs can be modified to signal *dual* (modification signalling that there are two referents), *trial* (three referents) and *plural* (three or more referents). For dual marking, there are two possible verb modifications. In a two-handed sign like QUESTION (Figure 6.12), the movement would be repeated, each time ending in a different location in the signing space. Each of the two locations would be associated with one of two referents. Alternatively, if the indicating verb sign is a one-handed sign in citation form, such as ASK or REMIND, then the verb may be produced as a double-handed sign with both hands moving simultaneously or sequentially to two different locations in the signing space associated with the two objects.

For trial marking, the sign is repeated, ending in three different locations associated with each referent. To indicate indefinite plural, there are two common inflections: the *multiple* and the *exhaustive* (Klima & Bellugi, 1979). The multiple inflection is used to represent a non-specific plural meaning, with number and location of the referents unspecified. This inflection involves adding a sweep of the hand(s) in an arc along a horizontal plane to the citation form (Figure 5.26). This means that all the referents are involved in the action or event, and that the action is viewed as a single event. The exhaustive inflection involves a multiple repetition of the verb along a horizontal arc towards the locations associated with referents (Figure 5.26). This means that many, but not necessarily all, referents are involved, and the action is viewed as repeated events of the same type. Like other verb modifications described in this chapter, although they are common, it is not clear if these markings of number are obligatory in any context in Auslan.

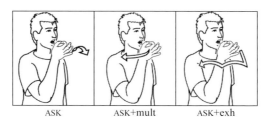

| ASK | ASK+mult | ASK+exh |

Figure 5.26: *The sign ASK with multiple (+mult) and exhaustive (+exh) modifications.*

5.4.2.4 Manner

It is important to distinguish manner from aspect (discussed in the next section). *Manner* refers to verb modifications that describe how an action is carried out, while *aspect* refers to how an action is performed specifically with reference to time.

In English, manner information is often contained in separate words and phrases that may appear next to the verb (i.e., adverbs or adverbial phrases), and not as a modification to the verb. In the following sentences, the words in italics contain information about how the action in the verb is performed.

(5.6)   He walked *quickly* across the room.
        She worked *cheerfully.*
        He watched the movie *with little interest.*
        She signs *like a deaf person.*

Manner information may also be signalled by the use of different words. English has many different lexical items that refer to human motion on two legs, each of them differing in how the motion is represented: *walk, run, skip, hop, jog, powerwalk, moonwalk, shuffle, stroll, hobble, limp, stagger* and *swagger.* All of these words provide information about the manner in which a person walked.

Auslan may also represent manner information by the use of separate signs (cf. Brennan, 1992). For example, a range of signs exists to describe human motion, many of which can express a similar range to the list of English verbs above: WALK, RUN, SPRINT, MARCH, TREAD or WALK ('from, to') (see Figure 5.27).

Separate adverbial signs and phrases can also occur next to the verb sign to signal manner, as in (5.7). Neither of these options would be considered examples of verb modification.

(5.7) MAN RUN FAST
       WOMAN WORK HAPPY
       TEACHER SIGN SAME DEAF

Auslan may, however, also include manner by modifying the way in which the verb itself is produced. This appears to be an option available in all signed languages documented to date. In particular, modifications to a verb sign's movement and its accompanying non-manual features are extremely common ways to represent manner information, as extensively discussed by Brennan (1992) in the introduction to the Dictionary of BSL/English. The sign WALK for example could be signed with a more rapid or a slower movement than in the citation form to signal changes in the speed of walking. It could be produced slowly, with a grimace and downward droop of the shoulders, to represent 'walking with difficulty', or with drawn-in lips and large outward movements to mean 'walking determinedly with huge strides'. This sign's movement could also be modified appropriately to mean 'limp' or 'stagger'. While signing TREAD, the signer's head could be pushed forward and moved slowly from side to side to signal 'creeping warily'. If the head and shoulders were thrust back and the hands moved relatively quickly while producing the sign MARCH, this would mean 'marching defiantly'.

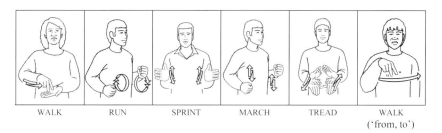

| WALK | RUN | SPRINT | MARCH | TREAD | WALK ('from, to') |

Figure 5.27: *Lexical signs representing manner information.*

Strictly speaking, many of these modifications are perhaps more appropriately treated as derivational rather than inflectional, since they actually result in signs with quite distinct meanings. As we have seen, inflection is usually used to refer to modifications of a word to signal grammatical information, such as notions of plurality or agreement in person and number. In the examples of manner modifications above, we can see that differences in movement and non-manual signals actually result in significant changes to the sign's meaning, but we are treating them together with other processes that resemble inflection simply because they are based on modifications to a citation form of the sign.

Many verbs can be produced with a non-manual adverb referred to as 'mm', as in (5.8).

(5.8)   <u>   mm </u>
    MAN DRIVE+rept
    The man is driving along (in a normal manner).

The 'mm' non-manual marker, also found in ASL (Liddell, 1980) and BSL (Sutton-Spence & Woll, 1999), is used to indicate that an action was performed in the normal and expected manner and that the signer is feeling relaxed and unhurried. As in these other signed languages, this contrasts with the non-manual signal 'th' that is used, in combination with changes to a verb sign's movement, to represent an action that is performed in a careless or inappropriate manner.

(5.9)   <u>   th </u>
    MAN DRIVE+rept
    The man is driving along carelessly.

Other non-manual signals can signal aspects of the emotions linked to an action, as examples (5.10), (5.11), and (5.12) illustrate (these would be examples of constructed action using role shift, as explained in Chapter 9). In each case, the signer produces the same string of signs, but the accompanying facial expression and movements of the head and body express contrasting emotions. In the first example, the signer uses a relieved facial expression, perhaps with an outward exhalation of air. In the second, the signer produces a sad facial expression, while in the third, the signs are accompanied by a look of disgust. Signers may interpret the emotional expressions in each case as linked to the manner in which the referent carried out the action. Equally, however, the emotions may reflect the feelings of the signer about the event, so these modifications are potentially ambiguous. The exact interpretation would, however, be clear in the specific context.

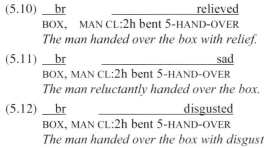

(5.10) <u> br   relieved </u>
    BOX,   MAN CL:2h bent 5-HAND-OVER
    The man handed over the box with relief.

(5.11) <u> br   sad </u>
    BOX, MAN CL:2h bent 5-HAND-OVER
    The man reluctantly handed over the box.

(5.12) <u> br   disgusted </u>
    BOX, MAN CL:2h bent 5-HAND-OVER
    The man handed over the box with disgust
.

5.4.2.5 Aspect

Before we discuss the notion of aspect, it may be useful to compare and contrast it with tense. English speakers are often more familiar with the notion of tense than they are with aspect, perhaps because tense is a common grammatical feature of English and other languages of European origin.

Tense inflections are modifications to verbs that indicate the time in which the action described by the verb took place, usually relative to the time of speaking. These morphemes may be used to signal that an event occurred in the past, will take place in the future, or is happening in the present. In English, an example would be the *-ed* suffix used to signal past tense, as in *she walked*. Strictly speaking, English has only two inflections for tense: past tense and the third person present tense marker *-s* as in *she walks*. In linguistics, however, the notion of grammatical tense has been extended to also include phrasal constructions (i.e., not just inflections) and so we often hear discussions of the future tense using *will*, as in *she will teach a class tomorrow*. Auslan has a sign WILL which might also be considered a tense marker, although it appears to be used less frequently to express futurity (as opposed to simple intention) than its English equivalent.

Aspect is used to represent information about the duration and frequency of an event rather than the actual time in which it occurred. Thus aspect describes how an event unfolded through time, rather than situating it at a particular time. An aspectual marker in English is the verb ending *–ing* which signals that an action continued for some time (known as *continuous* or *progressive* aspect), as in the phrase *I am talking for an hour*. The aspect marker *-ing* in English combines with past and future tense markers, as in *I was talking for an hour* or *I will be talking for an hour* to give complex representations of both when an action or event occurred, as well as how it unfolded in time. English also uses other phrasal constructions and inflections to show that an action or event was complete at the time of speaking (*completive* or *perfective* aspect), as in *I have eaten all the food* or that an event was just about to begin (*inceptive* aspect), as in *I was just about to start eating*.

Systematic inflections for tense do not appear to exist in any documented signed language (separate time signs and phrases are used to situate an action or event in time, as we will see in Chapter 7), but aspectual inflections have been reported for Auslan, ASL, BSL and a number of other signed languages (Fischer, 1973; Bergman, 1983; Brennan, 1992; Engberg-Pedersen, 1993). Example of modifications considered to be aspectual inflections can be seen below.

(5.13) PRO-1 GO-TO+fast-rept G-Y-M
     I go to the gym regularly.

(5.14) PRO-1 WAIT+fast-rept PRO-2
     I've been waiting a long time for you.

In the first example, the sign GO-TO is reduplicated with a relatively fast movement to represent going regularly (this might be considered an example of *habitual* aspect). In the second, WAIT is reduplicated a number of times to signal waiting for a long time (an example of *durational* aspect).

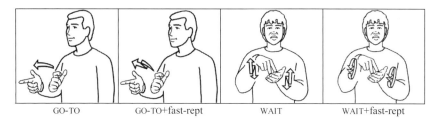

| GO-TO | GO-TO+fast-rept | WAIT | WAIT+fast-rept |

Figure 5.28: *Signs modified for aspect.*

Reduplication is one of the major ways in which aspectual distinction is signalled, but its meaning is different in the case of GO-TO and WAIT. This is because the interpretation of the reduplication interacts with the meaning of the verb itself (see Table 5.4).

Table 5.4 *The meaning of slow and fast reduplication in punctual and durative verbs.*

	punctual verb **(e.g., GO-TO)**	**durative verb** **(e.g., WAIT)**
fast reduplication	= habitual aspect PRO-1 GO-TO+rept-fast G-Y-M REGULAR FRIDAY *I go regularly to the gym every Friday*	= durational aspect PRO-1 WAIT+rept-fast YOU *I've been waiting a long time for* *you*
slow reduplication	= iterative aspect PRO-1 GO-TO+rept-slow G-Y-M *I go to the gym again and again*	= continuative aspect PRO-1 WAIT+rept-slow YOU *I've been waiting for you for ages* *and ages*

All verbs (and some adjectives) have some inherent time information in their meaning, and can be classified as *stative* or *dynamic* (Saeed, 1997). Stative verbs do not refer to an activity, but to a state of affairs. Examples in Auslan would include signs such as HAVE and KNOW. Reduplication is possible with these two signs but would be used to signal emphasis rather than aspect. Dynamic verbs refer to an activity and may be further subclassified into *durative* and *punctual* verbs. Punctual verbs represent the class of actions that are usually brief or instantaneous (e.g., KICK, HIT, THROW) and durative verbs those that usually require time to unfold (e.g., GROW, CONSIDER, WALK). When punctual verbs are reduplicated rapidly, it may signify an habitual action, while the same reduplication of durative verbs represents an action that continued for a long time (durational aspect). The slow reduplication of punctual verbs is usually read as meaning the action is repeated (*iterative* aspect), and the slow reduplication of durative verbs is usually understood as meaning the action endured or continued for a very long time (*continuative* aspect) A hold at the end of each slowly reduplicated movement may add extra emphasis. For iterative aspect, a forward rocking motion of the body and/or head with each movement adds a sense the signer had a negative feeling about the event, as in situations where one has to do something that is difficult over and over again.

Other modifications may be considered aspectual modifications. In her work on BSL, Mary Brennan (1992) pointed out that beginning a sign and then holding the handshape, orientation and location without any further movement can be used to signal something had just started to happen but does not (an example of inceptive aspect), as in (5.15).

(5.15) PRO₁ START-TO-SIGN LIGHTS-GO-OUT
I was just about to start signing when the lights went out.

Producing a sign with a movement 'in steps' can be used to show that something happens incrementally, as in the following example with BECOME-DARK.

(5.16) SUNSET BECOME-DARKER-BY-DEGREES
It slowly became darker as the sun went down.

All of these examples are verb modifications that are used to signal aspect, but signers also use phrasal constructions with FINISH to represent a completed action (perfective aspect), as in (5.17). This aspect marker is not an example of verb inflection, however, as it occurs sequentially with the verb, often following it.

(5.17) EAT FINISH PRO-2
Have you eaten?

In summary, we can see that Auslan (like other signed languages) has a rich system for aspect marking, but this area requires much more research as it remains unclear about whether there are any grammatical contexts in which such uses of verb modifications (or indeed of the perfective marker FINISH) are obligatory.

5.4.2.6 Intensification

In English, intensification of adjectives can be signalled by the addition of a separate word, such as *very* or *so*, as in *very happy*. It can also be signalled by lengthening the vowel in a word, as in *the movie was just too looong.* The latter, however, is generally considered a gesture-like modification of a linguistic item (Okrent, 2002), and thus many linguists would not treat it as part of the grammar of English (i.e., not as an inflection). We discussed issues related to linguistic and gestural features of communication in Chapter 1 and will revisit them in Chapter 10.

In Auslan, separate intensifier signs such as VERY and TRUE exist. Nevertheless, some adjective and verb signs may take a specific modification of their movement features to signal intensification. This modification involves the initial hold in the sign being lengthened, followed by a sharp release, as in signs BLACK vs. BLACK+intens, or TIRED vs. TIRED+intens. Because this is a systematic modification of the sign from its citation form to signal a particular grammatical meaning, and because it applies to a whole class of signs, it is usually considered an example of an inflection in signed languages (e.g., Sandler & Lillo-Martin, 2006).

BLACK	BLACK-intens

Figure 5.29: *An example of intensification.*

5.4.3   Non-manual features in Auslan

As is clear from the preceding discussion on verb modification, a variety of non-manual units are used extensively in Auslan. These non-manual components have been analysed by some researchers as bound morphemes (e.g., Sutton-Spence & Woll, 1999) because there appear to be very few non-manual signals that act as independent lexical items in signed languages. Instead, as pointed out in Chapter 4, most non-manual features tend to be produced in combination with signs, especially ones that have verbal or adjectival meanings, such as THIN or DRIVE. They less commonly co-occur with nominal signs, such as TABLE or HOUSE, although this may be acceptable in some contexts (e.g., when modifying a noun for size and shape as discussed in §5.4.1 above). For this reason, these non-manual features are sometimes referred to as *non-manual adverbs* (Liddell, 1980). They appear to play a productive role in the language, being used to modify the meanings of both core and non-core native signs (see Chapter 6).

In this section, we shall examine a small number of non-manual signals that have been identified in both ASL and BSL and which appear to have a similar role in Auslan. We have already discussed 'th' and 'mm'. Additional non-manual markers include the mouth gestures known as 'ee', the facial expressions 'puffed cheeks' and 'pursed lips' and the movement of the head and body known as 'cs' (mentioned in Chapter 4) (Liddell, 1980). Despite the fact that some of these non-manual features make use of particular movements of the mouth, these mouth gestures do not appear to be related to the mouthing of English words that occurs in other contexts. Some of these non-manual features do, however, appear to be similar to mouth gestures used by speakers of English, but more investigation of this is needed.

The 'ee' non-manual feature, as the name suggests, involves the lips being pulled tight in an 'ee' shape with the teeth showing. This signal is used with signs such as NEXT, SOON or THERE to produce forms meaning 'right next to', 'very soon' or 'right there'. Thus, 'ee' seems to have an intensifying function, signalling that something is very close in time or space. It often co-occurs with the use of the 'cs' movement, where the shoulder and cheek are brought together by raising the shoulder and tilting the head. This form is also used to intensify the meaning of temporal and spatial signs, as we have seen with the example RECENT+cs. These two non-manual markers can also be used in combination with a range of other signs to intensify their meaning. Combining 'ee' with the sign HOPE, for example, can mean 'to really hope something will happen'.

Two other non-manual signals seem to have an intensification function in Auslan. These both primarily involve the cheeks. The 'puffed cheeks' feature involves a puffing out of the cheeks, sometimes with an exhalation of air. It has a number of functions, including indicating that something is extremely large, as in the sign FAT+puff ('very fat'), or was done with great effort, as in the sign TOIL ('work hard'). It also co-occurs with signs to show that something occurred in a very distant location, as in FAR, or at a time in the distant past, as in AGO. It is often combined with aspectual modifications of signs, as in WAIT+rept-slow 'wait for ages' (Brennan, 1992). The 'pursed lips' feature is realised as a sucking in of the cheeks and an inhalation of air through the lips. It has a range of functions, including indicating that something has unpleasant or negative associations, often co-occurring with the signs TERRIBLE, RISKY and SORE to intensify their meaning. It is also used to emphasise that something is particularly small in size or width, as in the sign THIN. SASS classifier constructions (defined in Chapter 6) thus often occur with the either the 'pursed lips' or 'puffed cheeks' non-manual feature, depending on whether the signer wishes to draw attention to the relatively small or large dimensions of an object.

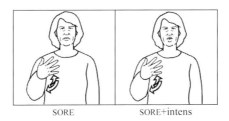

| SORE | SORE+intens |

Figure 5.30: *Intensification using non-manual signals.*

A range of other non-manual elements appear to act as meaningful units in the language, such as the 'puckered nose' which may be used to indicate a signer's disapproval and the 'tongue-in-cheek' gesture which has a range of meanings, such as suggesting an intention to deceive. Brennan (1994a) commented that it is not always clear, however, which of these non-manual components, and others, form a single meaningful unit. Often movements of the shoulders, trunk, and head accompany particular facial expressions, and groups of facial expressions frequently, although not consistently, co-occur. Given that the 'pursed lips' signal is sometimes produced with a 'squint', should we consider one as an intensifier of the other? If so, which is which? Brennan concluded that there are no clear answers to these questions at this stage, and explained that more empirical evidence is needed before firm conclusions can be reached.

5.5   Summary

In this chapter, we have introduced the notion of morpheme, and described the various types of morpheme that can be found in spoken and signed languages. We then discussed various processes of sign formation (or derivation) and modification (or inflection) in Auslan, as well as briefly sketching the role of non-manual features in the language. In the next chapter, we examine the properties of the Auslan lexicon.

5.6   Further Reading

Fromkin *et al.* (2005) provides a useful introduction to morphology of spoken languages, and Bauer (1988) is a more detailed overview. See Valli *et al.* (2005) for an introduction to ASL morphology, and both Brennan (1992) and Sutton-Spence & Woll (1999) for BSL. Sandler & Lillo-Martin (2006) provide a generative account. For alternative approaches, see Engberg-Pedersen (1993) and Liddell (2003).

6 Lexicon: the structure of Auslan vocabulary

In the previous chapter, we discussed the various types of morphological processes that can create new signs or modify existing signs in Auslan. In this chapter, we describe the structure of the Auslan lexicon, and the various different categories of signs that exist in the language.

6.1 The Auslan lexicon

Linguists believe that users of a particular language have a *mental lexicon* (i.e., a dictionary in the mind) that contains the words and morphemes of that language, along with their meanings and other important types of linguistic information (such as their word class, see Chapter 7). Together with the mental grammar (which contains the rules for combining the words and morphemes into complex lexical items, phrases and sentences), the mental lexicon enables users of a language to produce and comprehend utterances in that language.

An individual's mental lexicon, however, could not possibly contain *all* the words of a language, as the list is very large (see the discussion of creativity in Chapter 1). New words are being created all the time, many of which do not become established lexical items in the language. This aspect of the language means we need to draw a distinction between *potential* signs in Auslan and *actual* signs (cf. Spencer, 1991). Actual signs are those which have occurred and with which most of the signing community is familiar, as opposed to the limitless number of potential signs which are possible. In the signed language linguistics literature, the lexicon of actual (or *lexicalised*) signs is widely known as the *frozen*, *established* or *core* lexicon (e.g., Supalla, 1986; Sutton-Spence & Woll, 1999; Brentari & Padden, 2001).

6.1.1 The native and non-native lexicon

In signed languages such as ASL, it has been suggested that the lexicon may be divided into a sub-component that contains all the native sign vocabulary (called the *native lexicon*), and a non-native component (the *non-native lexicon*) mostly derived from contact with English (Padden, 1998; Brentari & Padden, 2001). In the case of Auslan, native lexicalised forms would include signs such as THINK, HOW-MUCH, MORNING, BLUE and CHECK discussed in earlier chapters. These are signs that have developed within Auslan, and conform to a set of *nativisation constraints*. Nativisation constraints include the symmetry and dominance conditions discussed in Chapter 4, and the tendency for signs to be monosyllabic (e.g., to have an upper limit of two handshapes in a single sign).

Non-native forms include lexical items that are fingerspelled representations of English words (or words from other languages that use a Roman script). The native sub-component may itself be subdivided into *core* and *non-core* components. Figure 6.1 shows that the non-core native lexicon is composed of depicting and pointing signs that have a close relationship to gestural communication. The area in the centre of the diagram is the core native vocabulary of lexicalised signs. As we see in the next section, lexical items may move from the non-core and non-native areas into the core lexicon through a process of lexicalisation (Johnston & Schembri, 1999). There is also a process of delexicalisation in which full fingerspelling replaces a sign derived from a manual letter, for example, or when the components of a sign are modified to depict characteristics of the referent (e.g., see Figure 5.19) (this is represented by the double-headed arrows in the figure).

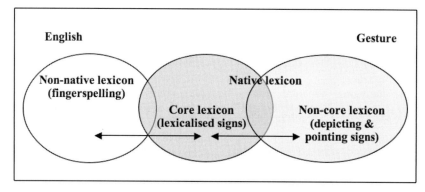

Figure 6.1: *A model of the Auslan lexicon.*

Although lexicalised signs, fingerspelled items and depicting signs form distinct categories of lexical items, they are regularly mixed together in signed utterances, as in (6.1) below. In this sentence, the sign CAR is an example of a sign from the core native lexicon, while the depicting signs CL:2-PERSON-LOCATED-IN-FRONT-OF-CAR and CL:B-CAR-LOCATED-BEHIND-PERSON are from the non-core lexicon. The fingerspelled name S-A-M is of course an example from the non-native lexicon. In the following sections, we will explore each type in turn, beginning with lexicalised signs.

(6.1) sh   CL:B-CAR-LOCATED-BEHIND-PERSON
       2h   CAR S-A-M
       dh   CL:2-PERSON-LOCATED-IN-FRONT-OF-CAR
       Sam is standing in front of the car.

6.2 The native lexicon

In the following section, we shall discuss the core native lexicon and the properties of lexicalised signs in detail, before turning to a discussion of depicting and pointing signs in the non-core native lexicon.

6.2.1 The core native lexicon

The core lexicon is the repository of lexicalised signs, including CAR in (6.1) above. This component is sometimes referred to as the *frozen* or *established* lexicon. It represents the heart of the lexicon of Auslan, and forms the basis of the vocabulary listed in dictionaries of Auslan (Johnston, 1989b, 1997, 1998). Many lexicalised signs in Auslan may be analysed as monomorphemic signs. We can refer to such monomorphemic signs as *completely specified* signs (cf. Liddell & Johnson, 1984). These appear to be listed in the signer's mental lexicon as single meaningful units and are thus equivalent to free morphemes in a spoken language such as English. Their formational features are completely specified: any significant change in the handshape, orientation, location or movement may alter the meaning of the sign, or result in a completely different sign (e.g., the sign CAR and DRIVE differ only in movement).

CAR   DRIVE

Figure 6.2: *Two completely specified signs that differ in only one feature (movement).*

An example of a completely specified morpheme (the sign PEOPLE) as it might be represented in a signer's mental lexicon is found in Table 6.1. Each cell of the table contains specific information about the sign's formational features.

The core lexicon, however, also consists of signs that are derived from a combination of more than one morpheme. Many lexicalised compound signs in Auslan are clearly derived from two morphemes, such as CHECK (SEE^MAYBE) and FEEL-BAD (WRONG^MIND), although such forms might more appropriately be considered monomorphemic forms because their meaning is not entirely predictable from their component parts. Generally, it appears that signs that are a compound of more than two signs are most often loan translations from English, such as DEAF^AWARE^TRAINING 'deafness awareness training', SIGN^LANGUAGE^LINGUISTICS 'signed language linguistics' or NATIONAL^DEAF^MEETING 'national deaf conference'. As can be seen from these examples, normally the number of signs in these compounds corresponds to the number of English lexical items upon which they are based. This latter type of loan translation is a highly productive process in Auslan, and is regularly used as a way of creating new compounds.

Table 6.1: *Specifications of the parameters of the sign* PEOPLE.

Parameter	Value
Handshape	1
Orientation	hand diagonally up, palm diagonally down
Location	nose
Movement	brush past twice
Non-manual features	n/a

Another group of signs we can call *incompletely specified* lexicalised signs (cf. Liddell & Johnson, 1984). Only some of the features of these signs appear to be specified in the mental lexicon, forming what might be considered a root or base morpheme. The rest of the sign's features contain open specifications that must be filled by other meaningful units to produce a modified form of the base sign. Examples of incompletely specified lexicalised signs would include the indicating verbs discussed in the previous chapter. There are a variety of such incompletely specified signs in the lexicon, ranging from those with only one or two features which are not specified to those that contain many unspecified cells that allow the base form to be combined with numerous kinds of meaningful unit.

Table 6.2, for example, shows three forms of the verb sign INVITE. As mentioned previously, changes in the orientation, location and movement specifications of the sign may be used to signal who is the actor and who is the undergoer. The base form of INVITE listed in the signer's mental lexicon has incomplete specifications for the modifications to show actor and undergoer, which are then filled in to produce the three forms shown in the table.

Thus we can see that the signs in the core native lexicon can be grouped into three main types: (1) completely specified lexicalised signs which may be monomorphemic, (2) compounds of two (or more) completely specified lexicalised signs and (3) incompletely specified lexicalised signs consisting of base morphemes which may be combined with other meaningful units to produce modified or inflected lexicalised signs.

Table 6.2: *Specifications of the parameters of three forms of the sign* INVITE *(for a right-handed signer).*

	No illustration of base form possible			
	INVITE	**f+INVITE+c**	**c+INVITE+f**	**lf+INVITE+rt**
Parameter				
Handshape	Bent7 > IrishT	Bent7 > IrishT	Bent7 > IrishT	Bent7 > IrishT
Orientation	fingers towards undergoer at x, palm facing x	fingers towards addressee, palm left	fingers towards signer, palm right	fingers towards left, palm towards signer
Location	at x	in neutral space	in neutral space	in neutral space
Movement	from undergoer at x to actor at y	from addressee to signer	from the signer to addressee	from signer's left to right
Non-manual features	n/a	n/a	n/a	n/a

6.2.1.1 Characteristics of lexicalised signs

Earlier we mentioned that lexicalised signs tend to conform to a set of nativisation constraints. In this section, we will outline some of the phonological, grammatical and semantic properties that appear to characterise signs in the core native lexicon (Johnston & Schembri, 1999; Brentari & Padden, 2001).

First, there appear to be general phonological constraints on lexicalised signs. Although the human body is possible of producing a vast array of gestures, signs in the core native lexicon tend to use a limited set of handshape, location and movement components, as we saw in Chapter 4. Although this is also true of the non-native components of the lexicon (i.e., fingerspelling in Auslan also uses a limited set of handshape, location and movement contrasts), this is less true of non-core native signs. In the discussion on depicting signs below, we will see that they make use of a much larger and more varied selection of locations and movements, for example. Furthermore, depicting signs, such as the sign in (6.1), also do not always follow the symmetry and dominance condition described in Chapter 4. Two-handed fingerspelling can involve handshape combinations (such as those in the manual letter -Q-) that do not follow the dominance condition.

An example of a more specific rule of lexical sign formation is the *selected fingers constraint* (Mandel, 1981). Selected fingers refer to the set of fingers that are involved in the handshape of a sign. For example, in the 1 and X handshape, the index finger is the selected finger. In the H and bent 2 handshapes, the selected fingers are the index and middle fingers. The selected fingers constraint means that lexicalised signs generally only have one set of active selected fingers involved in the production of a sign (although compounds and numeral signs such as TWENTY-ONE form an interesting exception to this tendency). Thus, if there is a change in handshape in a particular lexicalised sign, there will not be a change from a 2 handshape to a 1 handshape, for example. Instead, as in signs such as QUOTE, there is a change from a 2 to bent 2 handshape, or a change from 1 to X in TURKEY. This is different from the fingerspelled sign S-O-N (Figure 4.21), in which -S-, -O- and -N- involve quite different sets of selected fingers on the dominant hand.

QUOTE   TURKEY

Figure 6.3: *Selected fingers and change of handshape.*

Another phonological constraint was mentioned in Chapter 4, where it was pointed out that core signs tended to be monosyllabic or bisyllabic, at least in their citation form. This is the *two-type constraint* (Brentari & Padden, 2001). This means that there are generally no more than two types of handshape or movement in a lexicalised sign. In a sign such as FORGET, for example, we see that the handshape changes from an initial O handshape to a 5 handshape. Thus, in order to produce the sign, only two different handshapes are necessary. Lexicalised signs also tend to have no more than two movements in citation form. A sign can be specified, for example, for a single contacting movement on the body, such as the sign THINK, or two contacts, as in the sign MOTHER, but there are very few signs that are specified in the lexicon for three movements. Signs, such as PEOPLE, may be produced with multiple repeated movements, but this movement is not specified for any particular number of repetitions (and thus this Auslan sign would be analysed as a monosyllabic sign by many researchers, see Sandler & Lillo-Martin, 2006). This is in contrast with the fully fingerspelled lexical form of the lexical item

S-O-N that involves three different handshapes on the dominant hand (other fingerspelled items may involve many more than this), and three separate contacting movements.

Second, there are grammatical characteristics that distinguish lexicalised signs from depicting signs and fingerspelled items (cf. Brentari & Padden, 2001). Depicting verbs include classifier handshapes, as we will see below, and often involve simultaneous constructions in which each hand represents a different referent (as in (6.1) above). We will see in Chapter 7 that utterances with depicting verbs may have a syntax that is distinct from those that contain lexicalised verbs. Fingerspelled items take few of various types of sign modification described in Chapter 5 (e.g., fingerspelled verbs cannot usually be modified spatially to indicate person).

Third, there are semantic distinctions between lexicalised signs, fingerspelled items and depicting signs. In many lexicalised signs (e.g., PEOPLE), the parameters of handshape, orientation, location and movement may be identified separately, but they do not have their own separate meaning. This is different from depicting signs, as we saw in Chapter 5. In these signs, the same components may be both formational (i.e., equivalent to phonemes) and meaningful elements (i.e., morphemes). Similarly, manual letters have a dual function, as pointed out by Rachel Sutton-Spence (1995). Each manual letter can operate as a free morpheme when used as the name of the corresponding letter in the alphabet, but represents a phoneme (or more accurately a grapheme) rather than a morpheme in fingerspelled sequences that represent English words (where the total sequence of manual letters may represent a morpheme). Fingerspelled sequences in the non-native lexicon also tend to retain the meaning of the corresponding English word, whereas lexicalised signs and depicting signs do not necessarily have meanings based on English, and may be translated by a range of equivalents. Clearly, signs do not correspond to English words in meaning and use in the same way as fingerspelled items (see Chapter 8).

Lexicalised signs and depicting signs also differ in that the latter group of signs have a much closer relationship to gesture (Liddell, 2003; Kendon, 2004; Schembri *et al.*, 2005), as we will see in the following sections.

6.2.2   The non-core native lexicon

The distinction between the core native lexicon and the non-core native lexicon (also known as the *productive* lexicon) in signed languages has been explored in the work of several linguists, including Supalla (1978, 1982), Brennan (1990), Johnston & Schembri (1999), Cuxac (1999), and Brentari & Padden (2001). As we have seen, the core native lexicon consists of those completely and incompletely specified lexicalised forms which are frequently used and highly standardised in the language, while the non-core native lexicon is made up of meaningful units which are only partly specified, as we shall see below. The most important type of non-core native signs are depicting and pointing signs. Depicting signs differ from lexicalised signs because the former are traditionally considered to be actively created by signers from combinations of meaningful units (hence the term 'productive' lexicon used by Mary Brennan).

Auslan, like other signed languages, has a wide range of such meaningful units in the non-core native component of the lexicon: meaningful uses of handshape, orientation, location and movement, as well as a variety of non-manual signals, are available in the mental lexicon of the fluent signer. These units can be used by the signer to extend or modify the meaning of lexicalised signs, as we have seen with the use of space in indicating verbs. These features may also be combined in novel ways to produce entirely new depicting signs, which (as we saw in Chapter 5) have generally been analysed as polymorphemic constructions by sign language researchers (e.g., Brennan, 1990; Engberg-Pedersen, 1993; Brentari & Padden, 2001). The skilled signer is able to produce new forms by assembling the different meaningful units in different ways as the need arises. This may result in combinations of handshape, location and movement which may never have actually been used before, but which are fully understandable and meaningful in a particular context (Brennan, 1992). In Figure 6.4, examples of various depicting verbs using the 1 handshape (used to refer to the motion of a human being) combined with different location and movement units are shown.

This productive aspect of the language is very much a part of everyday interactions between signers. In any given sample of sign usage (particularly in creative story-telling, for example), there is most probably 'a significant number of signs which have been created or re-created, on the spot', as required by the topic or context of the discussion (Brennan, 1992:46). Some of these signs may remain nonce or 'one-off' lexical items. Other forms may move into the core lexicon of the language through processes of lexicalisation and nativisation, coming to be used by the wider community of signers in a standardised way. The lexical sign MEET shown in Figure 6.4, for example, appears to have been derived from a depicting verb using the 1 handshapes to refer to two individuals approaching each other.

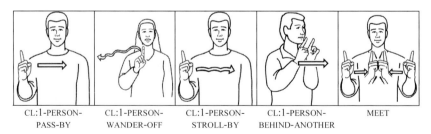

| CL:1-PERSON-PASS-BY | CL:1-PERSON-WANDER-OFF | CL:1-PERSON-STROLL-BY | CL:1-PERSON-BEHIND-ANOTHER | MEET |

Figure 6.4: *Various depicting verbs using CL:1 and the derived lexical sign MEET (on right).*

6.2.2.1 Depicting signs

6.2.2.1.1 Space and movement

Unlike lexicalised signs, depicting signs are complex lexical items in which each of the units of handshape, orientation, location and movement may have their own meaning. It is not clear whether all aspects of these signs ought to be treated as morphemes in the strictest sense (Cogill-Koez, 2000; Liddell, 2000; Schembri *et al.*, 2005), although it is clear that each of them is meaningful. In Chapter 5, for example, we discussed the use of space in indicating verbs. Liddell (2000, 2003) pointed out that the number of locations used in these verbs was potentially unlimited. As we will see below, sign language researchers encounter the same problem with all the many possible spatial arrangements found in depicting signs. It is also difficult to provide a complete list of all the movement components that are possible in these forms, because in many cases, a depicting verb of motion may imitate a large variety of types of possible movement. This makes the meaningful uses of location and movement unlike the identifiable and listable morphemes that may be found in a dictionary of English.

Drawing on the work of a number of researchers (Supalla, 1982; Liddell & Johnson, 1987; Schick, 1990; Brennan, 1992; Engberg-Pedersen, 1993), we will provide an outline here of the main uses of location and movement in these signs.

6.2.2.1.1.1 The use of space

Depicting signs make use of topographic space in two ways (see Emmorey, 2002, for an overview). First, topographic space may be used as if it was a scaled-down model or map of the physical environment. This is known as *diagrammatic space*. Second, signers may use the space around their bodies to reflect an individual's point of view on a life-size environment. This is known as *viewer space*.

Diagrammatic space (also known as *depicting space* in Liddell, 2003) can be used linguistically to describe the location and spatial relationships of people and objects in the real world. It can work as a kind of stage or map where the signer represents information in a schematic or analogue fashion, imitating the spatial relationships of objects in the real world. Thus, the place a depicting sign occurs in diagrammatic space can be used to refer to a point or place in real space. A signer may use the person 1 classifier handshape, for example, to describe the movement of a person from one location to another, and may show that the person paused on his or her journey by stopping the handshape at a point in between the two locations in the signing space. Similarly, the relative locations of two referents may be represented by the signer's positioning of two classifier handshapes in diagrammatic space. English generally uses prepositions to describe spatial relationships, as in the sentences 'the bird was *on* the roof' or 'the man was *beside* the car'. Auslan, however, may represent these relationships by using a classifier handshape for each referent and positioning them in the appropriate ways, one of which can be found in (6.1). A signer may place the B vehicle classifier handshape behind the upturned 2 legs classifier, as in this example. This means, of course, that the person the signer is talking about is in front of the car. Depending on where the legs classifier is placed in relation to the vehicle classifier, Auslan can represent a person as standing next to the front on the passenger's side, or next to the middle of the car on the driver's side, or several other specific locations, as shown below.

Figure 6.5: *Classifier handshapes used to represent the location of a person relative to a vehicle.*

With other depicting signs, signers can make use of viewer space (referred to as *surrogate space* in Liddell, 2003). The signer can act 'as if a specific object was actually present and locate the hand(s) with reference to that object' (Brennan, 1992:78). When explaining how to use a computer, for example, the signer may use a 1 handshape to indicate turning on the machine on the left, and a bent 7 extended to show how to use the mouse on the right side of space. Two bent 5 hands may then be used to indicate typing on the keyboard in the centre of space, while the signer's non-manual features imitate someone staring forward at the screen. Similarly, if a signer uses the bC handshape to indicate moving a cup from one location to another, viewer space may be used to signal that this location 'is relatively high or low in relation to the signer, for example, if the object is moved from a high shelf to a low shelf' (Brennan, 1992:78).

A summary of the uses of space discussed in this chapter and in Chapter 5 is presented in Figure 6.6.

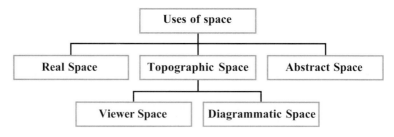

Figure 6.6: *The uses of space in signed languages.*

6.2.2.1.1.2   *The use of movement*

A number of different movement types can be identified in depicting signs: movement can represent a referent's *location*, *distribution*, *path* and *manner of motion,* or may *trace* its size and shape.

Locating movement involves the hand making a short sharp downward movement which ends with an abrupt stop at a specific location in the signing space. This stamping movement does not mean that the object is moving in this way, but is used to signal that it is located in a particular place. If the B hand vehicle classifier is produced with a locating movement, then this means something like 'a vehicle is located in this position', as in the following example.

(6.2)   TRUCK CL:B-VEHICLE-LOCATED-ON-THE-LEFT
      A truck is on my left.

In distributional movement, the hands move through space to represent the location and spatial arrangement of a number of objects, or the motion of objects to a number of locations in a particular spatial arrangement. This type of movement can also combine with other types of movement morphemes, such as locating, path and tracing movement. A particular arrangement of vehicles, for example, can be realised by combining a specific distributional arrangement (such as 'in-a-line' or 'in-an-arc') with the B vehicle classifier handshape and a repeated locating ('stamping') movement.

(6.3)   MANY CAR CL:B-MANY-VEHICLES-LOCATED-IN-A-LINE
      Many cars were parked in a line.

Path movement refers to the use of the hands to show the general movement of an object from one location in space to another. When the hand is moving, the movement means that the object being described is moving (regardless of the manner in which it actually did so), or that it appears to be moving. This movement may be a straight path between two points in space, or it may be an arcing, circling, or back-and-forth movement. If the 1 hand person classifier is produced with a path movement from a location on the left to one on the right, then this means something like 'a person moves from this place to another', as in (6.4).

(6.4)   STUDENT CL:1-PERSON-APPROACH-FROM-RIGHT
      The student came up to me from my right.

In contrast to the use of path movement, manner movement involves the use of the hands to represent the specific movement of an object. The particular way that the hand is moving means that the object being described is moving in this particular way or that it appears to be moving in this particular way. Manner movement thus can provide 'a stylised imitation of real-world action' (Schick, 1990:17). The 2 legs classifier can be moved in a variety of ways to represent the specific actions of a referent. It can be used to describe the movements of an athlete or acrobat jumping off platforms, bouncing on trampolines, flipping in the air, falling on the ground and tumbling over, diving into the water and swimming, etc., as in (6.5).

(6.5)   sh   CL:B-WIDE-FLAT-SURFACE
        2h J-E-T-T-Y GIRL
        dh   CL:2-PERSON-DOES-TRIPLE-SOMERSAULT-DIVE
        The girl dived from the jetty, doing a triple somersault on the way
        down.

Tracing movement is distinct from path and manner movement because, although the hand moves, this does not mean that the referent is moving. Rather the movement of the hand represents an iconic description of some aspect of the referent by tracing an outline of its size and shape. Thus, a B handshape may be used to show the lie of the land, as flat, gently undulating or extremely hilly. Again, the range of possible forms that may be used seems quite large.

(6.6)   ROAD CL:B-TRACE-GENTLY-UNDULATING-SURFACE
        The surface of the road was gently undulating.

6.2.2.1.2   *The types and inventory of handshapes*
This section will provide a brief overview of the different types of handshape classifiers that have been suggested by sign language researchers (Liddell & Johnson, 1987; Schick, 1990; Brennan, 1992; Engberg-Pedersen, 1993). We organise these various types into three general categories: *entity*, *handling* and *SASS* classifier handshapes. These three categories are based both on the patterns of resemblance each classifier handshape has to its meaning, the manner in which each combines with units of movement and location, as well as the specific role each has in the grammar of Auslan. As we shall see, entity classifiers represent the location and movement of people, animals or objects; handling classifiers indicate interaction with or movement of objects by an actor; and SASS forms provide descriptive information about the size and shape characteristics of people, animals or objects.

6.2.2.1.2.1   *Entity handshapes*
Entity classifiers are those handshapes that may refer to a category of objects. We have already seen two major entity categories in §6.2.2.1.1.1 above: the 1 entity classifier may represent a human being and the B can stand for vehicles. The handshapes used as entity classifiers often resemble the shape of the object, or some part of the object, which they represent. These handshapes are used in depicting verbs to show the movement and/or the location in space of objects. Combining with the appropriate location and movement units, they can indicate a referent's path and manner of movement, and spatial arrangement. A signer can also use two entity handshapes to simultaneously describe the relative locations and movements in space of two (or more) separate referents, as we saw earlier in (6.1).

Researchers have suggested four main subcategories of entity classifier handshapes (Liddell & Johnson, 1987). First, there are the *whole entity handshapes* which, as the name suggests, stand for an object as a whole. The person and vehicle handshapes are examples of whole entity classifiers. Other whole entity handshapes which represent objects would include the use of the horizontal 1 handshape or 2 legs for animals, the Y handshape for aeroplanes or telephones, the S for spherical objects (such as heads, balls, etc.), the F handshape for small flat round objects (such as buttons, coins, etc.), and the palm up B handshape for flat objects (such as pieces of paper, leaves, books, etc.). The second group are known as *collective* handshapes. The main handshapes in this group are used to represent large groups of objects or the movement of liquids, such as the 5 handshape which can be used to show the movement and location of a crowd of people, a herd of animals or swarm of insects. Third, there are the *body part* handshapes which indicate the motion of people or animals by representing the motion or actions of their limbs or other parts of the body. The most common would include the down-turned 1 and palm down B handshapes used to mimetically represent the actions of the legs and feet respectively. Lastly, there are the *extent* handshapes. Handshapes in this group represent amounts or volumes, such as the amount of water in a glass or pool, or a pile of books or papers. Changes in the amount or volume, such as rising or falling water, can be signalled using a B or 5 handshape, for example.

6.2.2.1.2.2 Handling handshapes

Handling classifiers imitate the hands interacting with an object. As a result, these handshapes form part of depicting verbs which focus on how a human or animal handles some referent, and what happens to it as a result of this handling.

There are three main kinds of handling classifiers discussed in the literature (Brennan, 1992). First, there is a group of *holding* handshapes. These occur in depicting verbs which describe the movement of objects by a human or animal, such as a bent 5 to describe picking up a box, an S for holding a bag or turning a door handle, a bC for holding a cup, an Irish T for turning a key, a flat O for holding a piece of paper, or an F for using a needle and thread. As these examples show, the handshape used varies according to the size and shape of the object being handled (directly reflecting how the hand would actually look when interacting with objects of various dimensions). If a signer is describing the handling of a round object, for example, the hand configuration will vary its formation: a bent 8 handshape for a small round object (such as a small stone or a marble), a bent 5 for a medium-sized round object (such as a piece of fruit or tennis ball), and two bent 5 handshapes for a large round object (such as a basketball or a melon), held far apart and combined with non-manual signals (such as puffed cheeks) which imply a large size or great weight.

Second, handling classifiers include a class of *touch* handshapes. Here the handshape used is based on the way in which the object is touched. The handshape does not reflect the shape of the object being handled, but the shape of the hands themselves when they touch different kinds of objects and when they touch the same kinds of objects in different ways. Thus, the wiggling 5 handshape may be used to represent using an automatic teller machine or a calculator, the 6 handshape for pressing a doorbell, the B handshape for patting a pet or the bent 5 for scratching a surface. Third, this category includes a group of *instrumental* handshapes. Iconically, instrumental handshapes often represent the shape of an instrument or tool (and thus share some characteristics of entity handshapes), as in the use of a 2 handshape to represent cutting with scissors, a Y for a teapot or telephone receiver, a 7 for a drill or an H for a screwdriver, but they may be used in depicting verbs which describe the way someone handles this object, or uses this object to act on another object. Thus, in the Auslan translation of the English sentence 'I cut the paper in half with scissors', the signer may use the 2 handshape as an instrumental handshape to show how the paper was cut.

6.2.2.1.2.3   *Size and shape specifier handshapes*

Size and shape specifiers (SASSes) refer to those classifier handshapes used to describe the referent object by outlining its shape and size. SASS classifier constructions appear to be adjectival, describing aspects of a referent's appearance and its dimensions. They may also act as nouns in some contexts. Like handling classifiers, the handshape used varies according to the characteristics of the object being described, so that a 1 handshape, for example, may be used to trace the shape of a relatively thin rectangular object (as in a credit card or photograph), while a B hand would be used to represent a relatively wide rectangular object (such as a box or television).

Three main categories have been suggested in the literature (Liddell & Johnson, 1987). First, there is the group known as *surface* handshapes. These can be used to describe the surface of objects, representing them as narrow or wide, flat or undulating (as in the use of the B hand to describe surface of the road in (6.6) above). Second, there are the *depth and width* handshapes. These handshapes show the relative depth and width of objects, such as two bC hands used to depict the dimensions of pipes, poles or tree trunks. The third group are known as the *perimeter-shape* handshapes. The handshapes in this group can trace an outline of the external shape of an object. If the object is a large symmetrical shape, such as a rectangular picture on a wall, the two hands may be used, as in the use of 1 handshapes to trace the size and shape of the picture's frame. If the object is asymmetrical, such as the irregular shape of a modular sofa, then one hand may remain stationary as the other hand traces out the shape.

6.2.2.1.3   Depicting signs and gesture

In his work on gesture, Kendon (2004) has noted that the uses of handshape, location and movement in depicting signs have much in common with gesture. Non-signers also use different hand configurations to represent different groups of objects, and movement of their hands to show the motion and location of referents, how they are handled, or to trace their size and shape. Recent research indicates, however, that signers use these meaningful units (particularly handshapes) in a more consistent and systematic manner than non-signers (Schembri *et al.*, 2005). Despite this, it is important to realise that the use of depicting signs in signed languages appears to represent a regularisation of visual representation strategies that are widely used in the gestures of non-signers.

Like many gestures used by hearing non-signers, depicting signs may be very general in meaning. Kendon (2004) explained that depictive gestures obtain their specific interpretation by being used in combination with spoken language. The specific meaning of many depictive signs also results from an interaction with lexicalised signs and fingerspelled items. The B handshape, for example, can be used to represent vehicles, or it can depict the movement and location of flat objects, such as pieces of paper, books, tiles, or walls. It can represent surfaces, tracing out the shape and dimensions of objects with flat exteriors. It can show how something is handled, representing the holding of flat objects, such as boxes or plates, or an instrument used in cutting or slicing an object. Often the precise function of the classifier handshape is determined, not by handshape alone, but by the combination of a particular hand configuration with a particular kind of movement in a specific linguistic context. Thus, the bC handshape can be used to represent an entity, as in CL:bC-CYLINDRICAL-OBJECT-FALL, how something is held in the hands, as in CL:bC-GIVE-CYLINDRICAL-OBJECT, or as a SASS handshape, as in CL:bC-TRACE-LONG-CYLINDRICAL-OBJECT. The nature of the referent being described in each example would need to be identified by the use of a lexicalised sign like CUP, or a fingerspelled item like C-A-B-L-E, which may precede the depicting sign in the discourse.

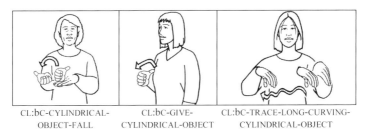

| CL:bC-CYLINDRICAL-OBJECT-FALL | CL:bC-GIVE-CYLINDRICAL-OBJECT | CL:bC-TRACE-LONG-CURVING-CYLINDRICAL-OBJECT |

Figure 6.7: *Examples of the use of the bC classifier handshape.*

6.2.2.1.4   *Depicting signs in close and distant focus*

Depicting verbs are used to produce what Supalla (1990) has called *serial verbs of motion*. Here, one motion event may be represented by two depicting verbs with different handshapes. In these forms, the path of movement and the manner of movement may be represented by different signs, even though the two forms refer to the same real-world event. To describe a person climbing up a cliff using their hands, for example, a signer may first use a 2 legs handshape to show the upwards path movement, followed by the use of the two-handed bent 5 handshapes to characterise the manner of climbing. Similarly, to represent a person tiptoeing past and away from the signer, a combination of the whole entity 1 for the path and two-handed palm down B handshapes to show the tiptoeing feet may be used. As a result, two depicting verbs of motion are used to represent the one motion event (although the use of such serial verb combinations is not obligatory in all contexts, as suggested by the work of Hawk & Emmorey, 2002, on ASL).

The use of two or more different depicting signs in these examples reflects the fact that signers may often switch between two different frames of reference while describing the same event (Schick, 1990; Brennan, 1992). This shift of scale is also known as *close* and *distant focus* (Brennan *et al.*, 1984). We can see that the 2 legs handshape in the example above may involve use of diagrammatic space (as a type of distant focus) to indicate the path movement from one location to another, while the use of the bent 5 handshapes in combination with role shift (see Chapter 9) uses viewer space (for close focus). This enables the signer to move from one frame of reference to another, 'sometimes zooming in to provide a close up view, at other times pulling back to provide a "long shot" on the action' (Brennan, 1992:51).

6.2.2.2 *Classifier handshapes: A note on terminology*

In this book, we have continued to use the term *classifier* to refer to the meaningful handshapes in depicting signs. Although this is a familiar term for students of Auslan, Brennan (1992:46) pointed out that the notion of *classifier* is not likely to be familiar to English speakers, partly because it is not a grammatical concept which is a particularly relevant to the language. She provided the following definition of the term *classifier*:

> Classifiers are linguistic units which indicate what kind of group or category a particular referent belongs to. They mark out what is referred to as belonging, for example, to the class of animate entities, the class of humans, the class of round things, the class of flat things, the class of vehicles and so on.

Some of the most well-known examples of languages which have classifier morphemes include Mandarin, Thai and Indonesian. In these languages, separate words and morphemes are used to show what category a referent belongs to, as shown in the Indonesian examples (6.7) and (6.8).

(6.7) dua   biji   bola
       two   *round-object-classifier*   *ball*

(6.8) dua   batang   potlet
       two   *long-narrow-classifier*   *pencil*

Classifiers, however, appear to play a role in many of these languages that is a little different from what is seen in signed languages. In signed languages, the main function of classifier handshapes appears to be to depict, rather than categorise, objects in the world. The use of classifier handshapes is very much part of the iconicity of signed languages (see Chapter 8), and their origin in the meaningful use of hand configurations in gesture is clear (Kendon, 2004; Schembri *et al.*, 2005). As a result, not all sign language researchers agree that the term *classifier* is the most appropriate one for signed languages (see Engberg-Pedersen, 1993; Schembri, 2003). Note, too, that strictly speaking, only the handshape in depicting signs is a classifier, even though many now use the term to refer to depicting signs in general. We have opted to use the term *classifier* here (although some researchers, such as Liddell, 2003, have abandoned it) partly because it has become widely known, especially among sign language teachers, and because no replacement term has yet gained acceptance.

6.2.2.3 Pointing signs

A range of pointing signs exists in Auslan. Each of these works by indicating its referent which may be physically present, located somewhere else, or imagined to be present.

Figure 6.8: *Pointing signs.*

In the standard pointing gesture in our culture, the extended index finger is usually directed towards the referent (see Kita, 2003, for an overview of research on pointing gestures). Pointing signs are often glossed as INDEX by many signed language linguists. This form is also widely used in Auslan, alongside lexicalised uses of the pointing gesture (e.g., pointing to the chest for PRO-1 'I/me', sweeping the index finger in an arc in front of the chest for PRO-1+PL 'we/us' and to the space immediately in front of the body for HERE). For example, lexicalised signs for many body parts do not exist in Auslan (as we will see in Chapter 8), because signers usually indicate the part of the body they wish to refer to using a variety of pointing gestures. In some cases, pointing gestures have become core signs. For example, a 1 handshape directed towards the ear is actually the sign HEAR. Thus, another form is used for EAR (the Irish T handshape grasps the ear lobe).

Like indicating verbs, we treat pronominal and possessive pointing signs as incompletely specified lexicalised signs, and thus this subset of pointing gestures belongs in the core native lexicon (Johnston & Schembri, 1999). This would include, for example, the two variants of the possessive sign (with the B and S handshapes respectively) that point at their referents with the palm side of the hand. These signs are discussed in more detail in Chapter 7.

6.2.3 Lexicalisation of depicting signs

A considerable number of lexicalised signs appear to imitate the physical features or actions of objects in the real world, as we will see in Chapter 8. These lexicalised signs appear to be derived from the combination of particular handshape, location and movement units in depicting signs. Signs such as AEROPLANE and TREE appear to involve entity classifiers, the signs TICKET and HOUSE resemble the use of various SASS classifier forms, while DRINK and WRITE seem to have developed from handling classifiers (Figure 6.9).

These signs can thus be considered examples of lexicalised forms of depicting signs. Lexicalisation refers to the process where signs composed of many separate meaningful units come to act as single morphemes. The term lexicalised means 'like a word', that is, like a free morpheme in the language. The English words *dishwasher* and *radar* are formed from the combination of separate morphemes (*radar* is made up of the initial letters from *radio detection and ranging*), but in each case, these combinations of morphemes come to act as a single meaningful unit. Although we can see how the word has been derived, we cannot predict the meaning of the word *dishwasher*, for example, from knowledge of the meaning of the words *dish* and *washer*. A *dishwasher* does not only wash dishes—it also washes cutlery, cups, cooking utensils and so forth. Although a dishwasher could refer to a person (the agentive suffix –*er* in English is often used to refer to people), it has come to refer specifically to a machine that washes eating and cooking utensils.

| AEROPLANE | TICKET | DRINK | MEET | MEETING |

Figure 6.9: *Lexicalised signs derived from depicting signs.*

Like these examples from English, depicting signs appear to be assembled out of smaller meaningful parts. Signers may combine classifier handshape morphemes with location, movement and non-manual components to create complex constructions. The Auslan lexicon, however, includes many examples of depicting signs that have become fully lexicalised, and many others that appear to be partly lexicalised (Engberg-Pedersen, 1993; Johnston & Schembri, 1999). Signers do not necessarily use these signs as productive constructions, and the meaning of the separate parts may no longer play a role in the meaning of the sign. If we think of the lexicalised sign MEET and MEETING (Figure 6.9), for example, we can see that the handshape appears to be derived from a classifier handshape for person. If we think about the meaning of the word, it is obvious that meetings involve people coming together. The signs MEET and MEETING, however, use only two individual classifier handshapes, and yet meetings can include many more than two people. The circular movement in MEETING does not have anything to do with the movement of people, and two individuals may meet without necessarily approaching each other face-to-face as is suggested by the sign MEET. The handshape morpheme is thus no longer productive in either sign, nor is the movement unit. Unlike depicting signs, the handshape in these signs does not change to reflect the number of people. These classifier-based signs have become fully lexicalised: the meaning of all the smaller units of handshape, location and movement is no longer productive in the meaning of the sign.

Lexicalised depicting signs are an important source of new signs for new concepts. There are a significant number of signs in Auslan which appear to be in the process of lexicalisation. In a project on signs for computer terminology, for example, researchers found that some depicting signs being used by deaf computer users for various types of computer technology are becoming incorporated into the established lexicon of the language (Parker & Schembri, 1996). Examples of such signs include those for MOUSE, TRACKBALL and JOYSTICK. Each of these partially lexicalised signs involves the use of particular classifier forms based on the handling of these objects. Handling classifiers are also important in the various signs that exist for other types of new technology, such as AUTOMATIC-TELLER-MACHINE and EFTPOS ('electronic funds transfer at point of sale'). Entity classifiers seem to be the basis of the signs LAPTOP-COMPUTER, VIDEO-CAMERA, MODEM, FAX and SATELLITE, while SASS classifiers play a role in signs for SPREADSHEET and MARGIN.

SASS depicting signs are also an important way in which signs for mathematical concepts have developed amongst deaf students (Spicer & Rogers, 1989). Many SASS constructions trace out the shape of particular mathematical symbols, and these have become lexicalised signs for these concepts (at least in educational contexts). Examples of such signs include INFINITY, EQUALS, MINUS, PARABOLA, RATIO, THEREFORE and INTEGRAL.

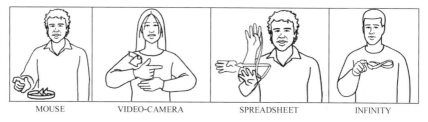

| MOUSE | VIDEO-CAMERA | SPREADSHEET | INFINITY |

Figure 6.10: *Recent frequently used depicting signs undergoing lexicalisation.*

The process of lexicalisation appears, however, to be a gradual one. For example, there are currently a number of variants of MOBILE-PHONE. One variant with a bent 5 represents holding the handset at the ear, while another uses a 1 handshape held with the palm side contacting the cheek to represent the shape of the mobile phone and its antenna. In addition, some signers now use a handling form in which the extended thumb of the 6 handshape repeatedly bends to represent creating a text message.

6.3   The non-native lexicon in Auslan

The non-native lexicon represents 'foreign' elements that have been borrowed into the native Auslan lexicon via fingerspelling (cf. Brentari & Padden, 2001). Lexical borrowing refers to the process in which lexical items from one language are incorporated into the lexicon of another language. The vocabulary of English, for example, includes many words borrowed from other spoken languages. A great number of loan words are part of the basic vocabulary of the language, and most English speakers use them every day without being aware of their origins in other languages. Fingerspelling is a form of indirect borrowing, however, because it is not a direct representation of English. Instead, fingerspelling is a manual representation of the written representation of English. Although fingerspelling is unique to signed languages (Lucas & Valli, 1992; Sutton-Spence, 1995), we will continue here to refer to it as an example of lexical borrowing to highlight some of the similarities between uses of the manual alphabet and the integration of foreign vocabulary in spoken languages.

Auslan borrows both from written and spoken English (via fingerspelling, loan translations and mouth patterns) and from other signed languages. In the following section, we focus on borrowing from English, with borrowing from other signed languages discussed in §6.3.2.

A variety of changes occur to a lexical item when it is integrated into one language from another (see Romaine, 1995, for an overview), but we will focus on just two here. First, the form of the foreign lexical item is often restructured (or phonologically nativised) to make it more closely resemble the phonological form of words in the language. In the case of Auslan, borrowed words are most commonly fingerspelled using the two-handed manual alphabet, or are translated into signed form. Mouthing of English words most often is accompanied by fingerspelling and signing. Note, however, that many signs borrowed from other signed languages do not appear to require restructuring and fit seamlessly into the language (Lucas & Valli, 1992). Second, the meaning of the borrowed lexical item is often modified. The borrowed item may come to have either a more general or a more specific meaning in Auslan. The fingerspelled D-O, for example, is most often used only as a main verb in Auslan (TOMORROW PRO-2 D-O WHAT? 'What are you doing tomorrow?'), and less often as an auxiliary verb (as in the English example 'what *do* you want?'). The ASL sign originally meaning SELL or SHOP is used by some signers to mean MARKET, or MARKETING. It has come to have a more restricted meaning in Auslan than in ASL, probably because signers use native Auslan signs for SELL and SHOP.

MARKET/MARKETING
(ASL SHOP/SELL)

SHOP

SELL

Figure 6.11: *A borrowed ASL sign taking on a more restricted meaning in Auslan.*

6.3.1 Borrowing from English

Some researchers have suggested that fingerspelling is a kind of *code-mixing* or *code-switching* between signed languages and spoken languages (Sutton-

Spence & Woll, 1993). Code-mixing generally refers to the mixing of different languages so that a single utterance may contain words and grammatical constructions from two or more languages. Code-switching occurs when a person produces part of an utterance in one language and then switches to another language for another part, thus changing from one language to another in the same conversation (although see Clyne, 2003, for a discussion of the difficulty of distinguishing code-mixing and code-switching). Fingerspelling one or two words in a signed utterance might be considered a type of code-mixing, while producing a complete phrase entirely in fingerspelled English and another in Auslan might be an example of code-switching. This type of language mixing is normal in all bilingual communities and is very common all over the world (Romaine, 1995).

Fingerspelling is often used for spelling common or proper nouns, or for other English words that do not have a lexicalised equivalent in Auslan. Fingerspelled forms may also often be preferred over a recently coined sign because 'they may refer to domains of knowledge whose centre is outside the deaf community, or because they refer to a discipline-specific term that may have not undergone broad discussion within the deaf community' (Brentari, 1995:42).

Fingerspelling is used to represent English words, but it is important to realise that characteristic changes take place when these letter signs are produced in sequence (Hanson, 1981; Akamatsu, 1985; Wilcox, 1992). In the rapid fingerspelling of native signers of Auslan, not all the letters of a word are fingerspelled and the parts blend together, so that it is often only the overall sign shape that is recognised, not the shapes of the individual letter signs themselves (Johnston, 1989a). Handshapes for a given letter may also vary, and this seems to depend on the surrounding letters. The fingerspelled letter -B-, for example, may be made with the third, fourth and fifth fingers open, but these fingers may be closed if the letter occurs at the end of a word (Sutton-Spence & Woll, 1993).

Because fluent signers do not fingerspell all the letters of a word, common fingerspelled words may become so modified over time that only a few letters of the word are usually produced by a signer. Often the first and last, or sometimes only the first letter is used, and the other letters are dropped. Other regularly fingerspelled words may already only have two or three letters. In such cases, the fingerspelled item may become part of the core native lexicon. These frequently fingerspelled items may change over time to obey the same phonological constraints as other Auslan signs. There are many examples of lexicalised signs in Auslan that have developed out of commonly fingerspelled words. These signs are examples of what is known as *lexicalised fingerspelling* (Lucas & Valli, 1992) or *fingerspelled loan signs* (Battison, 1978).

Sutton-Spence (1995) has produced a description of the various categories of lexicalised fingerspelling signs in BSL. Since BSL and Auslan are historically related languages, and because many of the examples they discuss also occur in Auslan, Sutton-Spence's description has been used here as a framework for the discussion of lexicalised fingerspelling in Auslan.

6.3.1.1 Fingerspelling

6.3.1.1.1 Lexicalised Fingerspelling

Lexicalised fingerspellings involve single letter signs, such as DAUGHTER (D-D), KITCHEN (K-K) and TOILET (T-T), acronyms such as A-A-D (Australian Association of the Deaf), abbreviations such as JANUARY (J-A-N), TUESDAY (T-U-E-S) and ADVERTISEMENT (A-D-V), as well as whole English words such as L-A-W, S-O-N and D-O.

Table 6.3 *Types of lexicalised fingerspelling.*

Single manual letter signs	Lexicalised acronyms, abbreviations and others	Whole English words
Common nouns:	*Common nouns:*	*Common nouns:*
A-A 'alcohol'	A-C 'air-conditioning'	A-P-R-I-L
D-D 'daughter'	A-C-C 'accident'	C-H-E-A-P
I-I 'insurance'	A-D-V 'advertisement'	C-L-U-B
K-K 'kitchen'	C-H-O-C 'chocolate'	C-R-E-A-M
F-F 'father'	C-O 'company'	L-A-W
G-G 'garage'	D-R 'doctor'	M-A-Y
M-M 'mother'	E-M-G 'emergency'	J-U-L-Y
T-T 'toilet'	P-O 'post office'	S-H-O-E-S
		S-O-A-P
Proper nouns:	*Proper nouns:*	S-O-N
B-B 'Brisbane'	A-A-D 'Australian Association of the Deaf'	
P-P 'Parramatta'	B-W-C-K 'Brunswick'	*Verbs:*
Q-Q 'Queensland'	D-R-A 'Deafness Resources Australia'	D-O
	N-R-S 'National Relay Service'	
Verbs:	R-I-C-H 'Richmond'	*Conjunctions*
R-R 'rather, prefer'	S-E-P-T 'September'	A-B-O-U-T
	T-A-S 'Tasmania'	I-F
Adjective/adverb:	V-I-C 'Victoria'	S-O
N-N 'normal'	W-A 'Western Australia'	

Some items are fully lexicalised phonologically (i.e., they follow all the same phonological constraints as lexicalised signs, such as the symmetry and dominance conditions, the selected fingers constraint, etc.), grammatically (i.e., they may undergo modifications for person, number or aspect) and semantically (i.e., they have taken on particular meanings within the language that may differentiate them from their English origins). Other fingerspelled loan signs may be only partially phonologically or semantically lexicalised, and yet others are examples of nonce ('one-off') borrowings which undergo only local lexicalisation for the duration of a particular signed exchange.

6.3.1.1.2   Single manual letter signs

These signs involve the use of the first letter of the English word. In informal signing, signers often fully fingerspell an English word when they first introduce it into the conversation, but then later simply fingerspell the first letter of the word to refer back to it. This often happens with the names of people and places. If the meaning is clear in a particular context, sometimes the single letter is used from the beginning. This is particularly true of signs of measurement, as in YEAR (-Y-), CENT (-C-) or WEEK (-W-). Because some of these single letter signs are only clear in context, or because English mouthing is often used to make the meaning clear, some of these items appear only to be semi-lexicalised. An example of this is the use of -M- to mean 'month', 'metre' or sometimes 'minute'.

Other single letter signs appear to work as fully lexicalised signs in Auslan. In many of these fingerspelling signs, the movement is reduplicated. Examples of this include DAUGHTER (D-D), FATHER (F-F), MOTHER (M-M), KITCHEN (K-K), ALCOHOL (A-A), RATHER/PREFER (R-R), TOILET (T-T), VERY (V-V), PARRAMATTA (P-P), QUEENSLAND (Q-Q) and BRISBANE (B-B). Some of these signs are fully nativised, and indistinguishable from core native signs (as also mentioned in Chapter 8, DAUGHTER is identical to a core native sign NEEDLE).

In some signs, a single letter is combined with a particular movement, as in ENGLAND, FRIDAY, MILLION, BILLION, GOLD and SILVER. In many of these cases, the movement seems to have no meaning of its own, and may simply have been added as a distinguishing feature. The recently coined sign for TELSTRA (a major telecommunications company in Australia) seems to be an additional example. Here the dominant 1 handshape in the fingerspelled -T- flicks open to a 5 handshape as it moves slightly down. There have been reports that this sign began as a combination of -T- plus STAR, based on an initial misunderstanding of the name. Now, however, the handshape change bears little relationship to the meaning of STAR and simply works to distinguish it from other fingerspelled forms based on the letter -T-, such as the sign TOILET.

Sometimes, however, the addition of movement to a fingerspelled form may reflect some aspect of Auslan grammar, as in the directional use of the -Q- and -A- in the indicating verbs QUESTION and ANSWER. In other cases, greater modifications may take place. The handshapes on both hands may become the same, so that the resulting sign is easier to produce, as in the signs AUNT and UNCLE.

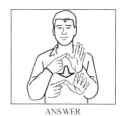

| FRIDAY | QUESTION | ANSWER |

Figure 6.12: *Signs with letter-movement combinations.*

In a small number of examples, it seems that the single letter has replaced the handshape of an Auslan sign with a related meaning, as in the signs FAMILY and CLASS from GROUP, or CHOCOLATE from LOLLY. There are also many examples of initialised signs which use one-handed fingerspelling handshapes but these are often signs borrowed from other signed languages (such as ASL) or from artificial sign systems (such as Australasian Signed English). In other signs, we see a manual letter compound with a sign, as in SUNDAY (-S-^PRAY) or GOD (-G-^UP).

| FAMILY | CLASS | SUNDAY | GOD |

Figure 6.13: *Signs involving initialisation and compounding.*

6.3.1.1.3   *Acronyms and abbreviations*

Fingerspelled acronyms (i.e., fingerspelling the initial letters, not the full word) are often used by Auslan signers. The wider English-speaking community may also use some of these acronyms, while some may only be known to members of the signing community. Acronyms may be signed while mouthing the individual letters, such as 'ay ess el' for A-S-L (American Sign Language), while others may be accompanied by the lip patterns of the words they represent. Widely used examples of acronyms would include: A-A-D for 'Australian Association of the Deaf', D-R-A for 'Deafness Resources Australia', N-A-B-S for 'National Auslan Booking Service', A-B-C and S-B-S for the television channels, N-S-W, W-A, S-A and T-A-S for the states, S-Y for 'Sydney', G-C for 'Gold Coast' and N-Z for 'New Zealand'.

Other English words are abbreviated. Once again, these may be similar to familiar abbreviations in English (e.g., the names of the months of the year or days of the week) or they may be forms only used in the signing community. Examples include MONDAY (M-O-N), TUESDAY (T-U-E-S or simply T-T),

SATURDAY (S-A-T), JANUARY (J-A-N), FEBRUARY (F-E-B), DECEMBER (D-E-C) and ADVERTISEMENT (A-D-V). Other abbreviations are those more commonly seen in print than heard in spoken English, such as E-G which is regularly used by signers to mean 'example' or 'for example'.

Many of these abbreviations are modified in particular ways, so that they are easier to produce. WEDNESDAY is often simply W-D, not W-E-D, and THURSDAY (T-H) is sometimes signed with the Mid handshape (not the 1) contacting the subordinate palm for the -T-. For WOLLONGONG, the fingers of the 5 hand often do not fully form a -W-, but simply brush past each other before forming the -G-.

6.3.1.1.4   Whole English words

Not all fingerspelling in Auslan involves acronyms and abbreviations. A number of whole English words are regularly used in Auslan and in BSL without the loss of any letters (Sutton-Spence, 1995). Examples of these include words such as B-U-S, S-O-N, L-A-W, S-O-N, C-L-U-B and J-O-B (although the articulation of the medial vowels in these forms may often be considerably reduced). Other frequently used English function words have been borrowed into Auslan and BSL. Examples of these include S-O, I-F, O-R and N-O. Perhaps because of their frequent use, many are often partly or fully phonologically nativised. For many Auslan signers #HOW, #BUT and #ABOUT are fully lexicalised signs in which little of the original fingerspelled sequence remains. This is especially true of #FOR.

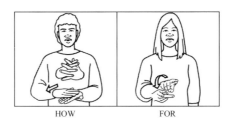

HOW   FOR

Figure 6.14: *Lexicalised signs derived from fingerspelling*

6.3.1.1.5   Local lexicalisation of fingerspelled forms

Lexicalised fingerspelling represents another example of the lexicalisation process discussed at the beginning of the chapter. Some forms come to act like core native signs. For example, as already noted, the longest monomorphemic signs in Auslan are generally disyllabic. Few monomorphemic signs have more than two movements (excluding transitional movements), or two changes in handshape, orientation, or location. As a result, fingerspelled signs like D-O and S-O tend to retain both elements, since the resulting form produces a relatively well-formed sign. Fingerspelled signs such as DECEMBER and WEDNESDAY are, however, formed from three or more letter signs. We have seen that some of the handshapes (particularly those for vowels) are usually dropped, or the number of parts tend to be reduced as they become more like Auslan signs. In fact, as Valli *et al.* (2005) pointed out, the process of lexicalisation actually operates on fingerspelling at all times, so that fully fingerspelled forms are often produced as increasingly reduced variants over the period of a single conversation. Signers will often fully fingerspell someone's name as they introduce them for the first time (e.g., D-A-V-I-D), but then the fingerspelling pattern quickly changes as the name is used over and over again in the conversation, with the medial -V- being reduced and the vowels almost disappearing (e.g., #DAVID). The changes that occur are examples of the process called *local lexicalisation* (Brentari, 1995b). In this process, a fully fingerspelled form becomes lexicalised for the duration of a single stretch of signed discourse. When the form appears for the first time, each letter is fully formed. Over successive productions, the form becomes 'temporarily' lexicalised for the rest of the exchange, achieving a stable form which more closely reflects the phonological constraints of the language.

6.3.1.2 *Loan translations*

Signers also borrow from English through a process called loan translation. Here, English words are translated literally into Auslan. This process is a highly productive one, creating signs that pass into the language without notice, such as SUPPORT^GROUP or SPORT^CAR 'sports car'. The use of some loan translations, however, has become controversial in the signing community, especially since deaf people have begun to teach their own language. An example of signs that cause contention might be the forms sometimes used for FEED^BACK, BACK^GROUND and BREAK^DOWN. Some signers translate these directly into Auslan, combining the signs for FEED and BACK, BACK and GROUND, BREAK and DOWN. This combination of the individual signs for BREAK^DOWN should be compared with the use of a single sign for BREAKDOWN which is not borrowed from English and which some signers prefer to use. Many consider loan translations unacceptable, since they use combinations of signs that reflect the grammatical and semantic patterning of English rather than those more typical of Auslan. There is no doubt, however, that loan translations such as these (and many others) are widely used in the signing community. It is also true that not all loan translations are considered unacceptable in this way. Many such signs, such as WORKSHOP and COPYRIGHT, are widely used by Auslan teachers. Other loan translations, such as the sign LOOK-AFTER, GIRLFRIEND or HIGH-SCHOOL are well established forms in the language. Many signs for place names are loan translations, such as BLACKTOWN (BLACK^TOWN), and others involve puns based on the sound or lip pattern of the English words, such as the sign name for the Sydney suburb LEICHHARDT (LIE^HARD). Many of these signs, even those originally coined as a joke, seem to be accepted by many members of the signing community.

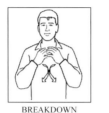
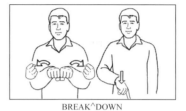

BREAKDOWN   BREAK^DOWN

Figure 6.15: *Example of a native sign and a loan translation.*

6.3.1.3 Mouthing

Most signers make some use of English or English-related mouth patterns while they sign and fingerspell. Mouthing must be distinguished from the use of particular mouth gestures described in Chapter 5 which appear to be unrelated to English words (Boyes-Braem & Sutton-Spence, 2001). Although the use of mouthing is widespread, it is clear that there is an enormous amount of variation from signer to signer, and that individual signers in different situations and with different conversational partners vary the amount and kind of mouthing that they use. It is thus difficult to say whether mouthing should be considered part of the formational structure of particular signs, or simply a result of contact between English and Auslan.

Research suggests that mouthing in signed languages occurs more often with noun signs than verbs (Schembri *et al.*, 2000), and more with core native signs than non-core (Engberg-Pedersen, 1993). It is not always clear, however, whether mouthing is an essential part of some core native signs, or simply an optional extra used in particular situations (thus, it has not been included in our diagram of the Auslan lexicon in Figure 6.1). For example, most Auslan signers use the same sign for 'husband' and 'wife', a sign we gloss as SPOUSE. Although the sex of one's spouse is usually quite clear in context, some signers will mouth the English word 'husband' or 'wife' while producing this sign. Sometimes this may simply involve forming some of the consonants on the lips, as in 'h-sb' and 'w-f'. British researchers point out that in mouthing, as in lexicalised fingerspelling, vowels are sometimes reduced and changes to the mouth shapes of the consonants can occur (Brennan, 1992). Some signers do not always produce mouthing of whole English words, apparently using this reduced mouthing simply as a means of distinguishing between the various meanings of a particular sign (see the discussion of polysemy in Chapter 8). Other signers may also use English mouthing as a means of explicitly extending the meaning of signs, so that the sign HAPPEN may co-occur with the mouthing of the English words 'opportunity' or 'event', or the sign DOCUMENT with 'story' or 'report'.

Mouthing often also co-occurs with fingerspelled items. It is frequently used in conjunction with fingerspelled abbreviations (see above), apparently to disambiguate the various meanings that may be associated with the one fingerspelled form. In the Sydney deaf community, the same form G-G is used by some signers to mean 'geography', 'generation', 'garage' and 'Gosford'. A similar form H-H is used for 'history', 'Hornsby' and 'Hurstville'. In each case, it appears that the accompanying mouth pattern may be used to ensure there is no misunderstanding, although once this meaning is established in a particular context, the mouthing may be dropped.

6.3.2 Borrowing from other signed languages

Auslan also regularly borrows from other signed languages, particularly ASL, and increasingly from IS. Greater opportunities for travel have naturally resulted in signed languages borrowing from each other (Brennan, 1992), and this has led to an growing trend to adopt other deaf communities' signs for their own place names (e.g., HONG-KONG, THAILAND, JAPAN, CANADA, AUSTRIA, SOUTH-AFRICA). As already noted, the ASL sign AMERICA has become widely known in Australia, replacing an older Auslan sign. In turn, some ASL signers now use the Auslan sign for AUSTRALIA, rather than the older American sign (Valli *et al.*, 2005). Similarly, increasing contact with deaf people in Britain has resulted in some BSL signs being introduced into Auslan. BSL signs for LONDON, WALES, DIAGNOSIS and DISABILITY, for example, are used by some signers. Recently, courses on linguistics at universities have begun to include deaf students for the first time. Deaf students, lecturers and interpreters have introduced BSL signs for terms such as LINGUISTICS (although the ASL sign is still more widely known), PHONOLOGY, MORPHOLOGY and ICONIC (Brien, 1992).

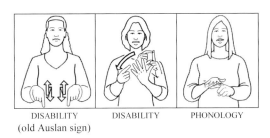

DISABILITY   DISABILITY   PHONOLOGY
(old Auslan sign)

Figure 6.16: *Some recent borrowings from BSL.*

The amount of borrowing from modern BSL, however, remains small compared with the number of ASL loan signs. Loan signs from ASL appear to have come from a number of sources. During the last few decades, a small number of influential members of the Australian deaf community were or are themselves of American origin, while others are Australian graduates of

Gallaudet University or the National Technical Institute for the Deaf in Rochester, New York. Many other Australian deaf people have worked or lived for periods in the USA or Canada. Partly for these reasons, many ASL signs (including signs originally from artificial sign systems used in American deaf education) have entered Auslan, such as COLLEGE, PHILOSOPHY, THEORY, MARKETING and INTERVIEW. This is particularly true of signs in the area of language teaching, such as CURRICULUM, SUBJECT, TEST, COURSE and EVALUATE. Some Australian deaf people are involved in American religious organisations where ASL signs, such as those for CHURCH, EVIL, LORD and MINISTRY, are used. The Australian Theatre of the Deaf has travelled considerably and established close links with American organisations. It is perhaps not surprising that the Auslan signs for STAGE, PRODUCTION and DIRECTOR have been borrowed or adapted from ASL.

Although greater contact between Americans and Australians has encouraged sign borrowing, there are other reasons for the large number of ASL loan signs in Auslan. The size and prestige of the American deaf community and the greater availability of materials on or in ASL have also played a role in this process. The signs used by many Auslan signers for INTERPRET, ORGANISATION, LANGUAGE, COMMUNITY, IDENTITY and CULTURE reflect the influence of the American deaf community on its much smaller Australian counterpart. In addition, educators of deaf children and sign language interpreters have sometimes introduced signs from ASL for technical terms where no widely accepted lexicalised Auslan sign existed.

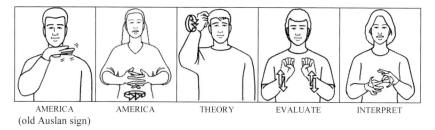

| AMERICA
(old Auslan sign) | AMERICA | THEORY | EVALUATE | INTERPRET |

Figure 6.17: Some recent borrowings from ASL.

Contact with ASL signers seems not only to have influenced the vocabulary of Auslan, but has also had some impact on the morphological system of the language. Some Auslan signers (particularly, it seems, from the northern dialect) now regularly use the ASL classifier handshape for vehicle, as shown in Figure 6.18, rather than the usual B handshape. Although this a recent phenomenon, its use has been documented amongst signers of different ages in the community (Schembri, 2001; de Beuzeville, 2006). Although a borrowing, there may be additional explanations for the use of this classifier. As we have seen, the B handshape plays a variety of roles in the classifier system, and the adoption of the ASL classifier handshape specifically for vehicles may reduce potential ambiguity.

Figure 6.18: *The ASL classifier handshape for vehicle.*

6.3.3 Non-native vocabulary and language attitudes

As Australian deaf people have become more aware of their language, many now strongly reject ASL signs that have been recently introduced into Auslan, especially if a sign for that concept already exists in the language. As with loan translations, however, there is no doubt that many signers in the community accept and use borrowed ASL signs. It is important to remember that all languages borrow from each other and that all languages change over time. Many American signs have become part of the language, and many signers use these signs without being aware of their origins.

It is interesting to note that the handshape of some ASL signs has been nativised by Auslan signers so that the sign more closely resembles a well-formed native sign. As we noted earlier, this happens only rarely, as most signs from other signed languages follow many of the same phonological constraints as Auslan signs. Nevertheless, some initialised signs, such as TEAM and THEORY, are usually produced by Auslan signers using handshapes which differ from those used in the ASL signs. Signers substitute the ASL manual letter T in these signs with an Irish T handshape. Just as *croissant* (French), *spaghetti* (Italian) and *kindergarten* (German) have been nativised and are now pronounced as if they were English words, so some ASL signs are produced by Australian signers as if they were Auslan signs.

6.4 Summary

In this chapter, we have discussed the Auslan lexicon. We have distinguished the lexicon of Auslan as including native signs that have developed within the language, and non-native signs that have developed as a result of language contact. We showed that the native signs may themselves be divided into two categories: core signs (i.e., lexicalised signs) and non-core signs (i.e., depicting and pointing signs). We discussed the various types of depicting signs, and looked at how they may become lexicalised signs. We then looked in detail at fingerspelling, loan translations and mouthing as part of the non-native lexicon, as well as borrowing from other signed languages. In the next chapter on Auslan syntax, we move on to discuss how signs from the lexicon are combined into the larger units we know as phrases, clauses and sentences.

6.5   Further Reading

Brentari (2001) is a collection of papers on signed language lexicons, although little of it is written at an introductory level. See Brennan (1990) and Liddell (2003) for more detailed explorations of depicting signs in BSL and ASL respectively, and Emmorey (2003) includes a range of other articles on these signs in different signed languages. Emmorey (2002) also provides an excellent discussion of different uses of space in signed languages. Battison (1978) is a classic study on fingerspelled loan signs in ASL, and Sutton-Spence's (1995) unpublished dissertation is the most complete account of fingerspelling in BSL (see Sutton-Spence & Woll, 1993, and Brennan, 2001, for published accounts).

7 Syntax: the structure of sentences in Auslan

The previous chapter examined the structure of the lexicon of Auslan. In this chapter, we discuss the syntax of Auslan. Syntax refers to the rules or conventions in a language that relate to the correct or acceptable ordering of words in a sentence. In English, for example, there is a syntactic rule that requires words such as *a* or *the* to precede a noun like *man* or *woman* in order to create phrases such as *the man* or *a woman*. Combinations such as *man the* are not acceptable phrase structures in English. Similarly, in Auslan, there conventionally accepted sign orders which we discuss below.

In contrast to descriptions of English syntax, however, the discussion of Auslan syntax in this chapter is very brief. There is also relatively more available information on the syntax of other signed languages, particularly ASL. Much of this research on ASL sentence structure, however, has been based on studies that elicit judgements about the acceptability of particular sentence structures from native signers (e.g., Neidle *et al.*, 2000; Sandler & Lillo-Martin, 2006). Recall from Chapter 2 that most signers, including native signers, live and communicate in a complex language contact situation. This makes acceptability judgements difficult to evaluate and researchers therefore need to take actual usage into account. However, research into usage requires a large amount of data (i.e., a *corpus*) to be collected, coded and analysed. Due to recent advancements in digital video and annotation technology (see Chapter 10), work of this kind has only recently begun in Australia (Johnston & Schembri, 2006), and thus a comprehensive account of Auslan syntax will only emerge in the future.

These qualifications understood, in this chapter we introduce word classes and then, after describing the basic sentence types, we describe some aspects of sentence structure in Auslan. We first look at simple clauses and then clause complexes. In simple constructions, we focus on the interaction between verb types (intransitive and transitive verbs, on the one hand, and plain, indicating and depicting verbs on the other) and sign order. A small number of other aspects of syntax, such as the use of negation, content questions topicalisation, pseudo-clefts and doubling are also discussed. In clause complexes, we briefly look at coordination and subordination, the latter with particular reference to conditionals and relative clauses.

7.1   Word classes in Auslan

Before we begin our discussion of sentence structure in Auslan, we need to understand the role played by specific categories of signs in sentences (i.e., whether they are acting as nouns, verbs, adjectives, etc.). These different categories of signs are called *word classes* or *lexical categories* (e.g., Finch, 2000). In spoken languages, they are often referred to as *parts of speech* (e.g., Fromkin *et al.*, 2005) but for obvious reasons, we will not use this term here.

Although the lexicon of Auslan has a large number of signs and fingerspelled items, each of these lexical items is not entirely unique in its form and function in the language. Lexical signs in Auslan may be grouped together into relatively few word classes based on shared meanings in the language and similar grammatical characteristics. The word classes described here are *nouns, verbs, adjectives, adverbs, determiners, auxiliary verbs, prepositions, conjunctions, pronouns* and *interjections*. Each class has a distinctive set of morphological properties (the relationship between the sign and the inflections that it can take) and syntactic properties (the relationship between the sign and other signs in a phrase or sentence). Many sign language researchers use both properties of a given sign to determine its lexical category. Note, however, that an individual sign may belong to more than one sign class, and thus may be able to act as a noun or a verb, for example (as we saw with the example of the sign WORK in Chapter 6). Terms such as *noun, verb, adjective,* etc. may thus sometimes refer to the role of the sign in a particular morphosyntactic context, not necessarily the sign itself outside that context.

Nouns, verbs, adjectives and adverbs each form an *open class*. This means that users of English or Auslan are able to create new words in each of these four categories. Determiners, auxiliary verbs, prepositions, conjunctions, pronouns and question signs each form a *closed class*. Ordinarily, users of English or Auslan cannot create new members of these categories.

The characteristics of the ten broad sign classes in Auslan are explained in the following section, defined both by their function (whether they refer to entities, for example, or actions) and their morphological and syntactic features (whether they can take specific sign modifications, for example). It is highly probable that further analysis or future investigations of Auslan grammar will make finer or different discriminations between the types of sign classes from those discussed here.

7.1.1 Nouns

Noun (or nominal) signs are used to refer to people (e.g., signs like MOTHER, fingerspelled names such as K-I-M) and other living creatures (e.g., CAT), places (e.g., SYDNEY) and concrete and abstract things (e.g., HOUSE, POLITICS).

Morphologically, English nouns may be recognised by the fact that most nouns signal plural by adding *-s* (*door* versus *doors*), but this is not true of nouns in Auslan. We saw in Chapter 5, for example, that only some nouns in

Auslan show plurality by being reduplicated in a series of different locations in the signing space. Thus, this is not a widespread morphological marker of plurality and cannot be used to recognise the class as a whole (unlike the plural suffix *-s* in English). Similarly, although we saw that some nouns may be distinguished from related verbs by differences in movement (having a characteristic repeated and/or restrained movement), this only applies to a relatively small subset of nouns.

Noun signs identify the *arguments* of a verb as well as *adjuncts* in a clause. A verb's arguments are the entities involved or affected by the action described by the verb. Adjuncts are non-arguments of the verb, such as nouns that represent a place in which the action described by the verb occurred. Some possible Auslan sentences including nouns are shown below. In (7.1), the noun WOMAN is the actor argument. The noun CAR is the undergoer argument in (7.2), and the noun SYDNEY is an adjunct.

(7.1) WOMAN   STAY
       N   V
       The woman stayed.

(7.2) WOMAN   BUY   CAR   D-A-R-W-I-N
       N   V   N   N
       The woman is buying a car in Darwin.

Syntactically, nouns in both English and Auslan can be identified by the fact that they occur in close relationships with two other lexical categories: determiners (POSS-1, SOME, etc.) and adjectives (OLD, NEW, CLEVER, etc.). In (7.3), the noun MAN is preceded by a pointing sign acting as a determiner (see the discussion on determiners in §7.1.5). In (7.4), the determiner MANY and the adjective BLACK (adjectives are discussed in §7.1.3) are used before the noun sign CAR (which is not marked morphologically for plurality). Determiners (including quantifiers like MANY, SOME, LOT and pointing signs, such as PT+mult, PT+exh) and number signs like THREE or FIVE-HUNDRED are the main ways Auslan signals information about more than one noun.

(7.3) PT+rt MAN   KNOW
       Det   N   V
       That man knows.

(7.4) MANY BLACK   CAR   DISAPPEAR
       Det   Adj   N   V
       Many black cars have disappeared.

7.1.2 Verbs

Verb signs describe an action or state (RUN, SLEEP, EAT, CHANGE, GROW, FEEL, etc.) and act as a *predicator* in a sentence. This means a verb may say (or *predicate*) something about the noun or nouns in a sentence. Verbs may act as a predicator for a single entity only, or for two or three entities. Note that in Auslan, adjectives (e.g., GREEN) and nouns (e.g., HOME) may also act as predicates as well as verbs, as we will see in §7.4.1 below, so this is not a unique characteristic of verbs in the language.

In (7.5), PLAY is a verb telling us something about the actor identified by the noun BOY. The sign PLAY here is acting as an *intransitive* verb. Intransitive verbs describe actions or states that only involve a single entity. In (7.6), LIKE is a *transitive* verb. Transitive verbs describe actions that involve two entities—an actor and an undergoer—which, in this example, are DOG and CAT respectively.

(7.5) BOY   PLAY
       N   V
       The boy is playing.

(7.6) DOG   LIKE   CAT
       N   V   N
       The dog likes the cat.

English verbs may be modified to show tense (*sing* vs. *sang*), aspect (*sing* vs. *singing*) as well as number and person (*he walks* vs. *they walk*). They can occur with auxiliary verbs (such as *will* or *may*) and may appear alone in a command (*Leave! Stop!*). As we saw in Chapter 5, verbs in Auslan may also be modified to show number (GIVE+dual, GIVE+exh, GIVE+mult), manner (DRIVE+carelessly) and aspect (GIVE+rept-slow).

As shown in examples (7.7) and (7.8), verb signs can also occur with auxiliary verb signs (such as WILL, CAN, SHOULD, CAN'T) and may appear alone in commands (as well as in many other sentence contexts). Example (7.9) shows a depicting sign that is often analysed as a sub-type of verb.

(7.7) WOMAN   SHOULD   LEAVE
       N   Aux   V
       The woman should leave.

(7.8) ____!
       FINISH
       V
       Stop it!

(7.9) MAN   CL:1-PERSON-APPROACH-ME
       N   V
       The man approached me.

7.1.3 Adjectives

Adjectives provide descriptive information about a person, place or thing referred to by a noun (e.g., SMALL, RED, FAT, OLD, etc.). This may include information about its size, quality, colour and type.

Syntactically, adjectives in English may occur before a noun (*the old woman*) or after a linking verb (*the woman is old*), such as *be, seem, become* or *look*. In English, many adjectives can also occur in comparative (e.g., *younger*) and superlative (e.g., *youngest*) forms that may be realised either morphologically (e.g. *tall, taller, tallest*) or syntactically (e.g., *beautiful, more beautiful, most beautiful*). In Auslan, adjectives may occur before or after a noun (e.g., BLUE CAR or CAR BLUE), as well as after some linking verbs, such as BECOME or LOOK (e.g., CAR LOOK NEW), as can be seen in examples (7.10) and (7.11). Note, that the *br* (brow raise) on the line above the glosses in (7.10) represents topicalisation (this is discussed in §7.4.6 below).

(7.10)
		br		
PT+rt	TALL+puff	WOMAN	POSS-1	TEACHER
Det	Adj	N	Det	N

As for the very tall woman, she's my teacher.

(7.11)
POSS-1	UNCLE	WORSE	OLD
Det	N	Adv	Adj

My uncle is older.

Many adjectival signs may also be modified for comparison by adverbial signs such as VERY, MORE, MOST or WORSE, as in (7.11), and may be modified to show intensification (the sign may be produced with an initial hold, then a rapid release), as described in Chapter 5.

7.1.4 Adverbs

Adverb signs modify the meaning of adjectives, verbs, other adverbs and entire sentences by describing manner, time and place (e.g., FAST, NOW, HERE). Many researchers also include intensifiers, such as VERY, BAD-LUCK and TRUE, and negatives, such as NOT, in the adverbial class, although these more closely resemble closed class rather than open class items.

A subset of adverbs in English are easily recognised by the ending *–ly* (e.g., *happily, quickly,* etc.), but many other adverbs do not take this ending (e.g., *well, westward,* etc.). There is no adverbial ending in Auslan and in many cases, identical signs may function as both adjectives and adverbs (e.g., SLOW, FAST, etc). In both English and Auslan sentences, adverbs often occur next to the adjective, verb, or adverb they are modifying, but sometimes adverbs may appear in many different places in a sentence, such as the beginning or the end if they are modifying the sentence as a whole. In Auslan, adverbs may be separate signs (e.g., NOW) or they may be modifications of signs (e.g., the intensification of the sign TALL in (7.10) above), or they may be non-manual features such as the 'th' mouth gesture described in Chapter 6 (and which accompanies the sign WRITE in (7.14) below).

(7.12) PT+lf JEANS VERY CHEAP
      Det N Adv Adj
      These jeans are really cheap.

(7.13) UNIVERSITY FINISH NEXT-WEEK
      N V Adv
      University finishes next week.

(7.14)   th
      MAN WRITE-CARELESSLY
      N V-Adv
      The man scribbled something down carelessly.

7.1.5 Determiners

Determiners provide information that helps to identify a noun, by specifying its location, quantity or possessor (e.g., PT+rt, PT-lf, OTHER, MANY, SOME, FEW, ALL, EACH, ENOUGH, MORE, MOST, LITTLE, LOT, ANY, BOTH, POSS-1, etc.). This helps to say how the noun relates to objects, events or concepts in the world (pointing signs used as determiners are discussed in Chapter 9).

In English, determiners (e.g., *a, the, this, some,* etc.) always occur before a noun. This is also the usual order in Auslan, as in (7.15) and (7.17), although some may also appear after a noun, as in (7.16).

(7.15) POSS-1 DAUGHTER SICK
      Det N Adj
      My daughter is sick.

(7.16) GIRL PT-lf FROM CANADA
      N Det Prep N
      That girl is from Canada.

(7.17) HAVE FEW M-A-C COMPUTER HERE
      V Det N N Adv
      There are not many Macintosh computers here.

7.1.6 Auxiliary verbs

Auxiliary verbs indicate information about the tense, aspect or mood of the main verb. Tense and aspect were discussed in Chapter 5. Mood refers to linguistic forms that express a speaker or signer's degree of commitment to a statement, as well as their attitude to and feelings about it. These may be used to express the extent to which a statement is believable, desirable or obligatory. They are also used when the speaker or signer wants the addressee to believe something, for example, or to commit to doing something. Auslan has the following auxiliaries: CAN, CAN'T, MAY, SHOULD, WILL, WON'T, FINISH, MUST and NEED.

In English, auxiliary verbs precede verbs (e.g., *he may go*) and invert with subject nouns and pronouns in questions (e.g., *may he go?*). They also show negation by combining with *n't* or *not*, as in *can't* or *cannot*. In Auslan, auxiliaries appear in similar positions in the sentence as English auxiliaries, but they may also appear at the ends of sentences, or may appear both before the main verb and at the end of the sentence, as in (7.18). There are also special negative forms of two auxiliaries (CAN'T and WON'T), although other main verbs also have special negative forms (such as NOT-WANT and NOT-KNOW).

(7.18)	WOMAN	CAN'T	UNDERSTAND	CAN'T
	N	Aux	V	Aux

The woman cannot understand at all.

7.1.7 Prepositions

Prepositions modify nouns, usually indicating direction and location in space as well as time. Auslan has lexical signs that can be glossed as ABOUT, AFTER, AROUND, BETWEEN, FOR, FROM, IN, NEAR, NEXT, ON, OPPOSITE, OUTSIDE, OVER, PAST, THROUGH, UNDER, UNTIL, WITH and WITHOUT. Some of these, however, may also act as verbs (e.g., IN may mean 'enter' or 'go into', and WITH can mean 'go with' or 'accompany').

In English, prepositions always appear before a noun (e.g., *in Japan*). The same is generally true in Auslan. Prepositions may, however, appear alone in other positions in the sentence, as in (7.20). It is possible that in this context, this sign might best be analysed as a verb (e.g., UNDER might be acting as a verb 'to be under' in this example).

(7.19)	FORGET	BUY	CAKE	FOR	POSS-1	BOSS
	V	V	N	Prep	Det	N

I forgot to buy a cake for my boss.

(7.20)	____br		
	TABLE	BALL	UNDER
	N	N	Prep

The ball is under the table.

Auslan actually appears to make far less use of prepositions than English. This is because direction and location can be shown by the placement of nominal signs in space, by the use of spatially modified verbs (especially depicting verbs) as in (7.59) and by use of the pointing sign 'PT' below.

(7.21) PRO-1 WORK PT+up+rt LAUNCESTON

I work (over there) in Launceston.

7.1.8 Conjunctions

Conjunctions link words and phrases (e.g., BUT, BEFORE, AFTER, UNTIL, OR, PLUS, THEN, NEXT, I-F, S-O, ANYWAY, BECAUSE, THROUGH (meaning 'because'), IN-CASE, IF, COINCIDENCE, etc.)

In English, conjunctions may occur between words, or between phrases and sentences. This is also true of Auslan. Some conjunctions in Auslan are borrowed from English and thus are fingerspelled (e.g., I-F, S-O) as in (7.22).

(7.22) _____ br

I-F	DAUGHTER	STILL	SICK	TOMORROW	GO	HOSPITAL
Conj	N	Adv	Adj	Adv	V	N

If my daughter is still ill tomorrow, we'll go to the hospital.

7.1.9 Pronouns

Pronouns stand for nouns (e.g. PRO-1, PRO-3, PRO-2+PL etc). In English, pronouns appear in the same positions in the sentence as nouns do, but some of the forms are different for subject roles (*I, he, she, we, they*) and object roles (*me, him, her, us, them*). There are different forms for first person (singular *I, me*; plural *we, us*), second person (singular and plural *you*), and third person (singular male *he, him*; singular female *she, her;* and plural *they, them*).

As we saw in Chapter 6, Auslan pronouns are most often pointing signs (e.g., the first-person singular sign PRO-1 – meaning 'I' or 'me' – is signed by a point to the chest). First-person forms point to the chest for singular and move in a circular manner near the chest for plural. These signs are relatively fixed in their location. Non-first person involves pointing in some other location. Usually, this involves pointing to the addressee for second person (the sign PRO-2 for 'you' is directed to wherever the addressee is located in space) and away from both the addressee and signer for third person (e.g., the sign PRO-3+pl meaning 'they' may be signed on the right or left of the signing space). The direction in which non-first-person pronouns point is thus not fixed, but is dependent on the context. Auslan pronouns do not have different forms to show actor and undergoer roles, but they may be modified to show differences in number (to signal 'you two', 'we three', etc.). Pronouns may occur before and after a verb. In fact, the order of pronominals (like the order of nouns) with regard to verbs is often used as one way to indicate actor and undergoer roles.

7.1.10 Interjections

Interjections are usually words that express strong feelings, such as surprise, anger, horror, or pain (e.g., HOW-DARE-YOU, INCREDIBLE, DAMN, SHIT, etc.). They are often used alone and thus do not always act as part of the sentence.

7.2   Sentences and their constituents

The core of most sentences is the verb. As we have seen, verbs act as a predicator in a sentence, because they say something about the arguments involved in the sentence (Van Valin & LaPolla, 1997). In (7.5), RUN is an intransitive verb telling us something about the actor GIRL. In (7.6), LIKE is a *transitive* verb. It relates to two arguments—an actor and an undergoer—which, in this example, are GIRL and MATHS respectively.

(7.23) GIRL   RUN
       N   V
       Subject   Predicate
       The girl is running.

(7.24) GIRL   LIKE   MATHS
       N   V   N
       Subject   Predicate
       The girl likes maths.

In these examples, the verb divides the sentence into two major parts (known as *constituents*): an entity and something that is said (or predicated) about it. These are traditionally known as the *subject* (which can be understood in the very general sense of 'subject or topic of discussion') and *predicate* (e.g., Lyons, 1968). In (7.24), the predicate itself consists of two parts—the verb LIKE and a second argument MATHS. Thus, verbs may have one argument (intransitive verbs), or two arguments (transitive verbs).

As we have seen in our discussion of sign classes earlier in this chapter, signs from the different classes tend to combine together in certain ways in particular types of constructions and these characteristics, together with potential morphological markings and semantic criteria, help us identify these classes. We have seen that determiners, for example, tend to occur before a noun (although some may occur after the noun) and do not just appear at random anywhere in a sentence. In other words, sentences are not simply combinations of one sign after another, as the simple examples given above may imply. Sentences may also be divided into smaller groups of signs, or phrases, which themselves form the constituents of a larger whole—the sentence.

If we look at (7.25), we can see that the subject and the predicate consist of two groups of signs.

(7.25) [PT+rt GIRL]   [LOOK-FOR POSS-2 CAT]
      Subject   Predicate
      That girl is looking for your cat.

The subject here is a *noun phrase* (NP). The pointing sign PT+rt is a determiner here that identifies the referent of the sign GIRL. It occurs before GIRL here, forming a unit with the noun. The noun phrase could have more signs within it, or it could consist only of a noun or pronoun. We could add an adjective, for example, as in (7.26).

(7.26) [PT+rt TALL GIRL]   [LOOK-FOR POSS-2 CAT]
      Subject   Predicate
      That tall girl is looking for your cat.

We know that a noun phrase acts like a unit because (whether it consists of just a noun or a noun together with determiners and adjectives, for example) it can be replaced by other signs, such as PRO-3 meaning 'she', or the sign WHO, as in (7.27) and (7.28) (note that the use of the furrowed brow non-manual feature in (7.28) is explained in §7.3 below). In response to this question, a signer can use the noun phrase alone as an answer, as in (7.28).

(7.27) [PRO-3] [LOOK-FOR POSS-2 CAT]
      She is looking for your cat.

(7.28) a.   ‾‾‾‾‾‾‾‾‾‾‾‾‾‾‾‾‾‾‾ bf
          [WHO] [LOOK-FOR POSS-2 CAT]
          Who is looking for your cat?
     b.   [PT+rt TALL GIRL]
          The tall girl.

We know that the predicate in (7.25) is also a unit because it can combine with the other units in (7.27) and (7.28), and it can also stand alone, as we see in the answer (7.29)b to the question in (7.29)a. The predicate here is actually an example of another type of phrase: a *verb phrase* (VP). Verb phrases always contain a verb that may appear with other constituents.

(7.29) a.   ‾‾‾‾‾‾‾‾‾‾‾‾‾‾‾‾‾‾‾ bf
          [PT+rt TALL GIRL] [D-O WHAT]
          What is the tall girl doing?
     b.   [LOOK-FOR POSS-2 CAT]
          (She is) looking for your cat.

The verb phrase in (7.29)b includes a noun phrase embedded within it (i.e., [LOOK-FOR [POSS-2 CAT]]). Noun phrases can function as actor or undergoer in a sentence. In the example noun phrase, there is a possessive determiner (POSS-2) and a noun (CAT). This noun phrase can be replaced by the question word WHAT, as in (7.30)a, and can stand alone in the response in (7.30)b.

(7.30) a.
<u>   bf</u>
[PT+rt TALL GIRL] [LOOK-FOR WHAT]
What is the tall girl looking for?

    b.   [POSS-2 CAT]
Your cat.

We can represent the overall constituent structure of (7.26) in the tree diagram in Figure 7.1. The 'tree' here is actually upside down with the 'root' at the top of the diagram, and the 'branches' underneath. Each of the branches represents a constituent of the sentence.

The S at the top of the tree represents the largest constituent: the sentence. This sentence is then divided into the first noun phrase (NP_1) and the verb phrase (VP). These correspond to the subject and predicate discussed above. The VP then is further subdivided into the verb (V) and a second noun phrase (NP_2). Sentences in many languages can be represented by tree diagrams. This is a very common way of showing how words may be grouped into constituents, and how sentences can be analysed as having a hierarchical structure (for signed languages, see Neidle *et al.*, 2000; Sandler & Lillo-Martin, 2006).

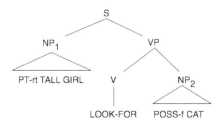

Figure 7.1: *Tree diagram of constituent order.*

7.3   Sentence types

In the examples above, we looked at the basic structure of sentences. Sentences have traditionally been categorised on the basis of their function, such as whether they are used to make statements or ask questions (Lyons, 1968). The type of sentence used to make a statement is known as a *declarative* (or *indicative*). Declarative sentences contrast with *interrogatives* (which are used to ask questions), *imperatives* (used to make orders, requests, etc.) and *exclamatives* (used to make an expression of shock, surprise, etc.). In order to understand the type of constituent order that is possible or typical of Auslan, we need to understand the types of sentences constituents can occur in, and the influence this can have on constituent order. We will briefly describe each of the four sentence types in turn here, beginning with the declarative because it is the most neutral type of sentence.

In English, a declarative sentence is usually made with the actor preceding the auxiliary and main verb, which may be followed by the undergoer (if the verb is transitive). A declarative is also usually produced with a falling intonation. In Auslan declaratives, the word order may be more varied (as we explain below) without any necessary non-manual marking. In both languages, declarative sentences work to provide information about some entity, as can be seen in the Auslan example and its English translation in (7.31).

(7.31) LEARN AUSLAN PRO-3
       She is learning Auslan.

Interrogative sentences in English and Auslan fall into two types: (a) *polar* questions and (b) *content* questions. Both types of interrogative sentences are used to ask questions, and are different in form from declaratives. Polar questions are also called *yes/no questions* because they are often answered by 'yes' or 'no', but they may be answered in other ways in Auslan (see (7.64) below). The term *wh-questions* is usually used for content questions because most content question words begin with 'wh' in English.

Polar questions in English may be produced with the noun phrase after the auxiliary verb, and/or with a rising intonation (the latter is often used alone in spoken English and is signalled in written English by the use of the question mark). In Auslan, the order of elements does not change (as can be seen in (7.32) below), but the sentence is often produced with a change in non-manual features. Polar questions are often signed with raised eyebrows (*br*) and the head tilted forward (*htf*) as in (7.32), and sometimes the last sign may be held.

(7.32) _____ br+htf
       LEARN AUSLAN PRO-3
       Is she learning Auslan?

Content questions involve the use of the Auslan signs WHERE, WHO, WHEN, WHAT, WHY, HOW, HOW-MANY, HOW-MUCH (traditionally used in reference to money only) and HOW-OLD. In English, content questions have the auxiliary verb preceding the noun phrase, and are produced with a falling intonation pattern. The order of signs does not necessarily change in Auslan, but (as we saw with polar questions) there may be a change in non-manual features, as in (7.33). Content questions are often produced with furrowed eyebrows (*bf*), with the head and the body perhaps tilting forward.

(7.33) _____ bf+htf
       LEARN WHAT PRO-3
       What is she learning?

Although it is most often the case that polar questions are signalled by raised eyebrows and content questions occur with furrowed eyebrows, these markings do not appear to be obligatory in Auslan, (nor for BSL, see Deuchar, 1984). Sometimes, a signer will produce a content question with little change in accompanying non-manual features (i.e., the facial expression may remain neutral). This may be because the context or the use of a question sign makes the request for information obvious. In some cases, polar questions may be accompanied by lowered brows, and content questions by raised brows. A polar question with lowered brows may signal that the signer is seeking more information than a simple yes/no response, while a content question with raised eyebrows may indicate that the signer is only seeking confirmation of some previously discussed information rather than additional content.

Imperatives are used for giving commands or making requests. In English, imperatives often occur without an actor noun phrase, and with various changes to intonation and stress depending on the mood of the speaker. In Auslan, the actor is often omitted as well, the signs may be produced with stress, and the non-manual signals may include direct eye gaze at the addressee and frowning (represented by the exclamation mark in (7.34) below).

(7.34) _____!
      LEARN AUSLAN
      Learn Auslan!

Exclamatives are usually used when the speaker or signer is reacting to something that has happened or that has been said. Usually, they express the excitement, pain, anger, surprise, shock or other strong feelings of the speaker or signer. Often, exclamations may consist of a single interjection, or they may be a whole sentence that has a structure similar to a declarative or interrogative sentence. Exclamatives are primarily signalled by changes in stress and intonation in English, and by stress and non-manual features in Auslan. The specific patterns of stress, intonation and non-manual features would depend on which emotion is felt, but the example in (7.35) shows an exclamation of surprise (represented by the *br!* symbols in Auslan and *?!* in English).

(7.35) _____br!
      LEARN WHAT PRO-3
      What is she learning?!

Having covered sign classes, constituent structure and sentence types, we will now examine the complex question of constituent order in Auslan in the next section. We will discuss simple sentences first, then turn our attention briefly to compound and complex sentences.

7.4   Constituent order in simple clauses

A clause is a group of words that includes a predicate, usually a verb. Often sentences are made up of a single clause. There appears to be an important relationship between verb type and the order of constituents in simple clauses in Auslan (Johnston, 1989a; Johnston *et al.*, in press). Different orders may be possible because indicating verbs, for example, can include information about actor and undergoer in their directionality, whereas plain verbs cannot. In the following sections, we will begin our discussion of constituent order in Auslan with clauses containing no verbs whatsoever ('verbless clauses'), and then examine intransitive and transitive plain verbs, followed by transitive indicating and depicting verbs (see Figure 5.25 for a summary of verb types in Auslan).

7.4.1   Verbless clauses

Auslan has no grammatical item that operates only as a linking word or *copula* (like *to be* in English) and it is thus possible to find constructions in Auslan in which two arguments are juxtaposed in a sentence that is essentially a verbless predication, as in these examples:

(7.36) WIFE   DENTIST
        N   N
        Carrier   Attribute
        The wife is a dentist.

(7.37)   ____hn
        POSS-1 FRIEND   DOCTOR
        N   N
        Carrier   Attribute
        My friend is a doctor.

(7.38) MAN   HOME
        N   N
        Carrier   Attribute
        The man is at home.

In these sentences, the entity about which the predication is made can be referred to as the *carrier* (the description *actor* is not appropriate here because there is no action and no verb). The carrier is placed first and is followed by the second lexical item, which we will refer to as the *attribute* (i.e., it is not an undergoer). The predicate may be accompanied by a head nod, as shown in (7.37), as has also been noted for ASL (Liddell, 1980), although this is not obligatory. This type of verbless predication is also frequently found when the second element is an adjective or adverb, rather than a noun, as in the following two examples:

(7.39) HOUSE   BIG
      N   Adj
      Carrier   Attribute
      The house is big.

(7.40) PT+rt CAR   HERE
      Det   N   Adv
      Carrier   Attribute
      This car is here.

7.4.2 Clauses with intransitive plain verbs

In clauses with intransitive plain verbs, the order of constituents most often appears to be the actor noun phrase before the verb phrase, as in examples (7.41) and (7.42). Note that the actor is a noun in the first case, and a pronoun in the second case.

(7.41) BABY CRY
      A   V
      The baby is crying.

(7.42) PRO-3 DANCE
      A   V
      She is dancing.

Often signers will include a pronoun that refers to the actor immediately at the end of the sentence, as in (7.43) and (7.44). This is known in the literature as *pronoun copy,* and has also been reported in ASL and other signed languages (Liddell, 1980; Bos, 1995). This repetition of the pronoun might be analysed as an example of a *sentence-final tag,* as explained in §7.4.5.

(7.43) BABY   CRY   PRO-3
      A   V   A
      The baby is crying, she is.

(7.44) PRO-3   DANCE   PRO-3
      A   V   A
      She is dancing, she is.

Some signers suggest that pronoun copy is most often used for emphasis, but it may also occur in other contexts where the signer is not being particularly emphatic, as in (7.46).

(7.45) PRO-1 MUST LEAVE   NOW   PRO-1
      A   Aux   V   Adv   A
      I have to leave immediately.

It is also common to find the verb followed by the actor noun phrase when the actor is a pronoun. Some researchers have suggested that this is actually a form of pronoun copy in which the first mention of the noun phrase has been omitted (Neidle *et al.*, 2000).

(7.46) DANCE PRO-3
      V   A
      She is dancing.

The pronoun copy in the examples above may be produced along with a head nod (represented by the abbreviation *hn*) and such a form is certainly more emphatic, as in (7.47). It has been claimed that the head nod is obligatory with this type of pronoun copy in ASL (Liddell, 1980). This does not appear to be true for Auslan. Even without the head nod, a constituent order like that in (7.47) would be clear in context, especially when the identity or location of the actor had been introduced earlier.

(7.47)   <u>   hn   </u>
      DANCE   PRO-3
      V   A
      She is dancing.

7.4.3 Clauses with transitive plain verbs

In clauses with transitive plain verbs, there are necessarily two arguments. Thus, the relationship of each noun phrase with the verb needs to be made explicit. This is because, unlike indicating verbs, plain verbs cannot be modified spatially to include information about the actor and undergoer. Instead, each may be represented by separate explicit noun phrases (e.g., noun or pronoun signs). A frequent order appears to be actor-verb-undergoer as in (7.48) and (7.49). Clauses with transitive plain verbs may also have pronoun copy, effectively adding a final constituent to produce the order in (7.50).

(7.48) WOMAN   KNOW MAN
      A   V   U
      The woman knows the man.

(7.49) CAT   LOVE DOG
      A   V   U
      The cat loves the dog.

(7.50) WOMAN   BUY   CAR   PRO-3
      A   V   U   A
      The woman is buying a car, she is.

The clause may not necessarily start with an actor (perhaps because it has been previously stated), as in (7.51), but a pronoun may nevertheless occur at the end. Again, a head nod may accompany the pronoun, but this non-manual signal does not appear to be obligatory in this context.

(7.51) <u>   hn   </u>
BUY   CAR   PRO-3
V   U   A
She is buying a car.

Verb final order also appears possible in sentences with transitive plain verbs. This may be especially the case when the roles of arguments are not reversible (i.e., when world knowledge means that one noun must be the actor and the other the undergoer), as in (7.52), but this issue has not yet been the focus of any corpus-based research (Fischer, 1975, made a similar observation for ASL). This pattern is also common if the verb is modified for aspect or number (Liddell, 1980) as in (7.53), although the reason for this is not clear.

(7.52) BOY CAKE EAT
The boy eats cake.

(7.53) GIRL HOUSE PAINT+rept-slow
The girl was painting the house for ages.

7.4.4 Clauses with indicating and depicting verbs

Clauses with indicating verbs seem to work a little differently from those with plain verbs because information about the actor and undergoer is represented by the directional modifications of the signs themselves. As a result, the constituent order may be freer, as also suggested for other signed languages (e.g., Fischer, 1975). Clauses in which no explicit mention of actor and undergoer is made are common (see §7.4.6 below).

Despite the fact that the directionality of the verbs marks who is doing what to whom, it is possible for separate noun phrases to appear, especially for emphasis, or if the actor or undergoer is not clear in the context. Thus, though the initial actor location is incorporated into the starting point and directionality of the sign HELP in (7.54), the pronoun is still explicitly signed before the verb to emphasise or clarify the actor.

(7.54) PRO-2 f+HELP+c
A   (A+)V(+U)
You *help me.*

Once again, pronoun copy is also possible with indicating verbs, as in (7.55).

(7.55) FINISH lf+GIVE+c   PRO-3
(Aux) (A+)V(+U)   A
(He) gave it to me, he did.

In cases where the actor and undergoer are actually introduced in the same sentence as the indicating verb, the constituent order is often actor-verb-undergoer, but may also be actor-undergoer-verb. Some native signers also accept undergoer-actor-verb in this context (Johnston, 1989a), but such constructions may be relatively rare. (This needs to be the focus of corpus-based research.) The clause-final verb is unambiguous because the indicating verb is able to move between locations in the signing space that are associated with the actor and undergoer. In some cases, a signer may chose to introduce these first, so that the verb is then articulated with reference to their locations in the signing space, as in (7.56). In such cases, the relative ordering of actor and undergoer appears less important. This is because the direction of the verb indicates who did what to whom (although, as we have seen, there may be a preference for the actor noun phrase to occur first in the sentence).

(7.56) DOG PT+rt   CAT PT+lf   rt+BITE+lf
      A   U   (A+)V(+U)
     The dog bites the cat.

Single indicating verbs that are only able to show the undergoer of the action (because they have a fixed beginning or end location, see Chapter 5) may be more likely to appear with a pronoun in contexts where the actor is not clear. In (7.57), for example, the actor is represented by a separate pronominal pointing sign because it cannot be incorporated into the form of the sign itself.

(7.57) PRO-3 THANK+rt
     A   V(+U)
     She thanks you.

In indicating verbs in which the modification is essentially locative in meaning, there may also be a verb final constituent order, as shown in (7.58) below.

(7.58) PRO-1 BOOK lf+PUT+rt
     A   U   (left+)V(+right)
     I moved the book from left to right.

Verb-final orders are also common in clauses containing depicting verbs of motion and location (Johnston *et al.*, in press), although here the actor may immediately precede the verb, as in (7.59) below.

(7.59) sh   CL:B-table-surface
     2h   TABLE
     dh   BOY   CL:2-human-jump-off
         Ground   Figure   Motion Event
     The boy jumped off the table.

The constituent order with depicting verbs of motion and location, as in (7.60), appears to reflect general cognitive principles in which the backgrounded, non-moving object (the *ground*) is produced first so that the foregrounded, moving object (the *figure*) may be described in relation to it (Talmy, 1985).

7.4.5 Sentence-final tags and doubling

Doubling of some constituents occurs often in Auslan. This involves the repetition of some material from the main part of the sentence. We have already seen that pronoun copy (which involves repetition of the actor) is one example. The repetition of the auxiliary is another common structure, as shown in (7.60). Like pronoun copy, the auxiliary may co-occur with a head nod, as in (7.61), but it does not appear that this non-manual feature is obligatory.

(7.60) ALL STUDENT CAN GO CAN
      All the students can go, they can.

(7.61) <u> hn </u>
      WOMAN WILL GO PARTY   WILL
      The woman will go to the party, she will.

As with actor pronouns, the auxiliary or question sign may also occur clause finally, producing sentence structures like those in (7.62).

(7.62) LEAVE TOMORROW WILL
      (I will) leave tomorrow, I will.

Like pronoun copy, these constructions are analysed by Neidle *et al.* (2000) as examples of sentence-final tags that repeat some other element of the clause, but the first element itself has been deleted. This analysis is motivated by a claim that there is a basic constituent order in ASL, and that all other possible orders represent clauses in which underlying elements are deleted or moved to another part of the sentence. It is not clear that this is the best analysis of these phenomena, however, for Auslan, or even for ASL, for two reasons. First, it is not clear if processes of deletion or movement need to apply to produce the different word orders we see in Auslan. Some linguists propose that a language user's mental grammar includes an inventory of different sentence structures as templates, with different sentence structures being used in different contexts (e.g., Van Valin & LaPolla, 1997). (We do not have sufficient space to explore this idea in more detail here, but we discuss differences of theoretical perspective on language in Chapter 10.) Second, sentence-final tags in spoken languages are usually set off from the main clause by a pause or by a change in intonation. Thus the example in (7.61), with its change in non-manual features, might qualify as a tag, but the others above do not (cf. Sandler & Lillo-Martin, 2006).

7.4.6 Ellipsis

Omitting a part of a sentence when it is understood from the context is known as *ellipsis*. Ellipsis is very common in Auslan (and in many other signed languages), and, in fact, may represent the normal way to create sentences in the language (unlike what may be found in many of the de-contextualised examples given in this book). A recent study by Wulf *et al.* (2002) on pronoun deletion in ASL narratives, for example, found that 65 per cent of plain verbs occurred without a noun or pronoun representing the actor (related work currently being undertaken suggests that this is also true for Auslan, see Schembri & Johnston, 2006). In all the rest, the pronoun marking for the actor was omitted because it was clear from the context (we will discuss this in Chapter 9).

With intransitive plain verbs, for example, if the actor is already known from the context, the clause with the plain verb may be produced simply with the verb on its own, as with CRY in (7.63).

(7.63) LAST-NIGHT BABY SICK. CRY+rept-slow. PRO-1 SLEEP NOTHING
Last night, the baby was sick. She cried and cried. I didn't sleep at all.

As with intransitive plain verbs, ellipsis is very common if the context makes the arguments of a transitive plain verb clear. In the dialogue in (7.64), for example, the actor is omitted in the interrogative sentence, and both the actor and undergoer are not produced in the declarative response.

(7.64) a. <u>   br </u>
         WANT TEA
         Do you want tea?
    b.   WANT
         Yes, I do.

As mentioned above, the ellipsis of actor and undergoer noun phrases may be much more common with indicating verbs because information about the actor and undergoer is represented by the directional modifications of the signs themselves. Thus the example in (7.65) would be equivalent to an entire sentence in English 'You blame me' (or 'second-person-actor-BLAME-first-person-undergoer'), although it consists only of a single sign.

(7.65) f+BLAME+c
You blame me.

7.5   Content questions

As has been reported by all ASL researchers (Sandler & Lillo-Martin, 2006), content question signs in Auslan may appear in the same positions in the clause as the constituents that they represent. Thus the question about the actor in (7.66) is produced with a clause-initial WHO, while the question about the undergoer in (7.67) has a clause-final WHAT.

(7.66)   bf

      WHO KNOW P-A-T

      Who knows Pat?

(7.67)   bf

      K-I-M EAT WHAT

      What does Kim eat?

Clause-initial question words asking about the undergoer also appear to be acceptable.

(7.68)   bf

      WHAT K-I-M EAT

      What does Kim eat?

Another example of a doubling structure in Auslan is the tendency for content question signs to appear at both the beginning and end of the sentence, as in (7.69). Like other types of doubling, this construction is so frequent that it is not necessarily only used for emphasis.

(7.69)   br

      WHAT SAY WHAT

      What did you say?

7.6   Topicalisation

Topicalisation refers to a process in Auslan for highlighting which constituent of a sentence represents the topic (the part of the sentence which the signer wants to make prominent or important—see Chapter 9 for more discussion). Many parts of the sentence can act as a topic.

In Auslan, as is also true of other signed languages, the constituent which is the topic of the sentence can be signalled by a change in non-manual features, a brief pause after the topic, or a combination of both (Liddell, 1980; Sutton-Spence & Woll, 1999). It is not clear if the non-manual features are obligatory to mark topicalisation—a brief pause before the rest of the sentence may be the only signal in some cases (cf. Sandler & Lillo-Martin, 2006, for ASL and Israeli Sign Language). The non-manual features associated with topicalisation include a brow raise (*br*) and a backwards head tilt (*htb*). We can see this in (7.70), where the actor has been topicalised.

(7.70)   br+htb

      POSS-1 DOG   HATE   POSS-2 CAT

      A   V   U

      My dog hates your cat.

Example (7.70) displays the typical order found in clauses with transitive plain verbs. Topicalisation, however, makes other word orders possible with plain verbs. The undergoer, for example, can be placed initially and marked as a topic, as shown in (7.71).

(7.71)
```
            br
POSS-2 CAT   POSS-1 DOG   HATE
U            A            V
```
As for your cat, my dog hates it.

It is possible for the entire verb phrase to be topicalised as in (7.72), although this is quite a rare sentence structure.

(7.72)
```
               br
HATE POSS-2 CAT    POSS-1 DOG
```
He hates your cat, my dog does.

As in ASL (Neidle *et al.*, 2000), Auslan can have topics which are neither the actor, the undergoer nor the verb, and are external to the main part of the sentence, as in (7.73).

(7.73)
```
                  br
ICE-CREAM FLAVOUR, PRO-1 PREFER BANANA
```
As for ice cream flavours, I prefer banana.

Questions may also be asked about topicalised constituents. Note that there is a change in the non-manual markings in (7.74) below, with brow raise over the topic and a furrowed brow over the polar question (this question also shows doubling).

(7.74)
```
   br                              bf
V-E-G   WHO NOT-WANT MUSHROOM WHO
```
As for vegetables, who doesn't want mushrooms?

7.7   Pseudo-clefts (or 'rhetorical questions')

A structure similar to topicalisation found in Auslan and ASL has been called a *pseudo-cleft* by some researchers (Wilbur, 1994a) or a 'rhetorical question' by others (Baker & Cokely, 1980).

In order to understand the term *pseudo-cleft*, we need to understand *cleft sentences*. A cleft sentence in English is a complex sentence in which one part serves to bring another part of the structure into focus as new information, as we see in (7.75).

(7.75) a. I really want to buy the linguistics book.

b. It is the linguistics book that I really want to buy.

If we compare these two sentences, we see that the meaning in both structures is similar, but that the second structure brings part of the information in the sentence (i.e., 'the linguistics book') into focus. This is called a cleft because the sentence actually is broken up into two sentences (i.e., 'it is the linguistics book' and 'I really want to buy') joined by 'that'. A pseudo-cleft is similar to a cleft structure, but it uses a question word, and does not look as clearly like two sentences joined together, as in the following English example.

(7.76) What I really want to buy is the linguistics book.

A similar structure appears in the following Auslan sentences.

(7.77) _____ br+htb
       PRO-1 LIKE WHO K-I-M
       Who I like is Kim.

(7.78)   br+htb _____ hn
       WOMAN PAINT WHAT OLD CHAIR
       What the woman painted was the old chair.

The first part of these sentences is similar to a content 'question' in its use of a question word, while the second part is composed of an 'answer'. The non-manual signals associated with this structure are the same as those for topicalisation (i.e., raised eyebrows and a backwards head tilt), and thus are different from what is often found in content questions. There may also be a slight pause after the question word, and the remainder of the phrase may be accompanied by a head nod. The non-manual signals may spread over the entire first part of the sentence as in (7.77), or may simply occur over the question word as in (7.78).

The similarity to the Auslan structures and the English pseudo-cleft is clear. Wilbur (1994a) pointed out the presence of the question word in both structures and has argued that, despite looking like a question and an answer, the resulting structure is a single sentence. It is thus best described as a pseudo-cleft. The term *rhetorical question* is inappropriate because this structure is actually neither rhetorical nor a question, but serves to bring the new information in the sentence into focus, as we shall see in Chapter 9.

7.8 Negation and affirmation

A sentence or phrase may be negated in Auslan by shaking the head from side to side while the sentence is being signed, as in (7.79) (the headshake is represented here by the abbreviation *hs*). Other non-manual signals may accompany this headshake, such as frowning, squinting or pouting.

(7.79) _____ hs
       PRO-1 LIKE TOMATO
       I do not like tomato.

The non-manual marking may accompany the predicate, rather than the entire sentence, as we see in (7.80) below.

(7.80)
　　　　　　　　　hs
　　　　PRO-1 LIKE TOMATO
　　　　I do not like tomato.

A manual sign of negation (or *negator*) may be added to the sentence in addition to the non-manual features, as in (7.81). Auslan uses two related forms to negate sentences: the signs NOT and NOTHING. These signs may occur before the verb, but NOTHING more frequently occurs after it, as in (7.82).

(7.81)　　　　　　　　　hs
　　　　PRO-1 NOT MARRY
　　　　I am not married.

(7.82)　　　　　　　　　　hs
　　　　PRO-2 LAUGH NOTHING
　　　　You did not laugh.

Auslan also includes other negators, such as NOT-YET and NEVER which may appear in the same sentence positions as NOT and NOTHING, as shown in (7.83). A number of signs have special negative forms, such as CAN'T, WON'T, NOT-HAVE (as in (7.84)), and NOT-KNOW, as has already been discussed in Chapter 5.

(7.83)　　　　　　　　　　　　hs
　　　　POSS-2 BROTHER NOT-YET ARRIVE
　　　　Your brother has not arrived yet.

(7.84)
　　　　　　　　hs
　　　　TEACHER NOT-HAVE
　　　　The teacher is not here.

Sometimes in response to a negated statement, a signer can respond by asserting the truth of what is being stated. This is *affirmation*, and it is signalled by accompanying the statement with a series of rapid head nods. In response to (7.84) above, a signer may produce a structure as in (7.85). Note that the nodding spreads over the entire sentence in just the same way as the negative headshake.

(7.85)　　　　　　　　　hn
　　　　POSS-1 BROTHER ARRIVE
　　　　*My brother **has** arrived.*

7.9　　Constituent order in clause complexes

In the sections above, we have only considered examples of sentences made up of a single *clause*. Sentences may, however, be composed of one or more clauses, as we will see in the following sections. These are known as clause complexes.

7.10   Coordination and subordination

In clause complexes, grammarians have long recognised that the relationship between clauses can either be one of *coordination* or *subordination* (Lyons, 1968). Co-ordination refers to a relationship between clauses in which they have an equal status, whereas subordination refers to relationships in which clauses may be *subordinate* in some way to a *main clause*.

In (7.86) below, we have an example of a simple sentence, while in (7.87) and (7.88) we see other types of sentences. The sentence in (7.86) is a simple sentence because it is main clause standing alone. It is not part of any other clause.

(7.86) K-I-M LIKE CAT
        Kim likes cats.

(7.87) K-I-M LIKE CAT BUT P-A-T PREFER DOG
        Kim likes cats but Pat prefers dogs.

(7.87) is an example of a *compound sentence* because it has two main clauses joined by the conjunction BUT. We can see that the two clauses are equal in status because we can reverse their order as in (P-A-T PREFER DOG BUT K-I-M LIKE CAT), and this does not change their meaning. The example in (7.88), however, is a *complex sentence* containing a main clause (the first clause) and a subordinate clause (the second clause).

(7.88) PRO-1 THINK P-A-T PREFER DOG
        I think that Pat prefers dogs.

The second clause is subordinate because it is acting as the second argument of the verb THINK. The second argument slot inside the verb phrase is filled by a clause rather than a noun phrase (i.e., the sentence has the same structure as PT+rt TALL GIRL LOOK-FOR POSS-2 CAT in Figure 7.1). This is shown by the tree diagram in Figure 7.2.

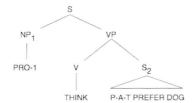

Figure 7.2: *Tree diagram of complex sentence.*

7.10.1 Conditionals

Conditional sentences involve another type of subordination in Auslan. These sentences are made up of a main clause that describes a possible event or state, and a subordinate clause that describes the conditions required for that event or state to come about. An example of a conditional structure is shown in (7.89). The first clause is subordinate clause. It may be marked by non-manual features (raised eyebrows, and a backwards head tilt) that are similar to those seen in topicalisation. The conditional clause in this example does not begin with a conjunction, but signers may also add a fingerspelled I-F or use the sign IF to indicate a conditional clause as well, as in (7.90). The main clause is a statement in (7.89), but it is a content question in (7.90).

(7.89)   _____br+htb

HOT TOMORROW   PRO-1 GO-TO BEACH

If it is hot tomorrow, I will go to the beach.

(7.90)   _____br+htb   _____bf

I-F WIN L-O-T-T-O   WHAT D-O PRO-2

If you won Lotto, what would you do?

7.10.2 Relative clauses

Relative clauses are another kind of subordinate clause. They may be either *restrictive* or *non-restrictive*, but we will discuss restrictive relative clauses first.

    Restrictive relative clauses are found inside a noun phrase. They work to modify the noun in some way by providing some additional information which enables the addressee to identify the referent, as we can see in (7.91). The entire noun phrase is marked by non-manual features which resemble those found in topicalisation (raised eyebrows, and a backwards head tilt). The clause LOOK SAME POSS-1 MOTHER is the relative clause inside the noun phrase.

(7.91)   _____br+htb

TODAY NEW TEACHER LOOK SAME POSS-1 MOTHER ARRIVE SCHOOL

The relief teacher who looks just like my mother came to school today.

    Unlike restrictive relative clauses, a non-restrictive relative clause is separated from the rest of the sentence by pauses and is not marked by any specific non-manual features, as shown in (7.92). They work to provide additional information about the referent which the signer assumes the addressee can easily identify.

(7.92)   _____br

TODAY NEW TEACHER, THINK FROM PERTH, ARRIVE SCHOOL

The new teacher, who I think is from Perth, came to school today.

7.11 Basic word order?

In summary, it appears that there are many possible constituent orders in Auslan sentences. The verb—the core element—may appear at the beginning, in the middle or at the end of a clause, as a result of a range of factors (including the potential for the verb to be modified in terms of its location and direction). In addition, some clauses in Auslan may actually be verbless. In most clauses, however, the pattern appears to be that the actor noun phrase of transitive and intransitive verbs is the first element, unless topicalisation occurs (Johnston *et al.*, in press). The only exception to this may be clauses with depicting verbs of motion and location in which the noun phrase representing the ground often precedes the figure noun phrase.

In verb-final clauses involving a transitive verb, the unmarked order of the two preceding arguments appears to place the actor before the undergoer. In all types of clauses, however, other orders are also possible which do not appear to be marked in any particular way. The most common example of this is the actor noun phrase in clause-final position when it is realised by a pointing pronoun sign. Although this frequently occurs as a copy of an initial actor noun phrase, it is also occurs even with no explicitly signed actor in the initial position.

When the order of signs is the only coding strategy used in Auslan (i.e., without exploiting space and direction), the common pattern with transitive verbs is actor-verb-undergoer. This order also appears to be a common order in clauses with transitive-indicating verbs (even if they are spatially modified), although this is less true of clauses with depicting verbs (Johnston *et al.*, in press). A predominantly actor-verb-undergoer pattern has been reported for ASL and BSL (Fischer, 1975; Brennan, 1992). Not only is this also one of the most common constituent orders in the world's languages (Comrie, 1989), it is also the order found in English. It is highly likely that this word order in Auslan is the result of influence from English (this may be why it is also found in other signed languages used in English-speaking countries), a point originally made by Fischer (1975) for ASL.

Spoken languages have been classified according to the way these elements are combined to form grammatical sentences. In these classifications, the terminology used usually refers to the actor as *subject* (S) and the undergoer as *object* (O) (we will see that these terms are not equivalent in Chapter 10, but this definition of subject and object will suffice for our purposes here). The most common way of combining subject (S), verb (V) and object (O) in a language is called the *basic word order*. There are six possible combinations–SOV, SVO, VSO, VOS, OVS and OSV. All have been documented in different spoken languages, but OVS, OSV and VOS are rare. The most frequent basic word orders in spoken languages are SVO, VSO and SOV (Comrie, 1989). Example (7.93) is from English (an

SVO language), while (7.94) is from Tongan (a VSO language) and (7.95) is from Guugu Yimidhirr, an Australian Aboriginal language (an SOV language) (Crowley *et al.*, 1995).

(7.93) The woman   drank the coffee
       S   V   O

(7.94) Na'e taipe   'e he tangata 'a e tohi
       typed   *the man*   *the letter*
       V   S   O
       The man typed the letter.

(7.95) Nyulu   nganhi   nhaadhi
       he   *me*   *saw*
       S   O   V
       He saw me.

However, many languages appear to have flexible or free word order. This is true of many Australian Aboriginal languages such as Dyirbal (Dixon, 1980), but this is also true of Latin (Crowley *et al.*, 1995). All the Latin sentences in (7.96) mean 'Mark likes the horse' (but reflect differences in information structure, see Chapter 9). This is possible because the suffix *–us* signals the subject of the verb, and *–um* marks the object.

(7.96) Marcus equum amat
       Equum Marcus amat
       Amat equum Marcus
       Marcus amat equum
       Equum amat Marcus
       Amat Marcus equum

As we have pointed out, Auslan appears to share some characteristics with SVO languages (undoubtedly, as a result of influences from English) but also with free word order languages (because sign order may be somewhat variable). However, it is difficult to say more about the 'basic word order' in Auslan, despite the fact that the actor-verb-undergoer constituent order is very common, for two reasons (cf. Mithun, 1992; Brennan, 1994b).

First, it is not clear that we can assume that declarative sentences with a transitive plain verb are in any sense 'basic' in the language, with all other patterns correctly interpreted as variations, modifications or transformations of a so-called 'basic word order'. As has already been mentioned, this is the approach taken by some ASL linguists (e.g., Neidle *et al.*, 2000), but it is not accepted by all researchers (e.g., Liddell, 2003). Clauses that contain only a verb are extremely common in signed languages, and research currently underway shows that ellipsis of noun phrases in Auslan representing actor arguments is frequent (Schembri & Johnston, 2006). This makes clauses in which transitive verbs appear alongside nouns representing both arguments appear more marked. Second, the grammatical roles of actor and undergoer in a language are not identical to the grammatical relations of subject and object (Palmer, 1994). It is not yet clear if we can say that Auslan, like English, has the grammatical relations of subject and object (see Chapter 10 for further discussion of the question of 'subject' and 'object' terminology in Auslan and signed language linguistics).

7.12   Summary

In this chapter, we have examined the structure of sentences in Auslan. We have introduced the notion of sign classes, shown how sentences are constructed out of smaller constituents, and how they fulfil different functions. We have discussed simple clauses of different types, as well as clause complexes, and ended with a discussion of the notion of basic word order in signed and spoken languages. In the next chapter on semantics, we will turn to a discussion of how signs and sentences in Auslan are used to create meaning.

7.13   Further Reading

Valli *et al.* (2005) cover many of the same topics presented here, but with a focus on ASL. Liddell (1980) is a classic text on the syntax of ASL, Sutton-Spence (1999) provide a very brief overview for BSL, and Brennan & Turner (1994) is collection of papers from a conference on word-order issues in signed languages. Neidle *et al.* (2000) and Sandler & Lillo-Martin (2006) present different accounts of ASL syntax from a generative perspective.

8 Semantics and pragmatics: sign meaning and sentence meaning

Semantics refers to the study of meaning in language (i.e., how words and sentences are used to convey particular meanings). But what is 'meaning'? How do we understand what the signs and sentences used in Auslan or other languages actually mean? Although most people may not be confused about what the word *meaning* refers to, providing a clear explanation of how language structure makes meaning is not an easy task. In fact, philosophers dating back to Aristotle and Plato have pondered the relationship between language, meaning and the world, and it is still an area in which there is much debate and diversity of ideas (Saeed, 1997). Understanding how language creates meaning is a highly complex task, because it needs to take into account all the different ways language structure is used to convey information. We shall look at some of the ways signed languages do this in this chapter, but we will begin by examining some of the misconceptions around the concept of meaning in language. We will then examine different types of meaning in Auslan signs, before moving on to look at iconicity. This is followed by a discussion of sentence meaning, and the chapter ends with an exploration of pragmatics (i.e., the study of meaning and context).

8.1.1 Auslan signs, English words and meaning

One very common misconception about the semantics of Auslan stems from a misunderstanding of the relationship between English and Auslan. We have already discussed this issue in some detail in Chapter 1, but we will revisit it briefly here. As already discussed, many people mistakenly believe that natural signed languages are artificial sign systems (i.e., signed codes for spoken languages). As a result, it is assumed that Auslan signs represent English words in the same way as writing does, and that they derive their meaning from the English words on which they are based (as represented in Figure 8.1).

Figure 8.1: *Incorrect representation of the relationship between referent, word and sign.*

As we have already explained, artificial sign systems and writing are secondary systems, while natural spoken and signed languages are primary systems of communication. Writing and artificial sign systems are the representation of spoken language in another medium, but natural signed languages are not simply representations of spoken language. It is appropriate to think of Auslan signs as having a direct relationship to their meaning in the same way as spoken words—they are not simply manually encoded words (Figure 8.2).

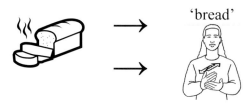

Figure 8.2: *Correct representation of the relationship between referent, word and sign.*

Of course, many signs do derive from English words, especially some of the examples of lexicalised fingerspelling we examined in Chapter 6. Many other signs are sometimes produced accompanied by English mouthing, and the meaning of other signs has undoubtedly been influenced by contact with the spoken language and culture of the surrounding community. But the influence of English on Auslan cannot account for the meaning of all signs in the language. One simple demonstration of this is that some signs in Auslan must be interpreted or translated into English by more than one word (see Figure 8.7). The reverse is also true—many English words do not have a single sign equivalent (recall the example of the word *light* in Figure 1.4). If signs were entirely based on the words of spoken languages, we would not expect to find such examples of lexical non-equivalence in the two languages.

It is clear then that signs do not derive their meaning entirely from English. How then do we understand the meaning of signs and sentences in Auslan? In the following sections, we shall consider some of the key misconceptions about meaning, drawing on a useful summary by Crabtree and Powers (1991).

8.1.2 Meaning and dictionaries

In our culture, many of us associate the meaning of a word with its dictionary definition. When we come across a lexical item that is unfamiliar, we consult a dictionary to find out what it means. If we are unsure about a word's spelling, pronunciation or its origin, we look to the dictionary as the source of this information. In playing word games, such as Scrabble, we use a dictionary as the ultimate authority about whether or not a word actually exists in our language. This creates an impression that the dictionary definition captures all that we need to know about a lexical item's meaning and use.

It is important to remember, however, that lexicographers create dictionaries by collecting information about how a word is used in a particular language community. In the case of signed languages, it is the community of signers that determines the meaning of a particular sign. The meaning of a sign listed in the dictionary reflects what signers use it to mean. A number of different dictionaries of Auslan are now available, and most of them attempt to record the meanings of signs used in the Australian deaf community. Thus, dictionaries and dictionary-makers do not determine the meaning of signs in Auslan, or words in English. The information they contain comes from the people who use these languages. But how do signers themselves understand how a sign is used in the community? How do they relate the form of the sign to its meaning?

8.1.3   Meaning and reference

We often think of the words of language as symbols that stand for actual people, places, things, events and states of affairs in the world around us. We use language to talk about things in the world, and we understand words because we know what their *referents* are (i.e., what they stand for). This aspect of a lexical item's meaning is known as *extension*. Furthermore, many signs in Auslan actually indicate their referent directly (e.g., EYE), or resemble some aspect of the referent (e.g., the bird's beak is suggested in BIRD), as we shall see in §8.5 below. Thus a sign's referent appears to be part of the sign's meaning in many lexical items in Auslan.

EYE   BIRD

Figure 8.3: *A referent shown directly (pointing to eye) or through resemblance (bird's beak).*

Reference does play an important role in meaning, but there is a problem with this notion as an explanation of the way all meaning works in signed and spoken languages—many words have referents that do not exist. There is nothing in the real world that the sign DRAGON or the words *tooth fairy* refer to, yet clearly both of these lexical items have meaning. This aspect of meaning is called *intension*—the meaning of these items relates to what they evoke in the mind of the language user, not to what they point to in the real world. Intension means that language can be used to tell stories that have no basis in fact (as in children's fairy tales, or in science fiction), so a theory of how language makes meaning must take this into account. In these examples, the meaning appears to come entirely from mental imagery—we can conceptualise referents for these lexical items, even though they do not exist in the real world.

8.1.4   Meaning and mental imagery

As we have seen, signed languages are visual-gesture languages in which the forms of signs often have some connection to their meaning. This is particularly true of depicting signs, but also of many lexicalised signs. Does the iconic nature of signed languages imply that the meaning of signs in Auslan is always derived from mental imagery? Does the use of a sign like TABLE create its meaning by causing a mental image to appear in the mind of the signer? Is this image somehow included in the meaning? Certainly, this may be partly true of this sign, and also of many other signs with concrete meanings (we discuss this point in §8.5 below). In fact, this may be why it appears that iconic signs are easier for adult second-language learners of signed languages to remember.

Although mental imagery does indeed have a significant role in signed languages, this cannot be the only way in which we understand the meaning of signs and sentences in Auslan. After all, people's mental imagery associated with signs and sentences may be different from one individual to the next. For example, the sign THEATRE may conjure up different conceptual imagery based on people's different experiences as a member of the audience, or as an actor on stage, or as someone working on the stage lighting. Despite all these different perspectives on the meaning of this lexical item, the way in which words are understood does not appear to vary a great deal from one person to the next. If mental imagery was the entire basis for meaning in language, it is difficult to understand how words could mean the same thing across an entire community of signers or speakers.

In addition to this problem, many words do not seem to be related to any particular kind of conceptual imagery. What mental imagery is associated with the sign SUPPOSE or the English word *must*? What image comes to mind when you see the sign IN-CASE, or read the word *if*? The meaning of these lexical items is quite abstract, so no concrete image appears to be linked to them (Figure 8.4, cf. BEACH and LIBRARY in Figure 1.5). Thus, mental imagery cannot fully explain how we use language to make meaning. Instead, the meaning of lexical items depends very much on their use in the appropriate linguistic context.

SUPPOSE IN-CASE

Figure 8.4: *Signs which do not evoke conceptual imagery.*

8.1.5 Meaning and truth

Thus far, we have concentrated on how words create meaning, but it is important to understand that words are rarely used on their own, so we need to consider also how phrases and sentences also make meaning. Although reference and conceptual imagery may not fully explain the semantics of individual words, perhaps the meaning of an entire sentence can be determined by understanding its referent in the real world. So, if a signer understands what the Auslan sentence in (8.1) means, perhaps this is because they know what it refers to.

(8.1)   <u>   br   </u>
         TODAY WORK PT+lf PRESIDENT A-A-D ARRIVE LATE
         The president of the Australian Association of the Deaf arrived late at
         work today.

Obviously, signers of Auslan would understand the meaning of the sentence in (8.1), but would they know what it refers to? Do they need to know who the president of the Australian Association of the Deaf (AAD) actually is, or what time he or she usually arrives at work? Do they need to know if the sentence in (8.1) is actually true? It should be clear that they do not need to know any of these things, so there is more to meaning than reference, even at sentence level.

But despite this, signers would need to understand exactly what this sentence would refer to if it **were** true. They would need to understand the conditions under which it could be true—the *truth conditions* of the sentence. This means that they understand that, for the sentence in (8.1) to be true, whoever actually is the president of AAD must have arrived at work later than his or her usual time today. Thus an explanation of the meaning of this sentence that includes both reference and truth conditions would go some way to explaining how it is meaningful, even to someone who does not know who it refers to or whether or not it is true.

Although it is easy to explain the truth conditions for a declarative sentence like (8.1), it is more difficult to specify them for an interrogative sentence, as in the following example:

(8.2)   <u>   br</u>
    TODAY A-A-D PRESIDENT ARRIVE LATE, RIGHT PRO-1
    The president of the Australian Association of the Deaf arrived late
    today, right?

We may not know whether this sentence is true or false and yet its meaning is clear, so there must be more to meaning than truth conditions, as we will see in the next section.

8.1.6 Meaning and language use

In addition to understanding the truth conditions of a sentence, we also need to understand something about how it used. So as well as knowing whether or not the sentence in (8.2) is true, we also need to know something about how its meaning relates to its function as a question. This is because language is not simply a way of communicating information about the world, it is also used as a means of making and maintaining contact with other people. Interrogatives have a different social function from declaratives, for example, and both are used in a different way to imperatives. Thus, in order to understand its meaning, we need to understand the social situation that must exist for a question like (8.2) to be used. *Pragmatics* is the study of the relation between language and its context of use, and this will also be explored in this chapter on semantics. Pragmatics is important because often an understanding of linguistic structure alone cannot account for all the meanings that we may convey when we use language.

8.2 Types of meaning

In the sections above, we have attempted to deal with some misconceptions about how language makes meaning. We have shown that making meaning is extremely complex, and cannot be explained by any simple assumptions about dictionary definitions, visual imagery, reference, truth conditions or language structure alone. In fact, all of these aspects play a role in how we use language to convey information about the world and communicate our feelings, ideas and intentions. In this section, we shall discuss three main types of meaning that have been identified by linguists, as summarised by John Lyons (1977). These types of meaning apply both to individual lexical items, as well as to sentences and stretches of discourse.

8.2.1 Descriptive meaning

Descriptive meaning refers to the use of language to describe people, things, events and states of affairs (it is also referred to as *propositional* or *referential* meaning). It is related to the notion of reference discussed in §8.1.3 above, and is typically the kind of meaning that is described in dictionaries. Thus, the descriptive meaning of a sign or sentence in Auslan conveys factual information about referents in the real world. As Lyons (1977) observed, descriptive meaning can be asserted, denied and objectively verified. Thus the descriptive meaning of the sign DEAF relates to its use as a sign that refers to people (or other living things) that cannot hear. This is either a verifiable fact about someone or it is not. In the sentence (8.3) below, we can see that the signer is asking if the teacher in the blue shirt is hearing or deaf.

(8.3)

	br		bf
TEACHER BLUE SHIRT PT+rt		DEAF HEARING WHICH	

Is the teacher in the blue shirt over there hearing or deaf?

This sign may have other types of meaning, however. The use of this sign may mean more than simply whether or not someone is hearing or not, as explained in the following section.

8.2.2 Social meaning

As well as being used to describe referents, events and states of affairs in the world, signs and sentences in Auslan may have social meaning. This refers to the fact that language can tell us something about the social characteristics of the signer and/or the addressee, or about the situation in which the language is being used (this is sometimes also called *evoked* or *interpersonal* meaning). For example, in sentence (8.3) above, the signer may have used the northern dialect sign BLUE or the southern dialect sign, depending on which region they live in or identify with. Thus the different forms of this sign can tell us something about the identity of the signer.

In this context, the signer who produced example (8.3) would have used the standard Auslan sign for DEAF (with the H handshape moving from ear to chin) because they are addressing the question to another signer who uses Auslan (the same sign would be used with a signer of BSL or NZSL). If they were communicating with a deaf person who used a signed language outside the BANZSL family (see Chapter 3), they might have used a sign in which a 1 handshape moved from ear to chin. When communicating with a hearing person who does not know any signed language (e.g., to let a hearing person know that the signer is deaf), a sign in which the B handshape touches the ear is commonly used. Thus, each of these forms has a different social meaning, providing us with information about the social characteristics of the addressee as well as the attitude of the signer to this individual.

8.2.3 Expressive meaning

Signs and sentences also have expressive meaning. In addition to descriptive and social meaning, language can convey something about the signer's feelings, attitudes or opinions (this is also known as *emotive* or *affective* meaning). Expressive meaning could be conveyed in Auslan by the choice of sign, the sentence structure or the non-manual features that accompany signing. In the reply to the question in (8.3) above, another signer produces a reply as in (8.4) below.

(8.4)

_____hn___

PT+rt TEACHER DEAF FLABBERGASTED EXCELLENT
The teacher is deaf! Wow, that's great

In the response above, the signs FLABBERGASTED and EXCELLENT reflect the expressive meaning of this sentence—the signer is clearly surprised and pleased that the teacher is deaf. The same response could have been included different signs, such as TERRIBLE or DISAPPOINT to signal that the signer was not pleased. The fact that different people may react differently to the same information and may use a sign like EXCELLENT in response to a range of different phenomena, shows that expressive meaning does not refer to a fact about the world, but to people's feelings and opinions about the world.

FLABBERGASTED   EXCELLENT

Figure 8.5: *Signs with expressive meaning.*

8.2.4 Denotation and connotation

Lyons (1977) pointed out that the terms *denotation* and *connotation* are sometimes used to refer to aspects of descriptive, social and expressive meaning. The descriptive meaning of a sign or sentence can also be referred to as its denotation, while social and affective meaning is also known as connotation. To illustrate the difference between denotation and connotation, we can return to the sign DEAF. As explained in §8.2.1 above, the denotation of the sign deaf is something like the following (from *The New Oxford Dictionary of English*, 1998:472): '**deaf**, *adjective,* lacking the power of hearing or having impaired hearing'. The sign in Auslan, however, has uses in the deaf community that reflect other, more positive connotations. Someone who is DEAF is not only a person who cannot hear, but also a person who uses a signed language and identifies with other deaf people. As such, phrases like VERY DEAF or TRUE DEAF applied to an individual may reflect the signer's positive feelings about that person's identification with the deaf community and use of signed language, as much as they do about the individual's audiological status. As a result, the sign DEAF in this context could even be applied to a hearing person if this individual's fluency in signed communication and degree of involvement in the deaf community were similar to that of a deaf person.

8.3   Sign, sentence and utterance meaning

In the following sections, we will examine aspects of meaning at the sign and sentence level. Although sign, sentence and utterance meaning are all inter-related, we will discuss each of these in turn, beginning with sign meaning.

8.4   Sign meaning

When discussing the meaning of signs, it is useful to make a distinction between *lexical meaning* and *grammatical meaning* (Matthews, 1997). Lexical meaning is primarily expressed in *content words* and grammatical meaning in *function words*. Content words include nouns, verbs, adjectives and adverbs. All content words, such as the signs CAT, RUN, YELLOW and QUICK, have descriptive meaning in that they refer to objects, events or states of affairs in the world. They may also have social and affective meanings. Function words, on the other hand, include determiners, prepositions and conjunctions. Many function words, such as the signs BUT and I-F, have no descriptive or expressive meaning at all, and appear to exist merely as part of particular grammatical constructions. Some function words, like IN or ON, do have some degree of descriptive meaning (i.e., they describe a spatial relationship between objects) and often may be used alone, but their meaning may sometimes be most clear at the phrase or sentence level and not at the level of the individual word (e.g., the meaning of the sign IN may be most clear in a phrase like CAT IN HOUSE PT+rt).

8.4.1   Reference and sense

In considering the meaning of words, it is also important to distinguish between two broad areas of lexical meaning: *reference* and *sense*, a distinction first proposed by Saussure (1983). We have already discussed reference above, and have seen that it reflects a sign's meaning based on its relationship to people, things, events and states of affairs in the world. Sense, on the other hand, stems from a word's relationship to other words. For example, if we return to our example of the sign DEAF, we have already established that it is used to refer to someone who cannot hear. We explained that its connotations in the deaf community, however, can also be positive because it also is used to refer to someone who identifies with the deaf community and communicates by means of a signed language. Part of this connotation comes from the sign's relationship to other signs and phrases in Auslan, such as ORAL, HEARING-IMPAIRED or HARD-OF-HEARING. These signs may all be used to refer to individuals who have some degree of deafness, but their use contrasts sharply with the sign DEAF in relation to indicating membership of the deaf community and use of a signed language—lexical items such as ORAL or HARD-OF-HEARING may sometimes be used for individuals outside the signing deaf community, and thus tend to have some negative connotations for signing deaf people. In some cases, people who are HEARING-IMPAIRED (i.e., have only a moderate degree of hearing impairment) may also be DEAF (i.e., members of the deaf community), but generally those who are ORAL (i.e., who use spoken language only) may not be considered DEAF at all.

In the following sections, we shall explore the notion of sense in Auslan, looking at *lexical relations*—that is, how the meanings of words are interrelated (Cruse, 1986). A number of different sense relationships between signs can exist in the lexicon: signs are organised into *lexical fields*, they can show *homonymy, polysemy, synonymy, antonymy, hyponymy* and *meronymy*.

8.4.2   Lexical fields

A lexical field is a group of signs and fingerspelled lexical items that are used to talk about a particular area of knowledge (such as the vocabulary used in linguistics or in medicine) or in a specific type of activity (such as playing football or cooking). Thus, the following signs would all be in the same lexical field (i.e., 'sport'): GOAL, COACH, FOOTBALL, CRICKET, SOCCER, NETBALL, TENNIS, COMPETITION, TEAM, WIN, LOSE and BEAT. The kinds of sense relationships that can exist between words in the same lexical field are explored in the following sections.

8.4.3   Homonymy

Homonyms are unrelated meanings of the same phonological form. In English, for example, the word *pupil* has two unrelated senses: it can refer to a school student or to part of the eye. Although these two homonyms have exactly the same pronunciation and spelling in English, these two meanings of this word do not appear to be related in any way. Historically, two words that may have once been separate have simply come to have the same form in the language.

Although homonymy may be somewhat rarer in the core native lexicon of Auslan than in the English lexicon (for a discussion of this claim in relation to ASL and English, see Emmorey, 2002), it is not difficult to find examples. Some signers use the same form for WHO (traditionally used in the northern dialect) and DINNER (originally a southern dialect sign which may also mean 'eat' or 'meal'). Other signers use the same form for AUNT and HOSPITAL,

HUNDRED and MELBOURNE, DAUGHTER and NEEDLE, FINLAND and ROCK. We can see that in all cases, the same phonological form is used, but the two signs appear to have little in common in terms of meaning.

| WHO/ | AUNT/ | HUNDRED/ | DAUGHTER/ | FINLAND/ |
| DINNER | HOSPITAL | MELBOURNE | NEEDLE | ROCK |

Figure 8.6: *Some homonyms in Auslan.*

Homonymy can also be found in lexicalised fingerspelled signs. Often the reduction of fully fingerspelled items to a single manual letter sign can create homonymy, so that forms such as MONTH, MINUTE and METRE (-M-), QUEENSLAND and QUESTION (Q-Q), or INFECTION and INSURANCE (I-I) are identical.

Of course, sociolinguistic variation in the language means that not all signers use these homonyms in the same way—lexical variants of WHO, DINNER, AUNT, NEEDLE, INSURANCE, ROCK and HOSPITAL also exist in the language.

8.4.4 Polysemy

Polysemy refers to the related meanings of the same phonological form. For example, the English word *head* can refer to the top part of your body, a person in the top job in an organisation, or the froth at the top of a glass of beer. Thus polysemy is used to describe the same sign having multiple related meanings. In contrast to homonymy, extensive polysemy seems quite common in signed languages (e.g., Wrigley *et al.*, 1990; Brien, 1992; Radutsky, 1992).

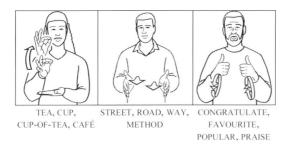

TEA, CUP,	STREET, ROAD, WAY,	CONGRATULATE,
CUP-OF-TEA, CAFÉ	METHOD	FAVOURITE,
		POPULAR, PRAISE

Figure 8.7: *Three polysemous Auslan signs.*

The three signs in Figure 8.7 are polysemous: sign (a) means 'tea', 'cup', 'cup of tea' and 'café', (b) means 'street', 'road', 'way' or 'method' and (c) means 'congratulate', 'favourite,' 'popular' and 'praise'. It is seems likely that these meanings are related due to processes of lexical extension, as discussed in Chapter 6.

The difference between homonymy and polysemy is not always clear cut, and this makes the design of dictionaries difficult because polysemous meanings are usually listed under the same lexical entry, while homonyms are usually given separate entries. Often, historical information about how a word's meaning has changed over time is used to decide whether polysemy or homonymy is involved. This is true for the signs ROCK and FINLAND, for example. The sign FINLAND appears to be a recent borrowing into the language, resulting from contact with foreign signers. Therefore, we know that its resemblance to the Auslan sign ROCK is probably coincidental. It thus makes sense to treat these two signs as homonyms. On the other hand, some signers use the same sign for PLAIN (as in 'undecorated' or 'ordinary') and SAD (as in 'unhappy'): is this an example of homonymy or polysemy? It could be suggested that these two meanings have something in common. In such cases, we have very few historical records for the language, so this makes tracing the history of Auslan signs and changes in their meaning over time very difficult. As a result, it is sometimes difficult to decide whether to treat identical forms with different meanings as examples of polysemy or homonymy.

8.4.5 Synonymy

Synonyms are lexical items with different phonological forms that have the same or similar meanings. For example, the words *lift* and *elevator* are synonyms, as they both have the same denotation. *Girl* and *lass* are two other examples from English. Examples in Auslan would include different variants of BLUE, MOTHER and AFTERNOON, or fingerspelled Y-E-S and N-O versus signed YES and NO.

Note, however, that true synonymy is rare. Although the descriptive meanings of the various forms of the sign BLUE are the same, for example, their social meanings are different. The variant of the sign BLUE with the 8 handshape is associated with the northern dialect, for example, and the form with the B handshape is used elsewhere in the country and in Australasian Signed English (see Chapter 2). Similarly, the two forms of the sign MOTHER appear to have differences in affective and social meaning: the form on the forehead appears to be more widely used in the southern dialect of Auslan than the two-handed sign, and some signers prefer it for use with small children (i.e., as the Auslan equivalent of 'mummy'). Fingerspelled Y-E-S and the sign YES may also reflect differences in social meaning—fingerspelled lexical items are clearly used more often by older signers, for example (Schembri & Johnston, in press). Similarly, as is also true of ASL (Valli *et al.*, 2005), signers will often move between fingerspelled and signed lexical items for particular communicative effects. A signer may, for example, fingerspell N-O as a form of emphasis rather than use the sign NO. Thus the expressive meaning of the two forms is different.

8.4.6   Antonymy

Two lexical items that have opposite meanings are referred to as *antonyms*. For example, the English words *big* versus *small* and the Auslan signs TALL versus SHORT are antonyms. Some antonyms in Auslan have related forms, such as WANT and NOT-WANT (which differ in movement only—WANT moves down the chest while NOT-WANT moves upwards), and HAVE and NOT-HAVE (which differ in the type of movement used—HAVE begins with a open handshape while the reverse is true of NOT-HAVE).

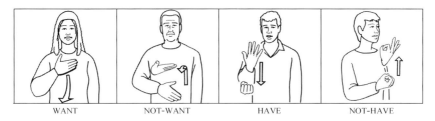

| WANT | NOT-WANT | HAVE | NOT-HAVE |

Figure 8.8: *Antonyms which are related forms.*

It is useful to identify several different types of antonymy. First, there are pairs of *complementary antonyms*. This is a relationship in which the positive of one sign implies the negative of the other. They have an either/or relationship. In Auslan, examples would include the signs PASS/FAIL, RIGHT/WRONG and LIVE/DIE. There are usually only two members in a complementary antonym pair (e.g., to say that someone is right means that they are not wrong, and vice versa), although signers may create alternatives to these pairs and say that someone is HALF RIGHT, for example.

Second, there are *gradable antonyms*. In this lexical relationship, the positive of one sign does not necessarily imply the negative of the other. Examples would include CLEVER/STUPID, DIFFICULT/EASY, INTERESTING/BORING, RICH/POOR and YOUNG/OLD. Although the two members of these pairs contrast in meaning, they are both gradable so that signers can emphasise the degree to which one or other sign is true (e.g., they can sign MORE OLD or VERY OLD). This is because the meanings are relative. Thus a thin pencil is going to be thinner than a thin girl, as Saeed (1997) pointed out.

Third, *relational antonyms* are those for which the same action or state of affairs may be seen from two different perspectives, such as FATHER/

DAUGHTER or TEACHER/STUDENT. These antonyms are said to have a *converse* relationship.

8.4.7 Hyponymy

A *hyponym* is a word that includes the meaning of a more general word. *Laptop computer* is a hyponym of *computer* which is itself a hyponym of *machine*. In Auslan, the signs DOG and CAT are hyponyms of the sign ANIMAL. The more general lexical item is called a *superordinate* or a *hypernym*. This relationship is illustrated in Figure 8.9. We can see that PERSON is the superordinate of WOMAN and MAN. WOMAN itself is the superordinate of SISTER, AUNT and MOTHER. Another example would be the hypernym LANGUAGE, with SIGN as a hyponym which includes the meaning of AUSLAN, A-S-L and B-S-L.

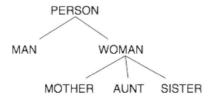

Figure 8.9: *Hypernyms and hyponyms.*

We can refer to the hyponyms SISTER, AUNT and MOTHER, or AUSLAN, A-S-L and B-S-L as *co-hyponyms*. This is a type of horizontal relationship (i.e., all the signs are at the same level in the relationship) as opposed to the vertical relationship between hypernyms and hyponyms.

8.4.8 Meronymy

Meronymy refers to a part-whole relationship between lexical items. Thus WHEEL, ENGINE, DOOR and WINDOW are meronyms of CAR because they refer to objects which form part of a car. This is different to a hyponymic relationship because a wheel is not a kind of car, it is part of a car. Another example suggested by Valli *et al.*, (2005) would be the relationship between the English words *phonology* and *linguistics*. *Phonology* is a meronym of *linguistics* because the meaning of the word *linguistics* includes the area of language study we call *phonology*.

8.5   Iconicity and metaphor in Auslan

In Chapter 1, we discussed the notion of iconicity as one of the kinds of relationship that can exist between a linguistic sign and its meaning. Iconicity exists at all levels of signed and spoken languages—in their phonology, morphology and syntax (Johnston, 1989a; Wilcox, 2004a). In this section, we shall discuss some kinds of iconicity that can be found in Auslan (although we will focus on lexical iconicity), and we will introduce the notion of metaphor.

There are a number of ways that spoken and signed languages can be iconic. Sarah Taub (2001:24) discussed the onomatopoeic English word *ding*, used to refer to the sound of a bell. She presents an amplitude waveform plot of the sound of a bell being struck. In the graph, there is a sharp onset of the sound, an initial loud tone, and then a long, gradual fade in the sound. If an amplitude waveform of the word *ding* is made, the resulting graph shows a very similar pattern. The word initial consonant /d/ 'provides a sharp onset', the word medial vowel /ɪ/ is 'a loud, clear tone', and the word final consonant /ŋ/ is a fading sound. Both the sounds of the English word and the time ordering of the sounds in combination resemble the acoustic properties of the referent.

Despite its iconicity, however, this iconic lexical item does have important linguistic aspects that it shares with other words in English. First, the form *ding* uses three of the possible sounds in English (i.e., it only uses sounds from the limited set of English phonemes): /dɪŋ/. Second, the form follows the same phonological constraints (i.e., the same rules of phoneme combination) as other words in English. As Taub (2001) points out, a sound like /dnnnngggggg/ could also be used to imitate the sounds of a bell, but it violates English phonological rules, such as the need for a vowel in a monosyllabic word and the standard length of English consonants, so this sequence is unlikely to become a lexical item. Third, the word *ding* is part of the English lexicon. It is conventionalised part of the English language (unlike other possible words for the sound of a bell such as *doon* or *pim*), and does not need to be recreated each time it is used.

Note, however, that other aspects of English can be considered iconic, such as chronological ordering of events in syntax which is assumed to directly reflect aspects of the real world (Haiman, 1985). Taub (2001) used the example in (8.5) to illustrate this point.

(8.5)   I jumped into the pool and took off my shoes.

On reading this sentence, the reader will naturally assume the jumping into the pool preceded the removal of the shoes. As Haiman (1985) observed, if the speaker wants to over-ride this default interpretation, then some explicit time-ordering word such as *after* or *simultaneously* must be added to one of two such phrases, as in (8.6).

(8.6)   a. I jumped into the pool *after* I took off my shoes.
         b. *Before* I jumped into the pool, I took my shoes off.

The iconicity is time-based but, it can be used to imply more than just the temporal order of events, especially in spoken English (Bolinger, 1989). Iconic temporal mapping may, for example, imply that the first event mentioned caused a second event ('It rained—I arrived late' meaning 'I arrived late *because* it rained') (see also 8.7.5 below). Thus, with appropriate intonation, it can also imply that the first event is the pre-condition for the second ('You give him an inch, he takes a mile' meaning '*If* you give him an inch, *then* he takes a mile'). Johnston (1992) pointed out this use of intonation and ordering of clauses in spoken languages is similar to the use of non-manual features and the order of Auslan conditionals (see Chapter 7 for a discussion of conditionals).

If we look at visual iconicity in signed languages, we can see that the form of an Auslan sign for TREE shown in Figure 8.10 gives an image of a tree. Taub (2001) suggested that this sign (which is the same in ASL and BSL) exemplifies the most typical case of iconicity between form and meaning because it is clear that the sign provides a visual image of the referent. She explained, however, that the relationship between the sign and its meaning is more complex than it may otherwise appear. First, note that not all trees look like the sign (i.e., not all trees have a straight trunk with branches growing in a semi-circular shape at the top). The sign TREE actually draws on a mental image of a *prototypical* tree, one that serves to exemplify all trees. This choice of image is conventional and not shared by all signed languages (other signed languages may use other images, as we saw in Chapter 1). Indeed, this sign is only one of three lexical variants of TREE in Auslan.

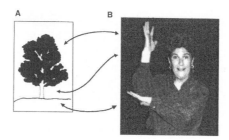

Figure 8.10: *Iconicity in the sign TREE.*

Second, note that this prototypical image could have been realised differently. The ground might have been ignored and not realised as the non-dominant hand and arm. The branching structure could have been realised with two handshapes, or with a 4 handshape, and the tall trunk could have been represented by a 1 handshape.

Third, TREE only uses acceptable formational aspects of Auslan (i.e., it draws on a limited set of handshapes, locations and movements possible in the language) and it follows the general phonological rules at work in both languages (e.g., the allowable contact between the dominant elbow and the back of the non-dominant hand).

Iconicity can also occur in the grammar of signed languages. We have seen that verb modifications for aspect, manner and number in Auslan, for example, use space and time iconically (Wilcox, 2004a, makes similar observations for ASL). In Chapter 5, it was shown that signers express the notion of walking quickly by producing the sign WALK at faster than normal speed. Similarly, to show that the action of the verb affects two people, an indicating verb can be directed towards two locations in the signing space.

Taub (2001) explains that iconicity involves what is known as *conceptual mapping*: there is a relationship between the linguistic forms in Auslan and imagery in the mind of the signer. We can see the link between aspects of the structure of these signs in Auslan and structure of the referents they represent. In the sign TREE, the non-dominant arm and hand represent the ground beneath the tree, the dominant arm stands for the trunk and the dominant hand and fingers represent the branches of the tree. Thus, there is a mapping between the sign's imagery and the concept of a prototypical tree in the mind of the signer.

To account for the iconicity of these aspects of signed and spoken languages, Taub (2001) proposed the *analogue-building model* of linguistic iconicity. This model is shown in the Figure 8.11, using the sign TREE as an example. In order to create an iconic linguistic item, first one *selects* aspects of the mental image of the referent that will be represented in the sign. In the case of TREE, the sign makes no reference to the smell or texture of trees, but focuses on aspects of its shape (perhaps because these are easiest to represent in a visual-gestural language). Second, these aspects are then modified or *schematised* so that the image can be represented by the language. The signs reflects a *schema* or mental image of the tree as a tall object growing from a flat surface with a branching structure at its top. Last, appropriate combinations of handshape, location, movement and so forth are used to show or *encode* each representable part of the image.

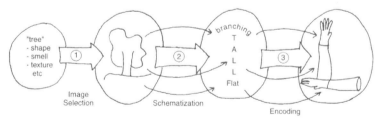

Figure 8.11: *Analogue-building model of linguistic iconicity.*

Although this model is represented as a sequence, this does not mean that a signer must move through these stages in this order, or even that a signer creating an iconic sign is conscious of these processes. It is possible that all of these occur simultaneously in the mind of the signer. Nevertheless, this model provides a useful summary of the kinds of processes that appear to be involved in creating iconic lexical items in signed languages.

8.5.1   Types of iconicity in Auslan

Building on earlier work by Mark Mandel (1977), Taub (2001) demonstrated that there is a range of iconic devices used in signed languages. Neither of these researchers has proposed an exhaustive list of iconic forms, but their ideas serve to provide an introduction to the iconic potential of signed languages. We will present an overview of their findings here.

One of the most direct forms of iconicity in signed languages, Taub (2001) explains, is based on the fact that physical entities may be used to represent themselves. For example, signers can take advantage of the fact that their body is always present during signing to point at body parts. Thus, in Auslan, the sign NOSE involves a point with the 1 handshape at the nose, the sign BODY involves the B handshapes moving down the trunk, and the sign EAR involves grasping the ear with the index finger and thumb. Similarly, pronominal signs used to represent people or objects can involve pointing at the referents if they are present at the time of signing. Thus the entities represented by signs such as NOSE or PRO-2 are called *presentable objects* by Mandel (1977) because they can be simply presented to the addressee by some kind of pointing sign. These signs are thus all examples of *deixis* (which we discuss in §8.7.2 below).

Another common form of iconicity involves using the shape of a signer's hands and other parts of the body to represent the overall shape of the whole referent. The sign TREE and AEROPLANE are examples of this. Signs can also represent the shape of part of the referent, so that the hands resemble the beak of a bird in BIRD, the rabbit's ears in RABBIT and the cow's horns in COW. Mandel (1977) referred to all these types of iconicity as *substitutive depiction* because the hands are in a sense substituting for the referent.

The movement of the signer's hands and other parts of the body may also be used to represent the movement of the referent. For example, in TAKE-OFF and LAND, the Y handshape can be moved in such a way as to suggest an aeroplane taking off and landing. Similarly, the 1 handshape can be moved from left to right in front of the signer to indicate a person moving in this way (cf. Wilcox, 2004a).

The location of the signer's hands can also represent the location of the referent. When describing locations around Australia, signers often make use of the signing space as if they were facing a large map of the country. A signer describing flying between Sydney, Darwin and Perth might move the sign AEROPLANE-FLY between a location in the upper part of the signing space to represent Darwin and locations on the right and left of the lower part of signing space for Perth and Sydney respectively.

The articulators can represent body parts of the same type, so that hands can be used to represent hands, or the body can represent itself. In signs such as SWIM or RUN, the hands represent themselves in a stylised representation of swimming or running. Mandel (1977) referred to signs of this type as based on *presentable actions* because the action referred to by these signs is 'enacted' for the addressee to see. The hands may also represent body parts of a related type on animals, so that the hands can represent paws as in KANGAROO.

In another category of signs, the shape of the signs' movement represents the shape of a referent. In such signs, such as ELEPHANT and TABLE, the movement of the hands does not refer to the movement of the referent, but traces its shape. This is very common in SASS depicting signs, as shown in Chapter 6. This type of iconicity is called *virtual depiction* by Mandel (1977). Both substitutive and virtual depiction have been shown to be central in the form and use of depicting signs (see Chapter 6).

The relative size of the articulation of a sign may also represent the relative size of a referent, as can be seen in the signs BIG and SMALL and the ways in which they can be modified (i.e., made larger or smaller respectively) to reflect characteristics of the referent. The number of articulators can also be used to show the number of referents. In pronoun signs meaning 'the two of you', 'the three of us', and 'the five of them', the number of fingers corresponds to the number of individuals.

These are just some of the ways in which signs may be iconic in signed languages. In the next section, we discuss degree of iconicity, another important variable in the relationship between form and meaning.

8.5.2   Degree of iconicity

Johnston (1989a), drawing on earlier work by Klima and Bellugi (1979), categorised signs into four groups according to their degree of iconicity, classifying them as *transparent, translucent, obscure* and *opaque*. Signs at the transparent end are the most iconic, and signs at the opaque end are the least visually motivated. Thus, the meaning of a transparent sign should be obvious to any observer who comes from the same social and cultural background as the community of Auslan signers. The number or percentage of transparent signs in the core lexicon is relatively small (perhaps no more than 5 per cent of the lexicon). We have previously referred to and illustrated many transparent signs, such as RUN, PRO-1, DRINK, GOOD, WRITE and CAR, and non-manual NO. Although these signs are transparent, they reflect conventional links between form and meaning found in Australia and other English-speaking communities. The fact that the hands held as if turning a steering wheel represents a car, or a point to the chest represents oneself, reflect gestural conventions that may not be understood by individuals of other sociocultural backgrounds. A point to the nose (rather than the chest) is, for example, the gestural convention for indicating oneself in some East Asian cultures.

Translucent signs include SCIENCE, SYDNEY, EXPLAIN, BORN, UNDERSTAND, FLOWER and HEARING. The meaning of a translucent sign may not be readily understood by a naive observer, but once told its meaning, the link between the sign's form and its meaning may become clear. For example, the link between the sign SCIENCE and pouring liquids from one test-tube to another would be readily apparent to anyone from our culture. Translucent signs make up a significant proportion of the Auslan lexicon.

 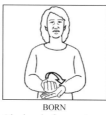 

SCIENCE	BORN	FLOWER
'pouring from test-tubes'	'the head of a new born emerging'	'holding and sniffing a flower'

Figure 8.12: *Translucent iconic signs with motivations.*

Obscure signs appear to be visually motivated, but the relationship between form and meaning is not clear. Such signs would include RICH, BISCUIT, WATER, WOMAN, FAMOUS, PROUD and SCHOOL. Often, there may be widely known explanations given for such signs within the deaf community. These are sometimes known as *folk etymologies* (*etymology* is the study of the origin and history of words). The southern dialect sign BISCUIT, for example, is claimed by some to be a mimetic sign representing the action of breaking a biscuit under one's elbow. It is sometimes suggested that the sign RICH represents stroking the fine garments worn by a rich person.

Unfortunately, because historical records of the origin and history of Auslan signs are lacking for all but a small number of signs (see Woll, 1987), we cannot be certain that these folk etymologies are in any way accurate. In some cases, the little historical evidence we have appears to contradict some popular explanations. Some signers suggest that the Auslan sign POLICE, for example, has some link to the notion of handcuffs. Historical sources, however, appear to indicate that the sign originally comes from a representation of stripes on a police officer's uniform. Unfortunately, this is one of only a handful of examples where historical documentation can be called upon to support or challenge folk etymology. Because of the lack of historical evidence in general, it is best to treat popular explanations for the origins of signs with some degree of scepticism.

| RICH | BISCUIT | WOMAN |
| 'stroking fur' | 'breaking a biscuit | 'stroking smooth cheek' |

Figure 8.13: *Obscure iconic signs with folk etymologies.*

Opaque signs have no apparent element of iconicity at all. Examples include WHY, PEOPLE, SIMPLE, WILL, NOT-YET and FLUKE. It is possible that such signs were at one time more iconic than they are now, and that processes of language change, such as those described by Frishberg (1975) for ASL and Kyle and Woll (1985) for BSL, have resulted in the form of signs losing their link to their meaning.

8.5.3   Metaphor in Auslan

Metaphor involves the extension of words beyond their primary meaning to describe referents that are different from the original referent of the word, often in order to suggest that there is some kind of resemblance between this referent and something else. It may, for example, involve describing abstract ideas and concepts as if they were concrete objects or actions. Studies have shown that 'metaphor is pervasive in everyday life, not just in language but in thought and action. Our ordinary conceptual system is fundamentally metaphorical in nature' (Lakoff & Johnson, 1980:3). For example, we frequently use spatial metaphors in English to express our understanding of time. As we 'approach' the end of a year, we may 'look forward' to things in the future, or 'look back' to events in the past. These examples illustrate Lakoff and Johnson's view that the 'essence of metaphor is understanding and experiencing one kind of thing in terms of another' (1980, p. 5).

Metaphors are very common in signed languages (e.g., Brennan, 1990; Wilcox, 2000). For example, the sign FLABBERGASTED uses the image and metaphor of the jaw dropping open, THRILLED that of someone jumping repeatedly in excitement and RAGE that of the top of some container exploding under pressure (see Figure 8.14).

Metaphor operates as a kind of 'as if' relationship between sign form and meaning (Brennan, 1992), establishing metaphorical chains of association between signs or sets of signs (Johnston, 1991c). Once we know that, in Auslan, a whole range of abstract concepts are understood as if they were physical entities which can be handled, then we understand the grasping metaphor at work in signs like REMEMBER, EXPERIENCE/ACQUIRE and BELIEVE, where ideas are treated as if they can be held in the mind. This same metaphor extends out to signs such as CATCH-UP (on work or studies), CATCH (signs), CATCH-SIGHT-OF or ACHIEVE-GOAL. The opposite movement occurs in the signs FORGET, GIVE-UP and WASTE, where a range of abstract concepts are treated as if they could be released from one's grip (see Figure 8.15).

'jaw dropping open'
☐ FLABBERGASTED

'jumping up and down'
☐ THRILLED

'lid coming off'
☐ RAGE

Figure 8.14: *Three lexical signs derived from metaphorical extensions of meaning.*

Fluent signers use the language's enormous potential for visual metaphor to modify and extend the meaning of existing signs, as well as to create new lexical items. Although the use of spatial metaphor is something both Auslan and English share, the potential for visual relationships between sign form and meaning is, as we have seen, one of the major differences between the lexicon and grammar of signed and spoken languages.

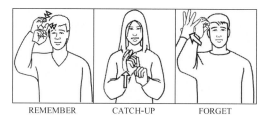

REMEMBER   CATCH-UP   FORGET

Figure 8.15: *Auslan examples with metaphorical imagery.*

Taub (2001) suggested that metaphor in signed languages involves a *double mapping*. In a sign like REMEMBER, we can see that there are two kinds of relationship between the form and the meaning of the sign. First, there is a link between the concrete act of holding something with your hand and the abstract meaning of keeping something in your memory. Second, there is a relationship between the concrete image (i.e., the image that remembering something is like holding something in your mind) and the handshape, location and movement in the sign itself. As in the sign HOLD, holding an object in Auslan may be represented by a tightly curled bC handshape closing into an S (i.e., the hand can represent itself holding something). As in other signs such as KNOW and UNDERSTAND, the forehead location represents mental processes. Thus, producing a holding action at the forehead is used to signify 'holding onto' something in your mind and this is conventionalised as an Auslan sign REMEMBER.

8.5.3.1 *Space is time: the time-line metaphor in Auslan*

In the English time-related expressions described above, time is understood as a physical substance in space through which we are moving (Lakoff & Johnson, 1980). This same 'time is space' metaphor can be found in Auslan and other signed languages, where the spatial metaphor can be realised by signs which actually occur in physical space. Thus, the signs FUTURE, TOMORROW, POSTPONE, HENCEFORTH and NEXT-WEEK all move forwards, while the signs for PAST, LAST-WEEK, PRIOR, LOOK-BACK and LONG-AGO move backwards. There is a small number of exceptions to this tendency, such as the sign YESTERDAY (and the related signs LAST-YEAR and LAST-WEEK) traditionally used in the southern dialect of Auslan. In these examples, the handshape actually moves forward off the cheek, but the orientation of the hand is nevertheless the opposite of that in the signs TOMORROW, NEXT-YEAR etc.

These signs, and other time-related uses of the signing space, are organised around three types of *time lines* in space, first identified by Brennan (1983), which we will refer to as the *deictic, anaphoric* and *sequence time lines* (Engberg-Pedersen, 1993). The deictic time line is a line perpendicular to the body that extends from the signer's dominant shoulder (deixis is explained in §8.7.2 below). Signs such as YESTERDAY, TOMORROW, NEXT-YEAR and LAST-YEAR are organised along this line. Their temporal meaning is related to the time in the discourse. Thus, in its default meaning, the sign YESTERDAY refers to the day before the time of signing. In relating a past event, however, this same sign may refer to the day before the event occurred (i.e., it would mean 'the day before'). The anaphoric time line extends diagonally across the space in front of the signer, and involves the use of the subordinate hand (anaphoric reference is explained in Chapter 9). Some signs along this line do not have a default interpretation, so that the interpretation of a sign like PRIOR needs to be established in the discourse. The sequence time line is parallel to the body, moving from left to right, probably reflecting the direction of writing in our culture (Johnston, 1989a). It is often used when signers want to compare the order of events, so that a sign like PERIOD can be moved along it in, and associated with a specific time or date.

As also reported for some other signed languages (Engberg-Pedersen, 1993), some signs appear to combine aspects of more than one of these time lines. For example, the signs NEXT-WEEK and HENCEFORTH move forward and away from the body, and may be used deictically or anaphorically. Brennan (1983) also claimed that the use of the space that extends from the foot to the head on the dominant side of the body (e.g., in signs like CHILD, ADULT or GROW-UP) should be considered an additional example of a time line. Johnston (1989a) pointed out, however, that it is only used in lexical items related to the increasing height of humans. Reversing the movement of GROW shows decreasing height, not movement backwards through time. This line is also not used for any specific time-related signs in Auslan, and thus is best not analysed as a time line at all.

8.6   Sentence meaning

In the sections above, we have looked at the meaning of words. In the following section, we shall examine sentence meaning. Sentence meaning is possible because signers and speakers understand the meaning of words in their language, but also because they understand the rules for combining the meanings of words into sentences.

8.6.1   Compositional meaning

Some of the meaning of sentences appears to come from knowing the meanings of the signs and words that make up the sentence. This is known as *compositional meaning* (e.g., Saeed, 1997).

(8.7)   PRO-1 TEACH INTERPRET TRAIN WORKSHOP PT+rt WITH TWO OTHER
TEACHER FROM SYDNEY
*I will be teaching an interpreter training workshop there with two
other teachers from Sydney.*

If we look at the example sentence in (8.7), we can see how its meaning is built up from a number of noun phrases (NP) and prepositional phrases (PP) together with a verb phrase (VP). These constituents are themselves composed of a number of signs with their own meanings. The compositional structure of the sentence can be clearly seen in the tree diagram in Figure 8.16. All of these parts contribute to the overall meaning of the sentence.

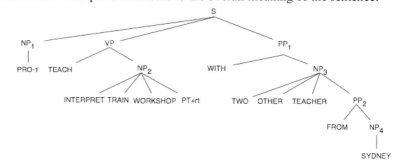

Figure 8.16: *Tree diagram of the compositional structure of a sentence.*

We will see below, however, that there is more to sentences than their compositional meanings. The meaning of the sentence is not simply the sum of its parts. As we saw in Chapter 7, the order in which these constituents are combined—the syntactic structure of the sentence—is also important to its meaning.

8.6.2   Semantic roles and sentence semantics

If we examine the sentences in examples (8.8) and (8.9), we will see that the two sentences have exactly the same signs, but very different meanings. This demonstrates that there is to more to the meaning of the sentences than simply compositional meaning.

(8.8)   DOG BITE+lf CAT
   A dog bit a cat.

(8.9)   CAT BITE+lf DOG
   A cat bit a dog.

As we have already seen in Chapter 7, the order of the signs is important for determining the meaning of these sentences. In (8.8), we can see that DOG is in the role of actor of the verb, while CAT is in the role of undergoer. More specifically, the dog is actually an *agent*, and the cat is *patient*. A noun in agent role is one that is the one carrying out some physical action, which directly affects the patient in some way. In example (8.9), we can see that these semantic roles have been reversed (i.e., the referent of CAT is now the agent, and that of DOG is the patient). Agent and patient are examples of *semantic roles* (also known as *thematic* or *theta roles*, see Saeed, 1997). The semantic role refers to the way the referent of the noun contributes to the event, process or situation described by the predicate in the sentence. These semantic roles are related to the meaning of the verb BITE. Listed in the mental lexicon of the signer would be the fact that BITE co-occurs with two nouns, one of which acts as an agent and the other as a patient.

Agent and patient are not the only semantic roles found in signed and spoken languages. A summary of some of the most common semantic roles recognised by linguists is shown in   Table 8.1.

We have already been introduced to *carrier* and *attribute* in Chapter 7. An example of a sentence with an *experiencer*, *stimulus* and *locative* is shown in (8.10). Here we can see that PRO-1 refers to the referent that experiences the feeling of pleasure, and that LINGUISTICS stands for the object that causes that feeling. The phrase S-Y UNIVERSITY gives a location for the state described by the verb.

(8.10)   PRO-1 LIKE LINGUISTICS PT+rt S-Y UNIVERSITY
   I like linguistics at Sydney University.

In (8.11), the DAUGHTER is the *beneficiary* of the action, and CAKE is the *theme*. Note that this semantic role may be marked by the use of a preposition in Auslan. In (8.12), we can see that the recipient role is played by the noun phrase POSS-3 SPOUSE.

(8.11) <u> br </u>

CAKE MAN BUY FOR DAUGHTER
The cake was bought by the man for his daughter.

(8.12) <u> br </u>

BOOK WOMAN GIVE+rt POSS-3 SPOUSE
The book was given by the woman to her husband.

Table 8.1: *Semantic roles.*

Role name	Role meaning
Agent	Performs an action
Patient	Affected by an action by an agent
Experiencer	Experiences some psychological state
Carrier	Has some characteristic
Attribute	Attributes some characteristic
Stimulus	Causes some psychological state
Recipient	Receiver of the result of some action
Beneficiary	Benefits from some action
Theme	Involved in motion or a change of state
Instrument	Used by an agent to perform some action
Locative	Place in which some action occurs
Goal	Where the action is moving towards
Source	Where the action begins

In (8.13), we see that the sign SCISSORS is in the instrumental role, as it is the object used to complete the action. Note that in Auslan and other signed languages, depictive signs of handling often include a handshape that reflects the shape of the instrument or the manner in which it is handled.

(8.13) <u> br </u>

PAPER SCISSORS rt+CUT-WITH-SCISSORS+rept+lf
The paper was cut up with the scissors.

In (8.14), SYDNEY is the source and PERTH is the goal. This is shown clearly in the spatial relationship between the signs. The source is signed on the left side of the signing space, and the goal on the right and then the sign FLY-TO is moved from left to right. The source and goal roles in Auslan are often realised iconically as the locations in which a spatial verb sign begins and ends its movement.

(8.14) <u>   br   </u>

SYDNEY+lf PERTH+rt PRO-1 lf+FLY-TO+rt FINISH
I have flown from Sydney to Perth.

We can see that semantic roles can reflect the particular relationships between verbs and their arguments. In the previous chapters, we have attempted to avoid this level of detail by using the semantic macro-roles of actor and undergoer because they group together a number of these more specific semantic roles (Van Valin & LaPolla, 1997). The notion of actor may refer, for example, to both agents and to experiencers, whereas undergoer includes patients, recipients, stimuli and themes. Regardless of whether or not we use the more general or specific terminology, it is nonetheless clear that the semantic relations between the verb signs and co-occurring noun signs are an important part of sentence meaning in Auslan.

8.6.3   Non-compositional meaning

In sentences with non-compositional meaning, the meaning cannot be based on knowing the meanings of the words that make up the sentence (this is a type of non-literal language, as discussed in §8.7.3). This is best illustrated by the particular type of non-compositional meaning found in *idioms*. Idioms are metaphorical phrases in which the meaning of the whole cannot be determined from its parts (e.g., Hudson, 2000). Examples from English include *raining cats and dogs* (i.e., raining very heavily), *kick the bucket* (i.e., to die) and *beat around the bush* (i.e., to avoid giving a direct answer). English idioms are sometimes translated literally into Auslan (e.g., NOT POSS-1 TEA 'not my cup of tea'), but there are very few idioms which are specific to Auslan itself. Some signs, such as the sign NONE-OF-ONE'S-BUSINESS, are sometimes mistakenly referred to as idioms in Auslan and other signed languages (as in Sutton-Spence & Woll, 1999). Although the translation of this sign may be an idiom in English, the sign itself is not an idiom because an idiom must be a phrase (i.e., more than one sign) with a non-compositional meaning.

One of the very rare examples of an idiom in Auslan actually appears to be borrowed from ASL (and is used in the title of a well-known book by Leah Cohen, published in 1994). It includes variants of the phrase TRAIN GO SORRY ('the train has left, sorry') or PRO-2 MISS TRAIN ('you missed the train'). This idiom is used when a conversational partner asks a signer to repeat what he or she has said, but the signer is not inclined to explain it again. We can see that this phrase has non-compositional meaning, because the overall meaning cannot be based on the signs TRAIN, GO, SORRY or MISS in combination. Because their meaning cannot be based on the meaning of their parts, idioms in English and Auslan must be stored in the signer's mental lexicon as whole phrases that are associated with particular non-compositional meanings.

Note that, although idioms are rare in Auslan, examples of other types of metaphor are extremely common, as we saw in §8.5.3 above.

8.6.4 Paraphrase, entailment and contradiction

Just as the meanings of words are inter-related, sentences have meanings that can be understood in relation to each other.

We have seen in §8.4.5 above that synonyms are words with similar meanings. In a similar way, *paraphrases* are sentences with similar meanings. The paraphrases in (8.15) and (8.16) have the same descriptive meaning, although they have different communicative effects. We can see, for example, that the semantic roles of the referents of CAT and FISH are the same (i.e., CAT is the actor and FISH refers to the undergoer).

(8.15) <u> br </u>
CAT, EAT FISH
Cats eat fish.

(8.16) <u> br </u>
FISH, CAT EAT
As for fish, cats eat them.

Similar to antonyms discussed in §8.4.6, sentences that have opposite meanings are examples of *contradiction*. Two sentences which contradict each other can be seen in (8.17) and (8.18).

(8.17) <u>   hs</u>
PT+rt WOMAN NOT FROM BRISBANE
That woman is not from Brisbane.

(8.18) PT+rt WOMAN FROM BRISBANE
That woman is from Brisbane.

Entailment, like the relationship between words known as hyponymy described in §8.4.7 above, involves one sentence describing a broader or more inclusive situation than another sentence. Therefore, we can see that the meaning of (8.19) is included in the meaning of (8.20). If the woman wants to buy a cat and a dog, then this includes the fact that she wants to buy a cat. We can say that 8.19 entails 8.20.

(8.19) PT+rt WOMAN WANT BUY CAT PLUS DOG
That woman wants to buy a cat and a dog.

(8.20) PT+rt WOMAN WANT BUY CAT
That woman wants to buy a cat.

8.7 Utterance meaning

All language use has a context. As explained in §8.1.6 above, the study of the relationship between language, meaning and context is known as *pragmatics*.

The context for words and sentences may be understood in three main ways. First, there is the *linguistic context* of an utterance. This refers to the language that comes before and after the utterance that helps to determine how the utterance is understood. For example, in sentence (8.21), we know who POSS-3 FRIEND 'her friend' refers to because it follows the lexical item J-A-N-E.

(8.21) S-A-M GO-TO RESTAURANT. POSS-3 FRIEND CAN'T AFFORD. STAY HOME
     Sam went to the restaurant. Her friend can't afford it and stayed at home.

We would also understand that the noun sign after GO-TO means 'restaurant' in this instance. This sign is polysemous: it can mean 'dinner', 'dine' or a 'restaurant' (i.e., 'the place where you dine') depending on the context. The use of the sign GO-TO suggests that Sam has gone to a place to have dinner, so one interpretation here would be that she has gone to a restaurant. This is reinforced by the following sentence in which it is explained that Sam's friend stayed home (i.e., he did not go to the restaurant) because he could not afford it (payment also suggests that Sam went to a restaurant rather than dinner at a friend's place).

The second important component of the context is the *situational context*. The situational context refers to other aspects of the communicative event that help us determine its the meaning. It includes *field, tenor* and *mode* (Halliday, 1978).

The ability to correctly interpret utterances involves the addressee in understanding not only the words and sentences used, but how their meaning depends on the *field* or subject matter being discussed. Specific subject areas often have their own specialist vocabulary, and familiar vocabulary may have subject-specific meanings. For example, a combination of a sign meaning 'silly' and another meaning 'stand' creates the compound SILLY-MID-ON. This refers to a fielding position in the game of cricket that is close to the batsman's wicket. Some signers use different signs to mean 'goal' when discussing rugby league, netball or Australian Rules football. Similarly, subject-specific signs such as MORPHOLOGY and PHONOLOGY may only be known to those who have studied signed language linguistics.

Field also includes the setting of communication—the time, place and occasion in which the communication occurs. The ability to interpret signs such as HERE and NOW correctly depends on an understanding of the signer's location in time and space. Signing HAPPY CHRISTMAS, for example, may mean something quite different on January 1 from what it does on December 25 (e.g., there may be something intentionally ironic or funny about using this phrase on New Year's Day).

Another crucial aspect of communication stems from the relationship between participants or *tenor*, such as whether a lecturer is addressing his or her students, a patient is consulting a doctor, or a mother is talking to her child. This also affects the way we understand uses of language, particularly in terms of how much background knowledge the conversational partners may have about each other, for example. Some linguists suggest that tenor has two sub-types: *personal tenor* and *functional tenor* (Finch, 2000). The first reflects the nature of the personal relationship between the participants, such as whether they are lovers, relatives, friends, acquaintances or strangers. The second involves the public relationship that they have, such as their relative status and social role in the community. A wife may be her husband's boss, for example, or a hearing friend may work as a deaf person's interpreter. Thus, the tenor in a particular situation will impact on the kinds of meanings language will be used to convey.

Mode is used to refer to the medium and purpose of the communication. The medium of communication refers to how meanings are created depending on whether the language is spoken, written or signed. If it is spoken, it may be a conversation on the telephone, a lecture at a university, or a radio interview. If it is written, it may be a poem, a novel, or a personal letter. If it signed, it may be a conversation over webcams on the internet, a face-to-face dialogue, a performance by Australian Theatre of the Deaf, or a song signed by a deaf school choir. All of these different modes of communication will impact on the kinds of meanings that will be understood. Mode also includes the purpose of the language being used: is the signer using language to inform (e.g., in a lecture), to exchange goods and services (e.g., in a shop), to persuade (e.g., in a debate), or for social (e.g., greetings) or aesthetic purposes (e.g., a poem)?

Lastly, there is the *context of culture*. This includes all the background knowledge relevant to the situation, such as shared values and beliefs, historical knowledge, awareness of customs and traditions and so forth. This is where language and the world outside language connect, so the context of culture includes all those assumptions outside the language system and the immediate situational context that have to be understood if language is to be produced or interpreted in the way that participants intend.

Although it is important to remember that all language has a context, Hudson (2000) provided a useful summary of five types of language that particularly require contextual cues in order to be interpreted correctly: (1) ambiguous words and sentences, (2) deictic words, (3) non-literal language, (4) indirect illocution and (5) presupposition. We explain each of these with examples from Auslan below.

8.7.1 Ambiguity

The polysemy of some signs and the existence of sign homonyms in Auslan can result in ambiguity. This is because the same combination of handshape, orientation, location and movement can have two or more meanings. Consider the examples in (8.22) and (8.23).

(8.22) <u>   br</u>
       BEACH, PRO-1 ARRIVE TWO-O'CLOCK
       As for the beach, I got there at two o'clock.

(8.23) <u>   br</u>
       YESTERDAY, PRO-1 ARRIVE TWO-O'CLOCK
       As for yesterday, I got there at two o'clock.

For some signers, these two sentences could look identical. This is because one variant of the sign BEACH (Figure 1.5) and the northern dialect variant of YESTERDAY are identical. This is an example of lexical ambiguity.

An entire sentence may also be ambiguous—this is known as structural ambiguity. In (8.24), there are two possible meanings of this sentence. Ellipsis of the pronouns referring to both the actor and undergoer in this context is possible, especially if the participants are already understood. If the sentence is taken out of context, however, it is structurally ambiguous. Topicalisation of both the actor and undergoer is also possible, so the brow raise over the noun phrase POSS-1 BOSS does not help us to disambiguate the sentence. Even the fact that the verb LOOK-FOR is articulated on the right hand of the signing space does not necessarily clarify the participant roles, because LOOK-FOR is not a double-indicating verb that can clearly signal actor and undergoer roles.

(8.24) <u>   br</u>
       POSS-1 BOSS LOOK-FOR+rt FINISH
       As for my boss, I/he/she looked for him/her/it.

In these particular examples of lexical and structural ambiguity, addressees might use information about the subject matter of the conversation or background knowledge about the participant's regional dialect to interpret these particular signs and sentences.

8.7.2 Deixis

Deictic lexical items (such as the pointing signs PRO-1, PRO-2 and HERE, or time signs such as NOW, TOMORROW and LAST-YEAR) have variable meaning that depends on the identity of the signer and addressee, and the location and time in which they are being used. The reference of a deictic sign will be different in each context in which it occurs. Thus, signer A might use PRO-2 (meaning 'the person addressed') to refer to signer B in one conversation, and then to refer to signer C in another. Each time, signer A, B or C use PRO-1 (meaning 'the person signing') to refer to themselves, the same form has a different referent. These signs are all examples of *personal deictics*, a category of signs that includes all the pointing signs used as pronouns (e.g., PRO-3) or possessives (e.g. POSS-1).

The sign HERE used by signer A when at work will refer to his or her place of work, while it will refer to his or her house if the signer uses it at home. Signs like HERE and THERE (which are also forms of pointing signs similar to pronouns) are examples of *spatial deictics*.

Lastly, there are *temporal deictics*, such as TODAY, YESTERDAY and NEXT-WEEK. The sign YESTERDAY refers to March 17, 2005 at the time this is being written, but this sign would have referred to September 25, 1985 if it were used on September 26, 1985.

All of these types of deixis are crucially dependent on the context of situation in which they are used, but we rarely have difficulty understanding what they refer to. In fact, pronominal signs in particular appear to be the most frequent signs used in signed languages (Kennedy & McKee, 1999; Morford & Macfarlane, 2003), so deictic signs would result in a great deal of confusion if their context of use did not make their meaning clear.

8.7.3   Non-literal language

Literal language refers to language used so that its primary descriptive and compositional meaning is the main focus. *Non-literal language* involves unexpected combinations of lexical items in which their descriptive and compositional meaning do not apply, or do not apply transparently. We have already discussed the example of phrases such as PRO-2 MISS TRAIN and the established ways in which metaphor is used in Auslan. Such uses of non-literal language are common in everyday communication as we see in examples (8.25) and (8.26). In (8.25), the signer is explaining in a neutral way that he or she does not want the addressee to know who is the source of his or her information. In (8.26), another signer has translated a well-known English idiom literally into Auslan. This idiom in (8.26) actually has the same meaning as the sentence in (8.25), although this may not be readily apparent to someone unfamiliar with this expression. The addressee may instantly recognise it as a non-literal use of language, or alternatively he or she would rely on the context to first reject the literal interpretation and then work out what the signer is actually saying.

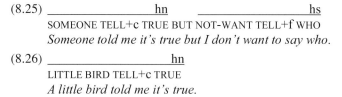

(8.25)   _____ hn   _____ hs
          SOMEONE TELL+c TRUE BUT NOT-WANT TELL+f WHO
          Someone told me it's true but I don't want to say who.

(8.26)   _____ hn
          LITTLE BIRD TELL+c TRUE
          A little bird told me it's true.

8.7.4 Indirect illocution

The philosopher John Austin (1962) introduced the notions of *locution* and *illocution*. To use language to describe something in the world or to express one's feelings are examples of locution. In contrast, using language to perform some social act, such as to make a request, promise, demand, command, apology, warning or threat are all examples of illocution. Illocution may be direct or indirect. Examples of direct locution would include commands, promises or requests in which the intention of the signer is very clear because of the choice of signs and sentence structure used, as in examples (8.27), (8.28) and (8.29) below.

(8.27) PLEASE SIT NOW
       Please sit down immediately.

(8.28) PROMISE WILL FINISH LATER WILL PRO-1
       I promise I will finish this later.

(8.29) _____ br
       CAN f+GIVE+c TEA PLEASE
       Could you give me the tea please?

Often, however, signers will use indirect illocution. In indirect illocution, signers use signs and sentence structures that do not make their intentions clear. Possible examples of indirect locution would include (8.30), (8.31) and (8.32) below.

(8.30) _____ bf
       ARRIVE R-U-N-D-L-E S-T HOW
       How do I get to Rundle St?

(8.31) PRO-1 THINK A-C HERE COLD+intens
       I think the air-conditioning here is too cold.

(8.32) DOG WANT P-A-R-K NOW
       The dog wants to go to the park now.

In (8.30), the question may be asked while a signer is visiting a friend in Adelaide. It looks like a question about the addressee's knowledge but the intention is actually to ask for assistance—the signer wants the other person to show them the way to Rundle Street. In (8.31), the visitor appears to be expressing their feelings but is actually indirectly requesting that the host turn down the air conditioning, and in (8.32), the signer is telling someone to walk the dog by making a statement about what the dog wants. Such strategies are actually very common in both signed and spoken languages, but we can see that the meaning relies on the addressee drawing on aspects of the situational context (such as the personal tenor) to correctly interpret these examples.

8.7.5 Presupposition

A presupposition refers to information that a signer assumes (or presupposes) to be understood by the addressee. Thus, in a declarative sentence like (8.33), the signer assumes that, at the time of signing this utterance, the addressee understands the daughter has been reminded at least once before.

(8.33) PRO-1 REMIND POSS-1 DAUGHTER AGAIN
I am reminding my daughter again.

If the first sentence (8.33) is negated, as in (8.34), then this does not affect the truth of the presupposition. But if the presupposition is not true, then the sentence (8.33) can no longer be true. This shows us that the information in sentence (8.33) must presuppose certain information.

(8.34)   hs
      PRO-1 REMIND POSS-1 DAUGHTER AGAIN
      I am not reminding my daughter again.

Thus, a presupposition involves background knowledge that the signer does not actually present, but that is assumed to be known by the addressee. A great deal of communication relies on assumed knowledge of this kind, and this can create confusion if information assumed to be known by both parties is actually not shared.

8.8   Summary

In this chapter, we provided an introduction to semantics, and looked at the distinctions between descriptive, social and expressive meaning on one hand, and between denotation and connotation on the other. Lexical relations and iconicity were also explored, as well as different types of sentence meaning. Finally, we looked at the relationship between meaning and context, and described a number of uses of language that depend on their context of use for interpretation. An understanding of the role of context is important for the next chapter, where we examine discourse in signed languages.

8.9   Further reading

Fromkin *et al.* (2005) and Finegan *et al.* (1997) are useful introductions to the semantics of spoken languages. Lyons (1977) is a classic text in this area, and Saeed (2003) a more recent introduction. Valli *et al.* (2005) provide a brief introduction to the semantics of ASL. Brennan (1990), Wilcox (2000), Taub (2001) and Wilcox (2004a) are studies of metaphor and iconicity in signed languages.

9 Discourse: structure and use above the sentence

Discourse is the term used to refer to any group of sentences in a language (either spoken, signed or written) that has a coherent meaning for someone who knows the language. An understanding of discourse structure depends on an understanding of language in use. In this chapter, therefore, we will focus on how aspects of the grammatical structure of Auslan are used to create clear and coherent communication.

The study of discourse is often defined as the study of texts (Crystal, 1997). Strictly speaking, *text* refers to any coherent sequence of written sentences, as in a letter, article or novel. Its use is often extended, however, so that it may also refer to any coherent series of spoken or signed sentences as well, such as a conversation, story or lecture (Matthews, 1997). This chapter looks at some of the features of signed and spoken language texts. First, we look at how the characteristics of text reflect aspects of the situation in which it is used, before looking at some specific features of different discourse types. In particular, we look at turn-taking structure and organisational principles of conversation, and the structure of narratives. We then discuss information structure and cohesion, two important features of discourse that enable addressees to recognise the background information needed to understand texts and identify who and what is being described in extended stretches of spoken and signed language.

9.1 Register, style and genre

Speakers and signers of a particular language recognise that the variety of that language used in a particular context will vary according to aspects of the social situation. For example, the type of language used varies according to whether one is chatting with family members, talking with work colleagues in the lunchroom, or making a formal presentation in a meeting or lecture. This variation in language according to situational context is known as *register* (e.g., Mesthrie *et al.*, 2000).

The term *register* is not used in the same way by all linguists. In this book, we will use a definition of register proposed by Halliday (1978). For Halliday, register reflects variation in the organisational structure of language according to differences in the field, tenor and mode of communication.

One aspect of register variation is the vocabulary used in a particular field (e.g., a specific subject area or occupation). The register of medicine, for example, involves the use of distinct specialist vocabulary (or *jargon*) which differs from the register of law, politics, engineering or linguistics. Specialist vocabulary may include subject-specific words, such as the English word *cardiomyopathy* in medicine or the Auslan sign CURRICULUM in education. Additionally, it may involve specialised senses of the same lexical item, such as the use of *morphology* to refer to the grammatical structure of words in linguistics, and to the structure of living things in biology. Similarly, the sign BETWEEN acts as a preposition but is also used to refer to a 'forward' position in a football game. Note, however, that Auslan has considerably less register variation in its native lexicon than English, reflecting the fact that it has not been used in as wide a range of occupations and subject areas. Research conducted by Parker and Schembri (1996) on computer-related terminology in Auslan, for example, showed that although new signs are emerging in this field, many native signers preferred to use fingerspelling to refer to specific computer terms in English (cf. Brentari, 1995).

Register is also used to refer to variation in grammar, vocabulary and pronunciation related to the tenor or social relationship between participants. This is often indicated by the level of formality, sometimes referred to as different *styles* (Joos, 1967) Thus, a paper at a professional conference will usually employ a more formal style than a chat with family members. We will explore aspects of variation in formality in English and Auslan below.

Lastly, variation in mode reflects aspects of the situational context. Different situations in the signing community require different choices in the medium of communication, such as speech, writing, sign, or fingerspelling. As well as differences in medium, different text types may be used for different purposes. Thus, the type of language used in a poem will be different from that found in a report in a newspaper, and a scientific conference paper will differ from a personal experience story told as part of a conversation with friends. *Genre* is the term used to refer to a particular text type that serves a specific function and has a characteristic pattern of grammar and vocabulary (Halliday, 1978). There has been very little research into genres in signed languages, and thus we will only deal with two very broad text types in this chapter: narratives and conversations.

9.1.1 Degrees of formality

Joos (1967) provided a useful summary of the main types of variation in formality in spoken languages, one of the dimensions of register. He suggested that there were five styles of English usage, from the most to the least formal: *frozen*, *formal*, *consultative*, *casual* and *intimate*. We will assume here that these five broad styles can also be applied to signed language use, although there has not yet been detailed research on this issue for Auslan.

A frozen style is used in written poems and other texts, and in ritualistic social situations using spoken and signed language (e.g., weddings, funerals, church services or when police recite someone's rights as they are arrested). The vocabulary and grammar in such situations is fixed and unchanging, and may even be archaic (e.g., as in the use of phrases such as *thou art in heaven* in prayer, or *our land is girt by sea* in the Australian national anthem). There are numerous examples in English, but fewer examples in Auslan. Frozen signed versions of prayers exist, for example, within particular deaf religious groups, and fixed versions of the national anthem and other signed songs are used in some schools for deaf children and by the Australian Theatre of the Deaf. Some fixed language use may occur in other situations, such as when proposing and seconding a motion in formal meetings of deaf political or sports associations.

Formal style refers to the language used in situations in which there is considerable social distance between the signer or speaker and the addressee. Often, the text of the formal exchange has been planned and perhaps rehearsed. Formal style might be used, for example, when a priest is delivering a sermon in church, an academic presenting a lecture, or the president of the Australian Association of the Deaf giving a report to its members. These uses of language are usually *monologic* (i.e., there is only one signer or speaker), and thus there is little interaction. The phonological production of signs and speech in this context is careful, with little assimilation or reduction. Fingerspelling will be slower, and specific lexical items may be fingerspelled in full. The choice of words may avoid *slang* (i.e., vocabulary suited to informal contexts) although it may be rich in jargon. The syntax is full and explicit, with less ellipsis.

Consultative style is similar to formal style but differs in that it involves more interaction. It reflects the kind of formality one might see in conversations between strangers, or between a sign language teacher and a small group of students in a classroom. The phonology, vocabulary and grammar are carefully selected and constructed, and conversational partners make background information and changes of topic explicit, but, because it is interactive, the language is somewhat less planned than what one might see in a formal situation.

Casual style is used in relaxed, unplanned conversation among friends who share more background knowledge. The phonological production of signs and speech is less careful, with significant assimilation and reduction. In Auslan, fingerspelling may be more rapid and incomplete, or sometimes used without the subordinate hand. The choice of words includes slang and fillers (e.g., phrases such as *you know* and *I mean*, or signs such as REALISE and RIGHT), and the syntax shows considerably more ellipsis and incomplete sentences than in more formal situations.

Intimate style refers to the style seen in conversations between people who know each other very well, such as couples, close friends, or members of the same family. This language is the least explicit because much more background information is shared. Exchanges may more often simply involve non-manual features or gestural communication, such as shrugs or facial expressions alone. The phonology is much reduced, with a great deal of assimilation and reduction. The vocabulary may include 'home signs' that are not understood by outsiders, nonsense words, or private terms for one's partner (e.g., *my little honey bunny*). Sentences may very often be incomplete, or may consist of single lexical items, such as 'cat' as a request to feed the cat, or COLD to mean that a cup of coffee has gone cold and it is time to make another.

9.1.2 Register variation in signed languages: An ASL case study

The work of June Zimmer (1989) on ASL represents one of the few studies on register variation in a signed language. Until further studies are carried out, no firm conclusions can be drawn about what register variation looks like in ASL (or Auslan, or indeed any signed language) on the basis of this study, but we will outline Zimmer's findings here because they suggest issues for future research into this area.

In Zimmer's (1989) study, data for her analysis came from three videotapes of one deaf native ASL signer (1) giving a lecture on linguistics, (2) presenting a talk to a small audience, and (3) conducting a television interview. All three texts are somewhat formal in style because each is planned and not spontaneous, and all are performed for an audience. However, the degree of formality in each text appears to be different. The lecture is the most planned and formal because it is based around a written paper. The genre of academic lectures is usually serious and impersonal in style. The talk is much less formal, and somewhat less planned (the signer uses notes to recall the main points he wishes to cover). The interview is less formal, more interactive and conversational, but it is taped for broadcast on television and is thus much more consultative than casual in style.

Zimmer (1989) found that the lecture was particularly different from the talk and interview, at all levels of structural organisation. A closer inspection also revealed that parts of each text were different from other parts, which she referred to as *intra-textual* register variation (also known as *register-mixing*).

A number of phonological differences between the texts were noted. For example, the signing space appeared to be much larger in the lecture, with signs being made beyond the top of the head, centre of the chest and shoulder width. Signs in the lecture also appeared to be longer in duration. Role shifts involved shifting of the entire torso or sideways movement by a step or two in the lecture, whereas only head movements were used in the talk and interview (*role shift* is explained in §9.3.1.5 below). Hand-switching (in which the non-dominant hand is used as the dominant hand) was used in all three texts, often with pronouns, but was used most frequently in the lecture. There was less assimilation of the handshape in pronoun signs in the lecture (e.g., fewer handshape changes in PRO-1 from 1 to B). Lastly, there was less perseveration and anticipation in the lecture (i.e., there were fewer instances in which the non-dominant hand in a two-handed sign appeared before the sign started or remained held in space after the sign had finished).

In terms of lexical and morphological differences in the three situations, Zimmer (1989) reported that certain colloquial ASL signs, such as WHAT-FOR and PEA-BRAIN, appeared in the talk and in portions of direct speech in the lecture but did not occur elsewhere. She also noted that conjunctions such as AND and THEN were used more in the lecture. Exaggerated reduplication of signs to indicate that some action was difficult and of long duration occurred more in the lectures, but similar meanings were realised through non-manual features, such as squinting eyes and 'ee', in the informal talk.

Several differences in syntactic and discourse features were found. For example, pseudo-cleft structures were used extensively in the lecture, but less so in the other two texts. Topicalisation was used more in the informal talk than the lecture. Discourse markers appeared more in the lecture, such as the use of the sign NOW not to talk about time, but to segment the lecture into smaller parts (*discourse markers* are defined in §9.3.3 below). Lastly, pointing with the non-dominant hand at a word fingerspelled on the dominant hand (e.g., D-E-A-F, A-T-T-I-T-U-D-E) only occurred in the lecture (of course, this is not possible in signed languages that use two-handed manual alphabets).

The most intra-textual variation occurred in the lecture, where there were three types of register variation. The body of the lecture was formal in style, but reported speech interspersed through the lecture had features of a more casual style. Some specific examples had a metaphorical and poetic style usually associated with signed theatre and poetry. The signer represented hearing researchers as a vehicle, for example, and deaf researchers as a boat, and then produced a simultaneous sign construction with two depicting verbs showing both moving along together.

Zimmer (1989) concludes that the five register styles suggested by Joos (1967) are too simplistic, since there is variation between these three types of text, yet all of these are basically formal in style, and because it does not take account of intra-textual variation.

9.1.3 Narrative structure

In this section, we shall focus on one particular text type: the personal experience narrative (i.e., stories people tell about experiences that they have had). In telling a story, a narrator needs to make choices about which events to include, which people and places to describe, and which linguistic structures to use. Mesthrie *et al.* (2000:191) noted that 'narratives cannot be regarded simply as neutral, factual accounts: they are always representations, constructed by the narrator to make a certain point. The choices made in narrating a story allow narrators to represent themselves in a certain light, and to evaluate other people and events in the story.'

In his study of American English, William Labov (1972) collected personal experience narratives from speakers in New York City. His research suggested that narrative structure consists of structured sequences of sentences that describe events in the order in which they actually occurred, at least for personal narratives in western, English-speaking cultures. Labov also claimed that prototypical narrative may include up to six parts. First, there is the *abstract* which provides a summary of the events to be described, and may include some sense of why the narrator feels this story is worth telling. This is followed by an *orientation* that describes the setting, characters and other background information that is necessary to understand the narrative. Next, there is the explanation of some *complicating action*. This recounts the basic details of the event or events that are the focus of the narrative. This may be followed by an *evaluation* that indicates some lesson to be learned from the story, or the reasons why the speaker thinks the events occurred. An evaluation may, however, be included at any point in the narrative, and is often interwoven with a description of the complicating action. Next, there is a *resolution* which explains the results of the events, and finally a *coda* that brings the story to a close and may link the events in the narrative to the present time.

Below we have given a basic transcription of an Auslan personal experience narrative (The carpentry class) from the video *Signs of Language* (Griffith University, 1992). We can see that this narrative appears to follow a similar overall pattern as the one suggested by Labov (1972). The first line appears to be an example of an abstract, although it does not provide a summary, simply an evaluation that the story is worth telling because it made a lasting impression on the signer. Lines 2-5 might be analysed as the orientation, describing the setting and characters. The complicating action occupies most of the remaining text, until the resolution in lines 17 and 18 explains the outcome. There is no clear evaluation section, although the fact that the students disapproved of their teacher's behaviour (but were unable to do anything about it) emerges clearly in several sections of the story. The coda at the end echoes the abstract at the beginning, linking the events described to the present. Thus, it appears that some of the general patterns of structural organisation in signed and spoken narrative may be very similar.

9.1.3.1 *The carpentry class narrative*

(9.1)　　<u>hn</u>　　　　　　　　<u>hs</u>
PT+f PRO-1 NEVER FORGET
Yes, I'll never forget this.

(9.2)
$$\overline{}^{\text{br}}$$
LONG-AGO WHEN PRO-1 YOUNG STILL A-T SCHOOL PRO-1P MUST LEARN
CARPENTRY
Back when I was young and still at school, we had to learn carpentry.

(9.3) ALL BOY CL:2H5-MANY-PEOPLE-GO-TO+lf CARPENTRY
All the boys had to go to carpentry class

(9.4)
$$\overline{}^{\text{mm}}$$
LEARN HAMMER PLANE+rept
where we learned how to use hammers, planes and so on.

(9.5)
$$\overline{}^{\text{th}}$$
LOOK-UP-AND-AROUND SOME PRO-1P YOUNG BOY SAME DREAM
Some of us, being young boys, would daydream.

(9.6)
$$\overline{}^{\text{rs:student}}$$
LOOK-AROUND CL:X-SMALL-THING-HIT-HEAD LOOK+rt WHAT SURPRISE
I was idly looking around the room, when something hit me on the head. I was shocked.

(9.7)
$$\overline{}^{\text{rs:teacher}}$$
TEACHER PT+rt THROW CL:X-SMALL-OBJECT-HIT-HEAD ORDER+lf WORK+rept
The teacher had thrown it! He ordered me to get on with my work.

(9.8)
$$\overline{}^{\text{rs:student}}$$
LOOK+rt IRRITATE LOOK+recip+lf WHAT-A-NERVE+rt PRO-3+rt
My classmates and I looked at each other, irritated—what a nerve he had!

(9.9)
$$\overline{}^{\text{rs:student}}$$
LOOK-DOWN WORK LOOK-DOWN WORK+rept HAVE-A-LOOK CA:wink LOOK+rt
We got back to work, but I became curious, winked at my classmate, and looked up.

(9.10)
$$\overline{}^{\text{rs:teacher}} \quad \overline{}^{\text{rs:student}}$$
CL:gC-GLASSES-TILT-DOWN LOOK+lf LOOK+recip +rt LOOK-DOWN
The teacher was staring back at me over his glasses and our eyes met, so I looked away.

(9.11)
$$\overline{}^{\text{rs:student}}$$
WRONG^MIND PRO-1 WORK+rept LOOK+rt
Feeling bad that he'd caught me, I got back to work, but took another look

(9.12)
$$\overline{}^{\text{rs:student}}$$
CA:startled CL:1 -PERSON-WALK-TOWARDS-ME-FROM-RIGHT
and was startled to see him striding towards me.

(9.13)
$$\overline{}^{\text{rs:teacher}}$$
WALK-IN-QUICK-ANGRY-MANNER LOOK+lf WALK-IN-QUICK-ANGRY-MANNER
He was approaching very quickly and staring straight at me,

(9.14)
$$\overline{}^{\text{rs:teacher}}$$
NOT HAPPY WALK-IN-QUICK-ANGRY-MANNER
and was clearly not pleased.

(9.15)   rs:teacher
ORDER+lf WORK ORDER+lf GRAB POSS-1P NECK ARM-OVER-SHOULDER
He ordered us to get back to work, grabbed our necks and signed over our
shoulders

(9.16)   rs:teacher   rs:student
LOOK-DOWN+rept CL:S-HEAD-AND-BODY-SHAKE HOW-DARE-YOU+rt
'Watch! Watch!'. Our heads were jerked back and forth as he signed.

(9.17)   rs:student
PUT-UP-WITH-IT CL:1 -PERSON-WALK-OFF-TO-RIGHT LEAVE+rt
We were shocked, but we just had to put up with it until he walked away.

(9.18) rs:student (with disgust)
LOOK+recip+lf
We exchanged disgusted looks,

(9.19)   rs:student   hs
LOOK-DOWN GRIN-AND-BEAR-IT WORK+rept NEVER FORGET PRO-1 PT+f
and then resigned ourselves to work. I'll never forget that.

9.1.4   Narratives in signed and spoken language compared

In work on comparing storytelling structure in different cultures, Dan Slobin (1996) argued that different languages provide their users with a different range of resources, and that this predisposed them towards particular ways of using language.

Jennifer Rayman (1999) was interested in investigating how English and ASL narratives represented characters, space and motion. She collected stories using a silent cartoon *The Tortoise and the Hare*. Five adult native signers of ASL and five adult speakers of English were individually shown the cartoon, and asked to retell the story to a deaf or hearing peer. The adults across each language group were matched for gender, age and educational background. She found a number of differences between the stories in ASL and those in English.

First, the signers and speakers tended to differ in the choice of perspective used to narrate the story. English-speaking participants told the majority of the story in narrator mode, while signing participants told the story mostly from the perspective of the characters involved. They represented the character's personalities by facial expressions and body movements using role shift (this is defined below). The ASL users also provided more visual and spatial details. They spent more time introducing the characters, and showed the characters' distinctive physical and personality characteristics using their own bodies. All of the deaf narrators, for example, imitated the rabbit in some way, by mimicking its gestures or manner of walking. Only two of the hearing narrators described the rabbit's manner of walking in any detail. Only one hearing person, an actress, used facial expressions to any extent, but not to the same degree as the deaf signers. All signers described how the race began by describing the contestants at the starting line and then mentioning the use of a starting gun, but this was only described by one hearing person. The ASL signers also showed the hare's hurried manner of running using the two 1 handshapes for 'legs' when he discovers that he has been overtaken by the tortoise. They also used depicting verbs to show the spatial relationship between the two animals as they ran, whilst the English speakers used prepositions like *behind*, *after* and *in front of* that did not communicate the same detail.

Many of these same characteristics appear also in narratives in Auslan, as can be seen from the carpentry class example. Rayman's (1999) work provides some evidence for Slobin's (1996) claim, suggesting that visual-gestural resources for describing characters, space and motion are more readily available to signers than to speakers because of the visual-spatial nature of signed languages, and that these resources thus shape the organisation of narratives in signed languages and create the differences we see between the signers and speakers in her study.

9.1.5 Conversation

Conversations between two or more people may be the most basic and important discourse type that exists in human communication. It is present in all societies across the globe, and is most probably the most common form of communicative event among human beings. This fact makes conversational structure difficult for linguists to study, because conversations occur in such a wide range of settings in so many diverse cultures, with so many different purposes and participants. Crystal (1997) has pointed out that, despite this diversity, there is little doubt that conversations are systematic in subtle ways. A conversation may be compared to a chess game—there appear to be ways of opening, conducting and ending conversations. Participants take turns, make moves and appear to follow rules. We will explore the turn-taking system and guiding principles for conversation in the next section.

9.1.5.1 Turn-taking in signed and spoken conversations
Conversations differ from narratives in that usually narratives are monologic, whereas conversations at minimum must be *dialogic* (i.e., two people talk). Conversational structure appears to differ in formal or consultative situations compared to casual or intimate circumstances (Sacks, Schegloff & Jefferson, 1974). In more formal conversations in Western culture, two or more people do not usually speak or sign at the same time. Instead, they often take turns at speaking, generally with only one person speaking or signing at any time. If two people begin at the same time, usually someone will stop. Silence between turns is generally avoided, although it may be completely acceptable in other cultures or in other less formal circumstances. In more casual situations, however, a different set of turn-taking rules may be followed, with

more overlapping turns and frequent interruptions. The rules for conducting conversational interaction are thus quite complex. The more formal model of conversational interaction is known as the *single floor*, while the more informal model is sometimes called the *collaborative floor* (Coates, 1997).

In the single floor model of conversation, a range of linguistic and non-linguistic signals are used to signal the start of a conversation, how to begin a turn and maintain it, how to interrupt someone else's turn, and how to end your turn. During an individual's turn, addressees also use linguistic and non-linguistic *back channels* (such as *mm* or *uh-huh*) to indicate that they understand the speaker (Sacks *et al.*, 1974).

In spoken languages, strangers may begin a conversation with socially recognised opening sequences, such as by using a greeting like *Hello, my name's Kim,* or an enquiry, such as *Excuse me, do you know the time?* Conversations between friends may use different opening sequences, such as *Guess what?* (Wardhaugh, 1985). In all cases, however, all that is required is that two speakers are able to hear each other. Thus, a speaker can simply begin talking to a stranger who might be reading a newspaper, or a family member in another room. In signed conversations, however, signers actually have to be looking at each other before any communication can take place. Thus, part of an opening sequence in signed language may include some means of gaining an addressee's visual attention. In early research on ASL, Baker (1977) found that signers may wave a hand within the addressee's field of vision, gently touch them on the upper arm or knee, or ask someone else to wave at or touch the person and direct their gaze to the signer. Signers may also use the vibration created by tapping on a tabletop around which others are sitting, or by stamping on the floor, to gain their addressee's visual attention. Once visual attention is gained, then an opening sequence such as signing HOW-ARE-YOU, HELLO or HI may be used.

Once speakers or signers have begun to converse, eye gaze is used as a way of holding the floor. In Western English-speaking cultures, for example, speakers do not normally stare at each other continuously when speaking. Instead, their eye gaze may alternate between their addressee and other points in space around the speaker (Wardhaugh, 1985). This is also true of signers. Signers can maintain a turn by looking away from their addressee while signing. They may also keep their hands in the signing space, or hold the last sign while pausing. They may use fillers, such as the sign UM, while they are thinking of what to say next. Speakers may also use fillers (such as *ah* or *um*), or hand gestures to maintain a turn.

Addressees usually maintain their eye gaze on the speaker or signer, although this is not necessary for all spoken language conversations (e.g., telephone conversations). They may wait their turn before beginning to speak or sign themselves, although the use of back channels may also occur. English speakers will use *mm*, *uh-huh* and *oh*, for example, or gestures such as head nodding. Signers may also use nodding and other non-manual features, or signs such as SURPRISE ('Oh, really!?', 'Uh-huh?'), TRUE ('Is that so!?'), RIGHT ('Yeah'), GOOD ('Yep', 'Hmm', 'Uh-huh'), or BAD ('Ooo!', 'Oh, no!', 'Oh dear' and so on and so forth).

UM   SURPRISE

Figure 9.1: *A filler and a back channel used in Auslan.*

Returning one's gaze to the addressee may indicate the termination of a turn. Signers and speakers may also signal the end of their turn by speeding up or slowing down their talking, by stopping their talking completely and/or returning their hands to rest position, or they may ask a question of an addressee. In multiparty conversations, the signer or speaker may allocate a turn to one individual by using gaze or indicating them in some way, or a turn may be requested by another person after a pause in the conversation. Signers may take the floor simply by raising their hands ready to sign, allowing time for others to turn their gaze towards them. They may also increase the frequency and size of their head nodding, or point towards the signer with an index finger or upturned palm (we can see an example of this at the beginning of the carpentry class narrative—in order to request a turn, the signer begins to nod and points forward before successfully taking the floor and beginning to tell the story). Conversational partners may interrupt by breaking their eye gaze with the signer, or by simply beginning to sign and repeating the first few lexical items until they gain the visual attention of their addressee. Signers may refuse to give up the floor by simply continuing, not turning their gaze towards the interrupter, or by explicitly directing a 'wait' gesture (such as an upturned palm or index finger) towards them. Many of these linguistic and gestural turn initiation and interruption strategies are also used by users of spoken languages (Wardhaugh, 1985).

In collaborative floor models of conversations, especially in casual situations among friends, the turn-taking system described above may not be followed (Coates & Sutton-Spence, 2001). Instead, the floor is shared by all participants. For example, signers may not check if they have their addressee's visual attention, but simply begin to sign. Signers may talk simultaneously, because participants can attend to more than one signer at a time. In such cases, participating in the floor is more important than having all of one's signing seen by all parties in the conversation.

9.1.5.2 Conversational maxims

The philosopher Herbert Paul Grice (1975) proposed that all communication, and particularly conversation, follows the *cooperative principle*. This principle states that conversational partners cooperate with each other so as to reduce the potential for misunderstanding, and will make contributions to the conversation that help fulfil its purpose. Obviously, the exact nature of this cooperation will vary from one conversation to the next. The way that the cooperative principle works in a business meeting (where time is limited and individuals are expected to keep to the topic) will be different from how it works in a casual conversation among colleagues in a pub after work (where changes in the topic of conversations are more welcome). Because of the cooperative principle, individuals involved in a conversation are able to infer what a conversational partner intends to say, even when it is not said directly. Thus, this is another aspect that can allow addressees to interpret language in context.

The cooperative principle consists of four sub-principles, known as *conversational maxims*. First, there is the *maxim of quantity* which states that (a) speakers and signers should make their contribution informative but (b) it should not be more informative than required. This is illustrated by example (9.20) below. The response here matches the requirements of the maxim of quantity. If the respondent were to explicitly mention the calendar date (with the month and year), it would most probably be considered excessive in this context, as we do not normally include the year in such responses.

(9.20) a.   <u>   bf   </u>

       NEW TEACHER ARRIVE WHEN
       When does the new teacher arrive?

   b.   NEXT-WEEK M-O-N
       Next Monday.

Next is the *maxim of relevance* which simply asserts that the speaker or signer should make a contribution that is relevant to the conversation. Again, the response in (9.20) fulfils this requirement. If in answer to the question about the arrival of the new teacher, the respondent were to begin to explain that Sihanoukville is a pleasant seaside town on the coast of Cambodia, and the addressee had not asked for this information in any of the preceding discussion, then this contribution would not be relevant in this context.

There is also the *maxim of manner* which states that the speaker or signer should (a) avoid ambiguity, (b) be brief and (c) be orderly. Although a possible response to the question in (9.20) that included the month, day and year would avoid ambiguity, it is not as brief as it could be, given that NEXT-WEEK M-O-N is sufficiently clear in this context.

Lastly, there is the *maxim of quality* which requires simply that signers or speakers should not say they believe to be false. Clearly, an answer to the question in (9.20) in which the signer deliberately gives misleading information, such as the wrong date, would not follow the cooperative principle.

These maxims represent principles on which the successful exchange of information between conversational partners is based. Grice (1975) recognised that there may be additional maxims at work in conversation, especially when individuals have aims other than the exchange of information. Speakers and signers can flout the maxim of quality, for example, by exaggerating or even lying when they are deliberately being humorous. This is completely acceptable when all conversational partners are aware that this is what is happening. Researchers in recent times have also recognised that other principles may be at work at other times, such as the *politeness principle* suggested by Leech (1983). In such cases, the need to avoid causing offence may take precedence over the maxim of manner, and these may result in the types of indirect illocution we saw in Chapter 8. The need to be polite may also flout the maxim of quality, causing individuals to tell 'white lies' in order to maintain communicative cooperation.

How the cooperative and politeness principles operate in conversation, however, undoubtedly varies from one socio-cultural group to the next. It is part of deaf community folklore that deaf signers sometimes seem to use language in a very direct way, commenting on aspects of the physical appearance of others that may be considered impolite by some hearing people. This anecdotal observation about differences between deaf and hearing communication has not, however, been the subject of any research. This possible difference may reflect divergence in the operation of the politeness principle between these groups, or simply the fact that signed languages, as visual languages, draw more commonly on types of visual description to identify individuals than a spoken language like English (this was discussed in §9.1.4 above).

9.2 Information structure

In the previous sections, we have looked at the patterns in the overall organisation of entire texts, such as conversations or narratives. In this section, we will look at the interaction between discourse and smaller grammatical units, such as clauses and combination of clauses. In Chapter 7 on syntax, we noted that the order of signs in Auslan appears to be more flexible than the order of words in English. We will now examine some of the discourse factors that influence the syntax of Auslan. Consider the sentences in (9.21), all of which have essentially the same descriptive meaning—'my friend has bought a house in Adelaide'.

(9.21) a.   POSS-1 FRIEND BUY HOUSE ADELAIDE
                   _____ br

    b.   ADELAIDE POSS-1 FRIEND BUY HOUSE PT+rt
                        _____ br

    c.   POSS-1 FRIEND BUY HOUSE ADELAIDE
                _____ br

    d.   HOUSE POSS-1 FRIEND BUY ADELAIDE
                        _____ br

    e.   POSS-1 FRIEND BUY WHAT HOUSE ADELAIDE PT+rt
                            _____ br

    f.   POSS-1 FRIEND BUY HOUSE WHERE ADELAIDE
                        _____ br

    g.   POSS-1 FRIEND D-O WHAT BUY HOUSE ADELAIDE
                        _____ br

    h.   BUY HOUSE ADELAIDE WHO POSS-1 FRIEND

Signers and speakers can use these different structures to emphasise some elements as being more or less important in a particular discourse context. This aspect of the organisation of language is known as *information structure* (Lambrecht, 1994). Information structure reflects aspects of the discourse context, such as whether the addressee already knows who or what is being discussed, or has already been told some of what the speaker is telling them. Because of its relationship to context, information structure is another aspect of pragmatics. We introduced the notion of pragmatics in Chapter 8, and defined it as the study of the relationship between context and meaning in language. Information structure is also relevant for our understanding of discourse, so we have included the discussion in this chapter.

Information structure is encoded in different ways in different languages, but the various factors we will discuss below appear to apply equally well to Auslan and English.

9.2.1   Given and new, topic and comment

One important aspect of information structure is the distinction between given and new information, and between topic and comment. These are known as *pragmatic* or *discourse roles* (Comrie, 1989).

In any natural discourse situation, speakers/signers and their addressees will share some background knowledge, but they may not be aware of other information. *Given information* is information that the speaker can assume the addressee already knows because it can be found in the immediate linguistic or situational context (Chafe, 1976). *New information* is information that the addressee may not know or which is introduced into the discourse context for the first time. In (9.22), we can see that the phrase FINISH READ BOOK PT+lf is given information. In this example, the signer assumes that the addressee knows that the book was supposed to be read (perhaps because this utterance is from classroom discourse in which the book is a set text, for example). In the reply, the fingerspelled sequence C-H-R-I-S is new information. Part of the given information (e.g., READ BOOK PT+lf) is simply omitted in this reply because it has already been introduced in the question. This is a typical pattern. Given information is commonly expressed in a more reduced or abbreviated fashion, or may be completely left out of the sentence.

(9.22)

a.
                                  br bf
FINISH READ BOOK PT+lf WHO
Who has read the book?

b.
                          hn
C-H-R-I-S FINISH PRO-3+rt
Chris has read it.

Like similar structures in spoken languages (Foley & Van Valin, 1985), the pseudo-cleft structure used in Auslan (discussed in Chapter 7) provides a clear syntactic marking of given and new information. A number of sentences using this structure appear as part of example (9.21). If we compare (e) and (h) in this example, we can see that there are differences in the given information in each context. For example, in (e), the signer first produces the sequence POSS-1 FRIEND BUY WHAT, showing that the addressee knows that the signer's friend bought something, but does not know what it is. In (h), however, the signer first produces BUY HOUSE PT+rt ADELAIDE WHO because the addressee knows that someone has bought a house in Adelaide, but does not know who. In each case, the new information follows the question sign.

The *topic* (or *theme*) of a sentence is what the sentence is about, while the *comment* (or *rheme*) gives some information about the topic (Li & Thompson, 1976; Halliday, 1985). The topic usually represents the first major element in a sentence. It is often the case that the topic is also given information, because the topic to be discussed will be something already known to the addressee. As a result, the comment will often be new information, and it will follow the topic in the sentence. We can see this clearly in the sentences (e) and (h) from (9.21) discussed above. In each case, the topic of these sentences (i.e., the string of signs produced with a brow raise) is the given information, while the comment is new information.

The topic does not, however, always represent given information. In (9.22) above, for example, we can see that sentence (b) begins with new information. So roles played by given and new information and by topic and comment structures are distinct.

Topics may also be marked by the non-manual signals for topicalisation, as discussed in Chapter 7. Some kind of non-manual marking of topics appears to be especially common if the undergoer noun phrase or the verb phrase is produced as the first element of a clause. This may be because the actor noun phrase is most often associated with the topic, although it is not clear if non-manual signals are actually obligatory when elements other than the actor noun phrase occur sentence initially in Auslan (cf. Sandler & Lillo-Martin, 2006 on ASL and Israeli Sign Language).

9.2.2 Contrastiveness and comparison

English often uses stress to signal that some element of a phrase or sentence is *contrastive* (Chafe, 1976). Contrast is used to highlight a statement in comparison to some previous statement or question. The contrasted element will be produced with more prominence by being longer in duration, louder and/or with a higher pitch (represented by bolding in (9.23)). This can be compared with the response in (9.24), which is not contrastive.

(9.23) a. I heard you really hate cats, right?
      b. No, I hate **dogs**.

(9.24) b. Yeah, I really can't stand them.

In signed language, stress is signalled in a very similar way. The stressed element may be longer in duration, produced with larger movements and more forceful articulation, and accompanied by specific non-manual features (Johnston, 1992; Wilbur, 1999). In (9.25) the sign is produced with stronger articulation (represented by bolding) and a forward lean ('fl') of the trunk, shoulders and head. These features are lacking in the non-contrastive reply in (9.26).

(9.25)

          cs   bf

    a.   HEAR POSS-2 CAT DIE RECENT POOR-THING BAD-LUCK
               I heard your cat died recently-the poor thing. Such a shame.
                   fl
    b.   NO POSS-1 **DOG** DIE
               *No, my **dog** died.*

(9.26)   YES BAD
               Yes, it's awful.

In addition to non-manual features for contrast, space may be used in *comparative* discourse. In order to compare two things or ideas, signers may produce the sign for each in a separate part of the signing space, usually on the right and left side of the signer's body (Johnston, 1992; Winston, 1995), as in (9.27). Here we see that the sign BUY has been produced on the left by means of a body lean in that direction as the sign was articulated ('ll'), while R-E-N-T has been fingerspelled accompanied by a body lean to the right ('rl').

(9.27) _____ br _____ bf
                                      ll _____ rl
HOUSE NEAR BEACH BUY R-E-N-T WHICH PREFER PRO-2
As for a house near the beach, would you prefer to buy or rent one?

The juxtaposition in space of the two referents allows the signer to highlight that there are only two available options if one wishes to live near the beach: buying or renting a house. In the remainder of this discourse, the signer may describe the pros and cons of buying compared to those for renting by using the comparative discourse frame established in this first clause complex. For example, by leaning to the left while signing about issues to do with buying a house, and then shifting to the right while discussing renting, the signer could draw the addressee's attention to the fact that a comparison between these options is being made.

9.2.3   Definite, specific and generic reference

Speakers and signers may mark a noun phrase as *indefinite* when they introduce it into the discourse and assume that the addressee cannot identify who or what is being referred to (Foley & Van Valin, 1985). Marking a noun phrase as *definite*, however, indicates that the addressee can identify its referent. In English, an indefinite noun phrase may be marked by the indefinite article *a* or *an*, as in (9.28). A definite noun phrase may use the definite article *the*, as in (9.29), where the speaker is talking about the family cat.

(9.28) I want to buy a cat.

(9.29) I can't find the cat.

In Auslan, indefinite noun phrases are usually not marked by any determiner, although sometimes a signer may use the sign ONE to talk about an indefinite singular referent, as in (9.30). Definite noun phrases may also occur without a determiner (especially if the noun phrase is a pronoun or a proper noun), but often signers will use a pointing sign as part of the noun phrase to signal that they assume the addressee can identify the referent being discussed, as in (9.31). This pointing sign is used even if the referent is not actually physically present, in which case it simply points away from the signer and addressee.

(9.30) HAVE ONE WOMAN WIN FIVE MILLION DOLLAR L-O-T-T-O
         There was a woman who won five million dollars in Lotto.

(9.31) SAME PT+rt WOMAN WIN L-O-T-T-O AGAIN
         The same woman won Lotto again.

A noun phrase can also show *specific* reference when it refers to a particular referent. In (9.32) and (9.33), the noun phrase MAN SHORT BLONDE 'the short blonde man' helps make the reference specific (i.e., because it refers to not just any man, but one who is short and blonde). A specific referent, however, may or may not be known to the addressee. In Auslan, a specific noun phrase with a referent that can be identified by the addressee (i.e., a specific and definite referent) may co-occur with a stress and/or repeated pointing sign, often accompanied by non-manual features, such as 'ee', as in (9.32). This is an emphatic way of indicating a specific referent that your addressee can identify. If the noun phrase has specific reference that may not be identifiable (i.e., a specific but indefinite referent) then no determiner may be used, as in (9.33).

(9.32)   ee   br
       PT+rt+rept   MAN SHORT BLONDE PT+rt LOOK-FOR PRO-2
       That short blonde man over there is looking for you.

(9.33)   cs
       RECENT HAVE MAN SHORT BLONDE LOOK-FOR PRO-2
       Just a minute ago there was a short blonde man looking for you.

Like indefinite noun phrases, non-specific noun phrases are not usually marked in any way, as in (9.34). The linguistic and situational context in this example would make it clear that the signer does not have any specific or definite dog in mind.

(9.34) PRO-1 CONSIDER BUY DOG PRO-1
       I'm thinking about buying a dog.

Noun phrases may also show *generic* reference. In (9.35), we can see that the signer is referring to elephants in a generic way—the sentence says something about in elephants in general. Like non-specific noun phrases, there is no formal way to mark a noun phrase as having generic reference in Auslan. Understanding that the noun ELEPHANT has generic meaning in (9.35) would come from the context (this sentence may come from a class in which a teacher is talking about animals in a general way, for example).

(9.35) ELEPHANT FROM FIRST-OF-LIST A-F-R-I-C-A SECOND-OF-LIST A-S-I-A
       Elephants are from Africa and Asia.

9.3   Cohesion

Cohesion in discourse refers to the features of the lexicon and grammar that link different parts of a text together. Cohesive devices make it possible for the addressee to keep track of who is being referred to and what is being described in a text, and they work to unify a text into a coherent whole. In English and Auslan, we can analyse cohesion as being achieved in four main ways: by means of *referential cohesion*, *ellipsis* and *substitution*, *discourse markers* and *lexical organisation* (Halliday, 1985; Schiffrin, 1987). We present a discussion of each of these aspects of cohesion in the following sections.

9.3.1 Referential cohesion

Referential cohesion works in two main ways (Halliday & Hasan, 1976). Lexical items, such as pronouns, can be associated with referents in the situational context, as in saying to the person next to you on a crowded train *Excuse me, could you please move a little to the side?* The referent of the pronoun *you* is completely clear in this situation, because the question has been directed towards the referent, so there is no need to actually identify who you are talking to in the discourse. This is known as *exophoric* (i.e., language external) reference. When indicating verbs are directed towards the addressee (i.e., to someone who is physically present), then this is also exophoric reference.

Lexical items may also refer to other lexical items in the discourse, as in (9.36) below. In the second sentence, we can identify who the possessive determiner *her* refers to because this person is identified in the first sentence. This is known as *endophoric* (i.e., language internal) reference.

(9.36) I need to phone the woman who called yesterday. What's her name?

Language internal reference may refer back (*anaphoric* reference) or forward (*cataphoric* reference) to something in the text. We will look at examples of this language internal reference in the following sections (most of which make referential use of space), drawing on a summary provided in Morgan (1999).

9.3.1.1 Full noun phrases
In signed narratives, third-person referents are often introduced by full noun phrases. Referents may be introduced using signs, as in TEACHER PT+rt 'the teacher' (9.7) and ALL BOY 'all the boys' (9.3) in the carpentry class narrative, or fingerspelling (e.g., in a personal experience narrative, a signer may use SHOP O-W-N-E-R to refer to a participant). These signed and fingerspelled items may then work as the beginning of a *reference chain* in a text (Martin, 1992). That is, they name the referent and introduce it into the discourse. Other cohesive devices may then refer back to this first instance, as we will see in the following sections.

9.3.1.2 Pronouns and determiners
In the example of TEACHER PT+rt, we see that the noun sign is accompanied by a determiner that points to a particular location in the signing space. This establishes an association between that referent and the right side of the signing space. Later, the signer uses a pointing sign as a pronoun. This is directed to the right and thus is used to refer back to the teacher, as we can see in the carpentry class narrative. In (9.8), PRO-3+rt is an example of

anaphoric reference, because the pronoun is referring back to a noun phrase TEACHER PT+rt in (9.7).

There is also an example of cataphoric reference in the text. In (9.2), the signer explains that 'we' had to learn carpentry. He uses the sign PRO-1+PL which is a very general pronoun meaning 'we' or 'us'. Although it is clear that he is referring to himself and his classmates, the exact referent of this sign is not clarified until (9.3) when he explains that only the boys had to go to carpentry class. Thus, the sign PRO-1+PL also refers forward to the noun phrase ALL BOY.

9.3.1.3 Verb modifications

We have reproduced part of the same example from the carpentry class narrative in (9.37) below, and we have highlighted how verb modifications work as part of referential cohesion. In the previous discourse, the signer has established the location on the right as representing the teacher, and the location on the left as associated with his classmates. Thus, when he signs LOOK directed towards the right, and LOOK+recip (a two-handed form in which each hand signs LOOK directed at the other hand) with the dominant hand directed towards the left, we know that the first sign means 'I looked at the teacher' and the second means 'My classmates and I looked at each other.' There are numerous other examples of spatially modified forms of LOOK in the text, as well as other signs, that help the addressee to keep track of who is doing what to whom.

(9.37) _____ rs:student
    LOOK**+rt** IRRITATE LOOK+recip **+lf** WHAT-A-NERVE+rt PRO-3+rt

9.3.1.4 Classifier handshapes

Classifier handshapes also add to the overall cohesion of a text. There are numerous examples in the carpentry class narrative. In particular, a 1 handshape representing a person is produced as part of a depicting sign that describes the teacher walking towards and away from the students. Like the verb modifications described in (9.37), this depicting sign moves towards the signer from a location on the right, and then later moves away towards the right. This location in space has already been associated with the teacher in the previous discourse, and the use of a 1 handshape (rather than a B handshape for a vehicle, for example) is also consistent with the referent being a person. As a result, it is clear to the addressee that these depicting signs refer to the motion of the teacher.

9.3.1.5 Role shift

Role shift (also known as *referential shift*) is another important aspect of referential cohesion, and is particularly important in the carpentry class narrative. Role shift is used to indicate that part of the discourse is presented from the point of view of a particular participant. The participant referred to may be the signer himself or herself at some time other than the present (e.g., if the signer is relating a story about a past event in which he or she were involved), or some other person. Role shift is signalled in three ways: *shifted expressive elements, shifted gaze and/or posture* and *shifted reference* (Engberg-Pedersen, 1993). In shifted expressive elements, signers may use their face and/or body to express the emotions and attitudes felt by someone other than the signer (or by themselves at some point in the past). Shifted gaze and posture may involve signers alternating between looking upwards and downwards, or to the left and the right, and turning their head and/or body in these directions. These shifts are often used to represent moving between two roles in a reported conversation, for example. Gaze and head positions that alternative between upward and downward directions are particularly common when reporting conversations between adults and children. Shifted reference refers to the use of pronouns and agreeing verbs to reflect the point of view of the participant role taken on by the signer. It is possible for each of these three elements to occur individually, but often shifted expressive elements, shifted gaze and shifted reference co-occur (the use of shifted head and body position appears to be a little less frequent).

We see all three elements in (9.13) from the carpentry class narrative. In this example, the signer is describing the actions of the teacher as he strode across the classroom towards the students. As the signer produced this part of the narrative, there is a break in his eye gaze with the addressee and his head turns to the left (i.e., shifted gaze and head position). His face takes on a stern expression, reflecting the emotions and attitude of the teacher (i.e., shifted facial expression). He directs the sign LOOK towards the left which is the location of the students (including himself) from the teacher's point of view (i.e., shifted reference).

The use of shifted expressive elements in this series of clauses is an example of *constructed action* (Liddell & Metzger, 1998). Constructed action refers to the gestures that imitate the actions of someone other than the signer at the time of signing. Thus, the sign WALK in this context is a lexical item (this sign is often used to mean 'march'), but the facial expression and posture are the constructed action. There are a number of other examples of constructed action in the carpentry class narrative, including when the signer represents himself winking at his classmates by winking during the narrative, and when he jerks his head and body backwards and forwards as he signs CL:S-HEAD-AND-BODY-SHAKE (9.16). The term *constructed action* was introduced by Winston (1991) because it refers to actions that are not just a direct imitation of the character's actions, but are a selective re-enactment (i.e., they are the signer's 're-construction' of another's actions).

Role shift can also be used to represent *constructed dialogue* (Tannen, 1986; Roy, 1989). Example (9.38) might form part of a narrative in which the signer is reporting a signed conversation with a friend.

(9.38)   rs:friend _____ rs:signer

    FRIEND ASK+c LIKE JAPAN FOOD PRO-2 YES LOVE PRO-1
    My friend asked me, 'Do you like Japanese food?' 'Yes, I love it', I
    replied.

While representing the question asked by the other person, the signer shifts his head and body slightly to the right, breaks eye gaze with the addressee, and produces the non-manual signals associated with a polar question. To represent the reply, the signer moves slightly to the left and emphatically nods, showing the attitude expressed in answer to the question at the time it was asked. Note the use of shifted reference when the pronoun PRO-2 in this example refers not to the addressee in the actual conversation, but to the addressee in the constructed dialogue. This is an extremely common way to represent reported verbal interaction in signed languages, and is an important part of referential cohesion.

9.3.1.6 *List buoys*

One further strategy for referential cohesion is the use of *buoys* (Liddell, 2003). Signers often produce a sign with the subordinate hand that is held in space as the dominant hand continues to produce other signs, and they may refer back to the subordinate hand as a way of keeping track of referents in the discourse. Liddell (2003:223) coined the term *buoy* to refer to such uses of the subordinate hand because 'they maintain a physical presence that helps guide the discourse as it proceeds'. One very common type of buoy is the *list buoy*. It can be used to keep track of a number of entities, usually from one to five. List buoys in Auslan involve listing referents on the subordinate hand (oriented with the fingers pointing horizontally) using the fingers starting from either the thumb or the index finger. For example, a signer may plan to refer to three things in a text. If the thumb is associated with the first thing, then the index finger will be associated with the second, and the middle finger with the third. Alternatively, the signer may choose to associate the first referent with the index finger, and then next two things with the middle and ring finger respectively. Either of these strategies is acceptable. The association between the fingers in the list buoy and the referents is made by touching the tip of the appropriate finger and producing the name or description of the entity (the contact may precede or follow the signed description). If the description is brief or only requires the dominant hand, then the list buoy continues to be held on the subordinate hand as each referent is described. This is shown in (9.39) in which the lines marked 'sh', '2h' and 'dh' represent the subordinate hand, the two hands used together, and the dominant hand respectively.

(9.39) sh   FIRST-OF-LIST SECOND-OF-LIST
      2h   DAUGHTER
      dh PRO-3 HAVE TWO   AGE-FOURTEEN   AGE-TEN
      She has two daughters. One is 14 years old and the other is 10.

Alternatively, if the description is long and/or both hands are required (as in fingerspelling), the buoy may be dropped temporarily. This occurred in (9.35) above, in which elephants are described as being from Africa and Asia, and the signer opted to fingerspell these lexical items.

9.3.2 Ellipsis and substitution

As we mentioned in Chapter 7, ellipsis refers to the omission of part of a sentence because it may be understood from the context. An example of ellipsis can be found in (9.40) below which is a sequence of two clauses from the carpentry class narrative. A number of aspects of the linguistic context make ellipsis work as part of referential cohesion, as shown by a recent study on ellipsis of pronouns in ASL (Wulf *et al.*, 2002). Ellipsis appears to be more common in the presence of role shift and when the referent is the same as in the previous clause. This is clear in (9.40). The signer uses role shift here to indicate that he is in a particular role, and the subject of the sign LOOK is the same as the subject of WORK (i.e., the signer himself was working in the class and then looked up at the teacher). As a result, these aspects of the linguistic context make it an easy task for the addressee to identify the referent of the second clause.

(9.40) _____ rs:student
      PRO-1 WORK+rept LOOK+rt

Substitution is another way to maintain cohesion (Halliday & Hasan, 1976). Substitution is similar to the use of pronouns in that another lexical item takes the place of the noun that identifies the referent. An example of substitution can be found in (9.41) below. Here the noun phrase OLD CAR is replaced by the sign OTHER (meaning 'another one') in the second clause, but both are associated with the same referent.

(9.41) FINISH SELL OLD CAR. NOW PRO-1 LOOK-FOR OTHER
      I've sold my old car. I'm looking for another one now.

9.3.3 Discourse markers

Discourse markers are lexical items that help to guide the direction of the discourse, including *conjunctions* and *fillers* (Schiffrin, 1987). These items help to bracket together subsections of the discourse so that it forms a coherent whole.

Conjunctions, such as BUT, S-O, THEN and COINCIDENCE, contribute to the cohesion of a text by linking clauses together into compound and complex sentences, as we saw in Chapter 7. An example is illustrated in (9.42) below. We can see that conjunctions do not work in the same way as referential cohesion, ellipsis and substitution. Unlike these cohesive devices, they are not involved in anaphoric or cataphoric reference. Conjunctions are not cohesive in themselves, but indirectly contribute to cohesion because of their meanings (Halliday & Hasan, 1976). Although they do not make specific reference to other lexical items in the discourse, their use presupposes the presence of other parts of the text. The use of sign COINCIDENCE in (9.42) is appropriate in this context because the preceding clause shows that something was already happening when the signer unexpectedly met his or her boss.

(9.42)
$$\overline{\qquad\text{mm}\qquad}$$

PRO-1 WALK HOME WALK+rept COINCIDENCE MEET POSS-1 BOSS
I was walking home when I unexpectedly ran into my boss.

Fillers like WELL, HOLD or UM also contribute to cohesion. For example, the sign UM may be used to maintain a turn in a conversation while a signer thinks of something else to say, or HOLD directed towards another signer also signals that a signer may not wish another conversational partner to interrupt. This helps cohesion by coordinating the interaction and guiding the discourse.

9.3.4 Lexical cohesion

Patterns of word choice can also contribute to cohesion. This is more subtle than the effects of other forms of cohesion, but it nevertheless contributes to ensuring a text has a coherent meaning. As we listen to a spoken text, or watch a signed text, we understand each particular lexical item because their meaning partly depends on the other lexical items that have been used in the preceding discourse.

These patterns are known as lexical cohesion (Halliday & Hasan, 1976). Lexical cohesion has two main forms. First, there may be *reiteration* of a lexical item. This may involve repetition of the same word. For example, the sign BOY appears twice in the carpentry class story. This repetition assists the addressee to identify an important group of characters in the story. Reiteration may also involve the use of a *synonym* or a *superordinate* term that is related in meaning. Thus, lexical relations (as discussed in Chapter 8) also help a text to hang together.

Second, *collocation* also plays a role in lexical cohesion. Collocation refers to the fact that words that are related in meaning tend to co-occur. Thus, we see that much of the vocabulary used in the carpentry class narrative (SCHOOL, BOY, TEACHER, CARPENTRY, WORK, ORDER and LEARN) is related to educational experiences. Once we know the subject of this story, we would be able to predict the use of many of these signs because they form part of the same lexical field. These collocation patterns thus add to the cohesion of the text by assisting addressees to make sense of the overall meaning.

9.4   Summary

In this chapter, we have examined some aspects of discourse in Auslan, focussing in particular on register and style, and on the characteristics of conversation and narratives. We also examined information structure and cohesion, two important organisational patterns above the sentence level in signed and spoken languages. In the next chapter, we will move away from the description of Auslan that has been the focus of the previous six chapters and step back to cast a critical eye at some of the issues and debates currently preoccupying the field of signed language research.

9.5   Further Reading

Finegan *et al.* (1997) cover some of the same topics presented here with a focus on spoken languages. Halliday & Hasan (1976) is a classic text on cohesion in English. Zimmer (1989), Engberg-Pedersen (1993), Winston (1995), Liddell & Metzger (1998), Rayman (1999), Coates & Sutton-Spence (2001) and Liddell (2003) all discuss issues related to signed language discourse, and Metzger & Bahan (2001) is an overview of the area.

10 Issues in the study of signed languages

Throughout this introduction to the linguistics of Auslan, we have attempted to point out that there are debates regarding the most appropriate analysis of some of the linguistic features we have presented. In many cases, it is not the presence or absence of specific phenomena in signed languages which is in question. For example, most researchers accept the existence of the dominance and symmetry conditions in signed language formational structure (Sutton-Spence & Woll, 1999; Sandler & Lillo-Martin, 2006). Instead, debate surrounds the status these phenomena have in a specific signed language such as Auslan or ASL, in signed languages generally, and even in the everyday use of speech and gesture (van Gijn *et al.*, in press). For example, are there aspects of the dominance and symmetry conditions that are unique to signed languages, or are they similar to what we see in the gesture that accompanies spoken language?

The areas that create the most debate appear to relate strongly to modality differences: signed languages are visual-gestural languages whereas spoken languages are auditory-oral languages (although they may be accompanied by gesture). Does this difference in modality impact on language structure in a fundamental way? For example, is the movement of indicating verbs in space best described as a system of verb agreement entirely comparable to that found in the morphology of verb agreement in spoken languages (e.g., Padden, 1988)? Alternatively, can it be understood as a blend of linguistic and gestural elements (which may or may not differ in degree or kind with the role of gesture in spoken languages) (e.g., Liddell, 2003)?

In this chapter, we will first discuss the influence of different theoretical assumptions on signed language research and issues in signed language data collection. We will then present some of the major issues in the study of signed languages that relate to each of the major topics taken up in Chapters 4 to 7. It is beyond the scope of this introduction to resolve the areas of debate around signed language structure. It is nonetheless important to be aware of these issues and the impact they have on the way that signed language grammars are presented by other linguists and on the direction of signed language research in the years ahead.

We conclude by returning to the topic of our introductory chapter, namely signed languages and linguistics.

10.1   Issues of theory

The grammarian Robert Van Valin (2001) has pointed out that many non-linguists would assume that the most important function of language is communication. They would therefore be surprised to learn than some leading linguists reject this view, or believe that the function of language is not directly relevant to the analysis of language structure. For example, the most well-known linguist, Noam Chomsky (1980:239), has suggested that 'human language is a system of free expression of thought, essentially independent of stimulus control, need-satisfaction or instrumental purpose'. He claimed that language form (i.e., phonology, morphology and syntax) is best described without reference to its function as a means of making meaning. This is because there is no necessary link, Chomsky claimed, between particular aspects of grammar and their communicative function. For example, in English, auxiliary verbs (e.g., *should, will,* etc.) are found in a sentence-initial position in questions, commands, offers and exclamations, as shown in the following examples.

(10.1) a. Can I fly Qantas from Sydney to Tokyo?
    b. Can you please pass the sugar?
    c. Can I help you?
    d. Can it be true!

Thus, examples such as these are believed to demonstrate that grammatical structures work independently of their function.

Chomsky (1965) argued that linguistic science needed a clearly defined methodology, and should primarily focus on describing language structure (i.e., grammar). What, however, is the best way to investigate the structure of languages? Simply recording how people use everyday language in social interaction is not sufficient, Chomsky claimed. He drew attention to the fact that speech is full of errors due to lapses in memory or attention. There are also pauses, hesitations and reformulations in which speakers fail to end one sentence before beginning another. Because of this fact, the work of linguists, he suggested, should focus on speakers' knowledge of the grammatical rules of their native language (i.e., their *competence*) and not how they use this knowledge on particular occasions (i.e., their *performance*).

The aim of the Chomskyan approach to linguistics is thus to produce a complete account of a speaker's knowledge of these underlying grammatical rules of a language (Chomsky, 1965). This description should indicate precisely what can and cannot be a well-formed sentence in a language. For example, consider the examples in (10.2). Although the form of the questions in (b) and (d) seems similar, there appears to be a specific rule which makes (d) ungrammatical in English. This is known as the Coordinate Structure Constraint (Ross, 1967). This rule allows a question to be made out of a noun phrase following a preposition (e.g., *with*), but prohibits one based on a noun phrase that is in a coordinated relationship with another noun phrase (e.g., preceded by *and*).

(10.2) a. Kim likes chicken wings with chilli sauce.
       b. What does Kim like chicken wings with?
       c. Sam likes fish cakes and spring rolls.
       d. *What does Sam like fish cakes and?

A Chomskyan description of a language would result in a set of specific rules (such as the Coordinate Structure Constraint) that could produce all the possible forms in that language without reference to their meaning. Because of this interest in rules that can 'generate' sentences, Chomskyan approaches are sometimes known as *generative linguistics* (Chomsky, 1965).

In addition to the focus on grammar rather than meaning, and on competence rather than performance, generative theory holds to a number of other assumptions about language (Newmeyer, 1998). First, Chomsky claimed that the rules of grammar are independent not only of meaning, but all language-external factors. Thus, they are not affected by the constraints of human cognition (e.g., by memory or reasoning), or by the social needs of communication. Second, the rules of grammar are produced and processed by a separate cognitive system in the mind that is distinct from other aspects of cognition (i.e., the so called 'language module' in the brain). Third, at least some of the rules of grammar are universal (i.e., true for all human languages) and innate (i.e., children are born with a knowledge of some grammatical rules). Generativists claim that a rule such as the Coordinate Structure Constraint, for example, may form part of an innate, universal grammar because it has been found to hold true of many languages, including ASL (Padden, 1988; Sandler & Lillo-Martin, 2006).

Theories of language that reject the Chomskyan perspective are widely known as cognitive and functionalist theories. Some of the most important functionalist approaches are Functional Grammar (Dik, 1989), Role and Reference Grammar (Van Valin & LaPolla, 1997) and Systemic Functional Grammar (Halliday & Matthiessen, 2004). Cognitive Grammar (Langacker, 1987) is another theory that has a particular focus on the relationship between language and the workings of the mind in general. All of these theories differ in their specific accounts of language structure, but they all agree that language is a system whose primary function is communication. Thus, in order to understand language, linguists working in cognitive-functionalist approaches believe it is necessary to investigate the interaction of language structure with meaning, social interaction, and with other areas of cognition. Thus, they reject the competence versus performance distinction, the notion of an innate universal grammar, and the separation of language from language-external factors.

In this book, we have adopted a broadly cognitive-functionalist perspective, although we have not presented our description in terms of any one specific theory. Much of contemporary signed language linguistics is, however, based within the generative tradition (Sandler & Lillo-Martin, 2006). Until recently, there had been little work from a cognitive-functionalist perspective, although this has begun to change quite rapidly over the last decade (e.g., Wilcox & Janzen, 2004). We will discuss some of these developments below. Next, we will turn to a discussion of the implications of different theoretical perspectives on signed language research methodology.

10.2   Issues in data collection

Conducting research into signed language linguistics is not an easy task. In this section, we will briefly discuss a number of important issues about the nature of research into signed languages (cf. Deuchar, 1984; Neidle *et al.*, 2000).

As we saw in Chapter 2, the sociolinguistic context of signed languages such as Auslan is very complex. Despite our attempt to present a clear overview of the varieties of signed communication, signed language use in the Australian deaf community is in fact extremely heterogeneous. Although distinct types of signed communication can be identified (i.e., Auslan, signing in English, contact signing and Australasian Signed English), these types are actually abstractions away from real language use in the community. All signed language use, even between deaf native signers, may actually reflect varying degrees of influence from English. This reflects the fact that, throughout its short history, Auslan has been affected by contact with the spoken and written language of the surrounding community and by the fact that the majority of its users are bilingual to some degree. During the twentieth century, we have seen the extensive use of oralist approaches, the Rochester Method (i.e., the exclusive use of fingerspelling as a means of instruction) and a standardised artificial sign system (i.e., Australasian Signed English) in schools for deaf children. These have all had an enormous impact on language use in the Australian deaf community. Moreover, observation suggests that many deaf people have internalised negative language attitudes towards signed language, because of the higher status of English in the wider community. Like all minority language users, signers thus regularly engage in code-mixing and code-switching (Lucas & Valli, 1992).

If we are to understand the natural sign language of a deaf community such as Auslan, however, such code-switching needs to be kept to a minimum when collecting data. Given that perhaps more than 95 per cent of Auslan signers are not native signers (i.e., they did not acquire the language from birth from signing deaf parents) and that many non-native signers only learn sign after extensive exposure to English, this is problematic. As a result, only individuals who have acquired a signed language from birth from signing deaf parents are our most genuine, expert and reliable sources of data for the natural signed language (Neidle *et al.*, 2000; Padden & Rayman, 2002). Data from all signers are essential in understanding signing deaf communities, but failing to separate data from native and non-native signers may confuse rather than illuminate the description of Auslan. When we describe signing deaf communities and their languages, we must be clear not only about the type of data we base our generalizations on (see below) but also about whom we are making a generalization—signers generally, deaf signers of various backgrounds, or native signers (deaf or hearing).

Although data can be collected from native signers, it needs to be naturalistic data. When videotaped, however, signing will be influenced by the presence of a camera, and thus such data can never be completely natural, and needs to be supplemented by other kinds of data, such as observation and elicitation. Data may be directly elicited from signers by asking questions about their signed language use, but signers need to have highly developed awareness of their own signed language use for this to be effective and reliable. Such skills are rare in the deaf community (Engberg-Pedersen, 1993; Neidle *et al.*, 2000).

Despite these problems, the elicitation of judgements about signed language structure is a common approach to signed language research, particularly among those who have a background in generative linguistics (e.g., Neidle *et al.*, 2000). Until recently is has been very difficult for linguists not to rely on the linguistic judgements of relatively few native signers because the means of gathering, documenting (both notating and transcribing) and describing visual recordings of large amounts of signed language data from many different signers has been expensive, if not simply impossible.

Although native signer/speaker intuitions provide valuable hypotheses as to shared norms regarding meaning or accepted usage in any language, linguists ought to expect data on the language background of participants and research assistants to be made available. Standardised approaches to providing such information have become available (Crasborn & Hanke, 2003). More importantly, as technological innovations make this increasingly feasible in the study of signed languages, researchers will also expect to be able to access annotated video recordings of the data (such as those available from the European Cultural Heritage Online (ECHO) website on signed languages).[4] This will allow other researchers to see the signed language data that is the basis of, or at least exemplifies, the generalizations being made.

---

[4] See http://www.let.kun.nl/sign-lang/echo/index.htm

The issue in the coming years will be the development of shared protocols and standards for linguists to be able to share data on signed languages in order to maximise the datasets upon which generalizations are made, allow for peer review and validation, and to facilitate cross-linguistic study (Crasborn, van der Kooij & Brugman, 2004).

10.3   Issues in signed language description

In the following sections, we explore some of the areas of current debate in signed language phonology, morphology, lexicon and syntax that are relevant to the description of Auslan presented in this book. Many of these arguments are far too complex to be taken up here in any detail, so the following sections aim merely to act as signposts to guide the reader into relevant areas in the extensive literature on signed language linguistics.

10.3.1 Phonology

We saw in Chapter 3 that signs are often made up of smaller elements, similar to the phonemes and/or distinctive features of spoken languages, which have no inherent meaning in themselves. Should this level of signed language structure actually be referred to as the 'phonology' of signed languages (the term is itself based on the Greek word *phone* meaning 'sound')? Stephen Anderson (1993) suggested that the use of this term was problematic and predisposed researchers to look for similarities rather than differences in signed and spoken language formational structure, but Mary Brennan (1994b) and Wendy Sandler (1995) argued that such an approach is appropriate. Given theoretical assumptions about universal grammar, many linguists in the generative school have thus adopted this position. Some have pointed out, however, the dangers of this 'test and transfer' approach in which findings about a particular phenomenon in signed languages are described in accordance with what is known about spoken languages (Uyechi, 1996).

Although most true of signs in the core native lexicon, it is not always accurate to say that the formational parameters of handshape, orientation, location and movement are meaningless (Boyes-Braem, 1981; Johnston, 1989a; van der Kooij, 2002). Thus, this may raise questions about the distinction between phonemes and morphemes in signed languages, particularly in depicting signs. This problem is further exacerbated by the iconicity of some of the meanings associated with many sign elements (i.e., similar elements have the same or similar meaning across many signed languages and may be used in similar ways in the gesture of non-signing spoken language users). The study of signed languages must develop an analysis of signed language phonology that does not simply ignore the possibly meaningful use of the basic building blocks of signs. Some descriptions of signed language phonological structure have attempted to take links between signed language phonology and semantics into account (Friedman, 1976; Stokoe, 1991; van der Kooij, 2002), but this relationship needs to be more fully explored.

On a more general level, the question has also been raised as to what other kind of phonological categories found in spoken languages may or may not be applicable to signed language structure. With respect to parallelisms between spoken language and signed language phonology, some other features of spoken language phonology seem to have no ready or unproblematic equivalents in signed languages (Uyechi, 1996). For example, spoken language words are made up of consonants and vowels. We have seen that these may be considered equivalent to the movement and holds of the Liddell and Johnson model of signs discussed in Chapter 4. Other researchers have argued that handshape and location together act in a similar way to consonants because these elements contain the most formational contrasts, while accepting the notion that movement is analogous to a vowel (e.g., Brentari, 2002).

Although the notion of the sign syllable has become increasingly accepted (Sandler & Lillo-Martin, 2006), researchers disagree about how best to characterise its structure. Does the sign syllable, for example, have internal structure, like spoken syllables such as *fro* in which the initial consonant cluster /fr/ forms an onset, and the following vowel /o/ is the nucleus? Might movement act as a nucleus with handshape and location as onsets and codas? We have already noted that core native signs in many signed languages appear to prefer a monosyllabic or bisyllabic structure (i.e., the two-type constraint). The likely universality of this phenomenon across different signed languages suggests that there may be some language-external factor influencing this constraint. For example, this may reflect the fact that signs appear to take longer to produce than words, and the need for rapid and efficient production and comprehension of communication favours this upper limit on sign size (Meier, 2002a). Alternatively, the two-type constraint may reflect the fact the more simultaneous contrasts of minimal elements are possible in visual-gestural languages because the visual system favours vertical (i.e., simultaneous) over horizontal (i.e., sequential) processing (Brentari, 2002). Although spoken languages generally only use 20-40 phonemes, signed languages like Auslan have a much larger number of possible handshapes, locations and movements that can be combined to form signs.

The traditional parameter model was 'flat' in that handshape, orientation, location and movement were considered formational elements of equal importance, but this has been largely abandoned for more hierarchical models of sign structure, such as the movement-hold model (Liddell & Johnson,

1989), the hand tier model (Sandler & Lillo-Martin, 2006), the dependency model (van der Hulst, 1993) and the prosodic model (Brentari, 1998). The traditional parameter model and a simplified version of the dependency model's account of sign structure are presented in Figure 10.1. These models attempt to understand the relative importance of each of these elements in signed language phonology, but debates about this issue continue. For example, Harry van der Hulst and his colleagues argue that movement is actually not one of the basic building blocks of core native signs. All examples of movement in lexicalised signs are analysed as the predictable result of changes in handshape, location and orientation (van der Hulst, 1993; van der Kooij, 2002).

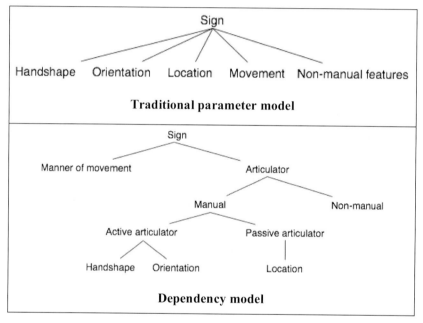

Figure 10.1: *Two models of sign structure.*

Finally, it would appear that some of the phonological rules describing the structure of signs (such as the symmetry and dominance constraint) may not be strictly linguistic constraints at all. As suggested in Chapter 4, it is possible that they reflect physical constraints rather than processes that operate on phonological features of a sign. A recent study, for example, has revealed that the symmetry condition also applies to the co-speech gestures produced by hearing users of spoken languages (van Gijn, Kita & van der Hulst, in press).

10.3.2 Morphology

One of the key issues in the study of signed language morphology is the degree to which sign modification is part of a systematic and abstract system of marking for person, aspect and number, and to what degree it can be adequately or better explained as a system that combines aspects of gestural and linguistic elements within the sign.

We will focus here on the morphology in indicating verbs. As we have seen, the process of directing these verbs towards present referents or towards locations in space associated with non-present referents is analysed as part of a fully linguistic system of person agreement by many linguists (e.g., Padden, 1988; Aronoff *et al*, 2003), while for others it represents the fusion of linguistic elements and gesture (e.g., Liddell, 2003).

Padden (1988) suggested that verbs in ASL could be divided into three classes based on their use of space: plain verbs, spatial verbs and agreeing verbs. She argued that each of these verbs differs with respect to which inflectional morphemes may be added to them. Agreeing verbs can be modified spatially to show person and number agreement while spatial verbs may be modified to signal the location of referents, but not person agreement. The analysis of agreement verbs as showing person and number agreement not unlike the inflectional affixes in spoken languages has been widely accepted by many sign language researchers, particularly those working in generative frameworks (e.g., Neidle *et al*, 2000; Aronoff *et al.*, 2003).

This three-way classification of verbs signs has been found to apply to all signed languages whose verbal systems have been documented. There are two main problems with this model. First, while not disputing the existence of these categories, some researchers have found that it is difficult to maintain a clear distinction between spatial and agreeing verbs, especially with respect to the underlying significance of spatial and directional modifications (Bos, 1990; Johnston, 1991b; Engberg-Pedersen, 1993). For example, a sign such as LOOK may be ambiguous (i.e., it is difficult to know if LOOK+rt means 'look at a location on the right' or 'look at a person on the right'). The division between plain and agreeing verbs is also problematic, because some verb signs do not consistently pattern with either group (see Chapter 6). Second, it is not clear whether all of the various meaningful units in Padden's class of agreeing verbs are best analysed as morphemes (Liddell, 2000, 2003). Liddell introduced the term *indicating verb* to replace *agreeing verb* because he claimed these signs point towards referents present in the environment or towards locations in the space around the signer associated with absent referents. Thus, he suggested that they do not take affixes in the same way as the examples of verb agreement in Spanish (discussed in Chapter 5). Referents may occupy any number of potential locations around the signer, and if the referent is absent, signers may direct the indicating verb towards any number of locations in space associated with the referent. This possibility makes problematic any attempt to consider such spatial locations as examples of morphemes because the number of locations is not listable. Morphemes generally do not have an unlimited number of potential forms. He suggested instead that directional signs in signed languages result from a blend of signs and pointing gestures.

A number of researchers have responded to Liddell's (2000) work, defending the analysis of indicating verbs as a verb agreement system (Lillo-Martin, 2002; Meier, 2002b; Rathmann & Mathur, 2002; Aronoff *et al.*, 2005). These scholars have pointed out that indicating verbs share many properties with verb agreement in spoken languages (both, for example, work as part of referential cohesion), although some agree that such signs may also include a gestural component (Rathmann & Mathur, 2002). Although Liddell's analysis is controversial, we have adopted this approach in this book because it appears to provide the most complete and economical description of the verb system in Auslan, and we share Liddell's theoretical assumptions about how best to approach the study of signed languages (see Liddell, 2002).

The notion that signed languages draw on linguistic and gestural elements dovetails nicely with extensive research which demonstrates that face-to-face spoken language also draws on gestural elements in making meaning (Kendon, 2004). As Liddell (2003) reminds us, hearing users of spoken languages often use pointing gestures directed towards people and objects in their environment as they speak. Gestural pointing can indicate any real or imagined location in space. An English speaker may point towards a location or referent with a gesture of the hand (or possibly head), sometimes in combination with a shift in eye gaze direction. In fact, it is almost impossible to imagine the following sentence uttered by a speaker in a marketplace without some pointing gesture: *No, I don't want to buy that one, I'd like* **this** *one.* Thus, the gestural use of pointing exists alongside the use of spoken language and may be an essential part of its meaning. Liddell argues that, in signed languages, this pointing gesture has become incorporated into the lexical item itself, but in many other respects, signed language makes use of gestural elements in ways that are similar to what we see in spoken languages.

If Liddell's (2003) analysis is correct, however, indicating verbs do not represent examples of inflection, because the use of pointing in these forms is not the same as adding grammatical morphemes to mark person agreement. In fact, a number of scholars have begun to raise doubts about other aspects of sign modifications that have been considered examples of inflection since work began on signed language grammars in the 1970s (e.g., Klima & Bellugi, 1979), such as the marking of plurality on nouns by reduplication, and of number and aspect on verbs (Engberg-Pedersen, 1993; Bergman &

Dahl, 1994; Liddell, 2003). One key aspect of inflectional morphemes is that their presence is required in certain contexts by the grammar (Bybee, 1985). We have seen, however, that the use of these modifications in Auslan appears to be optional in many cases. It may be that the grammar of Auslan is best characterised as one with a rich system of sign modifications, but that it is basically an inflection-less language.

10.3.3 Lexicon

In our model of the lexicon in Chapter 6, we showed that the core lexicon of Auslan may be augmented by the use of non-core native signs (such as depicting signs) on the one hand, and by non-core non-native signs that largely derive from English (usually via fingerspelling) on the other. The boundary between the native and non-native lexicon on the one hand, and the core and non-core lexicon on the other is, however, not always easily identifiable. This presents a significant challenge in signed language lexicography, as traditionally dictionaries only include fully lexicalised items (Johnston & Schembri, 1999; Johnston, 2003b).

Particularly problematic is the distinction between lexicalised and depicting signs. Recently, some scholars have claimed that the division of the lexicon into the core and non-core native lexicons should be abandoned (Liddell, 2003; Oviedo, 2004). They suggest that depicting signs may in fact be part of the core lexicon of signed languages. In particular, Liddell (2003) has found that depicting signs do not appear as productive as many have assumed. He found that many potential combinations of classifier handshape with movement and location features were considered by ASL signers to be unacceptable. For example, some signers reject the use of the 5 handshape in a depicting sign CL:5-FIVE-PEOPLE-APPROACH. This finding suggests that the signer's mental lexicon may have a list of acceptable combinations of such meaningful units. In this analysis, the handshape and movement component of a sign such as CL:1-PERSON-APPROACH represent a partially-specified root morpheme, like the handshape and movement of an indicating verb such as INVITE (Liddell, 2003; Oviedo, 2004). This root is then combined with different features, such as gestural uses of location and orientation, to create the range of depicting signs we discussed in Chapter 6.

Moreover, some researchers have pointed out that the meaningfulness of handshape, location and movement units is not completely lost as depicting signs move into the core lexicon (Brennan, 1990; Johnston & Schembri, 1999; Zwitserlood, 2003; Oviedo, 2004). In some recent psycholinguistic research, for example, signers of German Sign Language (Deutsche Gebärdensprache or DGS) appeared to be sensitive to the meaningful use of handshape in lexicalised signs (Grote & Linz, 2003). In previous work (Johnston & Schembri, 1999), we have discussed how many lexical signs in Auslan can be 'de-lexicalised' in context and the iconic depicting value of their components 're-activated' (hence the double-headed arrows in Figure 6.1).

We have not abandoned the division between core and non-core native lexicon in this book because, as we outlined in Chapter 6, there are a number of phonological, grammatical and semantic reasons for maintaining this distinction. However, like Engberg-Pedersen (1993, 2003), we believe that there is a continuum of lexicalisation. It is possible that some of the depicting signs in ASL that Liddell (2003) has discussed (and their equivalents in Auslan) may be partially lexicalised in the way he has suggested. This question, however, awaits further investigation.

In the meantime, much discussion and debate continues in the signed language linguistics literature about the nature of depicting signs (for example, see Emmorey, 2003). In particular, the Australian researcher Dorothea Cogill-Koez (2000) has argued that these signs may actually be best understood as visual representations (i.e., similar to drawings) rather than as linguistic representations, at least in the traditional sense. Recent work on the acquisition of depicting signs in Auslan is compatible with such an account (de Beuzeville, 2006). Wendy Sandler and Diane Lillo-Martin (2006) list characteristics of these signs that differentiate them from lexicalised signs, arguing that they do not fulfil the usual criteria for wordhood. Alternatively, researchers such as Ted Supalla (2003) maintain that these signs are fully linguistic constructions, analogous to complex, polymorphemic words. Other researchers, as we have seen, view them as combinations of linguistic and gestural elements (Liddell, 2003; Schembri *et al.*, 2005). While awaiting further developments in this area, we have attempted to present our discussion of these signs in Chapter 6 in neutral terms, although we have adopted Liddell's terminology to highlight the iconic nature of these signs.

Another important area of debate centres on the role of mouthing. As we have seen in Chapters 2, 5 and 6, it is possible to produce a sign at the same time as one utters a word from a spoken language. Some signs appear to have a general meaning that is made more specific by the simultaneous mouthing of one of a number of related spoken language words (e.g., with the sign in Figure 8.7 meaning 'street', 'road', 'way' or 'method'). In such cases, it is difficult to know the extent to which all of the resulting signs are truly distinctive separate lexical signs belonging to the core native vocabulary. Is the mouthing in this context obligatory for some signers? Is it an example of borrowing or an instance of code-mixing? Does the use of mouthing in this context reflect nothing more than negative attitudes towards signed languages that result from the dominance of oralism in deaf education? It is difficult to establish if mouthing has become an obligatory part of the form of a sign and thereby creates a new and distinctive lexicalised sign, or whether it remains an optional borrowing from the spoken language. Clearly, this area requires much more investigation, both for Auslan and other signed languages (Ebbinghaus & Hessman, 1996; Boyes-Braem & Sutton-Spence, 2001).

10.3.4 Syntax

An utterance in a signed language is likely to consist of several types of signs. These include lexicalised signs, depicting signs, fingerspelled items, constructed action and gestures. Despite this, some descriptions of signed language syntax in the literature are based on utterances that only consist of strings of lexicalised signs (e.g., Neidle *et al.*, 2000). Other studies have, however, documented an apparent association of indicating and depicting verbs with particular sign orders (Friedman, 1976; Liddell, 1980; Johnston, 1992; Sze, 2003; Johnston *et al.*, in press). Engberg-Pedersen (2002:8) observed that in DSL, for example, sentences with depicting signs and/or constructed action 'typically start by a presentation of the participants involved before the classifier predicate or the verb with the stylised imitation of one of the participants' action'. We have tried to incorporate some of these findings in our discussion of Auslan syntax in Chapter 7. The challenge for future work on the syntax of signed languages is, however, to create a unified account of sentence structure that does not simply exclude certain subcategories of signs.

Another issue relates to the establishment of clause boundaries in signed language discourse. In the absence of a standardised method for recognising clauses, differences in analysis can lead to differences in the constituent orders attributed to an utterance. Attempting to apply the traditional notion that a clause centres around a verb as a means of identifying clause boundaries is not always satisfactory, as it is difficult to know how to treat some sequences of two or more verb-like signs. For example, a verb may be repeated (often with some kind of modification), as in (10.3). Researchers disagree whether this repeated verb is best analysed as a separate clause (Liddell, 2003) or as some kind of 'verb sandwich' or verb doubling that creates a complex single clause (Fischer & Janis, 1990; Matsuoka, 1997).

(10.3) POSS-1 FRIEND READ BOOK READ+rept HOURS-AND-HOURS
    My friend was reading her book for hours.

Similar disagreements occur with the analysis of pseudocleft constructions, with some scholars treating them as one clause (Wilbur, 1994a) and others as two clauses (Neidle *et al.*, 2000). It has been suggested that non-manual features, such as changes in facial expression, head position, gaze direction and eye blinks signal clause and sentence boundaries (Baker & Padden, 1978; Wilbur 1994b). However, the analysis of signed language discourse indicates that these features are not always a reliable signal of these boundaries (Lucas *et al.*, 2001; Johnston *et al.*, in press).

The role of non-manual features in signed language syntax in general is an interesting area of on-going research (Sandler & Lillo-Martin, 2006). For example, researchers recognise that both signers and non-signers use facial expression to convey emotion, such as happiness, sadness and anger. But many also claim that signed languages use obligatory changes in facial expressions, eye gaze, and head and body positions to signal syntactic information (Neidle *et al.*, 2000). In Chapter 7, we have seen that non-manual features are used in interrogatives as well as in negation and topicalisation. It is not clear, however, how obligatory particular combinations of non-manual features are with specific syntactic structures in Auslan, and similar observations have been made for BSL (Deuchar, 1984) and ASL (Sandler & Lillo-Martin, 2006). Quantitative research on the role of non-manual markers of interrogatives, negation and topicalisation in Sign Language of the Netherlands (Nederlandse Gebarentaal or NGT), for example, shows that their use varies from 63 per cent (for brow raise in polar questions) to 99 per cent (for headshake in negations) of occurrences (Coerts, 1992). Furthermore, some researchers claim that grammatical uses of facial expression differ from emotional facial expressions in their timing (Liddell, 1980; Baker-Shenk, 1983). The use of non-manual features associated with topicalisation, for example, does indeed appear to be synchronised with specific constituents of the sentence, and they have a clear onset and offset. The NGT study found that this clear co-ordination was most true of brow raises only, however, and less true of headshake (Coerts, 1992). In any case, this clear onset and offset is similar to what is found in spoken language intonation (Bolinger, 1986, 1989; Ladd, 1996), yet linguists do not agree about whether intonational features are morphological, syntactic or pragmatic elements. Moreover, recent psycholinguistic research on the recognition of questioning facial expressions by deaf signers and hearing non-signers does not indicate that the two groups perceive them differently (Campbell *et al.*, 1999). Furthermore, the processing of non-manual negation by the brain also appears to occur in the right hemisphere of the brain, an area more typically associated with the production of intonation and gesture (Atkinson *et al.*, 2004). It is likely that non-manual features have a complex inter-relationship with the syntax of Auslan, but ultimately operate independently from it (Johnston, 1992; cf. Sandler & Lillo-Martin, 2006).

Another unique feature of signed languages is the ability to produce two signs simultaneously, one on each hand. We have seen in Chapter 6, that the use of simultaneity in depicting signs can be used to indicate spatial relationships between two referents. Other research has shown that the perseveration of the subordinate hand can maintain discourse topic (e.g., Emmorey & Falgier, 1999). When two signs are co-articulated in this way, one must ask if the concept of constituent order is meaningful. Importantly, it is difficult to know if linguists treat these simultaneous elements of sign production consistently when making generalizations about the grammar of a particular signed language and when comparing it to other signed languages. For example, in a recent overview comparing the syntax of signed and spoken languages, the issue of simultaneity was not mentioned at all (Lillo-Martin, 2002).

It is not yet clear if grammatical roles, such as subject and object, can be applied to signed languages such as Auslan. Grammatical roles are different from both the semantic roles (e.g., agent, patient, etc.) discussed in Chapter 8, and pragmatic roles (e.g., given, new, topic, comment) in Chapter 9. As we saw in these chapters, semantic roles are based on the meaning of verbs and their co-occurring nouns. Pragmatic roles reflect whether particular information can be assumed to be known by all participants, or is highlighted as the focus of the discourse. Grammatical roles, however, reflect morphological and syntactic properties of the sentence (Van Valin & LaPolla, 1997). All languages have semantic and pragmatic roles, but it is not clear if the notion of grammatical role applies to all spoken and signed languages (LaPolla, 1993; Engberg-Pedersen, 2002).

Subject clearly exists in English, for example, and can be identified by at least five distinctive morphological and syntactic characteristics. First, subject nouns are replaced by a specific set of first- and third-person pronouns (e.g., *I, we, he, she, they versus me, us, him, her, them*). Second, subjects usually precede the verb in statements (e.g., *Koalas eat leaves*, not *Eat koalas leaves*). Third, the third-person singular *-s* suffix on present tense verbs signals agreement with the subject noun in person and number (e.g., *A koala eats leaves*). Fourth, tag questions agree with the subject in person and number (e.g., *Koalas eat leaves, don't they?*). Fifth, the auxiliary verb precedes the subject in polar questions (e.g., *Can koalas climb trees?*). Although it has been claimed that subjects also have some distinctive grammatical properties in ASL (Padden, 1988; Wilbur, 1994c), it is not clear if the criteria used are sufficient for this claim. If the interaction of semantic and pragmatic roles can account for the same phenomena, then there is little evidence for grammatical roles, as suggested for Auslan by Johnston (1991b). Certainly, Engberg-Pedersen (2002) has argued against the existence of grammatical roles in DSL, and more investigation is needed to confirm whether this is also true of Auslan. If the evidence for grammatical roles is lacking, then this may undermine the claim that modifications in indicating verbs represent examples of subject and object agreement.

10.3.5 Signed languages, creolisation and grammaticalisation

For reasons discussed in Chapter 3, all of the natural signed languages that have been identified appear to be comparatively young, or newly emerging languages. Like signed languages, creoles are also young languages, having developed within the last five hundred years or so (McWhorter, 1998). In

Chapter 3, we have already mentioned that signed languages and creoles have many grammatical features in common. All known creole languages and signed languages have little affixation of any kind, for example (McWhorter, 1998; Aronoff *et al.*, 2003). Furthermore, the fact that so few users of natural signed languages are native signers raises the real possibility that the majority of deaf signers may actually have creolised their restricted language input at each generation (Fischer, 1978).

Though the small numbers of deaf native signers in deaf schools certainly have in the past facilitated the transmission of natural signed languages to deaf children who do not have signed language input at home, the grammatical aspects of many natural signed languages suggest that creolisation may have occurred. This has, in turn, impacted on the language used by native signers. Many researchers, however, claim that the rich, layered set of verb modifications of signed languages is evidence against this interpretation because creoles do not show complex morphology (Gee & Goodhart, 1985; Lupton & Salmon, 1996; Aronoff *et al.*, 2005). As we saw in §10.3.2 above, this observation is, however, put in doubt by alternative analyses of verb modification that suggest that such processes may represent fusions of language and gesture, and may actually not represent examples of inflection in the strictest sense of the word. This re-opens the debate about how the youth of signed languages may have relevance for an understanding of their structure.

One impact such a short history may have had on signed languages relates to the issue of grammaticalisation. This refers to a process of language change over time 'through which lexical words become grammatical morphemes (and eventually inflectional morphology)' (Givón, 1989:57). An example of grammaticalisation in English is shown in (10.4).

(10.4) a. I am going to Alice Springs.
        b. I am going to finish this essay soon.
        c. *I'm gonna Alice Springs.
        d. I'm gonna finish this essay soon.

Of the four examples, we can see that the English phrase *going to* retains its original lexical meaning as a verb describing motion in (a). However, it has also become a grammatical marker indicating immediate future tense in (b). In this context, the reduced form *gonna* is possible (d), but it sounds odd in example (c) where *going* is used as content word rather than grammatical item. Historical records suggest that the grammaticalisation of *going to* has been taking place since the time of Middle English (i.e., the fifteenth century) (Hopper & Traugott, 2003).

Grammaticalisation involves three main processes (Hopper & Traugott, 2003). First, there is semantic change. We see this in the change from *going to* as a lexical verb of motion to a grammatical marker indicating an action in the immediate future. Second, there is phonological reduction. Again, we see this in the loss of phonological elements in the change from *going to* to *gonna*. Lastly, the grammatical marker may become obligatory in specific contexts. The use of *going to* has not yet arrived at this stage (i.e., it is not obligatory in any context, as the auxiliary *will* can also indicate future actions). An example of a fully grammaticalised morpheme in English would be the use of *have* as a perfective aspect marker. In Standard English, it is clearly obligatory in the context in the following example.

(10.5) I ____ been to Alice Springs.

There are only a few studies of grammaticalisation in signed languages. They include the analysis of the evolution of two auxiliaries in TSL from the signs MEET and SEE (Smith, 1990), the development of the sign FINISH in ASL into a marker of perfective aspect (Janzen, 1995) and the grammaticalisation of WRONG in ASL as a conjunction meaning something like 'suddenly' or 'then unexpectedly' (MacFarlane, 1998). Particularly interesting have been studies showing the evolution of auxiliary signs like CAN and WILL in ASL from lexical signs STRONG and GO (Wilcox, 2004b). These in turn appear to have developed from emblematic gestures used by hearing people (Janzen & Schaffer, 2002). Though they remain lexical items to varying degrees, such signs have nonetheless also become grammatical markers in these languages.

The question some researchers have raised is not so much the existence of these pathways of grammaticalisation, but the degree to which various gestural and/or lexicalised signs have become grammaticalised in particular signed languages, given their relatively recent emergence (Johnston & Schembri, 2001; Zeshan, 2003; Schembri *et al.*, 2005). A major issue in these studies is establishing the degree to which such grammatical markers are systematic and obligatory in the grammar of a particular signed language (e.g., the discussion of the noun-verb distinction in Auslan in Chapter 5). This is a question that awaits future research, but it seems clear that the comparative youth of signed languages and the length of time required for grammaticalisation processes to take hold (often several centuries) may partly explain the reason that many of the morphological and syntactic features of Auslan discussed in this book appear to be optional in most contexts.

10.4   Conclusion: signed languages and linguistics

Research during the 1960s and 1970s into signed languages aimed to establish them as real languages with language-like characteristics (for an overview, see Woll, 2003). Much of the subsequent research has aimed to establish the validity of the linguistic universals proposed by generativist theory. Although these are based on the study of spoken languages, researchers have focused on exploring their application to signed languages (e.g., Sandler & Lillo-Martin, 2006). Other research has attempted to determine the impact of modality on language structure (e.g., Meier, Cormier, & Quinto-Pozos, 2002), and has sought to acknowledge the degree to which signed languages are different from spoken languages. Depending on how the dynamics of spoken language are understood (and particularly whether gesture, intonation and speech are seen as working in tandem), the differences (such as the grammatical use of non-manual features and space in signed languages) have been perceived as either additional special characteristics peculiar to language in the visual-gestural modality, or as differences of degree only which have been occasioned by modality. For some linguists, the use of a spatial and iconic morphology has been regarded as unique to signed languages but nonetheless analysed as a part of a fully linguistic system (Aronoff *et al.*, 2003). For others it represents a fusion of elements of language and gesture (Liddell, 2003). In fact, the so-called unique resources of signed languages may actually be best understood as face-to-face communicative resources available to all language users—even if they are under-exploited in spoken languages and are ignored in most grammatical descriptions of languages like English. The only real difference—not without important consequences—is that these 'unique' resources saturate the grammar and lexicon of signed languages because they are always available in languages which are embodied and, of necessity, always in view.

Today the task for linguists is how to interpret the emerging facts of signed language description and integrate them into an overall and coherent model of human language. In particular, current accounts of the role of gesture in signed communication that suggest possible solutions to some of the descriptive problems encountered by sign language researchers have been highlighted in this book. This reflects developments that show our definition of language has been too narrow, and that we now need to acknowledge that speech and gesture work together as part of the same communicative package (McNeill, 1992; Kendon, 2004). Insofar as it may contribute to the redefinition of what is 'language' or what is properly 'linguistic', the short history of the study of signed languages belies its relative importance to linguistics.

References

Aitchison, J. 1992. *Teach Yourself Linguistics* (4th edn.). London: Hodder & Stoughton.

Akamatsu, C. T. 1985. 'Fingerspelling Formulae: A Word Is More or Less Than the Sum of Its Letters'. In W. C. Stokoe & V. Volterra (eds.), *SLR '83: Sign Language Research* (pp. 126-132). Silver Spring, MD: Linstok Press.

Anderson, S. R. 1993. 'Linguistic Expression and Its Relation to Modality'. In G. R. Coulter (ed.), *Phonetics and Phonology: Current Issues in ASL Phonology* (pp. 273-290). New York: Academic Press.

Ann, J. 2001. 'Bilingualism and Language Contact'. In C. Lucas (ed.), *The Sociolinguistics of Sign Languages* (pp. 33-60). Cambridge: Cambridge University Press.

Antzakas, K., & Woll, B. 2002. 'Head Movements and Negation in Greek Sign Language'. In I. Wachsmuth & T. Sowa (eds.), *Gesture and Sign Language in Human-Computer Interaction: International Gesture Workshop GW 2001, London, UK, April 18-20, 2001 Proceedings.* (pp. 193-196). Berlin: Springer-Verlag.

Arends, J., Muysken, P., & Smith, N. 1995. *Pidgins and Creoles: An Introduction.* Amsterdam: Benjamins.

Aronoff, M., Meir, I., Padden, C. A., & Sandler, W. 2003. 'Classifier Constructions and Morphology in Two Sign Languages'. In K. D. Emmorey (ed.), *Perspectives on Classifier Constructions in Sign Languages* (pp. 53-84). Mahwah, NJ: Lawrence Erlbaum Associates.

Aronoff, M., Meir, I., & Sandler, W. 2005. 'The Paradox of Sign Language Morphology'. *Language, 81*(2), 301-344.

Atkinson, J., Campbell, R., Marshall, J., Thacker, A., & Woll, B. 2004. 'Understanding "Not": Neuropsychological Dissociations between Hand and Head Markers of Negation in BSL'. *Neuropsychologia, 42*, 214-229.

Austin, J. L. 1962. *How to Do Things with Words.* New York: Oxford University Press.

Bailey, C. S., & Dolby, K. (eds.) 2002. *The Canadian Dictionary of ASL.* The University of Alberta Press: Edmonton, Alberta, Canada.

Baker, C. 1977. 'Regulators and Turn-Taking in American Sign Language'. In L. A. Friedman (ed.), *On the Other Hand: New Perspectives on American Sign Language* (pp. 215-236). New York: Academic Press.

Baker, C., & Cokely, D. 1980. *American Sign Language: A Teacher's Resource Text on Grammar and Culture.* Silver Spring, MD: T. J. Publishers.

Baker-Shenk, C. 1983. *A Microanalysis of the Non-Manual Components of Questions in American Sign Language.* Unpublished doctoral dissertation, University of California, Berkeley, CA.

Battison, R. 1978. *Lexical Borrowing in American Sign Language.* Silver Spring, MD: Linstok Press.

Battison, R., & Jordan, I. K. 1976. 'Cross-Cultural Communication with Foreign Signers: Fact and Fancy'. *Sign Language Studies, 10*, 53-68.

Bauer, L. 1988. *Introducing Linguistic Morphology.* Edinburgh: Edinburgh University Press.

Bellugi, U., & Fischer, S. D. 1972. 'A Comparison of Sign Language and Spoken Language'. *Cognition, 1*, 173-198.

Bellugi, U., & Klima, E. S. 1975. 'Aspects of Sign Language and Its Structure'. In J. F. Kavanagh & J. E. Cutting (eds.), *The Role of Speech in Language* (pp. 171-203). Cambridge, MA: MIT Press.

Bender, R. E. 1970. *The Conquest of Deafness*. Cleveland & London: Case Western Reserve University Press.

Bergman, B. 1983. 'Verbs and Adjectives: Morphological Processes in Swedish Sign Language'. In J. Kyle & B. Woll (eds.), *Language in Sign: An International Perspective on Sign Language* (pp. 3-9). London: Croom Helm.

Bergman, B., & Dahl, O. 1994. 'Ideophones in Sign Language? The Place of Reduplication in the Tense-Aspect System of Swedish Sign Language'. In C. Bache, H. Basboll & C. E. Lindberg (eds.), *Tense, Aspect and Action: Empirical and Theoretical Contributions to Language Typology* (Vol. 12, pp. 397-442). Berlin, New York: Mouton De Gruyter.

Bernal, B., & Wilson, L. (eds.) 2004. *Dictionary of Auslan: English to Auslan (with Regional Sign Variations)*. Melbourne: Deaf Children Australia.

Bezzina, F. (ed.) (n.d.) *Niftiehmu bis-sinjali: Gabra mil-Lingwi tas-Sinjali Maltin*. Malta: Gozo Association for the Deaf.

Blackmore, H. 1996. *The House on the Hill: The First Hundred Years of the School for Deaf Children in Western Australia 1896-1996*. Perth, WA: The Western Australian School for Deaf Children Inc.

Bloomfield, L. 1933. *Language*. New York: Henry Holt.

Bogaerde, B. van den 2005. 'Everybody Signs in Kosindo Also?' *Deaf Worlds, 21*(1), 103-107.

Bolinger, D. L. 1986. *Intonation and Its Parts: Melody in Spoken English*. Stanford, CA: Stanford University Press.

Bolinger, D. L. 1989. *Intonation and Its Uses: Melody in Grammar and Discourse*. Stanford, CA: Stanford University Press.

Bornstein, H. 1990. 'A Manual Communication Overview'. In H. Bornstein (ed.), *Manual Communication: Implications for Education* (pp. 21-44). Washington, DC: Gallaudet University Press.

Bos, H. 1990. 'Person and Location Marking in Sign Language of the Netherlands: Some Implications of a Spatially Expressed Syntactic System'. In S. Prillwitz & T. Vollhaber (eds.), *Current Trends in European Sign Language Research. Proceedings of the 3rd European Congress on Sign Language Research, Hamburg, July 26-29, 1989* (pp. 231-248). Hamburg: Signum Verlag.

Bos, H. 1995. 'Pronoun Copy in Sign Language of the Netherlands'. In H. Bos & T. Schermer (eds.), *Sign Language Research 1994: Proceedings of the Fourth European Congress on Sign Language Research, Munich, September 1-3, 1994* (pp. 121-147). Hamburg: Signum Press.

Boyes-Braem, P. 1981. *Distinctive Features of the Handshape in American Sign Language*. Unpublished doctoral dissertation, University of California, Berkeley.

Boyes-Braem, P., & Sutton-Spence, R. (eds.) 2001. *The Hands Are the Head of the Mouth: The Mouth as Articulator in Sign Languages*. Hamburg: Signum Press.

Branson, J., & Miller, D. 1991. 'Language and Identity in the Australian Deaf Community: Australian Sign Language and Language Policy–an Issue of Social Justice'. *Australian Review of Applied Linguistics, 8*, 135-176.

Branson, J., & Miller, D. 1995. *The Story of Betty Steel: Deaf Convict and Pioneer*. Sydney: Deafness Resources Australia.

Branson, J., Miller, D., Marsaja, I. G., & Negara, I. W. 1996. 'Everyone Here Speaks Sign Language, Too'. In C. Lucas (ed.), *Multicultural Aspects of Sociolinguistics in Deaf Communities* (pp. 39-57). Washington, DC: Gallaudet University Press.

Branson, J., Toms, J., Bernal, B., & Miller, D. 1995. 'The History and Role of Fingerspelling in Auslan'. In H. Bos & T. Schermer (eds.), *Sign Language Research 1994: Proceedings of the Fourth European Congress on Sign Language Research, Munich, September 1-3, 1994* (pp. 53-67). Hamburg: Signum Press.

Brennan, M. 1983. 'Marking Time in British Sign Language'. In J. G. Kyle & B. Woll (eds.), *Language in Sign: An International Perspective on Sign Language* (pp. 10-31). London: Croom Helm.

Brennan, M. 1990. *Word Formation in British Sign Language*. Stockholm: University of Stockholm Press.

Brennan, M. 1992. 'The Visual World of BSL: An Introduction'. In D. Brien (ed.), *Dictionary of British Sign Language/English* (pp. 1-133). London: Faber & Faber.

Brennan, M. 1994a. 'Pragmatics and Productivity'. In I. Ahlgren, B. Bergman & M. Brennan (eds.), *Perspectives on Sign Language Usage: Papers from the Fifth International Symposium on Sign Language Research* (pp. 371-390). Durham, UK: International Sign Linguistics Association.

Brennan, M. 1994b. 'Word Order: Introducing the Issues'. In M. Brennan & G. H. Turner (eds.), *Word-Order Issues in Sign Language: Working Papers Presented at a Workshop in Durham, 18-22 September 1991* (pp. 9-45). Durham, UK: International Sign Linguistics Association.

Brennan, M., Colville, M. D., & Lawson, D. 1984. *Words in Hand: A Structural Analysis of the Signs in British Sign Language*. Edinburgh: Moray House College of Education.

Brennan, M., & Turner, G. H. (eds.) 1994. *Word-Order Issues in Sign Language: Working Papers Presented at a Workshop in Durham, 18-22 September 1991*. Durham, UK: International Sign Linguistics Association.

Brentari, D. 1995. *Prosodic Constraints in American Sign Language: Evidence from Fingerspelling and Reduplication*. Hamburg: Signum Press.

Brentari, D. 1998. *A Prosodic Model of Sign Language Phonology*. Cambridge, MA: MIT press.

Brentari, D. 2001. *Foreign Vocabulary in Signed Languages: A Cross-Linguistic Investigation of Word Formation*. Mahwah, NJ: Lawrence Erlbaum Associates.

Brentari, D. 2002. 'Modality Differences in Sign Language Phonology and Morphophonemics'. In R. P. Meier, K. A. Cormier & D. Quinto-Pozos (eds.), *Modality and Structure in Signed and Spoken Languages* (pp. 35-64). Cambridge: Cambridge University Press.

Brentari, D., & Padden, C. A. 2001. 'Native and Foreign Vocabulary in American Sign Language: A Lexicon with Multiple Origins'. In D. Brentari (ed.), *Foreign Vocabulary in Signed Languages: A Cross-Linguistic Investigation of Word Formation* (pp. 87-120). Mahwah, NJ: Lawrence Erlbaum Associates.

Brien, D. (ed.) 1992. *Dictionary of British Sign Language/English*. London: Faber & Faber.

Brun, T. 1969. *The International Dictionary of Sign Language: A Study of Human Behaviour*. London: Wolfe Publishing Ltd.

Burns, S. E. 1998. 'Irish Sign Language: Ireland's Second Minority Language'. In C. Lucas (ed.), *Pinky Extension and Eye Gaze: Language Use in Deaf Communities* (pp. 233-273). Washington, D.C.: Gallaudet University Press.

Bybee, J. L. 1985. *Morphology: A Study of the Relation between Meaning and Form.* Amsterdam: Benjamins.

Campbell, R. 1999. 'Language from Faces: Uses of the Face in Speech and in Sign'. In L. S. Messing & R. Campbell (eds.), *Gesture, Speech, and Sign* (pp. 57-73). Oxford: Oxford University Press.

Carmel, S. J., (ed.) 1982. *International Hand Alphabet Charts*: Published by the author.

Carty, B. 2000. 'John Carmichael: Australian Deaf Pioneer'. In A. Schembri, J. Napier, R. Beattie & G. R. Leigh (eds.), *Proceedings of the Australasian Deaf Studies Research Symposium, Renwick College, Sydney, August 22-23, 1998* (pp. 9-20). Sydney: North Rocks Press.

Carty, B. 2004. *Managing Their Own Affairs: The Australian Deaf Community During the 1920s and 1930s.* Unpublished doctoral dissertation, Griffith University, Brisbane.

Chafe, W. L. 1976. 'Givenness, Contrastiveness, Definiteness, Subjects, Topics, and Points of View'. In C. Li (ed.), *Subject and Topic* (pp. 25-55). New York: Academic Press.

Chomsky, N. 1965. *Aspects of the Theory of Syntax*. Cambridge, MA: MIT Press.

Chomsky, N. 1980. *Rules and Representations*. New York: Columbia University Press.

Clyne, M. 2003. *Dynamics of Language Contact*. Cambridge: Cambridge University Press.

Coates, J. 1997. 'The Construction of a Collaborative Floor in Women's Friendly Talk'. In T. Givon (ed.), *Conversation: Cognitive, Communicative and Social Perspectives* (pp. 55-89). Amsterdam: John Benjamins.

Coates, J., & Sutton-Spence, R. 2001. 'Turn-Taking Patterns in Deaf Conversation'. *Journal of Sociolinguistics, 5*(4), 507-529.

Coerts, J. 1992. *Non-Manual Grammatical Markers: An Analysis of Interrogatives, Negations and Topicalizations in Sign Language of the Netherlands*. Amsterdam: University of Amsterdam.

Cogill-Koez, D. 2000. 'Signed Language Classifier Predicates: Linguistic Structures or Schematic Visual Representation?' *Sign Language and Linguistics, 3*(2), 153-207.

Cohen, L. H. 1994. *Train Go Sorry*. Boston: Houghton Mifflin.

Collins-Ahlgren, M. 1989. *Aspects of New Zealand Sign Language.* Unpublished doctoral dissertation, Victoria University of Wellington.

Comrie, B. 1989. *Language Universals and Linguistic Typology: Syntax and Morphology* (2nd edn.). Chicago: University of Chicago.

Corina, D. P. 1990. 'Handshape Assimilation in Hierarchical Phonological Representations'. In C. Lucas (ed.), *Sign Language Research: Theoretical Issues* (pp. 27-49). Washington, DC: Gallaudet University Press.

Corina, D. P., & Sandler, W. 1993. 'On the Nature of Phonological Structure in Sign Language'. *Phonology, 10*, 165-207.

Corker, M. 1997. 'Deaf People and Interpreting—the Struggle in Language'. *Deaf Worlds, 13*(3), 13-20.

Crabtree, M., & Powers, J. 1991. *Language Files: Materials for an Introduction to Language*. Columbus, OH: Ohio State University Press.

Crasborn, O., & Hanke, T. 2003. *Additions to the IMDI Metadata Set for Sign Language Corpora.* Agreements at an Echo Workshop, May 8-9, 2003, Nijmegen University.

Crasborn, O., Kooij, E. van der, Broeder, D., & Brugman, H. 2004. 'Sharing Sign Language Corpora Online: Proposals for Transcription and Metadata Categories'. In O. Streiter & C. Vettori (eds.), *Proceedings of the LREC (Language Resources and Evaluation) 2004 Satellite Workshop on Representation and Processing of Sign Languages* (pp. 20-23). Paris: ELDA.

Crean, E. J. 1997. *Breaking the Silence: The Education of the Deaf in Ireland 1816-1996*. Dublin: Irish Deaf Society Publications.

Critchley, M. 1939. *The Language of Gesture*. London: Edward Arnold.

Crowley, T. 1992. *An Introduction to Historical Linguistics*. Oxford: Oxford University Press.

Crowley, T., Lynch, J., Siegel, J., & Piau, J. 1995. *The Design of Language: An Introduction to Descriptive Linguistics*. Auckland: Longman Paul.

Cruse, D. A. 1986. *Lexical Semantics*. Cambridge: Cambridge University Press.

Crystal, D. 1995. *The Cambridge Encyclopedia of the English Language*. Cambridge: Cambridge University Press.

Crystal, D. 1997. *The Cambridge Encyclopedia of Language* (2nd edn.). Cambridge: Cambridge University Press.

Cuxac, C. 1999. 'The Expression of Spatial Relations and the Spatialization of Semantic Relations in French Sign Language'. In C. Fuchs & S. Robert (eds.), *Language Diversity and Cognitive Representations* (pp. 123-142). Amsterdam/Philadelphia: John Benjamins.

Day, L., & Elton, F. 1999. *Comparison of British Sign Language (BSL) and Australian Sign Language (Auslan).* Paper presented at the XIII World Congress of the Word Federation of the Deaf, Brisbane, Queensland, Australia.

Deaf Society of New South Wales. 1989. *Operation Knock Knock: A Profile of the Deaf Community of NSW*. Parramatta, NSW: Deaf Society of New South Wales.

Deaf Society of New South Wales. 1998. *Hands up NSW: A Profile of the Deaf Community of NSW*. Sydney: Deaf Society of New South Wales.

de Beuzeville, L. 2006. *Visual and Linguistic Representation in the Acquisition of Depicting Verbs: A Study of Native Signing Deaf Children of Auslan (Australian Sign Language).* Unpublished doctoral dissertation, University of Sydney, Sydney.

Deuchar, M. 1978. 'Sign Language Diglossia in a British Deaf Community'. *Sign Language Studies, 17*, 347-356.

Deuchar, M. 1984. *British Sign Language*. London: Routledge & Kegan Paul.

Dik, S. C. 1989. *The Theory of Functional Grammar*. Dordrecht, The Netherlands: Foris Publications.

Dixon, R. M. W. 1980. *The Languages of Australia*. Cambridge: Cambridge University Press.

Drasgow, E., & Paul, P. 1995. 'A Critical Analysis of the Use of MCE Systems with Deaf Students: A Review of the Literature'. *Association of Canadian Educators of the Hearing Impaired, 21*(2), 80-93.

Eastman, C. M. 1983. *Language Planning: An Introduction*. San Francisco, CA: Chandler & Sharp.

Ebbinghaus, H., & Hessman, J. 1996. 'Signs and Words: Accounting for Spoken Language Elements in German Sign Language'. In W. H. Edmondson & R. B. Wilbur (eds.), *International Review of Sign Linguistics, 1* (pp. 23-56). Mahwah, NJ: Lawrence Erlbaum Associates.

Emmorey, K. D. 2002. *Language, Cognition, and the Brain: Insights from Sign Language Research*. Mahwah, NJ: Lawrence Erlbaum Associates.

Emmorey, K. D. (ed.) 2003. *Perspectives on Classifier Constructions in Sign Languages*. Mahwah, NJ: Lawrence Erlbaum Associates.

Emmorey, K. D., & Falgier, B. 1999. 'Talking About Space with Space: Describing Environments in ASL'. In E. Winston (ed.), *Story Telling and Conversations: Discourse in Deaf Communities* (pp. 3-26). Washington, DC: Gallaudet University Press.

Emmorey, K. D., & Lane, H. (eds.) 2000. *The Signs of Language Revisited: An Anthology to Honor Ursula Bellugi and Edward Klima*. Mahwah, NJ: Lawrence Erlbaum Associates.

Engberg-Pedersen, E. 1993. *Space in Danish Sign Language: The Semantics and Morphosyntax of the Use of Space in a Visual Language*. Hamburg: Signum Press.

Engberg-Pedersen, E. 2002. 'Grammatical Relations in Danish Sign Language: Topic and Subject'. In A. Pajunen (ed.), *Mimesis, Sign, and the Evolution of Language (Publications in General Linguistics 3)* (pp. 5-40). Turku, Finland: University of Turku.

Engberg-Pedersen, E. 2003. 'How Composite Is a Fall? Adults' and Children's Descriptions of Different Types of Falls in Danish Sign Language'. In K. Emmorey (ed.), *Perspectives on Classifier Constructions in Sign Languages* (pp. 311-332). Mahwah, NJ: Lawrence Erlbaum Associates.

Finch, G. 2000. *Linguistic Terms and Concepts*. Basingstoke, UK: Palgrave.

Finegan, E., Blair, D., & Collins, P. 1997. *Language: Its Structure and Use* (Second Australian edn.). Sydney: Harcourt Brace & Co.

Fischer, R. 1995. 'The Notation of Sign Languages: Bébian's Mimographie'. In H. Bos & G. M. Schermer (eds.), *Sign Language Research 1994: Proceedings of the Fourth European Congress on Sign Language Research, Munich, September 1-3, 1994* (pp. 285-302). Hamburg: Signum Press.

Fischer, S. D. 1973. 'Two Processes of Reduplication in American Sign Language'. *Foundations of Language, 9*, 469-480.

Fischer, S. D. 1978. 'Sign Language & Creoles'. In P. Siple (ed.), *Understanding Language through Sign Language Research* (pp. 309-331). New York: Academic Press.

Fischer, S. D. 1998. 'Critical Periods for Language Acquisition: Consequences for Deaf Education'. In A. Weisel (ed.), *Issues Unresolved: New Perspectives on Language and Education* (pp. 9-26). Washington, DC: Gallaudet University Press.

Fischer, S. D., & Gough, B. 1978. 'Verbs in American Sign Language'. *Sign language studies, 18*, 17-47.

Fischer, S. D., & Janis, W. 1990. 'Verb Sandwiches in ASL'. In S. Prillwitz & T. Vollhaber (eds.), *Current Trends in European Sign Language Research: Proceedings of the 3rd European Congress on Sign Language Research Hamburg July 26-29, 1989* (pp. 279-294). Hamburg: Signum Verlag.

Fitzgerald, S. 1999. *Open Minds, Open Hearts: Stories of the Australian Catholic Deaf Community*. Lidcombe, NSW: CCOD.

Flynn, J. W. 1984. *No Longer by Gaslight*. Melbourne: Adult Deaf Society of Victoria.

Foley, W. A., & Valin, R. D. V. 1985. 'Information Packaging in the Clause'. In T. Shopen (ed.), *Language Typology and Syntactic Description* (Vol. 1: Clause structure, pp. 282-364). Cambridge: Cambridge University Press.

Foran, S. J. 1996. *Irish Sign Language*. Dublin: National Association of the Deaf.

Forman, W. 2003. 'The ABCs of New Zealand Sign Language: Aerial Spelling'. *Journal of Deaf Studies and Deaf Education, 8*(1), 92-96.

Friedman, L. A. 1976. *Phonology of a Soundless Language: Phonological Structure of the American Sign Language*. Unpublished doctoral dissertation, University of California, Berkeley.

Frisch, K. v. 1967. *The Dance Language and Orientation of Bees* (L. E. Chadwick, Trans.). Cambridge, MA: Harvard University Press.

Frishberg, N. 1975. 'Arbitrariness and Iconicity: Historical Change in American Sign Language'. *Language, 51*, 696-719.

Frishberg, N. 1986. 'Ghanian Sign Language'. In J. van Cleve (ed.), *The Gallaudet Encyclopedia of Deaf People and Deafness*. Washington, DC DC: Gallaudet University Press.

Fromkin, V., Rodman, R., Hyams, N., Collins, P., & Amberber, M. 2005. *An Introduction to Language* (Fifth Australian edn.). Sydney: Thomson.

Gee, J. P., & Goodhardt, W. 1985. 'Nativization, Linguistic Theory, and Deaf Language Acquisition'. *Sign Language Studies, 49*, 291-341.

Gijn, I. van, Kita, S., & Hulst, H. van der. In press. 'How Phonetic Is the Symmetry Condition in Sign Language?' In V. J. van Heuven, H. van der Hulst & J. M. van de Weijer (eds.), *Phonetics and Phonology — Selected Papers of the Fourth Hil Phonology Conference*. Amsterdam, Philadelphia: John Benjamins.

Givón, T. 1989. *Mind, Code and Context: Essays in Pragmatics*. London: Lawrence Erlbaum Associates.

Goldin-Meadow, S. 2003. *The Resilience of Language: What Gesture Creation Can Tell Us About How All Children Learn Language*. Philadelphia, PA: Psychology Press.

Grice, H. P. 1975. 'Logic and Conversation'. In P. Cole & J. L. Morgan (eds.), *Speech Acts* (Vol. 3, pp. 41-58). New York: Academic Press.

Griffith University. 1992. *Signs of Language (Video)*. Brisbane: QUT Educational TV Facility for Centre for Deafness Studies and Research, Griffith University.

Groce, N. E. 1986. *Everyone Here Spoke Sign Language: Hereditary Deafness on Martha's Vineyard*. Cambridge, MA: Harvard University Press.

Grosjean, F. 1982. *Life with Two Languages*. Cambridge, MA: Harvard University Press.

Grote, K., & Linz, E. 2003. 'The Influence of Sign Language Iconicity on Semantic Conceptualization'. In W. G. Muller & O. Fischer (eds.), *From Sign to Signing: Iconicity in Language and Literature 3* (pp. 23-40). Amsterdam: John Benjamins.

Guerra Currie, A.-M. P., Meier, R. P., & Walters, K. 2002. 'A Crosslinguistic Examination of the Lexicons of Four Signed Languages'. In R. P. Meier, K. A. Cormier & D. Quinto-Pozos (eds.), *Modality and Structure in Signed and Spoken Languages* (pp. 224-236). Cambridge: Cambridge University Press.

Haiman, J. 1985. *Natural Syntax: Iconicity and Erosion*. Cambridge: Cambridge University Press.

Halliday, M. A. K. 1978. *Language as Social Semiotic*. London: Edward Arnold.

Halliday, M. A. K. 1985. *An Introduction to Functional Grammar*. London: Edward Arnold.

Halliday, M. A. K., & Hasan, R. 1976. *Cohesion in English*. London: Longman.

Halliday, M. A. K., & Matthiessen, C. 2004. *An Introduction to Functional Grammar* (3rd edn.). London: Arnold.

Hanson, V. L., & Feldman, L. B. 1991. 'What Makes Signs Related?' *Sign Language Studies, 70*(35-46).

Hawk, S., & Emmorey, K. 2002. Serial Verbs of Motion in ASL Re-Examined: Paper presented at the Linguistic Society of America Meeting, 3-6 January, 2002, San Francisco.

Herbst, J. M. 1987. 'South African Sign Language'. In J. van Cleve (ed.), *Gallaudet Encyclopedia of Deaf People and Deafness* (pp. 106-108). New York: McGraw-Hill Book Company, Inc.

Hockett, C. 1960. *A Course in Modern Linguistics*. New York: Macmillan.

Hopper, P. J., & Traugott, E. C. 2003. *Grammaticalization*. Cambridge: Cambridge University Press.

Horvath, B. 1985. *Variation in Australian English: The Sociolects of Sydney*. Cambridge: Cambridge University Press.

Hudson, G. 2000. *Essential Introductory Linguistics*. Oxford: Blackwell.

Hulst, H. van der 1993. 'Units of Analysis of Signs'. *Phonology, 10*(2), 209-241.

Humphrey, J. H., & Alcorn, B. J. 1996. *So You Want to Be an Interpreter?: An Introduction to Sign Language Interpreting*. Amarillo, TX: H & H Publishers.

Hyde, M., & Power, D. J. 1991. *The Use of Australian Sign Language by Deaf People*. Brisbane: Centre for Deafness Studies and Research, Griffith University.

Jackson, P. 1990. *Britain's Deaf Heritage*. Haddington: Pentland Press.

Jackson, P. W. 2001. *A Pictorial History of Deaf Britain*. Winsford, UK: Deafprint.

Janzen, T. 1995. *The Polygrammaticalization of Finish in ASL*. Unpublished master's thesis, University of Manitoba, Winnipeg.

Janzen, T., & Shaffer, B. 2002. 'Gesture as the Substrate in the Process of ASL Grammaticization'. In R. P. Meier, K. A. Cormier & D. Quinto-Pozos (eds.), *Modality and Structure in Signed and Spoken Languages* (pp. 199-223). Cambridge: Cambridge University Press.

Jeanes, D. R., Jeanes, R. C., Murkin, C. C., & Reynolds, B. E. 1972. *Aid to Communication with the Deaf*. Melbourne: Victorian School for Deaf Children.

Jeanes, R. C., & Reynolds, B. E. 1982. *Dictionary of Australasian Signs for Communication with the Deaf*. Melbourne: Victorian School for Deaf Children.

Johnson, R. E. 1991. 'Sign Language, Culture and Community in a Traditional Yucatec Maya Village'. *Sign Language Studies, 70*, 461-475.

Johnston, T. 1987a. *A General Introduction to Australian Sign Language (Auslan)*. Adelaide: TAFE National Centre for Research and Development.

Johnston, T. 1987b. *A Preliminary Signing Dictionary of Australian Sign Language (Auslan)*. Adelaide: TAFE National Centre for Research and Development.

Johnston, T. 1987c. *A Curriculum Outline for Teaching Australian Sign Language (Auslan) as a Second Language*. Adelaide: TAFE National Centre for Research and Development.

Johnston, T. 1989a. *Auslan Dictionary: A Dictionary of the Sign Language of the Australian Deaf Community*. Sydney: Deafness Resources Australia.

Johnston, T. 1989b. *Auslan: The Sign Language of the Australian Deaf Community.* Unpublished doctoral dissertation, University of Sydney, Sydney.

Johnston, T. 1991a. 'Autonomy and Integrity in Sign Languages'. *Signpost, 4*(1), 2-5.

Johnston, T. 1991b. 'Transcription and Glossing of Sign Language Texts: Examples from Auslan (Australian Sign Language)'. *International Journal of Sign Linguistics, 2*(1), 3-28.

Johnston, T. 1991c. 'Spatial Syntax and Spatial Semantics in the Inflection of Signs for the Marking of Person and Location in Auslan'. *International Journal of Sign Linguistics, 2*(1), 29-62.

Johnston, T. 1992. 'The Realization of the Linguistic Metafunctions in a Sign Language'. *Language Sciences, 14*(4), 317-353.

Johnston, T. 2001. 'Nouns and Verbs in Auslan (Australian Sign Language): An Open and Shut Case?' *Journal of Deaf Studies and Deaf Education, 6*(4), 235-257.

Johnston, T. 2002. 'The Representation of English Using Auslan: Implications for Deaf Bilingualism and English Literacy'. *Australian Journal of Education of the Deaf, 8*, 23-37.

Johnston, T. 2003a. 'BSL, Auslan and NZSL: Three Signed Languages or One?' In A. Baker, B. van den Bogaerde & O. Crasborn (eds.), *Cross-Linguistic Perspectives in Sign Language Research, Selected Papers from TISLR 2000* (pp. 47-69). Hamburg: Signum Verlag.

Johnston, T. 2003b. 'Language Standardization and Signed Language Dictionaries'. *Sign Language Studies, 3*(4), 431-468.

Johnston, T. 2004. 'W(h)ither the Deaf Community? Population, Genetics, and the Future of Australian Sign Language'. *American Annals of Deaf, 148*(5), 358-375.

Johnston, T. (ed.) 1997. *Signs of Australia on CD-ROM: A Dictionary of Auslan (Version 1.0 for Windows).* Sydney: North Rocks Press.

Johnston, T. (ed.) 1998. *Signs of Australia: A New Dictionary of Auslan.* Sydney: North Rocks Press.

Johnston, T., Adam, R., & Schembri, A. 1997. 'Research in Progress: The Auslan Lexicography Project at Renwick College'. *Australian Journal of Education of the Deaf, 3*(1), 42-46.

Johnston, T., & Schembri, A. 1999. 'On Defining Lexeme in a Sign Language'. *Sign Language & Linguistics, 2*(1), 115-185.

Johnston, T., & Schembri, A. 2001. *Grammaticalization in Auslan (Australian Sign Language): Evidence from the Test Battery of Auslan Morphology and Syntax.* Paper presented at the Conference on Sign Linguistics, Deaf Education and Deaf Culture in Asia, Chinese University of Hong Kong, December 17-19.

Johnston, T., & Schembri, A. 2006. *The Use of Elan Annotation Software in the Auslan Archive/Corpus Project.* Paper presented at the Ethnographic Eresearch Annotation Conference, University of Melbourne, Feburary 15-16.

Johnston, T., Vermeerbergen, M., Schembri, A., & Leeson, L. in press. '"Real Data Are Messy": Considering Cross-Linguistic Analysis of Constituent Ordering in Australian Sign Language (Auslan), Vlaamse Gebarentaal (VGT), and Irish Sign Language (ISL)'. In P. Perniss, R. Pfau & M. Steinbach (eds.), *Visible Variation: Cross-linguistic Studies on Sign Language Structure*. Berlin: Mouton de Gruyter.

Joos, M. 1967. *The Five Clocks.* New York: Harcourt Brace & World.

Katamba, F. 1989. *An Introduction to Phonology.* London & New York: Longman.

Kegl, J. A. 1994. 'The Nicaraguan Sign Language Project: An Overview'. *Signpost,*

7, 24-31.

Kegl, J. A., Senghas, A., & Coppola, M. 1999. 'Creation through Contact: Sign Language Emergence and Sign Language Change in Nicaragua'. In M. DeGraff (ed.), *Language Creation and Language Change: Creolization, Diachrony & Development* (pp. 179-237). Cambridge, MA: MIT Press.

Kendon, A. 1980. 'A Description of a Deaf-Mute Sign Language from the Enga Province of Papua New Guinea with Some Comparative Discussion: Part 1—the Formational Properties of Enga Signs'. *Semiotica, 32*, 1-32.

Kendon, A. 1988. *Sign Languages of Aboriginal Australia: Cultural, Semiotic and Communicative Perspectives*. Cambridge: Cambridge University Press.

Kendon, A. 2004. *Gesture: Visible Action as Utterance*. Cambridge: Cambridge University Press.

Kennedy, G., Arnold, R., Dugdale, P., Fahey, S., & Moskovitz, D. (eds.) 1997. *A Dictionary of New Zealand Sign Language*. Auckland: Auckland University Press with Bridget Williams Books.

Kennedy, G., & McKee, D. 1999. 'The Distribution of Signs in New Zealand Sign Language'. In G. Kennedy (ed.), *New Zealand Sign Language: Distribution, Origins, Reference* (pp. 3-16). Wellington: Occasional Publication 2, Deaf Studies Research Unit, Victoria University.

Klima, E. S., & Bellugi, U. 1979. *The Signs of Language*. Cambridge, MA: Harvard University Press.

Kooij, E. van der. 2002. *Phonological Categories in Sign Language of the Netherlands: The Role of Phonetic Implementation and Iconicity*. Utrecht, The Netherlands: LOT.

Kuschel, R. 1973. 'The Silent Inventor: The Creation of a Sign Language by the Only Deaf-Mute on a Polynesian Island'. *Sign Language Studies, 3*, 1-27.

Kyle, J. G., & Woll, B. 1985. *Sign Language: The Study of Deaf People and Their Language*. Cambridge: Cambridge University Press.

Labov, W. 1972. *Language in the Inner City*. Philadelphia: University of Pennsylvania Press.

Ladd, P. 2003. *Understanding Deaf Culture: In Search of Deafhood*. London: Multilingual Matters.

Ladd, R. 1996. *Intonational Phonology*. Cambridge: Cambridge University Press.

Ladefoged, P. 1982. *A Course in Phonetics* (2nd edn.). San Diego, CA: Harcourt Brace Jovanovich.

Lakoff, G., & Johnson, M. 1980. *Metaphors We Live By*. Chicago: University of Chicago Press.

Lambrecht, K. 1994. *Information Structure and Sentence Form: Topic, Focus and the Mental Representations of Discourse Referents*. Cambridge: Cambridge University Press.

Lane, H. 1984. *When the Mind Hears: A History of the Deaf*. New York: Random House.

Lane, H., Boyes-Braem, P., & Bellugi, U. 1976. 'Preliminaries to a Distinctive Feature Analysis of Handshapes in American Sign Language'. *Cognitive Psychology*(8), 263-289.

Lane, L. G. 1993. *Gallaudet Survival Guide to Signing*. Washington, DC: Gallaudet University Press.

Langacker, R. W. 1987. *Foundations of Cognitive Grammar, Vol. 1: Theoretical*

Perspectives. Stanford, CA: Stanford University Press.

LaPolla, R. J. 1993. 'Arguments against 'Subject' and 'Direct Object' as Viable Concepts in Chinese'. *Bulletin of the Institute of History and Philology, 63*(4), 759-813.

Lee, D. M. 1982. 'Are There Really Signs of Diglossia? Re-Examining the Situation'. *Sign Language Studies, 35*, 127-152.

Leech, G. N. 1983. *Principles of Pragmatics.* London & New York: Longman.

Leigh, G. R. 1995. *Teacher's Use of Australasian Signed English System for Simultaneous Communication with Their Hearing-Impaired Students.* Unpublished doctoral dissertation, Monash University, Melbourne.

Leith, D. 1997. *A Social History of English* (2nd edn.). London & New York: Routledge.

LeMaster, B., & Foran, S. 1987. 'Sign Languages: Ireland'. In J. van Cleve (ed.), *Gallaudet Encyclopedia of Deaf People and Deafness* (pp. 82-84). New York: McGraw-Hill Book Company, Inc.

Li, C., & Thompson, S. A. 1976. 'Subject and Topic: A New Typology of Language'. In C. Li (ed.), *Subject and Topic* (pp. 457-489). New York: Academic Press.

Liddell, S. K. 1980. *American Sign Language Syntax.* The Hague: Mouton.

Liddell, S. K. 1990. 'Structures for Representing Handshape and Local Movement at the Phonemic Level'. In S. D. Fischer & P. Siple (eds.), *Theoretical Issues in Sign Language Research. Volume 1: Linguistics.* (pp. 37-66). Chicago: University of Chicago Press.

Liddell, S. K. 1993. 'Holds and Positions: Comparing Two Models of Segmentation in ASL'. In G. R. Coulter (ed.), *Phonetics and Phonology, 3: Current Issues in ASL Phonology* (pp. 189-211). New York: Academic Press.

Liddell, S. K. 1996. 'Numeral Incorporating Roots & Non-Incorporating Prefixes in American Sign Language'. *Sign Language Studies, 92*, 201-225.

Liddell, S. K. 2000. 'Indicating Verbs and Pronouns: Pointing Away from Agreement'. In K. D. Emmorey & H. Lane (eds.), *The Signs of Language Revisited: An Anthology to Honor Ursula Bellugi and Edward Klima* (pp. 303-320). Mahwah, NJ: Lawrence Erlbaum Associates.

Liddell, S. K. 2002. 'Modality Effects and Conflicting Agendas'. In D. F. Armstrong, M. A. Karchmer & J. van Cleve (eds.), *The Study of Signed Languages* (pp. 53-81). Washington, DC: Gallaudet University Press.

Liddell, S. K. 2003. *Grammar, Gesture, and Meaning in American Sign Language.* Cambridge: Cambridge University Press.

Liddell, S. K., & Johnson, R. E. 1984. 'Structural Diversity in the ASL Lexicon'. In D. Testen, V. Mishra & J. Drogo (eds.), *Papers from the Parasession on Lexical Semantics: Chicago Linguistics Society* (pp. 173-186). Chicago: Chicago Linguistic Society.

Liddell, S. K., & Johnson, R. E. 1987. *An Analysis of Spatial-Locative Predicates in American Sign Language.* Paper presented at the Fourth International Symposium on Sign Language Research, July, Lappeenranta, Finland.

Liddell, S. K., & Johnson, R. E. 1989. 'American Sign Language: The Phonological Base'. *Sign Language Studies, 64*, 195-277.

Liddell, S. K., & Metzger, M. 1998. 'Gesture in Sign Language Discourse'. *Journal of Pragmatics, 30*, 657-697.

Lieberth, A. K., & Gamble, M. E. B. 1991. 'The Role of Iconicity in Sign Language

Learning by Hearing Adults'. *Journal of Communication Disorders, 24*(2), 89-99.

Lillo-Martin, D. 2002. 'Where Are All the Modality Effects?' In R. P. Meier, K. A. Cormier & D. Quinto-Pozos (eds.), *Modality and Structure in Signed and Spoken Languages* (pp. 237-240). Cambridge: Cambridge University Press.

Lo Bianco, J. 1987. *National Policy on Languages.* Canberra: Australian Government Printing Service.

Lombardino, A. J., & Nottebohm, F. 2000. 'Age at Deafening Affects the Stability of Learned Song in Adult Male Zebra Finches'. *The Journal of Neuroscience, 20*(13), 5054-5064.

Lucas, C., Bayley, R., & Valli, C. 2001. *Sociolinguistic Variation in American Sign Language.* Washington, DC: Gallaudet University Press.

Lucas, C., & Valli, C. 1992. *Language Contact in the American Deaf Community.* San Diego: Academic Press.

Lupton, L., & Salmons, J. 1996. 'A Re-Analysis of the Creole Status of American Sign Language'. *Sign Language Studies, 90,* 80-94.

Lyons, J. 1968. *Introduction to Theoretical Linguistics.* Cambridge: Cambridge University Press.

Lyons, J. 1977. *Semantics.* Cambridge: Cambridge University Press.

MacDougall, J. 1988. 'The Development of the Australasian Signed English System'. *The Australian Teacher of the Deaf,* (29), 18-36.

MacFarlane, J. 1998. 'The Grammaticization of WRONG in American Sign Language'. In C. Berkenfield, D. Nordquist & A. Grieve-Smith (eds.), *Proceedings of the First Annual High Desert Linguistics Society Conference, April 3-4, 1998* (Vol. 1, pp. 17-23). Albuquerque, NM: High Desert Linguistics Society.

Maher, J. 1996. *Seeing Language in Signs. The Work of William C. Stokoe.* Washington, DC: Gallaudet University Press.

Mandel, M. A. 1977. 'Iconic Devices in American Sign Language'. In L. A. Friedman (ed.), *On the Other Hand: New Perspectives on American Sign Language* (pp. 57-107). New York: Academic Press.

Mandel, M. A. 1981. *Phonotactics and Morphophonology in American Sign Language.* Unpublished doctoral dissertation, University of California, Berkeley.

Marentette, P., & Mayberry, R. I. 2000. 'Principles for an Emerging Phonological System: A Case Study of Early ASL Acquisition'. In C. Chamberlain, J. Morford & R. I. Mayberry (eds.), *Language Acquisition by Eye* (pp. 71-90). Mahwah, NJ: Lawrence Erlbaum Associates.

Martin, J. R. 1992. *English Text: System and Structure.* Philadelphia, PA: John Benjamins.

Massone, M. I., & Curiel, M. 2004. 'Sign Order in Argentine Sign Language'. *Sign Language Studies, 5*(1), 63-93.

Matsuoka, K. 1997. 'Verb Raising in American Sign Language'. *Lingua, 103*(2-3), 127-149.

Matthews, P. H. 1974. *Morphology.* Cambridge: Cambridge University Press.

Matthews, P. H. 1997. *The Concise Oxford Dictionary of Linguistics.* Oxford: Oxford University Press.

Matthews, P. A. 1996. *The Irish Deaf Community Volume 1: Survey Report, History of Education, Language and Culture.* Dublin: Linguistics Institute of Ireland.

Mayberry, R. I., & Eichen, E. B. 1991. 'The Long-Lasting Advantage of Learning Sign Language in Childhood: Another Look at the Critical Period for Language

Acquisition'. *Journal of Memory and Language, 30*, 486-512.

McCrum, R., Cran, W., & MacNeil, R. 1986. *The Story of English*. London: Faber & Faber.

McDonald, B. 1982. *Aspects of the American Sign Language Predicate System.* Unpublished doctoral dissertation, State University of New York at Buffalo.

McIntire, M. L. 1977. 'The Acquisition of American Sign Language Hand Configurations'. *Sign Language Studies, 16*, 247-266.

McKee, D., & Kennedy, G. 2000. 'Lexical Comparison of Signs from American, Australian, British and New Zealand Sign Languages'. In K. D. Emmorey & H. Lane (eds.), *The Signs of Language Revisited: An Anthology to Honor Ursula Bellugi and Edward Klima* (pp. 49-76). Mahwah, NJ: Lawrence Erlbaum Associates.

McKee, R. L. 2000. *People of the Eye: Stories from the Deaf World*. Wellington, NZ: Bridget Williams Books.

McKee, R. L., & Napier, J. 2002. 'Interpreting into International Sign Pidgin: An Analysis'. *Sign Language & Linguistics, 5*(1), 27-54.

McNeill, D. 1992. *Hand and Mind: What Gestures Reveal About Thought*. Chicago: University of Chicago Press.

McNeill, D. (ed.) 2000. *Language and Gesture*. Cambridge: Cambridge University Press.

McWhorter, J. H. 1998. 'Identifying the Creole Prototype: Vindicating a Typological Class'. *Language, 74*(4), 788-818.

Meier, R. P. 2002a. 'Why Different, Why the Same? Explaining Effect and Non-Effects of Modality Upon Linguistic Structure in Sign and Speech'. In R. P. Meier, K. A. Cormier & D. Quinto-Pozos (eds.), *Modality and Structure in Signed and Spoken Language* (pp. 1-25). Cambridge: Cambridge University Press.

Meier, R. P. 2002b. 'The Acquisition of Verb Agreement: Pointing out Arguments for the Linguistic Status of Agreement in Signed Languages'. In G. Morgan & B. Woll (eds.), *Directions in Sign Language Acquisition* (pp. 115-141). Amsterdam/Philadelphia: John Benjamins.

Meier, R. P., Cormier, K. A., & Quinto-Pozos, D. 2002. *Modality and Structure in Signed and Spoken Languages*. Cambridge: Cambridge University Press.

Mesthrie, R., Swann, J., Deumert, A., & Leap, W. L. (eds.) 2000. *Introducing Sociolinguistics*. Edinburgh: Edinburgh University Press.

Metzger, M., & Bahan, B. 2001. 'Discourse Analysis'. In C. Lucas (ed.), *The Sociolinguistics of Sign Languages* (pp. 112-144). Cambridge: Cambridge University Press.

Mitchell, R. E., & Karchmer, M. A. 2004. 'Chasing the Mythical Ten Percent: Parental Hearing Status of Deaf and Hard of Hearing Students in the United States'. *Sign Language Studies, 4*(2), 138-163.

Mithun, M. 1992. 'Is Basic Word Order Universal?' In D. L. Payne (ed.), *Pragmatics of Word Order Flexibility.* (pp. 15-61). Amsterdam and Philadelphia: John Benjamins.

Morford, J., & MacFarlane, J. 2003. 'Frequency Characteristics of American Sign Language'. *Sign Language Studies, 3*(2), 213-225.

Morford, J., & Mayberry, R. I. 2000. 'A Reexamination of "Early Exposure" and Its Implications for Language Acquisition by Eye'. In C. Chamberlain, J. Morford & R. I. Mayberry (eds.), *Language Acquisition by Eye* (pp. 111-128). Mahwah, NJ:

Lawrence Erlbaum Associates.

Morgan, G. 1999. 'Event Packaging in British Sign Language Discourse'. In E. Winston (ed.), *Storytelling & Conversation: Discourse in Deaf Communities* (pp. 27-58). Washington, DC: Gallaudet University Press.

Mühlhäusler, P. 1986. *Pidgin & Creole Linguistics*. Oxford: Basil Blackwell.

Nakanishi, K. 1994. 'The Influence of Japanese Word Order on Japanese Sign Language'. In M. Brennan & G. H. Turner (eds.), *Word-Order Issues in Sign Language: Working Papers Presented at a Workshop Held in Durham, 18-22 September 1991* (pp. 171-192). Durham, UK: International Sign Linguistics Association.

Neidle, C., Kegl, J. A., Maclaughlin, D., Bahan, B., & Lee, R. 2000. *The Syntax of American Sign Language: Functional Categories and Hierarchical Structure*. Cambridge, MA: MIT Press.

Newmeyer, F. J. 1998. *Language Form and Language Function*. Cambridge, MA: MIT Press.

Newport, E. L. 1990. 'Maturational Constraints on Language Learning'. *Cognitive Science, 14*, 11-28.

Newport, E. L., & Supalla, S. J. 2000. 'Sign Language Research at the Millennium'. In K. D. Emmorey & H. Lane (eds.), *The Signs of Language Revisited: An Anthology to Honor Ursula Bellugi and Edward Klima* (pp. 103-114). Mahwah, NJ: Lawrence Erlbaum Associates.

O'Rourke, T. J. 1978. *A Basic Vocabulary: American Sign Language for Parents and Children*. Silver Spring, MD: T.J. Publishers.

Okrent, A. 2002. 'A Modality-Free Notion of Gesture and How It Can Help Us with the Morpheme Vs. Gesture Question in Sign Language Linguistics (or at Least Give Us Some Criteria to Work with)'. In R. P. Meier, K. A. Cormier & D. Quinto-Pozos (eds.), *Modality and Structure in Signed and Spoken Language* (pp. 175-198). Cambridge: Cambridge University Press.

Ostapenko, O. 2005. 'The Optimal L2 Russian Syllable Onset'. In *LSO (Linguistis Studens Organisation) Working Papers in Linguistics 5: Proceedings of WIGL (Workshop in General Linguistics) 2005* (pp. 140-151). Madison, WI: Department of Linguistics, University of Wisconsin-Madison.

Oviedo, A. 2004. *Classifiers in Venezuelan Sign Language*. Hamburg: Signum Press.

Ozolins, U., & Bridge, M. 1999. *Sign Language Interpreting in Australia*. Melbourne: Language Australia.

Padden, C. A. 1988. *The Interaction of Morphology and Syntax in American Sign Language*. New York: Garland.

Padden, C. A. 1998. 'The ASL Lexicon'. *Sign Language & Linguistics, 1*(1), 39-60.

Padden, C. A., & Gunsauls, C. 2003. 'How the Alphabet Came to Be Used in a Sign Language'. *Sign Language Studies, 4*(1), 10-33.

Padden, C. A., & Humphries, T. 2005. *Inside Deaf Culture*. Cambridge, MA: Harvard University Press.

Padden, C. A., & Humphries, T. (eds.) 1988. *Deaf in America: Voices from a Culture*. Cambridge, MA: Harvard University Press.

Padden, C. A., & Rayman, J. 2002. 'The Future of American Sign Language'. In D. F. Armstrong, M. A. Karchmer & J. van Cleve (eds.), *The Study of Signed Languages* (pp. 247-261). Washington, DC: Gallaudet University Press.

Palmer, F. R. 1994. *Grammatical Roles and Relations*. Cambridge: Cambridge

University Press.

Parker, D., & Schembri, A. (eds.) 1996. *Technical Signs for Computer Terms: A Sign Reference Book for People in the Computing Field.* Sydney: North Rocks Press.

Parkhurst, S., & Parkhurst, D. 2003. 'Lexical Comparisons of Signed Languages and the Effects of Iconicity'. In A. J. Bickford (ed.), *Work Papers of the Summer Institute of Linguistics, University of North Dakota Session* (Vol. 47). SIL International.

Pearsall, J. (ed.) 1998. *New Oxford Dictionary of English.* Oxford: Oxford University Press.

Perlmutter, D. 1993. 'Sonority and Syllable Structure in American Sign Language'. In G. R. Coulter (ed.), *Phonetics and Phonology, 3: Current Issues in ASL Phonology* (pp. 227-259). New York: Academic Press.

Petitto, L. A. 2000. 'On the Biological Foundations of Human Language'. In K. Emmorey & H. Lane (eds.), *The Signs of Language Revisited: An Anthology in Honor of Ursula Bellugi and Edward Klima.* (pp. 447-471). Mahwah, NJ: Lawrence Erlbaum Associates.

Pinker, S. 1994. *The Language Instinct.* New York: W. Morrow and Co.

Pizzuto, E., & Corazza, S. 1996. 'Noun Morphology in Italian Sign Language (LIS)'. *Lingua, 98*(169-196).

Poizner, H., Klima, E. S., & Bellugi, U. 1987. *What the Hands Reveal About the Brain.* Cambridge, MA: MIT Press.

Power, D. J. 1987. 'Australian Sign Language'. In J. van Cleve (ed.), *The Gallaudet Encyclopedia of Deaf People and Deafness.* Washington, DC: Gallaudet University Press.

Prillwitz, S., Leven, R., Zienert, H., Hanke, T., & Henning, J. 1989. *HamNoSys Version 2.0, Hamburg Notation System for Sign Languages, an Introductory Guide.* Hamburg: Signum Press.

Radutsky, E. (ed.) 1992. *Dizionario Della Lingua Italiana Dei Segni.* Rome: Edizioni Kappa.

Rathmann, C., & Mathur, G. 2002. 'Is Verb Agreement the Same Crossmodally?' In R. P. Meier, K. A. Cormier & D. Quinto-Pozos (eds.), *Modality and Structure in Signed Language and Spoken Language* (pp. 370-404). Cambridge: Cambridge University Press.

Rayman, J. 1999. 'Storytelling in the Visual Mode: A Comparison of ASL and English'. In E. A. Winston (ed.), *Storytelling and Conversation: Discourse in Deaf Communities* (pp. 59-82). Washington, DC: Gallaudet University Press.

Rée, J. 1999. *I See a Voice: A Philosophical History.* London: Flamingo (HarperCollins).

Reilly, J. S., & McIntire, M. L. 1980. 'American Sign Language and Pidgin Sign English: What's the Difference?' *Sign Language Studies, 27*, 151-192.

Romaine, S. 1995. *Bilingualism.* Cambridge, MA: Blackwell.

Rosenstock, R. 2004. *An Investigation of International Sign: Analyzing Structure and Comprehension.* Gallaudet University, Washington DC.

Ross, J. R. 1967. *Constraints on Variables in Syntax.* Unpublished doctoral dissertation, Massachusetts Institute of Technology.

Roy, C. 1989. 'Features of Discourse in an American Sign Language Lecture'. In C. Lucas (ed.), *The Sociolinguistics of the Deaf Community* (pp. 231-252). San Diego, CA: Academic Press.

Sacks, H., Schegloff, E. A., & Jefferson, G. 1974. 'A Simplest Systematics for the Analysing of Turn-Taking in Conversation'. *Language, 50*, 696-735.

Saeed, J. I. 1997. *Semantics*. Cambridge, MA: Blackwell.

Sandler, W. 1989. *Phonological Representation of the Sign: Linearity and Nonlinearity in American Sign Language*. Dordrecht, The Netherlands: Foris Publications.

Sandler, W. 1995. 'One Phonology or Two? Sign Language and Phonological Theory'. *Glot International, 1*(3), 3-8.

Sandler, W., & Lillo-Martin, D. 2001. 'Natural Sign Languages'. In M. Aronoff & J. Rees-Miller (eds.), *The Handbook of Linguistics* (pp. 533-562). Oxford: Blackwell.

Sandler, W., & Lillo-Martin, D. 2006. *Sign Language and Linguistic Universals*. Cambridge: Cambridge University Press.

Sandler, W., Meir, I., Padden, C., & Aronoff, M. 2005. 'The Emergence of Grammar: Systematic Structure in a New Language'. *Proceedings of the National Academy of Sciences, 102*(7), 2661-2665.

Saussure, F. de. 1983 [1915]. *Course in General Linguistics* (R. Harris, Trans.). London: Duckworth.

Schein, J. D. 1968. *The Deaf Community: Studies in the Social Psychology of Deafness*. Gallaudet: Gallaudet College Press.

Schein, J. D. 1987. 'Deaf Population'. In J. van Cleve (ed.), *Gallaudet Encyclopedia of Deaf People and Deafness* (pp. 251-256). New York: McGraw-Hill Book Company, Inc.

Schein, J. D., & Delk, M. T. J. 1974. *The Deaf Population of the United States*. Silver Spring, MD: The National Association of the Deaf.

Schembri, A. 1996. *The Structure and Formation of Signs in Auslan (Australian Sign Language)*. Sydney: North Rocks Press.

Schembri, A. 2001. *Issues in the Analysis of Polycomponential Verbs in Australian Sign Language (Auslan)*. Unpublished doctoral dissertation, University of Sydney, Sydney.

Schembri, A. 2003. 'Rethinking "Classifiers" in Signed Languages'. In K. D. Emmorey (ed.), *Perspectives on Classifier Constructions in Sign Languages* (pp. 3-34). Mahwah, NJ: Lawrence Erlbaum Associates.

Schembri, A., & Johnston, T. in press. 'Sociolinguistic Variation in the Use of Fingerspelling in Australian Sign Language: A Pilot Study'. *Sign Language Studies, 7*(3).

Schembri, A., & Johnston, T. 2006. *Sociolinguistic Variation in Australian Sign Language Project: Grammatical and Lexical Variation*. Paper presented at the Ninth International Conference on Theoretical Issues in Sign Language Research, Universidade Federal de Santa Catarina, Floriannopolis, SC Brazil, December 6-9 2006.

Schembri, A., Johnston, T., & Goswell, D. in press. 'NAME Dropping: Location Variation in Australian Sign Language'. In C. Lucas (ed.), *Multilingualism and Sign Languages: From the Great Plains to Australia*. Washington, DC: Gallaudet University Press.

Schembri, A., Jones, C., & Burnham, D. 2005. 'Comparing Action Gestures and Classifier Verbs of Motion: Evidence from Australian Sign Language, Taiwan Sign Language, and Nonsigners' Gestures without Speech'. *Journal of Deaf Studies and Deaf Education, 10*(3), 272-290.

Schembri, A., Wigglesworth, G., Johnston, T., Leigh, G., Adam, R., & Barker, R. 2000. 'The Test Battery for Australian Sign Language Morphology and Syntax Project: Noun-Verb Pairs in Auslan'. In A. Schembri, J. Napier, R. Beattie & G. Leigh (eds.), *Deaf Studies, Sydney 1998: Selected Papers from the Australasian Deaf Studies Research Symposium, Renwick College, August 22-23, 1998* (pp. 99-118). Sydney: North Rocks Press.

Schembri, A., Wigglesworth, G., Johnston, T., Leigh, G. R., Adam, R., & Barker, R. 2002. 'Issues in Development of the Test Battery for Auslan Morphology and Syntax Project'. *Journal of Deaf Studies and Deaf Education, 7*(1), 18-40.

Schick, B. S. 1990. 'Classifier Predicates in American Sign Language'. *International Journal of Sign Linguistics, 1*(1), 15-40.

Schiffrin, D. 1987. *Discourse Markers*. Cambridge: Cambridge University Press.

Sebeok, T. A., & Umiker-Sebeok, D. J. (eds.) 1978. *Aboriginal Sign Languages of the Americas and Australia. Volumes 1 and 2*. New York & London: Plenum Press.

Seyfarth, R. M., Cheney, D., & Marler, P. 1980. 'Vervet Monkey Alarm Calls: Semantic Communication in a Free-Ranging Primate'. *Animal Behaviour, 28*, 1070-1094.

Singleton, J. L., & Newport, E. L. 2004. 'When Learners Surpass Their Models: The Acquisition of American Sign Language from Inconsistent Input'. *Cognitive Psychology, 49*(4), 370-407.

Siple, P. (ed.) 1978. *Understanding Language through Sign Language Research*. New York: Academic Press.

Slobin, D. I. 1996. 'From "Thought and Language" to "Thinking for Speaking"'. In J. J. Gumperz & S. C. Levinson (eds.), *Rethinking Linguistic Relativity* (pp. 70-96). Cambridge: Cambridge University Press.

Smith, W. 1990. 'Evidence for Auxiliaries in Taiwan Sign Language'. In S. D. Fischer & P. Siple (eds.), *Theoretical Issues in Sign Language Research. Volume 1: Linguistics.* (pp. 211-228). Chicago, IL: University of Chicago Press.

Smith, W. H., & Li-fen, T. 1979. *Your Hands Can Become a Bridge*. Taipei: The Sign Language Club.

Spencer, A. 1991. *Morphological Theory: An Introduction to Word Structure in Generative Grammar*. London: Basil Blackwell.

Spicer, P., & Rogers, I. 1989. *Technical Signs for Mathematics*. Sydney: The NSW Department of Technical and Further Education.

Stokoe, W. C. 1960. *Sign Language Structure: An Outline of the Visual Communication Systems of the American Deaf* (Vol. 8). Silver Spring, MD: Linstok Press.

Stokoe, W. C. 1969. 'Sign Language Diglossia'. *Studies in Linguistics, 21*, 27-41.

Stokoe, W. C. 1974. 'Classification and Description of Sign Languages'. In T. Sebeok (ed.), *Current Trends in Linguistics, Vol 12* (pp. 345-371). The Hague: Mouton.

Stokoe, W. C. 1991. 'Semantic Phonology'. *Sign Language Studies, 71*, 107-114.

Stokoe, W. C., Casterline, D. C., & Croneberg, C. G. 1965. *A Dictionary of American Sign Language on Linguistic Principles*. Washington, DC: Gallaudet College Press.

Supalla, S. J. 1991. 'Manually Coded English: The Modality Question in Signed Language Development'. In S. D. Fischer & P. Siple (eds.), *Theoretical Issues in Sign Language Research: Linguistics* (Vol. 2: Psychology, pp. 85-110). Chicago, IL: Chicago University Press.

Supalla, S. J., & McKee, C. 2002. 'The Role of Manually Coded English in Language

Development of Deaf Children'. In R. P. Meier, K. A. Cormier & D. Quinto-Pozos (eds.), *Modality and Structure in Signed and Spoken Languages* (pp. 143-165). Cambridge: Cambridge University Press.

Supalla, T. 1978. 'Morphology of Verbs of Motion and Location in American Sign Language'. In F. Caccamise & D. Hicks (eds.), *American Sign Language in a Bilingual, Bicultural Context. Proceedings of the Second National Symposium on Sign Language Research and Teaching, Coronado, California, Oct 15-19, 1978* (pp. 27-46). Coronado, CA: National Association of the Deaf.

Supalla, T. 1982. *Structure and Acquisition of Verbs of Motion and Location in American Sign Language.* Unpublished doctoral dissertation, University of California, San Diego.

Supalla, T. 1990. 'Serial Verbs of Motion in ASL'. In S. D. Fischer & P. Siple (eds.), *Theoretical Issues in Sign Language Research. Volume 1: Linguistics* (pp. 127-152). Chicago, IL: University of Chicago Press.

Supalla, T. 2003. 'Revisiting Visual Analogy in ASL Classifier Predicates'. In K. D. Emmorey (ed.), *Perspectives on Classifier Constructions in Sign Languages* (pp. 249-257). Mahwah, NJ: Lawrence Erlbaum Associates.

Supalla, T., & Newport, E. L. 1978. 'How Many Seats in a Chair? The Derivation of Nouns and Verbs in American Sign Language'. In P. Siple (ed.), *Understanding Language through Sign Language Research* (pp. 91-132). New York: Academic Press.

Supalla, T., & Webb, R. 1995. 'The Grammar of International Sign: A New Look at Pidgin Languages'. In K. D. Emmorey & J. S. Reilly (eds.), *Language, Gesture, and Space* (pp. 333-352). Hillsdale, NJ: Lawrence Erlbaum Associates.

Sutton-Spence, R. 1995. *The Role of the Manual Alphabet and Fingerspelling in British Sign Language.* Unpublished doctoral dissertation, University of Bristol.

Sutton-Spence, R., & Woll, B. 1993. 'The Status and Functional Role of Fingerspelling in BSL'. In M. Marschark & D. Clark (eds.), *Psychological Perspectives on Deafness* (pp. 185-207). Hillsdale, NJ: Lawrence Erlbaum Associates.

Sutton-Spence, R., & Woll, B. 1999. *The Linguistics of British Sign Language: An Introduction.* Cambridge: Cambridge University Press.

Sze, F. Y. B. 2003. 'Word Order of Hong Kong Sign Language'. In A. Baker, B. van den Bogaerde & O. Crasborn (eds.), *Cross-Linguistic Perspectives in Sign Language Research, Selected Papers from TISLR 2000* (pp. 163-192). Hamburg: Signum Verlag.

Talmy, L. 1985. 'Lexicalization Patterns: Semantic Structure in Lexical Forms'. In T. Shopen (ed.), *Grammatical Categories and the Lexicon* (Vol. 3, pp. 57-149). Cambridge: Cambridge University Press.

Taub, S. 2001. *Language from the Body: Iconicity and Metaphor in American Sign Language.* Cambridge: Cambridge University Press.

Tchernichovski, O., Mitra, P. P., Lints, T., & Nottebohm, F. 2001. 'Dynamics of the Vocal Imitation Process: How a Zebra Finch Learns Its Song'. *Science, 96*(22), 2564-2569.

Tennant, R. A., & Brown, M. G. 1998. *The American Sign Language Handshape Dictionary.* Washington, DC: Clerc Books, Gallaudet University Press.

Trask, L. 1999. *Language: The Basics.* London: Routledge.

Turner, G. H. 1999. '"Ungraceful, Repulsive, Difficult to Comprehend":

Sociolinguistic Considerations of Shifts in Signed Languages'. *Issues in Applied Linguistics, 10*(2), 131-152.

Uyechi, L. 1996. *The Geometry of Visual Phonology*. Stanford, CA: CSLI Publications.

Valli, C., Lucas, C., & Mulrooney, K. J. 2005. *Linguistics of American Sign Language: A Resource Text for ASL Users* (4th edn.). Washington, DC: Gallaudet University Press.

Van Valin, R. D. 2001. 'Functional Linguistics'. In M. Aronoff & J. Rees-Miller (eds.), *The Handbook of Linguistics* (pp. 319-336). Oxford: Blackwell.

Van Valin, R. D., & LaPolla, R. J. 1997. *Syntax: Structure, Meaning and Function*. Cambridge: Cambridge University Press.

Vashishta, M., Woodward, J. C., & De Santis, S. 1985. *An Introduction to the Bangalore Variety of Indian Sign Language*. Washington, DC: Gallaudet Research Institute.

Wallin, L. 1983. 'Compounds in Swedish Sign Language in Historical Perspective'. In J. Kyle & B. Woll (eds.), *Language in Sign: An International Perspective on Sign Language* (pp. 56-68). London: Croom Helm.

Wardhaugh, R. 1985. *How Conversation Works*. Oxford: Blackwell.

Washabaugh, W. 1986. *Five Fingers for Survival*. Ann Arbor, MI: Karoma.

Watson, J. 1809. *Instruction of the Deaf and Dumb*. London: Darton and Harvey.

Wilbur, R. B. 1987. *American Sign Language: Linguistic and Applied Dimensions* (2nd edn.). Boston, MA: Little, Brown and Company.

Wilbur, R. B. 1990. 'Why Syllables? What the Notion Means for ASL Research'. In S. D. Fischer (ed.), *Theoretical Issues in Sign Language Research, 1: Linguistics* (pp. 81-108). Chicago, IL: University of Chicago.

Wilbur, R. B. 1993. 'Syllables and Segments: Hold the Movements and Move the Holds!' In G. R. Coulter (ed.), *Phonetics and Phonology* (pp. 135-168). New York: Academic Press.

Wilbur, R. B. 1994a. 'Foregrounding Structures in American Sign Language'. *Journal of Pragmatics, 22*, 647-672.

Wilbur, R. B. 1994b. 'Eyeblinks and ASL Phrase Structure'. *Sign Language Studies, 23*(84), 221-240.

Wilbur, R. B. 1994c. 'Arguments for Sentential Subjects in ASL'. In I. Ahlgren, B. Bergman & M. Brennan (eds.), *Perspectives on Sign Language Structure: Papers from the 5th International Symposium on Sign Language Research. Vol. 1, Salamanca, Spain, 25-30 May 1992* (pp. 215-235). Durham, UK: International Sign Linguistics Association.

Wilbur, R. B. 1999. 'Stress in ASL: Empirical Evidence and Linguistic Issues'. *Language and Speech, 42*, 229-250.

Wilcox, P. 2000. *Metaphor in American Sign Language*. Washington, DC: Gallaudet University Press.

Wilcox, S. 1992. *The Phonetics of Fingerspelling*. Amsterdam/Philadelphia: John Benjamins.

Wilcox, S. E. 2004a. 'Cognitive Iconicity: Conceptual Spaces, Meaning, and Gesture in Signed Languages'. *Cognitive Linguistics, 15*(2), 119-147.

Wilcox, S. E. 2004b. 'Gesture and Language: Cross-Linguistic and Historical Data from Signed Languages'. *Gesture, 4*(1), 43-73.

Wilcox, S. E., & Janzen, T. 2004. 'Introduction: Cognitive Dimensions of Signed

Languages'. *Cognitive Linguistics, 15*(2), 113-117.

Wilkins, D. P. 2003. 'Why Pointing with the Index Finger Is Not a Universal (in Sociocultural and Semiotic Terms)'. In S. Kita (ed.), *Pointing : Where Language, Culture, and Cognition Meet* (pp. 171-215). Mahwah, N.J: Lawrence Erlbaum Associates.

Wilson, D., Walsh, P. G., Sanchez, L., & Read, P. 1998. *Hearing Impairment in an Australian Population*. Adelaide, South Australia: Centre for Population Studies in Epidemiology, South Australian Department of Human Services.

Winston, E. 1991. 'Spatial Referencing and Cohesion in an American Sign Language Text'. *Sign Language Studies, 73*, 397-410.

Winston, E. 1995. 'Spatial Mapping in Comparative Discourse Frames'. In K. D. Emmorey & J. S. Reilly (eds.), *Language, Gesture, and Space* (pp. 87-114). Hillsdale, NJ: Lawrence Erlbaum Associates.

Woll, B. 1983. 'The Comparative Study of Different Sign Languages'. In F. Loncke, Y. LeBrun & P. Boyes-Bream (eds.), *Comparing Sign Languages: Research in European Sign Language*. Ca. Lisse. Swets.

Woll, B. 1987. 'Historical and Comparative Aspects of BSL'. In J. G. Kyle (ed.), *Sign and School* (pp. 12-34). Clevedon, U.K.: Multilingual Matters.

Woll, B. 1990. 'Sign Language'. In N. E. Collinge (ed.), *An Encyclopedia of Language* (pp. 740-783). London: Routledge.

Woll, B. 2003. 'Modality, Universality and the Similarities among Sign Languages: An Historical Perspective'. In A. Baker, B. van den Bogaerde & O. Crasborn (eds.), *Cross-Linguistic Perspectives in Sign Language Research: Selected Papers from TISLR 2000* (pp. 17-30). Hamburg: Signum Press.

Woll, B., Sutton-Spence, R., & Elton, F. 2001. 'Multilingualism: The Global Approach to Sign Languages'. In C. Lucas (ed.), *The Sociolinguistics of Sign Languages* (pp. 8-32). Cambridge: Cambridge University Press.

Woodward, J. C. 1973. 'Some Observations on Sociolinguistic Variation and American Sign Language'. *Kansas Journal of Sociology, 9*(2), 191-200.

Woodward, J. C. 1980. 'Some Sociolinguistic Aspects of French and American Sign Languages'. In H. Lane & F. Grosjean (eds.), *Recent Perspectives on American Sign Language* (pp. 103-118). Hillsdale, NJ: Lawrence Erlbaum Associated, Inc.

Woodward, J. C. 2000. 'Sign Languages and Sign Language Families in Thailand and Viet Nam'. In K. D. Emmorey & H. Lane (eds.), *The Signs of Language Revisited: An Anthology to Honor Ursula Bellugi and Edward Klima* (pp. 23-47). Mahwah, NJ: Lawrence Erlbaum Associates.

Woodward, J. C., Erting, C. J., & Oliver, S. 1976. 'Facing and Hand(l)ing Variation in American Sign Language'. *Sign Language Studies, 10*, 43-52.

Woodward, J. C., & Markowicz, H. 1980. 'Pidgin Sign Languages'. In W. C. Stokoe (ed.), *Sign and Culture: A Reader for Students of American Sign Language* (pp. 55-79). Silver Spring, MD: Linstok Press.

Wrigley, O., Suwanarat, M., Ratanasint, A., Rungsrithong, V., & Anderson, L. B. (eds.) 1990. *The Thai Sign Language Dictionary: Revised and Expanded Edition*. Bangkok: National Association of the Deaf in Thailand.

Wulf, A., Dudis, P. G., Bayley, R., & Lucas, C. 2002. 'Variable Subject Presence in ASL Narratives'. *Sign Language Studies, 3*(1), 54-76.

Yule, G. 1996. *The Study of Language* (2nd edn.). Cambridge: Cambridge University Press.

Zeshan, U. 2003. '"Classificatory" Constructions in Indo-Pakistani Sign Language: Grammaticalizaton and Lexicalization Processes'. In K. D. Emmorey (ed.), *Perspectives on Classifier Constructions in Sign Languages* (pp. 113-141). Mahwah, NJ: Lawrence Erlbaum Associates.

Zimmer, J. 1989. 'Toward a Description of Register Variation in American Sign Language'. In C. Lucas (ed.), *The Sociolinguistics of the Deaf Community* (pp. 253-272). San Diego, CA: Academic Press.

Zwitserlood, I. 2003. *Classifying Hand Configurations in Nederlandse Gebarentaal (Sign Language of the Netherlands)*. Utrecht, The Netherlands: LOT.

Index